Counter Terrorism Issues

Counter Terrorism Issues: Case Studies in the Courtroom, Second Edition presents a panoramic view of the American judiciary's handling of domestic terrorism in the last 30 years. As has played out in recent history, the American legal profession and judicial system bear a unique responsibility to set and maintain the balance between defending homeland security and protecting the civil liberties outlined in the Bill of Rights. These competing interests will continue to collide as the threats to our safety grow.

The book examines some of the most notorious cases—the two attacks on the World Trade Center, the Oklahoma City bombing, and the Fort Hood massacre. Updates from the *First Edition* include a reflection on the Boston Marathon bombing, as well as an examination of the events of January 6, 2021, the subsequent legal proceedings and convictions of those involved in the assault on the U.S. Capitol, and the danger arising from increased domestic extremism and violent rhetoric from the right.

Drawing extensively upon trial transcripts, witness statements, and judicial opinions, the book reviews the events and cases to demonstrate how the criminal justice system has grappled with conflicting facts and countervailing legal rights and responsibilities. Through the words of witnesses, judges, and the attorneys who tried these cases in America's courtrooms, coverage provides important commentary on the historical/political contexts of these events, enabling readers to understand the significance of these infamous attacks on U.S. soil.

Counter Terrorism Issues

Case Studies in the Courtroom

Second Edition

James Ottavio Castagnera

CRC Press
Taylor & Francis Group
Boca Raton London New York

CRC Press is an imprint of the
Taylor & Francis Group, an **informa** business

Designed cover image: Shutterstock

Second edition published 2025
by CRC Press
2385 NW Executive Center Drive, Suite 320, Boca Raton FL 33431

and by CRC Press
4 Park Square, Milton Park, Abingdon, Oxon, OX14 4RN

CRC Press is an imprint of Taylor & Francis Group, LLC

First edition published by CRC Press 2013

Library of Congress Cataloging-in-Publication Data
Names: Castagnera, James, author.
Title: Counter terrorism issues : case studies in the courtroom / James Ottavio Castagnera.
Description: Second Edition. | Boca Raton : CRC Press, 2025. | Includes bibliographical references and index.
Identifiers: LCCN 2024017477 (print) | LCCN 2024017478 (ebook) | ISBN 9781032754628 (hardback) | ISBN 9781032754604 (paperback) | ISBN 9781003474104 (ebook)
Subjects: LCSH: Terrorism—Prevention—Law and legislation—United States. | Terrorism—Prevention—Law and legislation—United States—Cases. | Terrorism—Law and legislation—United States—Cases. | Capitol Riot, Washington, D.C., 2021. | Political violence—Washington (D.C.) | Presidents—United States—Election—2020. | Contested elections—United States. | Trump, Donald, 1946–
Classification: LCC KF9430 .C37 2024 (print) | LCC KF9430 (ebook) | DDC 345.73/02317—dc23
LC record available at https://lccn.loc.gov/2024017477
LC ebook record available at https://lccn.loc.gov/2024017478

ISBN: 978-1-032-75462-8 (hbk)
ISBN: 978-1-032-75460-4 (pbk)
ISBN: 978-1-003-47410-4 (ebk)

DOI: 10.4324/9781003474104

Typeset in Minion
by Apex CoVantage, LLC

Access the Support Material: www.routledge.com/9781032754604

To my wife Joanne Mary Cain and our children,

Marc James Castagnera and Claire Castagnera Holland

Contents

Foreword xi
Preface xvii
Acknowledgments xxi
Introduction xxiii
About the Author xxxix

1 The Fire Bell in the Night: The 1993 World Trade Center Bombing 1

1.1 The 1993 World Trade Center Bombing 2
1.2 Background 3
1.3 Pretrial Proceedings 5
1.3.1 Mohammad Salameh's Bail Application 5
1.3.2 Motions to Suppress Evidence 6
1.4 The First Criminal Trial 8
1.5 The Subsequent Criminal Trials 12
1.6 The Civil Trial 16
1.7 Conspiracy Theories 16
1.8 The Last Words 18

2 Homegrown Terrorists Timothy McVeigh and Terry Nichols (1995) 22

2.1 Background 22
2.2 Pretrial Proceedings 25
2.3 McVeigh's Trial 27
2.4 Appeals and Execution 43

3 Should Zacarias Moussaoui Die for Usama Bin Laden's Sins? (2006) 47

3.1 Background 47
3.2 Early al Qaeda Attacks 50
3.3 Planning and Execution 51
3.4 Pretrial Legal Maneuvers 59

3.5 The Trial: Phase 1 59
3.6 The Trial: Phase 2 64
3.7 Aftermath 66
3.8 Conspiracy Theories 67

4 It Shouldn't Happen to a Dog? The Trial of the SHAC 7 (2006) 76

4.1 The Roots of the Animal Rights Movement 76
4.2 Animal Activist Philosophy and Tactics 78
4.2.1 Federal Legislation to Protect Scientists Using Animals 81
4.3 Stop Huntington Animal Cruelty (SHAC) 84
4.4 SHAC's Website 85
4.5 Indictments and Trial 89
4.5.1 Andrew Baker 89
4.5.2 Sally Dillenback 90
4.5.3 Marion Harlos 92
4.5.4 Robert Harper 93
4.6 Conviction and Appeal 94
4.7 Aftermath 94
4.8 Current Status of the Radical Animal Rights Movement 100

5 All My Trials Soon be Over? Sami Al-Arian (2005–2010) 108

5.1 Al-Arian's Terrorism Trial 110
5.2 Al-Arian's Civil Contempt Case 112
5.3 Al-Arian's Criminal Contempt Case 116
5.4 The Final Chapter? 118

6 Victims Fight Back: The Persian Antiquities Cases (2001–2018) 125

6.1 The Museum of Fine Arts 128
6.2 The Arthur M. Sackler Museum of Harvard University 128
6.3 The Field Museum 130
6.4 The Oriental Institute 131
6.5 2010 Developments 134
6.6 Who Does Own Antiquity? 139
6.7 Three Postscripts 140
6.8 The Supreme Court Declined, Then Agreed to Intervene 142

7 At the Tipping Point on the Scales of Justice: National Security vs. Civil Liberties (When a U.S. Citizen is Declared an Unlawful Enemy Combatant) 152

7.1 Introduction: The Laws of War, War Crime Trials, and Combatants' Rights 152
7.2 Children of a Lesser God? Second-Class Citizens and Unlawful Enemy Combatants 157
7.3 Enter Jose Padilla 158
7.4 The Litigation Carnival Moves South 162
7.5 Padilla's Pretrial Perambulations 163
7.6 Padilla's Trial and Post-Trial Proceedings 163
7.7 Conspiracy Theories 165

8 Of Wannabes and Bumblers: The Fort Dix Conspirators and the Underwear Bomber 170

8.1 The Fort Dix Wannabes 170
8.2 The Target 172
8.3 The Plotters 173
8.4 The Underwear Bomber 177

9 Lone Madman or Freelance Jihadist? Nidal Malik Hasan and the Fort Hood Shootings (2009) 182

9.1 Background 183
9.2 The Shootings and the Legal Proceedings That Followed 186
9.3 Anwar al-Awlaki and the Yemeni Connection 188
9.4 Postscript 198

10 The Times Square Bomber (2010) 203

10.1 Background 206
10.2 Legal Proceedings and Trial 208
10.3 Accomplices and Co-Conspirators? 213

11 The Age of Trump 218

11.1 President Donald Trump and the Triumph of the Radical Right 220
11.2 Charlottesville, August 2017 221
11.3 Jason Kessler, et al. 222

11.4 James Alex Fields, Jr. 225
11.5 Aftermath 227

12 The January 6, 2021 Insurrection 230

12.1 The Stories Behind the Data 234
12.2 *United States v. Mario Mares* 236
12.3 *United States v. David Krauss* 238
12.4 Henry "Enrique" Tarrio 239
12.5 Stewart Rhodes 242
12.6 Conclusion 246

Index 251

Foreword

It is commonly said that the United States of America is a nation born in war. The Founding Fathers may have laid the political groundwork for our break with Great Britain, and some of them penned noble sentiments that continue to inspire their progeny, but it was the Continental Army—augmented by a widespread popular insurgency—that checked the re-imposition of George III's authority and vindicated the principles expressed by the Declaration of Independence.

Despite such bellicose beginnings, Americans view themselves as a peace-loving people. That comforting self-image is belied by the fact that the United States has regularly resorted to force to ensure its security, expand its borders, and advance other interests. Americans like to depict their wars as crusades in defense of freedom. The great irony is that the republic's freedoms have sometimes faced graver threats from the American people and their leaders than they have from external foes.

One of the enduring paradoxes in American history is that free societies at war must often abridge freedom to preserve it. Victory demands quick responses. A nation fighting for its survival cannot always afford the luxury of prolonged debate before choosing a course of action. The enemy will not politely wait for democracy to run its normal course. Likewise, an embattled state must not allow its tolerance for domestic dissent to undermine the public's will to win or threaten domestic order. In more than one conflict, the American government has had to strike a balance between its most cherished values and the imperatives of victory.

This unavoidable predicament prompts thoughtful people to ponder how much freedom a free society can suppress before it ceases to be free. There also remains the danger that any rights surrendered in the name of wartime expedience may not always be reclaimable on the return of peace. As Alexander Stephens, the vice president of the Confederacy, warned the citizens of the short-lived Southern nation that came so close to Balkanizing our republic: "Away with the idea of getting independence first, and looking for liberty afterwards. Our liberties, once lost, may be lost forever."[1]

These tensions have been inherent in the American way of war from the beginning. The revolutionaries who established the republic moved ruthlessly to neutralize Americans loyal to George III, and they also persecuted those who preferred to sit on the fence until it became clear which side was going to win. During the Quasi-War of 1798–1800, the Federalist majority in the U.S. Congress passed legislation to stifle public criticism of President John Adams' policies. Not only did the Sedition Act of July 1798 forbid conspiracies to oppose the measures of the central government by unlawful means, but it also outlawed printing or speaking "any false, scandalous, and malicious writing or writings against the government of the United States, or the President of the United States, with intent to defame . . . or to bring them or either of them, into contempt or disrepute." At least two dozen men—most of them editors of opposition newspapers—faced prosecution under this repressive law, and ten were convicted. Although Adams succeeded in pressuring France into respecting American rights without resorting to a full-fledged war, his administration's assault on freedom of expression provoked a backlash that ruined his chances for re-election and killed the Federalist Party as a national political force.

The Civil War that broke out in April 1861 confronted Abraham Lincoln with 11 slave states in rebellion, and disturbing manifestations of disloyalty within many states that never seceded from the Union. Firm in the belief that the American experiment in self-government served as the beacon that would lead all humanity to a freer future, Lincoln decided that the Union had to be saved at all costs. His love of liberty caused him to curtail civil liberties. He suspended the writ of habeas corpus and subjected suspected Confederate sympathizers to arrest without warrant and trial by military tribunals. The Lincoln administration temporarily closed hostile newspapers and kept others from mailing issues to their subscribers. A British protest in the summer of 1864 revealed that Union jailers subjected certain political prisoners to a form of water torture. Lincoln went along with having his most vociferous Congressional critic, Representative Clement L. Vallandigham of Ohio, tried for treason and exiled to the Confederacy. When critics raised objections to Lincoln's bold but unorthodox actions, the president responded with the hoary argument that the ends justify the means. As Lincoln put it on July 4, 1861, in a message to Congress: "Are all the laws, *but one*, to go unexecuted, and the government itself go to pieces, lest that one be violated?"(emphasis added)[2]

In April 1917, Woodrow Wilson led the United States into World War I, urging his fellow citizens that "the world must be made safe for democracy." Intent on forging the national unity necessary to defeat a state as powerful as imperial Germany, Wilson ended up jeopardizing freedom at home. The Espionage Act of 1917 authorized 20 years in prison and $10,000 fines for spying; sabotage; obstructing the war effort; causing "insubordination, mutiny, or refusal of duty"; or impeding "the recruitment or enlistment service."[3] Congress went further at Wilson's request with the Sedition Act of 1918, which basically outlawed criticism of the government, the armed forces, America's allies, and the war effort in general. Federal authorities arrested more than 1,500 people for either seditious utterances or the slightest suspicion of disloyalty.[4] The most conspicuous victim of this purge was Eugene V. Debs, the head of America's Socialist Party and a perennial presidential candidate. Debs received a ten-year sentence for delivering an antiwar speech.[5]

Whipped into frenzy by government propaganda that depicted Germans as "Huns" intent on replacing civilization with an age of barbarism, many Americans reinforced the Wilson administration's repressive policies with community action and vigilantism. Groups of thugs harassed German Americans. Professional orchestras ceased playing music by German composers, public libraries removed German books from their shelves, and some localities even forbade teaching or speaking the German language. In the 1919 case *Schenk* v. *United States*, the Supreme Court rejected a challenge to the Sedition Act, ruling that the government had the authority to place limitations on free speech during a national emergency. In an opinion that summed up the thinking of a unanimous court, Justice Oliver Wendell Holmes, Jr. framed a famous and often paraphrased pronouncement: "The most stringent protection of free speech would not protect a man falsely shouting fire in a theater and causing a panic."[6]

Although American strategists considered Adolf Hitler's Germany their country's most dangerous enemy during World War II, German Americans suffered far less persecution in 1941–1945 than did their parents in 1917–1918. Outrage over the Pearl Harbor attack and the racism that poisoned the American heart caused the federal government to target another segment of the nation's population. In Hawaii, where Japanese immigrants and their children constituted the islands' largest ethnic group and an indispensable part of the work force, they went largely unmolested. On the other hand, the 37,000 first-generation Japanese immigrants (*Issei*) and 75,000 native-born Japanese Americans (*Nisei*) who lived along the West Coast—2,000 miles further away from Japan—were deemed security risks. These people were rounded up and confined in relocation camps guarded by armed soldiers deep in the country's interior. Once again, the Supreme Court upheld the government's conduct in *Korematsu* v. *United States* (1944).[7] The subsequent triumph of the civil rights movement in the generation following the "Good War" altered popular attitudes, however, and the weight of American shame finally induced Congress to award $20,000 in compensation to each of the 62,000 internees still alive in 1988.

The suicide attacks of September 11, 2001 (9/11), on New York's Twin Towers and the Pentagon committed a grief-stricken nation to a long undeclared war with an elusive and unscrupulous foe. In strictly military terms, al Qaeda, the Taliban, and similar terrorist organizations did not represent as formidable an opponent as Revolutionary France, the Confederate States of

America, Wilhelm II's Germany, or the Japanese Empire, but those Islamic non-state actors have proven resolute, resourceful, and capable of striking down Americans both at home and abroad. Faced with such a threat, the administrations of George W. Bush and Barack Obama took unprecedented steps to safeguard America from terrorism.

During the first decade of the 21st century, civil libertarians raged over the Patriot Act, rendition, torture (or "enhanced interrogation techniques"), racial profiling, interminable confinement at Guantanamo, trial by military tribunal, depriving American citizens of due process by targeting them as enemy combatants, and war by assassination with aerial drones.[8] Such controversies seem to have subsided since the United States ended its wars in Iraq and Afghanistan.

Since the release of the *First Edition* of *Counter Terrorism Issues* in 2013, Americans face a terrorist menace not only from without, but increasingly from within. As Christopher A. Wray, the director of the Federal Bureau of Investigation, told the Senate Judiciary Committee on August 4, 2022:

> The greatest terrorism threat to our Homeland is posed by lone actors or small cells who typically radicalize to violence online and look to attack soft targets with easily accessible weapons. We see these threats manifested within both Domestic Violent Extremists ("DVEs") and Homegrown Violent Extremists ("HVEs"), two distinct threats, both of which are located primarily in the United States and typically radicalize and mobilize to violence on their own.

DVEs take their inspiration from domestic influences, particularly ethnic bias, and antigovernment conspiracy theories, while HVEs are radicalized by international terrorist actors who recruit lone wolf types via the Internet.

Since 2015, the thinly coded and overt rhetoric of Donald J. Trump has given license to white supremacists, antisemites, and other hate groups to broadcast their poisonous messages in the public square. The self-styled militias that espouse such beliefs actively plan attacks on the national and local governments and individuals who represent creeds, ideologies, and ethnicities that the haters despise. The fact that many Republican politicians refer to the insurgents of January 6, 2001, as "tourists" and political hostages, while seeking to neuter the Justice Department and the Federal Bureau of Investigation (FBI), reveals that the most un-American Americans have become a dominant part of the base that dictates the policies of the Grand Old Party.

Only time will tell if terrorism—which has long been regarded as a dangerous but manageable problem—will drastically change the republic and strip Americanism of its noblest attributes. Living as we do in an era when confidence in government and public institutions stands at an all-time low—when lying has become the default setting for the political party that represents nearly half of the American population—this vision should fill the rest of us with alarm.

In this gutsy book, *Counter Terrorism Issues: Case Studies in the Courtroom*, James Ottavio Castagnera casts the eyes of an experienced attorney on many perplexing problems, describing their impact on the American legal system since 9/11 while promoting a greater awareness of the rising threat from the American right. Castagnera's first edition adopted a realistic but essentially optimistic tone. This update is considerably more somber. The future of the United States is up for grabs. One can only hope that the republic can complete its voyage through today's stormy waters—as it has so many times in the past—before the third edition of this valuable study sees print.

Dr. Gregory J. W. Urwin
Professor of History, Center for the Study of Force and Diplomacy
Temple University
Philadelphia, Pennsylvania
January 12, 2024

Preface

A common complaint, voiced particularly by corporate America, is that the United States has too many law schools and too many lawyers. A typical, recent gripe (this one from a blog) goes like this:

> To get an idea of the proliferation of attorneys in the U.S., try looking in the phone book of any size city, large or small, and see who has the most number of full-page ads. Odds are, the attorney section of every telephone book across the country dominates the Yellow Pages to such an extent that there isn't even a close second category, save perhaps that of medical doctors. It is estimated that the U.S. has 70% of the world's attorneys, leaving the rest of the world with the remaining 30%. Given the overwhelming domination of the profession in the Yellow Pages and the sheer number of attorneys in America, is it any wonder that Americans have the most litigious society on the face of the planet?[9]

The complaint is not only common. It also is of long standing. In 1991, *TIME* magazine observed:

> As a political gambit, the method is tried and true. If you are an unpopular Vice President, refurbish your image by deriding an occupational group with an even lower approval rating than your own. Spiro Agnew popularized the ploy back in 1969 with his bitter denunciations of the news media. Following the same playbook, Vice President Dan Quayle—a lawyer—wangled an invitation to the American Bar Association convention in Atlanta and last week used the forum to mount a blistering attack on the legal profession.[10]

Coincidentally, these two observations roughly bracket the two decades dealt with in the first edition of this book (published in 2013). Between the day when Dan Quayle took the American Bar Association to task and the 2008 blog entry—both of which asked essentially the same question in their titles: Are there too many lawyers?—a series of terrorist attacks have shaken the legal foundations upon which America was founded. How America responded to that new crisis was in some sense a direct result of the nation having "too many lawyers."

To appreciate this point, we must look into the rearview mirror, which we call history. To begin, we might note that America has always been a litigious society, ever since colonial times. "When frontier became hinterland [and] there was no common enemy, [Americans] started taking one another to court over trifles."[11] They sued over ownership of a dead fox[12] and a beached whale.[13] But, I ask you, isn't calling Americans "litigious" just a negative way of saying a very positive thing: that America is a land where the rule of law prevails? I think so.

Some would have the Second Amendment stand as the American citizen's shield against tyranny.[14] While a well-armed citizenry might very well discourage a tyrannical regime,[15] the proliferation of guns in American society has resulted in one of the highest homicide rates in the world, as well as the flourishing of private, right-wing militias,[16] such as the organizations that spawned and supported Timothy McVeigh, the 1995 Oklahoma City bomber (see Chapter 2).

Isn't the rule of law to be preferred over such violence and carnage? The central theme of this book is that the American legal system—the nation's courts, its judges, and its attorneys—has held firmly to traditional principles of due process of law and the fair trial in the face of severe terrorist attacks upon our homeland security. Whereas the intelligence community in 2001 proved itself to be substantially inept at predicting and preventing the attacks, and the executive and legislative branches of our federalist system have flopped from relative indifference to the threat in the early 1990s to the opposite extreme of aggressive warfare, arbitrary incarceration, and torture,[17] the American judiciary and bar adhered to first principles, handing down substantial justice. A robust, extensive legal profession is in no small part to be credited for this. Thus, I stand by my view, expressed nearly 30 years ago,[18] that Americans can use every lawyer our law schools produce.

A second theme of this book is that, just as a robust and active bar is a feature of American society dating to colonial times, so too is domestic terrorism. While those who would strip us of our civil liberties in the name of national security contend that the 9/11 terrorist attacks were unprecedented and demanded unprecedented replies—such as the launching of a war of aggression in Iraq and the incarceration of American citizens without clear charges or competent legal counsel at home—in fact, such attacks occurred in the 19th and early 20th centuries, albeit without so extensive a loss of lives and property as in the 9/11 attacks.

The express purpose of this book's Introduction is to demonstrate that, in the words of H. Rap Brown (the 1960s African American radical activist), "Violence is as American as cherry pie."[19]

The Molly Maguire trials, which occurred in the hard coal region of eastern Pennsylvania in the early 1870s, involved an alleged secret society of Irish miners, accused of a long reign of terror involving murder, assault, and arson attacks upon the mines, railroads, and their managers. Echoing these trials some

30 years later, the trial of Western Federation of Miners (WFM) leader Bill Haywood for the "roadside bomb" murder of ex-governor Frank Steunenberg in Idaho resulted in a dramatically different result (acquittal as opposed to hanging) primarily because the latter enjoyed the counsel of legendary lawyer Clarence Darrow. The Molly and Haywood trials illustrate three important points about America a century before the terrorist trials recounted in the present volume.

First, domestic terrorism was no stranger to America during our nation's earlier history. Second, as in our post-9/11 nation, the terrorist activities occurring in late-19th– and early-20th–century industrial America led to efforts by the executive branches of government and the corporate sector—the "military–industrial complex" of its era—to manipulate and subvert the judiciary to achieve its ends.

Third, in contrasting the Molly Maguire trials to the Haywood trial, we find that the quality of legal representation of the defendants has been a crucial factor, whereby a fair trial was conducted to a just result.

The Introduction also includes a look back at the first terrorist attack on New York City by alien actors. The Black Tom Island explosion of 1916, perpetrated by German saboteurs, is barely recalled and almost never discussed today. And yet it was a devastating explosion that destroyed a major American ammunition depot, brought down the ceiling of the Great Hall on nearby Ellis Island, and shattered windows on Wall Street.

Some of Wall Street's windows were once again shattered by a bomb blast in the early 1920s, the post–World War I "Red Scare" episode, which led directly to the arrest, trial, conviction, and execution of anarchists Nicola Sacco and Bartolomeo Vanzetti.

In short, the Introduction demonstrates that—contrary to the claims of those who would convert 21st-century America into a police state in the name of homeland security—we've "been there and done that" many times before. And the republic has survived. Where the judiciary and bar have adhered to their first principles, we can look back with pride and satisfaction. Where, as with the Molly Maguires, the judicial process has been hijacked by external interests, we now blush at the brash miscarriage of justice.

Having hopefully established these themes in my Introduction, I proceed in the 12 chapters that follow to present the major terrorist trials of the past 30 years.

Appropriately, Chapter 1 recalls the first attack on the World Trade Center in 1993, one that was a fire bell in the night, but sadly a warning bell that failed to awaken those charged with protecting us.

Chapter 2 retells a tale of domestic terrorism, the Oklahoma City bombing of 1995. This tragic event reminded us that disaffected fellow Americans could be just as dangerous as any alien terrorists, be they German spies or radical Islamic militants.

Chapter 3 recounts the trial of the only living defendant to be brought to court following 9/11. Then, Chapter 4 returns to my domestic terrorism thread, looking at a trial that took place in Trenton, New Jersey, in 2006, involving radical animal rights activists.

Chapter 5, Chapter 7, and Chapter 8 cover the law enforcement and legal proceedings surrounding attempts to deal with Islamic terrorists and their American sympathizers, ranging from the radical college professor Sami Al-Arian to the Islamic engineer who tried to bomb Times Square in 2010. Much of the material in these chapters is concerned not with the trials themselves but rather with the efforts of dedicated American attorneys to provide adequate representation to defendants who often were held incommunicado, deprived of legal counsel, and incarcerated indefinitely without being charged with any crime. The outcomes of these cases are at the heart of my central theme that, by and large, the U.S. judiciary and bar have met the test and have been found to be worthy shields for our civil liberties.

A special word is in order about Chapter 6. This chapter deals with a long-standing, highly complex collection of cases in which the plaintiffs—American victims of international terror—won a massive default judgment against Iran, which they successfully characterized as a state sponsor of the terror that victimized them. The ongoing legal battles concerned their novel attempts to execute their judgment upon Persian artifacts held by various American museums and universities. To my knowledge, the cases are unique and test the important issue of the individual citizen's ability to gain justice in our courts of law against our international enemies. The seemingly endless litigation *may* finally have been resolved in March 2023, as revised Chapter 6 explains.

New to this *Second Edition* are Chapter 11 and Chapter 12, which recount the efforts of former President Donald Trump on January 6, 2021 to disrupt the counting of the Electoral College ballots and thereby prevent Joseph Biden's ascension to the presidency, dislodging Trump from the White House. That I feel comfortable leaping over the decade between the first and second editions of this book is a tribute to the U.S. military, police, and intelligence communities. Thankfully, there is no major terrorist incident to be reported prior to the January 2021 assault on the U.S. Capitol building.

This is not to say there was no violence. Mass shootings have proliferated during the past decade—and some of these mass shootings have been motivated by political and/or religious convictions. The gap my editorial judgment creates should not, therefore, be mistaken for an assertion of political quietude in America. Violence remains "as American as cherry pie."

Finally, a word about the intent of this *Second Edition*. In contrast to the original 2013 book, which was a freestanding contribution to homeland security studies, this new edition comes equipped with an Instructor's Manual and PowerPoint slides for each chapter. My hope is that faculty in law, political science, and security studies will see fit to adopt it for appropriate undergraduate and graduate courses.

Acknowledgments

The author thanks the Foundation for Defense of Democracies for the 2007 Academic Fellowship on Terrorism, which took him to Israel and opened his eyes to the challenges of counter terrorism. He also thanks Rider University (where he worked for 23 years until retirement in 2019) for providing him with the opportunity, as legal counsel, to hone his risk management skills, and the equally important opportunity to develop and teach the course in counter terrorism law, which led directly to the writing of this book. Finally, he thanks Professor Gregory J.W. Urwin of Temple University, whom he first met on their FDD Fellowship visit to Israel in June 2007, for his insightful foreword to this volume.

Introduction

Terrorism is the crucible in which the rule of law is tested. Sometimes in American history, our justice system has acquitted itself admirably. At other times, it has failed miserably.

The test I'm talking about is comprised of two parts. Part 1 concerns the effectiveness of our law enforcement agencies in solving the crime. Part 2 involves the climax of the legal process—that is, the trial. Let me illustrate my point by contrasting two famous cases involving accusations of terrorism leveled at early labor leaders in the late 19th and early 20th centuries. I am referring to the Molly Maguire trials in the hard coal region of eastern Pennsylvania in the 1870s and the Steunenberg murder trials in Idaho's Coeur d'Alene mining region during the first decade of the 20th century. These two cases have intrigued me for more than 50 years.

The Molly Maguires and the Western Federation of Miners

The summer of 1968 was an exciting time for my hometown of Jim Thorpe, Pennsylvania. Paramount Pictures brought Sean Connery, Richard Harris, Samantha Edgar, and Anthony Zerby to the hard coal region to film *The Molly Maguires*. What premiered about a year and a half later in early 1970 was the classic tale of capitalist oppression, reprisals by a secret society of Irish terrorists, betrayal by an undercover agent, and—inevitably—the day of the rope. Connery, looking to escape being typecast as a certain British spy, brought his license to kill over to the character of Black Jack Kehoe, presented to filmgoers as a coal miner with a pickax to grind against the mine owners, bosses, and coppers. Harris was James McParland, a.k.a. Jamie McKenna, the Pinkerton detective on the make, who befriends and then betrays Kehoe and his cohorts.

Not a bad movie, except that it got much of the story wrong. Although he mined coal in his salad days, Kehoe was a Girardville tavern keeper and political leader when he was arrested, tried, and hanged as the alleged King of the Mollies. And McParland, well, was he an undercover detective who later testified honestly to the Molly Maguire crimes he had witnessed, or was he an agent provocateur who instigated crime and violence in the mine patches, providing an opportunity for his masters—the likes of Alan Pinkerton and

President Franklin Gowan of the Philadelphia & Reading Railroad—to break the power of organized labor and the Irish immigrants' own Ancient Order of Hibernians? These questions have bedeviled historians and stirred controversy for generations.

Historian James Ford Rhodes recapitulated the traditional answer, the answer given by the juries who condemned the alleged Mollies in the 1870s, in his seminal 1919 volume on the subject:

> Many of the Mollies were miners and the mode of working the mines lent itself to their peculiar policy. Miners were paid by the cubic yard, by the mine car, or by the ton, and (in the driving of entries) by the lineal yard. In the assignment of places, which was made by the mining boss, there were "soft" jobs and hard. If a Molly applied for a soft job and was refused, his anger was aroused and not infrequently in due time the offending boss was murdered. If he got employment, there was a constant chance of disagreement in measuring-up the work and in estimating the quality of the coal mined, for it was the custom to dock the miners' wages for bad coal with too much slate and dirt, and a serious disagreement was apt to be followed by violence. Little wonder was it that, as the source of the outrages was well understood, mining bosses refused to employ Irishmen, but this did not ensure their safety, as they might then be murdered for their refusal. A good Superintendent of any colliery would, in his quality of superior officer, support an efficient mining boss and would thus fall under the ban himself. John T. Morse, Jr., who made a contemporaneous study of the Molly Maguires, wrote in his vivid account of their operations: "The superintendents and 'bosses' in the collieries could all rest assured that their days would not be long in the land. Everywhere and at all times they were attacked, beaten, and shot down, by day and by night; month after month and year after year, on the public highways and in their own homes, in solitary places and in the neighborhood of crowds, these doomed men continued to fall in frightful succession beneath the hands of assassins."
>
> The murders were not committed in the heat of sudden passion for some fancied wrong: they were the result of a deliberate system. The wronged individual laid his case before a quasijudicial tribunal demanding the death, say, of a mining boss and urging his reasons. If they were satisfactory, as they usually were, the murder was decreed; but the task was not assigned to the aggrieved person or to any one in his and the victim's neighborhood: perhaps directly-aggrieved parties might be tempted to use more force or more cruelty than necessary. Two or more relatively disinterested Mollies from a different part of the county or even from the adjoining county were selected to do the killing because, being unknown, they could the more easily escape detection. Refusal to carry out the dictate of the conclave was dangerous and seldom happened, although an arrangement of substitution, if properly supported, was permitted. The meeting generally took place in an upper room of a hotel or saloon and, after the serious business, came the social reunion with deep libations of whiskey.

In attempting to give precise figures, some writers have undoubtedly exaggerated the number of murders by this order from 1865 to 1875; but no one can go through the evidence without being convinced that a great many men were killed to satisfy the vengeful spirit of the Molly Maguires. Some of the victims were men so useful, so conspicuous, and so beloved in their communities that their assassinations caused a profound and enduring impression. In some cases, so Dewees (who has written a very useful story) asserts, robbery was added to murder: superintendents, who were carrying the money for the monthly pay of the miners and laborers, were waylaid as they drove along some lonely road in the desolate country. While the murders were numerous, still more numerous were the threats of murder and warnings to leave the country written on a sheet of paper with a rude picture of a coffin or a pistol and sometimes both. One notice read: "Mr. John Taylor—We will give you one week to go, but if you are alive on next Saturday you will die." Another, to three bosses, charged with "cheating thy men" had a picture of three pistols and a coffin and on the coffin was written, "This is your home." In other mining districts and in manufacturing localities, during strikes and times of turbulence similar warnings have been common and have been laughed at by mining bosses, superintendents, and proprietors; but, in the anthracite region between 1865 and 1876 the bravest of men could not forget how many of his fellows had been shot and suppress a feeling of uneasiness when he found such a missive on his doorstep or posted up on the door of his office at the mine. Many a superintendent and mining boss left his house in the morning with his hand on his revolver, wondering if he would ever see wife and children again. The young men of the order were selected for the commission of murder; above them were older heads holding high office and, in a variety of ways, displaying executive ability. They were quick to see what a weapon to their hand was universal suffrage, and, with the aptitude for politics which the Irish have shown in our country, they developed their order into a political power to be reckoned with. Numbering in Schuylkill county only 500 or 600 out of 5,000 Irishmen in a total population of 116,000, the Molly Maguires controlled the common schools and the local government of the townships in the mining sections of the county. They elected at different times three county commissioners and came near electing one of their number, who had acquired twenty thousand dollars worth of property, Associate Judge of the Court of Oyer and Terminer. In one borough a Molly was Chief of Police; another in Mahanoy township, Jack Kehoe, was High Constable. In the elections were fraudulent voting, stuffing of the ballot-boxes and false returns; in the administration of the offices, fraud and robbery. In Mahanoy township, $60,000 were drawn for the schools and eleven-twelfths of it stolen. Exorbitant road taxes were a fruitful means by which township officials robbed the taxpayers and put the money in their own pockets. In August 1875 an ex-county commissioner, a Molly, and two commissioners then in office, not actually belonging to the order but in sympathy with it, had been convicted of stealing the county funds and each had been sentenced by a full bench [September 6] to two years' imprisonment. At the fall election for governor in this year [1875] the

> Molly Maguires, who were naturally Democrats, foresaw Republican success and sold their vote in Schuylkill and Luzerne counties to the Republicans for a certain amount of money in hand and an implied agreement that these convicted commissioners and other criminals who were called by a leading Molly "our men" should be pardoned. It is hardly to be supposed that the Republican politicians who made this bargain were aware of the thoroughly criminal nature of the Molly Maguires, for they had astutely covered themselves with a virtuous cloak, securing from the Legislature in 1871 a charter for the Ancient Order of Hibernians whose motto was "Friendship, Unity and Christian Charity." On October 10, 1875, in a letter to the Shenandoah Herald Jack Kehoe denied with indignation that the Molly Maguires were synonymous with the Ancient Order of Hibernians, which latter was "composed of men who are law abiding and seek the elevation of their members." Kehoe was crafty enough to see the advantage of throwing dust in the eyes of the public and, when the outside world was bargained with, the A.O.H. was put forward; but, as matter of fact, it was the old story of ravening wolves in sheep's clothing.[20]

But did the jurors—did Rhodes—get it right? Clues pointing to a different answer may be found more than a quarter century and a couple of thousand miles from the Molly Maguire trials, in the Coeur d'Alene mining district of north Idaho early in the 20th century. The murder of Idaho governor Frank Steunenberg on December 30, 1905, in Caldwell, Idaho, has faded into history's mists, its lessons largely lost to our policy makers today. But Steunenberg's murder, caused by a terrorist's bomb tied to his garden gate, has a lesson to teach us about conspiracy and the two-edged nature of terrorism. Coeur d'Alene was a region rich in precious metals and in labor union agitation. The WFM was militant and bare-knuckled. During work stoppages, union terrorism took the form of dynamiting company mines and mills, capturing and imprisoning scab labor in the union hall, and hijacking trains. The dynamiting of the Bunker Hill Mining Company's major processing facilities in Wardner, Idaho, in May 1898, led Gov. Steunenberg to call in federal troops, who arrested "every male—miners, bartenders, a doctor, a preacher, even a postmaster and a school superintendent," in the nearby union bastion of Burke, Idaho. All together, about 1,000 men were herded into the "Cow Pen," a kind of makeshift concentration camp, and held for weeks without trial.

It has long been said, "Revenge is a dish best served cold."[21] Fully 7½ years later, the ex-governor, back home in Caldwell, opened his garden gate at 6 o'clock on the second-to-last snowy evening of 1905. The explosion of a homemade bomb, fastened to the gate by a fishing line, took off Steunenberg's legs. He lingered an hour before bleeding to death in a downstairs bedroom, conscious to the bitter end.

A waitress at Caldwell's Saratoga Hotel identified a long-term guest, one Thomas Hogan, as a possible suspect. A warrantless search of Hogan's hotel room turned up plaster of Paris in his chamber pot. Other detritus that could have comprised bomb components was found in his valise. On New Year's Day 1906, Hogan, a.k.a. Harry Orchard, was arrested and charged with first-degree murder. Less than a week later, the state of Idaho hired America's most famous detective: none other than James McParland, who headed the Pinkerton Agency's Denver office.

McParland, the famed Molly Maguire catcher, rushed to Boise and interrogated Hogan/Orchard relentlessly. The result? An astonishing 64-page confession to the killing of Frank Steunenberg and 17 others, all ordered, said Orchard, by the leaders of the WFM. On the strength of this confession, McParland led a posse by special train to Denver, where Colorado Gov. Jesse Fuller McDonald had a warrant waiting for the arrest of WFM officers William "Big Bill" Haywood, Charles Moyer, and George Pettibone. Denied any opportunity to contact their loved ones and lawyers, the three union leaders were kidnapped aboard the Idaho "special," a train specifically designated for the secret mission, and hauled to Boise for trial. The U.S. Supreme Court subsequently sanctioned their kidnapping to Idaho.

Luckier than Black Jack Kehoe and Yellow Jack Donohue, Big Bill Haywood and his comrades had Clarence Darrow on their side. Already a rising star, and later to win international fame in the Scopes Monkey Trial and Leopold-Loeb thrill killing case, Darrow was the darling of the American Federation of Labor.

Looking for three bites at the union apple, the prosecution brought Big Bill to trial first. Harry Orchard—like another alleged turncoat, Kelly the Bum, in the Molly trials—told his lurid tale of a life of crime, terrorism, and murder on the witness stand. In a long and passionate closing argument, Darrow told the jury of ranchers and businessmen,

> I don't believe that this man [Orchard] was ever really in the employ of anybody. I don't believe he ever had any allegiance to the Mine Owners Association, to the Pinkertons, to the WFM, to his family, to his kindred, to his God, or to anything human or divine. I don't believe he bears any relation to anything that a mysterious and inscrutable Providence has ever created . . . . He was a soldier of fortune, ready to pick up a penny or a dollar or any other sum in any way that was easy . . . to serve the mine owners, to serve the Western Federation, to serve the devil if he got his price, and his price was cheap.[22]

Darrow's theory was that Orchard acted alone in belated revenge for being squeezed out of a lucrative silver mine deal by Steunenberg years earlier.

In a direct attack on McParland and his methods, Darrow recalled for the jury the great detective's ambiguous role in bringing the Mollies "to justice," and expressly drew the parallel between the two cases, especially the

Pinkerton's production of the snitch known as Kelly the Bum, to bolster McParland's testimony for the prosecution.

Some say the jury's unanimous "not guilty" verdict was the result of Darrow's silver-tongued oratory. Less kind critics claim the terrorist tactics of the WFM intimidated the 12 jurors. But when George Pettibone was likewise acquitted, the prosecutors gave up the ghost and released the three defendants.

Were the WFM union officers guilty or innocent? Were Black Jack Kehoe and the other alleged Molly Maguires guilty or innocent? Or, in a climate of violence and terroristic tactics, did beleaguered government officials in league with influential corporations lay indisputable acts of violence at the feet of opponents they preferred to see removed from the stage? Worse yet, did they infiltrate agent provocateurs to instigate acts of violence for the express purpose of accusing and convicting these labor leaders?[23]

Black Tom Island

Less than two years after 9/11, I was part of a tour group being shown around Ellis Island by a federal park ranger. At the time, I could be counted among the vast majority of Americans who had no idea that lower Manhattan had been the target of terrorist bombs at least twice before in its history. The ranger enlightened me and my group. He told us the story of the Black Tom Island explosion.

From September 11, 2001—when the World Trade Center was attacked and destroyed by al Qaeda terrorists—until only just recently, tourists had been barred from climbing to Lady Liberty's crown. Since July 30, 1916, visitors to Liberty Island have been barred—and are still barred—from climbing into the Lady's torch. At about 2 o'clock on that Sunday morning, an explosion of such severity rocked adjacent Black Tom Island that Philadelphians felt the shock wave. The Statue of Liberty sustained $100,000 (in 1916 dollars) worth of damage from a shotgun blast of shrapnel. One long-term result was the closing of her torch to tourist traffic, according to the U.S. Park Service officer who led my tour. "Another," he added, "was the founding of the Federal Bureau of Investigation."

Black Tom Island, today comprising a portion of Liberty State Park's south side, was connected to Jersey City by a long pier used by the Lehigh Valley Railroad Company and the National Dock and Storage Corporation as a munitions depot for trans-shipment to the Allies on the Western Front. The night Black Tom blew, its warehouses held more than 2 million pounds (1,000 tons) of TNT, gunpowder, dynamite, and shrapnel. One vessel, Johnson Barge 17, alone accounted for 100,000 pounds of TNT. As with the airliners hijacked by al Qaeda in 2001, the railroad and barges on and around Black Tom were poorly guarded. The United States was still formally neutral in 1916, albeit British control of the Atlantic shipping lanes ensured that the Allies were America's main customers for our munitions production. Germany resolved to do something about that.

The park ranger said the main blast damaged neighboring Ellis Island, where he leads his tours, to the tune of $500,000 or "half the $1 million it cost the government to build the facility." In the immediate aftermath of the Black Tom disaster, spontaneous combustion was suspected. Guards spotted several small fires and ran for their lives. One watchman had the mental presence to pull the alarm that alerted the Jersey City Fire Department—but too late. The fires set off a series of shrapnel shells. As if part of a nuclear chain reaction, the small explosions culminated in a giant blast. And as if to record the blast for history, a chunk of metal hit the Jersey Journal's clock tower, stopping it at exactly 2:12 a.m. Readers of the Journal were told in 2-inch headlines later that morning that damage amounted to $75 million. Damage estimates vary, but windows were shattered within a 10-mile radius; the vast, vaulted concrete ceiling of Ellis Island's main hall collapsed, and "the shock wave set off burglar and fire alarms all over Manhattan," according to my guide. In sharp contrast to the thousands killed in the 9/11 tragedy, the Black Tom death toll was mercifully low—50 at most. Fortunately, no immigrants were in the Ellis Island great hall at that early hour; ultimately, all those in transit at the time had to be evacuated to Battery Park at the tip of Manhattan.

Since spontaneous combustion was the initial suspect, the first defendants brought to trial were not suspected terrorists. Rather, they were corporate officials charged with "criminal and gross negligence." And civil litigation concerning who should shoulder the losses dragged on through both World War I and World War II, including a 1941 decision by the U.S. Supreme Court.

However, local police actually apprehended a suspected saboteur shortly after the disaster. His name was Michael Kristoff (sometimes identified as Krisoff in court records). Aged 23 in 1916, he boarded with a distant relative, the elderly Anna Rushnak, a Czechoslovak who ran a half-dollar-a-night boarding house in Bayonne, N.J. According to an article published in American Legion Magazine in August 1964, Mrs. Rushnak—tossed from her bed like so many others in the path of the Black Tom shock wave—subsequently encountered Kristoff seated on the edge of his bed, mumbling, "What I do? What I do?"

After consulting with her daughter, Mrs. Lulu Chapman, who also had boarded Kristoff for a time and who found his comings and goings mysterious, the elder landlady approached a friend, Captain John J. Rigney of the Bayonne Police Department. Kristoff was arrested and questioned. A Slovakian subject of the Austro-Hungarian Empire—Germany's chief ally in the

Great War—he had emigrated in 1899 and was employed at the Tidewater Oil Refinery near Black Tom shortly before the explosion. All the same, he was released, viewed by the authorities as "insane but harmless."

Kristoff actually enlisted in the U.S. Army after America joined the Allied cause in April 1917. He and the Black Tom disaster were temporarily forgotten, their celebrity eclipsed by the war news from "over there." But after the November 11, 1918, armistice ended the "war to end all wars," the Lehigh Valley Railroad—itself buffeted by multiple civil suits, similar to the owners and operators of the Trade Center today—wanted to recoup its losses and, if possible, shift the blame onto other shoulders.

The railroad's chance came due to the occurrence of other alleged acts of sabotage in the years immediately before America's entry into the war. For example, on New Year's Day 1915, a fire had damaged Trenton's Roebling Steel Foundry. And on January 11, 1917, the Canadian Car and Foundry plant in Kingsland had suffered an act of arson. Congress finally acted to address these claims in 1922 by passing the Settlement of War Claims Act. The statute established a "German special deposit account" and a Mixed Claims Commission.

The commission's creation and the assertion of the Black Tom claim brought Michael Kristoff back into the judicial spotlight. Located in an Albany jail, serving time for theft, Kristoff admitted to being employed "for a few weeks" by Germany back in 1916. Released before this tantalizing but inconclusive statement could be followed up, he was fitfully pursued, until in 1928 he turned up in a potter's field on Staten Island. Even after exhumation of the corpse, however, Kristoff remained an enigma. The body carried papers identifying it as Kristoff's, but its teeth failed to match dental records purported to be the suspect's.

Consequently, in the words of one of many federal judges to consider aspects of the railroad's claim over more than two decades of litigation, District Judge Goddard of the Southern District of New York, sitting in Manhattan,

> After extensive investigation by Lehigh, Federal, State and local agencies, evidence was obtained tending to show that the explosions had been caused by one Krisoff. Although it was suspected that Krisoff was acting as an agent of the German Government, . . . Lehigh did not have the evidence to establish the fact.[24]

A former German agent, Lothar Witzke, was trailed to South America and then to China. Interviewed when he was beyond the reach of the U.S. law's long arm, and therefore voluble, he said yes, he "did the work in New Jersey with [an accomplice, Kurt Jahnke] when the munitions barges were blown up and the pier wrecked."[25]

Despite such evidence, the commission dismissed the Black Tom claims in 1930. Attorneys for Lehigh Valley Railroad and its co-claimants moved to reopen the case, contending that the commissioners had been misled by "fraudulent, incomplete, collusive and false evidence" provided by Germany's witnesses. The motion was heard by the commission's umpire, Justice Roberts of the U.S. Supreme Court, who decided in December 1933 that "while the Commission was without power to reopen a case merely for the presentation of after-discovered evidence, the Commission was still sitting as a court and did have power to consider the charge that it had been misled by fraud and collusion."

After that, the commission—comprised of its umpire plus one American and one German commissioner—reopened the Black Tom case. Proceedings dragged on into 1939 and became so contentious that the German commissioner ultimately withdrew, and the German ambassador challenged the commission's continuing jurisdiction in the absence of its member. The American commissioner contended that the tribunal enjoyed jurisdiction to determine the claim, even if reduced to a duet. Mr. Justice Roberts, as umpire, asserted his power to resolve the jurisdictional disagreement. He then held that the commission, having agreed six years earlier to retain jurisdiction and reopen the hearings, and having heard evidence that established fraud by the German side, was obliged to render an award.[26]

Following subsequent proceedings, Roberts ruled that the claims had been accurately calculated and, at a hearing boycotted by the Germans, he joined the American commissioner in an order awarding $50 million to the Lehigh Valley Railroad and its co-claimants.

The award was immediately certified by Secretary of State Cordell Hull and Treasury Secretary Henry Morgenthau, and almost as quickly challenged by the holder of an earlier commission award. Z. & F. Assets Realization Corporation challenged the cabinet members' decision to sanction the huge award, realizing that its payment would so deplete the fund that the plaintiff's own award would not be completely covered. Z. & F. lost its case all the way up the judicial ladder. On January 6, 1941, in a decision penned by Chief Justice Hughes and supported by the concurring opinion of Justices William Douglas and Hugo Black, the Supreme Court affirmed the trial and appellate courts, holding that Lehigh Valley's award should stand.

But even this seeming swan song by the "Supremes" did not put the claim completely to rest. An attorney named Lewis A. McGowan sued Lehigh Valley Railroad for a contingent fee, based on his efforts to implicate the German government in Michael Kristoff's misdeeds. McGowan finally lost his case in 1944, with District Judge Goddard of the federal court in Manhattan holding that the lawyer's contract with the defendant railroad required that the plaintiff actually prove Germany's complicity in order to qualify for a fee. Since the defendant had succeeded in establishing German culpability by other evidence, after Justice Roberts reopened the claim, McGowan was out of luck. And at last, the long saga that started on July 30, 1916, ended.

The Black Tom blast and related acts of German terrorism resulted in the passage of the federal Espionage Act in June 1917. The statute went beyond its principal purpose of curtailing Teutonic terrorists. Section 2 embargoed from the U.S. mails "every letter, writing, circular, postal card, picture, print, engraving, photograph, newspaper, pamphlet, book or other publication . . . containing any advocating or urging of treason, insurrection, or forcible resistance to any law of the United States," and subjected the authors to a $5,000 fine and five years' imprisonment. A potent precedent favoring the constitutionally questionable provisions of the USA Patriot Act, passed shortly after the 9/11 attacks, the 1917 law was given the Supreme Court seal of approval in *Schenk v. United States*, for which no less a civil libertarian than Oliver Wendell Holmes wrote for the high court majority, "When a nation is at war many things that might be said in times of peace are such a hindrance to its efforts that their utterance will not be endured so long as men fight."[27]

Additionally, the U.S. Justice Department was given a Bureau of Investigation, which would soon be rechristened the FBI. Shortly after the 1918 armistice, the new agency launched the now notorious Palmer Raids against suspected Communists and other "subversives," initiating the nation's first Red Scare. Immigrants deemed to be pro-communist or else anarchists—including Sacco and Vanzetti, now viewed by many civil libertarians as martyrs to a hysterical attack on First Amendment free speech and free association—were targeted for deportation and worse.

Walk the south side of Liberty State Park today and you will find a marker memorializing the Black Tom terrorist attack of July 30, 1916. A circle of American flags complements the plaque, which stands just a bit east of the visitor center.

Said my Ellis Island tour guide, "People have pretty much forgotten the Black Tom explosion. They don't know that, as bad as the Twin Towers tragedy was, it wasn't the first time terrorists attacked lower Manhattan." He added that to this day, Black Tom stands as one of the three worst terrorist attacks on U.S. soil, the other two being the bombing of the federal building in Oklahoma City by Timothy McVeigh and Terry Nichols in 1995 and the 9/11 attacks, which are covered in Chapter 2 and Chapter 3 of this book, respectively.

Anarchy on Wall Street

Wall Street was the direct target of an attack, which came just four years later. The Black Tom Island attack proved to be a prelude to the first Red Scare of the American century. In 1917, the Russian Revolution put the Bolsheviks in power in the new Soviet Union. In the United States, anarchists sent chills of fear down the spines of millions of ordinary Americans. Waves of immigrants—not familiar types from England, Ireland, Scandinavia, and Germany, but swarthier sorts from Southern and Eastern Europe—flooded onto Ellis Island in New York Harbor. Many espoused the cause of anarchism.

From 1901, when he arrived in the United States, until he was deported in 1919, anarchist Luigi Galleani inspired his followers to commit a series of deadly bombings in several American cities. This reign of terror, occurring mostly in 1919, climaxed with an explosion that shook Wall Street just past noon on September 16, 1920. Prefiguring the 1993 World Trade Center bombing and the 1995 Oklahoma City attack, in which the explosives were transported in vans, this early terrorist atrocity involved a wagon loaded with 100 pounds of dynamite and several pounds of cast iron. The 38 victims, most of whom were said to have died instantly or within moments of the blast, were mostly young adults working as messengers, stenographers, clerks, and brokers. Many of the wounded suffered severe injuries. The bomb caused more than $2 million in property damage and wrecked most of the interior spaces of the Morgan building.

As federal agents strove mightily to put an end to these anarchist attacks, caught up in their net were two recent Italian immigrants, Sacco and Vanzetti. Accused of a payroll robbery in which the payroll clerk was shot to death, they were tried and condemned to death. Thereafter, their fates became the cause of thousands around the globe, who contended that they were condemned not for crimes of which their guilt seemed far from certain, but for their political beliefs. More than 80 years after their executions, their guilt or innocence—like that of the Molly Maguires—remains a topic of controversy and curiosity.[28]

International Islamic Terrorism

Although the United States has been Israel's staunchest and most generous ally since its founding in 1948, the 1970s was the decade that brought international terrorism into American homes. Palestinian hijackers, the murder of Israeli Olympians in Munich, and the 1980 U.S. embassy hostage crisis in Tehran—which significantly influenced the presidential elections—replaced Vietnam on the nightly news. John LeCarre, famous for writing *The Spy Who Came in from the Cold* and other Cold War spy novels, turned his attention to international terrorism with *The Little Drummer Girl*, later a 1984 major motion picture starring Diane Keaton and more recently a 2018 TV miniseries starring Florence Pugh.

Still, the thrust of U.S. President Ronald Reagan's foreign policy remained anticommunism. The focus changed dramatically in the 1990s, as Uncle Sam's triumph in the First Gulf War was followed in a few short years by the first terrorist attack on the World Trade Center. And yet the years of Bill Clinton's presidency were marked by a sort of casual indifference at the highest levels of the American government to terrorism. Even Timothy McVeigh's devastating 1995 bombing of Oklahoma City's federal building failed to elicit the sort of response that might have anticipated—and perhaps averted—the cataclysmic events of September 11, 2001.

On that day, life in America changed. The course of U.S. foreign and domestic policy was set in new and dramatic directions. On the international front, two military incursions were initiated, the first in Afghanistan, the second in Iraq. As this is written, more than 19 years after the second of these invasions, these wars have finally wound down. President Joe Biden pulled U.S. troops out of Afghanistan early in his presidency, leaving that land of endless warfare to the Taliban.

On the home front, a new, cabinet-level Department of Homeland Security grouped such diverse agencies as the Coast Guard and the Immigration and Naturalization Service (INS) (now two distinct agencies) under one large umbrella. The USA Patriot Act and other new legislation endowed these agencies, as well as the FBI, National Security Agency (NSA), and others with enhanced powers of surveillance and enforcement.

All of this was lumped under the rubric of the War on Terror, a term that critics on the left hotly contested. The first World Trade Center bombing, covered in Chapter 1, and the Oklahoma City bombing, the topic of Chapter 2, were preludes to the first decade of the 21st century. They were early warning signals, omens of the worse to come. But as such, they provided only limited insight into what would happen during the first decade of the new millennium. As the War on Terror gained momentum, detainees poured into the U.S. military's Guantanamo Bay detention camp in Cuba, and even a few U.S. citizens were incarcerated without access to legal counsel or any prospect of a speedy trial. At the same time, the executed McVeigh was succeeded by new breeds of domestic terrorists, motivated by environmental rather than political and religious concerns, but organized—or not—around the same principle of "leaderless resistance." The Animal Liberation Front (ALF) and the Earth Liberation Front (ELF) are the best known of these loosely knit eco-terrorist outfits.

With the Bush administration maintaining that indefinite detention and techniques such as waterboarding—viewed by many experts to be a form of torture—lay within the government's legal purview, U.S. courts, especially federal courts, were faced with cases that cut to the quick of traditional civil liberties which once were presumably secured for all time by the Constitution.

As stated at the start of this Introduction, this book aims to assess how well America's justice system in the last decade of the 20th century and the first decade of the 21st century performed in the face of the new terrorist challenges that disrupted the all-too-brief *Pax Americana* at the end of the Cold War. In the 12 chapters that follow, as I present the main features of each trial within the context of the events leading up to it and the inevitable appellate court decisions surrounding it, I also keep one eye—and ask my readers to do the same—upon the two questions first posed here:

1. How well did law enforcement perform in the wake of each particular terrorist attack?
2. How well did our courts perform in trying the accused terrorists?

At times, I will make express referrals back to the early cases—the Molly Maguires, the Steunenberg murder, Black Tom Island, Sacco and Vanzetti—discussed briefly in this Introduction. At all times, I suggest that our consideration of the modern cases covered in this volume should be informed by the checkered history of American justice's handling of terrorism and its alleged perpetrators in our early modern industrial era (i.e., from the end of the Civil War to approximately the New Deal). In that context, the ultimate question this book asks is: Has American justice improved upon past performances?

Chapter 11 and Chapter 12 add additional perspectives on this question in the context of the January 6, 2021 assault on the Capitol and the varied official responses to it.

Notes

1. See "16.3 Wartime Politics," *LibreTexts: Humanities,* https://human.libretexts.org/Bookshelves/History/National_History/United_States_History_to_1877_(Locks_et_al.)/16%3A_The_Civil_War/16.03%3A_Wartime_Politics (accessed May 6, 2024).
2. "Clement Vallandigham and the Constitution," *Bill of Rights Institute* (emphasis added), https://billofrightsinstitute.org/essays/clement-vallandigham-and-constitutionalism (accessed May 5, 2024).
3. "Espionage Act of 1917 and Sedition Act of 1918 (1917–1918)," *National Constitution Center,* https://constitutioncenter.org/the-constitution/historic-document-library/detail/espionage-act-of-1917-and-sedition-act-of-1918-1917-1918 (accessed May 6, 2024).
4. Ibid.
5. See Eugene V. Debs, "Wikipedia," https://en.wikipedia.org/wiki/Eugene_V._Debs (accessed May 6, 2024).
6. *Schenck v. United States,* 249 U.S. 47 (1919); for an excellent discussion of *Schenck, see* "Schenck v. United States," *Laws,* https://kids.laws.com/schenck-v-united-states (accessed May 6, 2024).

7. 323 U.S. 214; *see also,* "Facts and Case Summary: Korematsu v. U.S.," *United States Courts,* https://www.uscourts.gov/educational-resources/educational-activities/facts-and-case-summary-korematsu-v-us (accessed May 6, 2024).
8. See, generally, Martin Henn, *Under the Color of Law* (Lanham, MD: Lexington Books, 2010).
9. Joe Cuervo, "Does America Have Too Many Lawyers?" August 4, 2008, http://www.associatedcontent.com/article/913093/does_america_have_too_many_lawyers.html?cat=17 (accessed October 24, 2010).
10. Julie Johnson and Ruth Kamlin, "Do We Have Too Many Lawyers?" *TIME,* August 26, 1991, http://www.time.com/time/magazine/article/0,9171,973684,00.html (accessed October 24, 2010).
11. Ted Morgan, *Wilderness at Dawn: The Settling of the American Continent* (New York: Simon & Schuster, 1993), p. 186.
12. *Pierson v. Post*, 3 Cai. R. 175, 2 Am. Dec. 264 (N.Y. 1805).
13. *Ghen v. Rich*, 8 F.159 (D. Mass. 1881).
14. The Second Amendment to the U.S. Constitution states, "A well regulated Militia, being necessary to the security of a free State, the right of the people to keep and bear Arms, shall not be infringed."
15. This argument was suggested by Humphrey Bogart's character, Rick, to a Nazi officer in the 1943 film *Casablanca*. Bogey tells the German officer, who wonders if Rick can imagine the German army in New York City, that there are some neighborhoods of New York that the Nazis would be ill advised to enter. The same contention was voiced in Leon Uris's 1963 novel *Armageddon* by a character who contended that if every Jew met the Gestapo at his front door with a loaded pistol, the roundup of Germany's Jewry for the camps would not have lasted very long.
16. See Barton Gellman, "Locked and Loaded: The Secret World of Extreme Militias," *TIME*, October 11, 2010, p. 24.
17. See Martin Henn, *Under the Color of Law: The Bush Administration's Subversion of U.S. Constitutional and International Law in the War on Terror* (Lanham, MD: Lexington Books, 2010).
18. James Ottavio Castagnera, "Why the Nation Needs More Lawyers," *Thurgood Marshall Law Review*, 22, 1, Fall 1996, p. 19.
19. "Crime: Cherry Pie," *TIME*, October 25, 1971, http://www.time.com/time/.magazine/article/0,9171,877306,00.html (accessed October 24, 2010).

> Last week, after 17 months on the FBI's Most Wanted list, Brown, 28, reappeared. The dramatic episode was a bitter elaboration on his mordant dictum: "Violence is as American as cherry pie." About 2:30 one morning, four black men, heavily armed, robbed a black after hours bar called the Red Carpet Lounge on Manhattan's upper West Side. They ordered about 25 customers to lie on the floor, assaulted some of them, took their wallets and laid down a barrage of fire as they left. As the robbers were scattering outside, they were pursued by six carloads of police who had been alerted by the bar's lookout men. In a running gun battle, two cops were wounded, one of them by a shotgun

blast. A patrolman chased one robber to a nearby rooftop and shot him twice in the abdomen. Identified by fingerprints, police said, the wounded man was H. Rap Brown, and he was holding a .357 Magnum revolver when hit. At week's end, he lay in fair condition in a New York hospital.

20. James Ford Rhodes, *History of the United States from Hayes to McKinley, 1877–1896* (Vol. 8 of the series *History of the United States of America: From the Compromise of 1850 to the McKinley-Bryan Campaign of 1896*) (New York: MacMillian, 1919), pp. 52–58.
21. See "Revenge Is a Dish Best Served Cold," *Wikipedia*, https://en.wiktionary.org/wiki/revenge_is_a_dish_best_served_cold ("Earliest known metaphorical reference to revenge as food in English is 'And then revenge is *very good eaten cold*, as the vulgar say,' from a 1846 translation of Eugène Sue's *Mathilde: Mémoires d'une Jeune Femme*. The passage suggests that it was an existing expression. Similar proverbs are known as early as the 17th century with 'Revenge is not good in cold bloud' in a translation of *Don Quixote*.") (emphasis in original) (accessed May 6, 2024).
22. Charles Darrow, "Comments on Harry Orchard during the Trial of Charles Moyer, William Hayward (sic) and George Pettibone (1907)," quoted and cited in "Murder of Frank Steunenberg," *Spatacus Educational*, https://spartacus-educational.com/USAsteunenberg.htm, note 3 (accessed May 6, 2024).
23. The absolute best source on the Steunenberg murder trials is J. Anthony Lukas, *Big Trouble: A Murder Trial in a Small Western Town Sets off a Struggle for the Soul of America* (New York: Simon & Schuster, 1997). Numerous books have debated the existence or nonexistence, the guilt or innocence, of the men hanged as Molly Maguires. Among those currently available, the most recent and perhaps best is Kevin Kenny, *Making Sense of the Molly Maguires* (New York: Oxford University Press, 1998). More obscure, but often informative and provocative, and available with some effort, are Thomas Barrett, *The Mollies Were Men: Final Chapter* (2nd ed.) (Bloomington, IN: First Books Library, 2003) (available as of August 24, 2010, http://www.amazon.com/exec/obidos/ASIN/1403396841/coalregiononline); and Anthony Bimba, *The Molly Maguires* (New York: International Publishers, 1970) (available as of August 24, 2010, http://www.amazon.com/exec/obidos/ASIN/0717802736/coalregiononline). Alan Pinkerton, founder of the Pinkerton Detective Agency, which allegedly infiltrated agents into the Molly Maguire secret society, published a nearly contemporary account of the exploit, *The Molly Maguires and the Detectives* (1880) (http://www. archive.org/details/mollymaguiresdet00pink). For a fictionalized treatment of the relationship between the Molly Maguire and Steunenberg cases, see James Castagnera, *Ned McAdoo, Attorney at Large*, *https://www.amazon.com/Ned-McAdoo-Attorney-at-Large, ebook/dp/B07ZBMF5N7/ref=sr_1_1?crid=131UWJV7PGR1&keywords=ned%20McAdoo%2C%20Attorney%20at%20Large&qid=1697970429&s=books&sprefix=ned%20mcadoo%2C%20attorney%20at%20large%2Cstripbooks%2C55&sr=1-1* (accessed May 6, 2024).
24. "Reports of International Arbitral Awards: Lehigh Valley Railroad Company, Agency of Canadian Car and Foundry Company, Limited, and Various

Underwriters (United States) v. Germany (Sabotage Cases)," 8, p. 226, June 15, 1939, reprinted by United Nations (2006), https://legal.un.org/riaa/cases/vol_VIII/225-460.pdf (accessed May 6, 2024).

25. James Ottavio Castagnera, "85 85 Ears before 9–11. . . Manhattan Was Blasted in a Now-Forgotten Act of Terrorism," *History News Network*, https://www.historynewsnetwork.org/article/85-years-before-9-11-manhattan-was-blasted-in-a-no (accessed May 6, 2024).
26. See, op. cit., Note 11.
27. *Schenck v. United States*, 249 U.S. 47 (1919).
28. See "Sacco and Vanzetti," *Wikipedia*, http://en.wikipedia.org/wiki/Sacco_and_Vanzetti; "The Trial of Sacco and Vanzetti," *Famous Trials*, http://www.law.umkc.edu/faculty/projects/ftrials/saccov/saccov.htm; Bruce Watson, *Sacco and Vanzetti: The Men, the Murders and the Judgment of Mankind* (New York: Viking, 2007); Nicolo Sacco and Bartolomeo Vanzetti, *The Letters of Sacco and Vanzetti* (New York: Penguin Books, 2007).

About the Author

Dr. James Ottavio Castagnera, Esq., holds an M.A. in journalism from Kent State University (Ohio), and a J.D. and Ph.D. (American studies) from Case Western Reserve University (Ohio). He worked for ten years as a labor, employment, and intellectual property (IP) attorney with the Saul Ewing law firm and 23 years as associate provost and legal counsel for academic affairs at Rider University (New Jersey), where in 2018 he received the university's highest annual award for distinguished service. He was also a full-time law professor at the University of Texas-Austin and Widener University Law School (Pennsylvania).

Having retired from Rider in 2019, he is engaged in a portfolio of activities: President of Dr. Jim's One-Stop HR Shop, a freelance writing, webinar and training company in the HR space; CEO of the International Artificial Intelligence Association, a think tank dedicated to understanding the effects of Generative AI; an Adjunct Professor of Law in the Kline School of Law at Drexel University (Pennsylvania) and the University of Miami (Florida) School of Law.

He has 25 published books.

The Fire Bell in the Night[1] The 1993 World Trade Center Bombing

1

> On a snowy day, Friday, February 26, 1993, a massive car bomb nearly toppled the World Trade Center. The unthinkable had happened, an instantly recognizable American landmark had become the target of a terrorist attack . . . . There had been terrorist acts before 1993,[2] but the Trade Center attack was unique. These were not Americans killed on an airplane or in a foreign land. These were Americans killed on their own soil. And the scariest element may have been not the explosion, the scale of the destruction, nor even the number of dead but the sense of vulnerability ushered in by the arrival of guerilla tactics in America.[3]

The writer of these words is Robert E. Precht, who in 1993 was a public defender appointed to represent one of the Muslim men accused of the bombing. In the first sentence of his book, he asks, "Is a fair trial possible in the war on terrorism?"[4] This is a question I will be asking—and, I hope, answering—throughout this book. In 1993, before the "War on Terrorism" was a cliché, but radical Muslim terrorism was already commonplace in the world at large (if not yet in the United States), the answer was a clear "yes."

On November 5, 1990, Rabbi Meir Kahane was shot dead in a Marriott Hotel in Manhattan, following a speech he had just given there. Kahane headed the Jewish Defense League, a radical Zionist organization linked to numerous terrorist activities. Accused of the assassination was El Sayyid Nosair, who was shot by an officer of the U.S. Postal Inspection Service as he fled the scene.[5]

Born on November 5, 1955, in Egypt, Nosair was a naturalized U.S. citizen. He had emigrated from Port Said in 1981, arriving in the United States with an engineering degree. He worked at various jobs in New York and New Jersey, notably as a heating, ventilation and air conditioning (HVAC) repairman in the Big Apple's criminal court buildings. He was granted U.S. citizenship in 1989. However,

> Nosair expressed dislike for American culture and what he perceived to be rampant moral corruption. Nosair became involved with the al-Farouq Mosque in Brooklyn, which was supported by the Maktabal-Khadamat (Services Office), which was established in 1984 by Osama bin Laden and Abdullah Azzam in Peshawar, Pakistan. The purpose of the Services Office was raising funds for the Arab mujahadeen during the Soviet war in Afghanistan, as well as recruitment.

DOI: 10.4324/9781003474104-1

> Ali Mohamed, a sergeant at Fort Bragg, provided United States Army manuals and other assistance to individuals at the al-Farouq Mosque, and some members including Mahmoud Abouhalima and Nosair practiced at the Calverton Shooting Range on Long Island, many of the group wearing [T]-shirts reading "Help Each Other in Goodness and Piety . . . . A Muslim to a Muslim is a Brick Wall" with a map of Afghanistan emblazoned in the middle.[6]

Nosair's defense was undertaken by the flamboyant "radical lawyer" William M. Kunstler.[7] Kunstler wrote in 1994—shortly after the trial and only a year before his death—"When I first took on Nosair, I believed he was guilty, so I suggested an insanity defense."[8] However, Kunstler explained, from the time he first met Nosair in a hospital, shortly after the shootings, his client consistently professed his innocence. Kunstler and his trial team eventually decided to withdraw the insanity plea and force the prosecution to prove beyond a reasonable doubt that Nosair had killed Kahane. Recalled Kunstler,

> During the trial, the prosecutors from the Manhattan district attorney's office presented a case with serious weaknesses. For example, although several people testified that they had seen Nosair near Kahane when the rabbi was killed, the videotape made by a Kahane supporter moments before the assassination showed that not a single one of the "eyewitnesses" was standing where they said they were when the shooting occurred. During the deliberations, the jury several times requested that the videotape be played back for them frame by frame.[9]

The jury's verdict has been called "bizarre."[10] Nosair was acquitted of Kahane's murder but convicted of assault and possession of an illegal firearm. The presiding judge, Alvin Schlesinger, opined that the jury's acquittal of Nosair on the murder charge "was against the overwhelming weight of evidence and was devoid of common sense and logic."[11]

Kunstler, of course, held a different view. Noting inconsistencies in the prosecutors' case, as well as some bizarre events in the aftermath of the killing,[12] he called the acquittal "a thrilling victory."[13] Judge Schlesinger called it "a rape of this country, of our Constitution and of our laws, and of people seeking to exist peacefully together." But he also conceded on the record, "The one thing that persists is the fairness and vitality of our system of law."[14]

Indeed, the outcome of the Nosair trial suggests that—at least in the early 1990s—a fair trial was possible for a Muslim terrorist in America.

1.1 The 1993 World Trade Center Bombing

In a 1997 Home Box Office docu-drama entitled *Path to Paradise*, Nosair is depicted plotting from prison with the convicted perpetrators of the 1993 bombing.[15] And, in fact, he was convicted in 1994 of seditious conspiracy for his role in planning the attack. The actual attackers—presuming that the right guys were arrested and convicted—included Ramzi Yousef, Mahmud Abouhalima, Mohammad Salameh, Nidal Ayyad, Ahmad Ajaj, and Eyad Ismoil. All were said to be impassioned followers of an imam, the so-called blind Sheik, Omar Abdul-Rahman.

At 17 minutes past noon on February 26, 1993, a Friday, a thunderous explosion—like the Black Tom Island blast nearly 75 years earlier—rocked Manhattan. This time the epicenter was the parking garage beneath the World Trade Center. The explosion, officially attributed to a 1,500-pound urea nitrate and hydrogen gas truck bomb, dug a 100-foot crater. It killed six. More than 1,000 more were injured, mostly in the chaos of the subsequent evacuation.[16]

1.2 Background[17]

On April 24, 1992, Ahmad Mohammad Ajaj departed from his home in Houston, Texas, and traveled to the Middle East to attend a terrorist training camp, known as Camp Khaldan, on the Afghanistan-Pakistan border. There he learned how to construct homemade explosive devices. During his time in Pakistan, Ajaj met Ramzi Ahmed Yousef. Together, the two plotted to use their newly acquired skills to bomb targets in the United States.

In the fall of 1992, after formulating a plan, Ajaj and Yousef traveled to New York City under assumed names. Ajaj carried with him a so-called terrorist kit that he and Yousef had assembled in Pakistan. The kit included, among other things, handwritten notes Ajaj had taken while attending explosives courses, manuals containing formulas and instructions for manufacturing bombs, materials describing how to carry off a successful terrorist operation, videotapes advocating terrorist action against the United States, and fraudulent identification documents.

On September 1, 1992, Ajaj and Yousef, using false names and passports, arrived at John F. Kennedy International Airport in New York. As they attempted to clear customs, Immigration and Naturalization Service (INS) inspectors discovered that Ajaj's passport had been altered. They searched his belongings. When the agents discovered his terrorist kit, Ajaj became belligerent. The INS seized the kit and placed him under arrest. Ajaj was later indicted in the U.S. District Court for the Eastern District of New York for passport fraud. He pled guilty and was sentenced to six months' imprisonment.

During Ajaj's encounter with the INS inspectors, he denied that he was traveling with Yousef, who proceeded unmolested to the secondary inspection area, where he presented an Iraqi passport and claimed political asylum.

Yousef was arrested for entering the United States without a visa. In this still innocent age, he subsequently was released by the INS on his own recognizance, promising to appear for a hearing some months hence.

Once in New York, Yousef assembled his team, which allegedly included Mohammed Salameh, Nidal Ayyad, Mahmoud Abouhalima, and Abdul Rahman Yasin. Together, the conspirators implemented the bombing plot that Ajaj and Yousef had hatched overseas. Ayyad and Salameh opened a joint bank account into which they deposited funds to finance the bombing plot. Some of that money was later used by Salameh to rent a storage shed in Jersey City, New Jersey, where the conspirators stored chemicals for making explosives. Yousef also drew on that account to pay for materials described in Ajaj's manuals as ingredients for bomb making.

The first target of the conspirators' plot was the World Trade Center. Ayyad used his position as an engineer at Allied Signal, a large New Jersey chemical company, to order the necessary chemical ingredients for bomb making, and to order hydrogen tanks from ALG Welding Company that would enhance the bomb's destructive force. Abouhalima obtained "smokeless powder," which the conspirators used to make explosives. Smokeless powder, along with all the other chemicals procured by the conspirators for the bomb, was stored in the shed rented by Salameh.

Abouhalima helped Salameh and Yousef find a ground-floor apartment at 40 Pamrapo Ave. in Jersey City. The apartment fit the specifications in Ajaj's manuals for an ideal base of operations. In the 40 Pamrapo apartment, Abouhalima, Salameh, Yousef, and Yasin mixed the chemicals for the World Trade Center bomb, following Ajaj's formulas. Abouhalima also obtained a telephone calling card, which the conspirators used to contact each other and to call various chemical companies for bomb ingredients.

During this entire period, although Ajaj remained incarcerated, he kept in telephone contact with Yousef. By doing so, Ajaj stayed abreast of the conspirators' progress in carrying out the terrorist plot and attempted to get his terrorist kit into Yousef's hands. Because Ajaj was in jail and his telephone calls were monitored, Ajaj and Yousef spoke in code when discussing the bomb plot.

On February 23, 1993, Salameh rented a yellow van at DIB Leasing, a Ryder dealership in Jersey City. The conspirators loaded their homemade bomb into that van. On February 26, 1993, the conspirators drove the bomb-laden van into a belowground parking lot on the B-2 level of the World Trade Center Complex and, using a timer, set the bomb to detonate. At approximately noon, the bomb exploded, killing six people, injuring over 1,000 others, and causing hundreds of millions of dollars in damage.

The explosion opened a hole seven stories deep; one FBI agent called the small number of deaths "a miracle."[18]

After the explosion, Ayyad took credit for the bombing on behalf of the conspirators by, among other things, writing an anonymous letter to *The New York Times* explaining that the attack was undertaken in retaliation for American support of Israel. The letter threatened future terrorist "missions."

Immediately after the bombing, Yousef, Abouhalima, and Yasin fled the country. Abouhalima was apprehended in Egypt prior to the trial and turned over to federal agents by Egyptian authorities, but Yousef and Yasin remained fugitives. Salameh arranged to flee, as well, but was arrested the day before he planned to depart when he made the ludicrous mistake of going back to the Ryder truck rental office to get his rental deposit back. On March 1, 1993, Ajaj completed his term of imprisonment on the passport fraud conviction and was released. Approximately one week later, on March 9, Ajaj was taken into government custody on an INS detainer.

In September 1993, Ayyad, Abouhalima, Ajaj, Salameh, Yousef, and Yasin were indicted in the U.S. District Court for the Southern District of New York on an assortment of charges relating to their participation in the plot to bomb the World Trade Center (Yousef and Yasin were still fugitives at the time of trial)

1.3 Pretrial Proceedings

1.3.1 Mohammad Salameh's Bail Application

Robert Precht had been a public defender for a dozen years when by chance he was appointed to represent Salameh. Harking back to the celebrated conspiracy trials of a bygone era to which I referred in the Introduction, Precht reminisced, "I had started the job fired with dreams of becoming the next Clarence Darrow, valiant defender of the underdog." But, he added, "my sense of mission had withered over the years in the face of the grim realities of the practice: a conveyor belt of small cases and broken lives, rude judges, arrogant prosecutors, and public contempt."[19] Six days after the bombing, all that changed. As he tells his tale, he was hauled into a courtroom to represent Salameh at his arraignment with virtually no opportunity to prepare. He tried to tell his client that bail in a case such as this was beyond the pale, but Mohammad was not hearing it. He insisted, "I want you to try. You are lawyer." Precht reproduced the following record of the hearing that followed before Federal District Judge Richard Owen.

Judge Owen: Counselor, I don't intend to be here all night.

Precht: Yes, I understand your Honor, just one more minute. Yes, your Honor, I have consulted my client and I am going to make a bail application. In the circumstances, your Honor, I . . . we will be asking for $5 million bail, secured by 10% cash and 20 consignors. Given the flimsy evidence in the complaint and the fact that . . .

Judge Owen: Counselor, don't you know how serious this crime is? Denied! Case adjourned to March 27 for assignment of trial judge.[20]

None of the other four defendants tried to make bail.

1.3.2 Motions to Suppress Evidence

While Ayyad, Abouhalima, Ajaj, and Salameh sat in jail awaiting trial, on October 6, 1993, Ahmad Ajaj pled guilty in the U.S. District Court for the Eastern District of New York to one count of passport fraud. After the guilty plea, Federal Judge Reena Raggi ordered the government to return Ajaj's belongings or to come forward with a reason for failing to do so.

On December 22, 1993, an assistant U.S. attorney for the Eastern District of New York served a grand jury subpoena on Ajaj calling for production of many of the terrorist materials seized at Kennedy Airport. When Ajaj's counsel in the passport fraud case inquired about whether the subpoena, styled *ad testificandum*, really sought Ajaj's testimony as well as the evidence listed in the rider, the government explained that the subpoena sought only the specified physical evidence. At the time, Ajaj did not move to quash the subpoena.

After Ajaj learned that the government was planning to introduce the terrorist materials in the World Trade Center bombing trial, however, he moved to suppress the materials held pursuant to the grand jury subpoena. Ajaj argued that the subpoena was illegal since: (1) he could not have been under investigation when the subpoena was issued because it was issued after the completion of the passport fraud case but before the World Trade Center was bombed; and (2) the subpoena was a subpoena *ad testificandum*, not a subpoena *duces tecum*. The trial judge denied Ajaj's motion to suppress, finding that the use of the subpoena was proper.[21] In total, District Judge Duffy allowed to be admitted into evidence:

- A videotape of the bombing of a U.S. embassy, complete with instructions on how to build bombs and timers.
- Ajaj's own notebooks on how to make explosives, such as urea nitrate and improvised weapons.
- A videotaped chemistry lesson on the concoction of explosive compounds.
- Manuals dealing with catalysts, detonators, and other bomb components.

- A pamphlet entitled "Facing the Enemies of God: Terrorism Is a Religious Duty and Force Is Necessary."
- A book entitled *Rapid Destruction and Demolition.*

Judge Duffy also admitted copies of similar books and pamphlets seized from Defendant Abouhalima's place and bearing his fingerprints. In a motion to exclude this evidence, Abouhalima argued that the highly prejudicial nature of the materials unfairly outweighed their probative value.[22]

The defendants also moved to suppress evidence of the contents of their storage shed. The shed was part of a facility called Space Station, located in Jersey City. On March 5, 1993, a magistrate judge in the federal district of New Jersey issued a search warrant, based on the probable cause affidavit of FBI Special Agent Eric Pilker. Pilker's affidavit in support of the search warrant began by stating the obvious, i.e., an explosion had occurred at the World Trade Center, and an FBI explosives expert had determined that a bomb caused it. It went on to relate that the expert knew from examining an auto part (a piece of an axle) recovered at the crime scene that the part belonged to whatever vehicle carried the bomb. Using the part's vehicle identification number (VIN), investigators traced it to a yellow Ford Econoline 350 van registered in Alabama to the Ryder truck rental company and leased by Mohammad Salameh at a rental office in Jersey City for a one-week period beginning three days before the explosion.

Elsewhere in the affidavit, Pilker related that a Space Station employee informed the FBI that storage shed No. 4344 was under lease to "Kamil Ibrahim." The employee told the FBI that on February 25, 1993, one day before the bombing, he observed Kamil Ibrahim, along with other males, making numerous trips to the shed using a yellow Ryder van. This same Space Station employee stated that on March 4, less than one week after the bombing, he let himself into the shed and saw containers marked "sulfuric acid," "nitric acid," and "urea." A forensic chemist at the Bureau of Alcohol, Tobacco and Firearms (ATF) informed the FBI that those three substances could be combined to produce a powerful bomb.

Finally, the affidavit asserted that when renting the Ryder van, Salameh had given a telephone number that belonged to one Jodie Hadas at 34 Kensington Ave., Apartment 4, in Jersey City. When investigators searched that apartment on March 4, 1993, they found tools, wiring, and manuals concerning antennae, circuitry, and electromagnetic devices. A law enforcement bomb technician advised the FBI that these items indicated that a bomb maker lived in that apartment.[23] Judge Duffy held that the government had probable cause to permit admission of the shed's contents into evidence.

Abouhalima's lawyers also moved to suppress some statements made by their client after his arrest. Abouhalima made two incriminating remarks during his post-arrest interview. Shortly after being taken into U.S. custody, he was informed that he was under arrest for his participation in the World Trade Center bombing. Once FBI agents advised him of his constitutional rights, they interviewed him about the apartment at 40 Pamrapo. During the interview, Abouhalima asked an officer whether he knew an individual by the name of Rashid. Yousef's nickname was Rashed. Abouhalima also corrected an FBI agent's pronunciation of "Pamrapo." At trial, Abouhalima requested a suppression hearing directly before these remarks were admitted into evidence. The court, however, found that such a hearing was unnecessary. After introducing these statements into evidence, the government used them to assert that Abouhalima had linked the questioning about 40 Pamrapo to the World Trade Center bombing to Yousef.[24]

Abouhalima's attorneys also moved for a separate trial, contending that Ajaj's Holy War materials would have a spillover effect that would bias the jury against him, since some of the same stuff was seized from his residence. This motion, too, was denied by Judge Duffy.[25]

Last, but hardly least, was Judge Duffy's denial of Salameh's motion for a change of venue grounded upon the vast amount of publicity the bombing had generated inside the Big Apple. "The judge ruled that the publicity engendered by the World Trade Center explosion was so widespread that there was no place where the case could be more fairly tried than in New York City."[26]

1.4 The First Criminal Trial

The trial ran for six months. The jury was treated to 1,000 physical exhibits and the testimony of some 200 witnesses. Few juries—and in fact, few attorneys—ever experience such an ordeal. The term trial truly applied. I myself have never tried a case running longer than three or four consecutive days. Every time I was left exhausted, regardless of its outcome. Laypeople, who experience courtroom proceedings through the lens of such television series as *Law and Order* and films like *A Few Good Men*, get only a glimpse of the intense preparation demanded by each day in court. Such dramatic glimpses fail to convey the grueling ordeal of six or eight hours inside the courtroom, followed by another four or more that night, prepping for the next day's joust. For a case like this, both sides will have war rooms bursting with exhibits and staffed by associate attorneys, paralegals, and legal secretaries. The costs—whether paid by clients, the taxpayer, or in the volunteer attorneys' own sweat equity—are astronomical. The pressure is intense.

When the pretrial motions have been decided, the next step is jury selection. In cases concerning large corporations, this process has become both a cottage industry and something between an art and a science. It can involve public opinion polling, intensive investigation of potential jurors in the pool, and the application of academic research. However, nothing in the record of this case indicates that either side indulged in such techniques—what many pundits would call excesses.[27]

Judge Duffy had already taken Salameh's lawyer, public defender Precht, to task during the hearing on his change-of-venue motion. The judge had lectured him:

> Counsel for Salameh points a finger at the Government for this state of affairs. The fault, as counsel knows full well, however, does not lie with the Government. This court attempted to prevent the dissemination of prejudicial publicity by imposing a "gag order" upon the attorneys and their agents at the time the matter initially came before me. Counsel for Salameh strenuously objected to this order, and successfully had it vacated by the Court of Appeals. In effect, counsel is really complaining that he was unable to "control" the publicity.[28]

Now, consistent with that admonition, Judge Duffy rejected Precht's request for a jury questionnaire. Ruled Duffy, "There has been . . . absolutely no showing that jury questionnaires are of any particular help in the selection of a jury in highly publicized cases where a searching voir dire is conducted."[29] Traditional jury selection usually takes one of two possible forms. I have tried cases in which the potential jurors were brought into the courtroom, where counsel for both sides conducted the voir dire without the interference of the trial judge. The judge was called from chambers only if the two lead counsels could not reach mutual agreement on the suitability of a particular juror.

Judge Duffy took the opposite path, taking the lead in conducting selection, introducing counsel for both sides and asking the potential jurors as a group some general bias questions, such as: "OK, now I want to introduce the defense lawyers. Will you stand up? Anybody know either of these two gentlemen? No, OK."[30]

His honor then questioned each candidate individually, dismissing—often with comments that dripped sarcasm—those who claimed conflicting personal or professional obligations, and those who expressed doubts about their impartiality. For instance, Duffy told a Wall Street broker, who said serving for several months would hurt his career, "If I possibly could, I'd lift your license and put you back on the street." To a woman who claimed bias because a friend worked in a building near the World Trade Center:

> Let me suggest to you the following: suppose, instead of arresting the four guys who are outside, the FBI arrested your friend because they knew that your friend was on Vesey Street and knew exactly all about her movements and how she was seen leaving the Trade Center. Suppose the FBI said your friend was responsible for blowing the Trade Center up. Would you think people should duck jury service if your friend was here on trial?[31]

In the third and final stage, the judge questioned each remaining candidate individually in the robing room with counsel—but not the other jurors—present. Each juror then was excused and the attorneys asked by Duffy to suggest other questions. One juror was dismissed after she told him:

> I believe that I could be fair and impartial. I believe, however, as I have listened to the religious preferences of the people who have been on this panel, that I am the first person who is Jewish. I don't think that my anonymity could be preserved. And so after much thought . . . , I think under these circumstances that I am not willing to serve on the jury.

Judge Duffy: Understandable. Understandable. I never ask the reason why.[32]

Most of the last batch who made it into the robing room made it onto the jury. Together, they faced six months of argument, evidence, and testimony. While, as I suggested previously, a trial is an intensive test of endurance for legal counsel, for laypeople, it is often a tedious affair. From personal experience, I can attest that even one's clients can find the day-to-day laying of evidentiary foundations for admission of exhibits, discussions at sidebar with the judge (out of the jury's hearing) of the finer points of the rules of evidence, and other aspects of courtroom procedure—considered essential to according the defendants due process of law—extremely boring. The thousands of pages of trial transcripts in this case confirm it was no exception.

However, the trial certainly had its dramatic moments. Some of the most dramatic occurred during the first week, when the government elicited first-hand testimony from witnesses who could describe events before, during, and immediately after the explosion. As some recounted their experiences, such as seeing the panicked faces of people fleeing the buildings, they cried. The prosecutors also presented half a dozen photographs of those who were killed. Wounds were visible and one of the dead was obviously pregnant. The photos were introduced in support of the medical examiner's testimony that the dead were killed by "blunt impact trauma" from objects hurled at high speed.[33]

From this dramatic opening move, the federal prosecutors proceeded to forge the chain of evidence they hoped would eliminate in the jurors' minds all reasonable doubts about the defendants' guilt. Evidence included:

- Photographs linking various defendants to the incarcerated Nosair.
- Testimony, fingerprints, and deoxyribonucleic acid (DNA) evidence linking a letter to *The New York Times*, claiming responsibility for the bombing, to defendants.
- Eyewitness testimony tying the defendants to the apartment where the bomb was built and to the storage facility where the components were stored.

Absent any confessions, proof beyond a reasonable doubt of each defendant's *mens rea* (guilty mind), a crucial element of the conspiracy charges in particular, posed a problem. Judge Duffy's jury instructions sought to assist the jurors over this hump, explaining that circumstantial evidence can be used to infer motive and intent.

> Knowledge and intent exists in the mind. No way, even with wonderful machines, with our [CAT] scans and all the rest of it that we can ever crawl into someone's head and figure out what's going on exactly, what is in his mind. You can't take a [CAT] scan of someone's brain and say, so, he was thinking this or that sometime. You can't conclude from that, and yet we draw a conclusion from actions of the person, what his knowledge was, what his intent was. You do it all the time. You do it from circumstantial evidence.
>
> When you were a kid and you were in school, do you remember there was a bully? There was a bully in every kid's class, I am sure of it. Some kid, he'd come along and he'd step on the toe of the person beside him. The victim would yell. And the bully would look at the teacher and say, oh, it was a mistake. I didn't mean to do that. That was an accident. Every other kid in the neighborhood knew that it was no mistake. Right?
>
> The direct evidence would be his declaration that it was a mistake and an accident. But by circumstantial evidence, ladies and gentlemen, you knew that it wasn't a mistake. It was him being a bully. You know, grown-ups are just big kids. We think the same way. You can conclude from circumstantial evidence what someone's intent or knowledge was. Direct evidence i[s] often misleading. Circumstantial evidence is quite sufficient. One thing you should recognize, it still must be proved beyond a reasonable doubt.[34]

Salameh's lawyer objected to the charge, stating, "I just don't think [it is] a good example and I object to that." Abouhalima's counsel also objected to the charge on the ground that it purported to give circumstantial evidence more weight than direct evidence. No other objections were articulated. Ajaj's attorney merely asked the court to instruct the jury on reasonable inferences again, to ensure that the jury understood it was not required to draw any inferences from the evidence. Judge Duffy acquiesced, giving the following reminder:

> I suggest to you that there are times when different inferences may be drawn from facts, whether they are proved by direct or circumstantial evidence. The government asks you to draw one set of inferences. The defendant asks you to draw another set.
>
> [It is] for you and for you alone to decide what inferences, if any, you are willing to draw. If you decide to draw no inferences, that's fine. That's up to you. That's a determination that you are to make.[35]

The jury drew the inferences the government wanted. The defendants were convicted on all counts—notably conspiracy, explosive destruction of property, and interstate transportation of explosives—and subsequently were sentenced to 240 years apiece in federal prison. In 1998, the U.S. Court of Appeals for the Second Circuit—which, like the U.S. District Court where the case was tried, sat in downtown Manhattan not far from the World Trade Center itself—released its 161-page opinion, reviewing the myriad objections raised by the defendants in their attempt to have the convictions overturned. Bottom line, the appellate panel held,

> We have conducted a thorough review of all the arguments raised by appellants, and find no basis for reversal in any of them. Accordingly, and for the reasons presented above, we AFFIRM the judgments of conviction as to all four defendants.[36]

The issue of sentencing was a somewhat different story. In their omnibus challenge, the defendants had thrown in an argument about their 1994 sentencing session with Judge Duffy. The Court of Appeals observed:

> All the defendants seek vacatur of their sentences on the ground that the district court erred in allowing them to proceed pro se at their sentencing hearing. After renouncing their trial counsel, the four defendants participated in their May 24, 1994, sentencing proceeding without counsel. The government admits that the record does not reflect a knowing, intelligent and voluntary waiver of the defendants' right to counsel as mandated by *Faretta v. California*, 422 U.S. 806, 834, 95 S. Ct. 2525, 45 L.Ed.2d 562 (1975), and does not object to vacatur. We have reviewed the record and agree that the defendants do not appear to have waived their right to counsel at the sentencing hearing. Accordingly, we vacate and remand for resentencing.
>
> Although Abouhalima has at times indicated that we should consider reassigning the remanded proceedings to a different judge, such a measure is rarely taken. See *United States v. Gaviria*, 49 F.3d 89, 92 (2d Cir., 1995) ("[R]emanding to a different district judge is an extraordinary remedy . . . [to] be reserved for the extraordinary case.") . . . More important, at oral argument all four appellants were expressly asked if they had any objection to matters being returned to Judge Duffy, and no such objections were raised. Under the circumstances, we believe the sentences in all four cases should be vacated and the matter remanded to Judge Duffy.[37]

1.5 The Subsequent Criminal Trials

Four of the six perpetrators of the 1993 bombing had been brought to justice. Two—arguably the two most culpable—had managed to flee the United States immediately following the attack. As noted previously, the conspiracy to bomb the World Trade Center began in the spring of 1992, when Yousef met Ahmad Mohammad Ajaj at a terrorist training camp on the border of Afghanistan and Pakistan. After formulating their terrorist plot, Yousef and Ajaj traveled to New York together in September 1992. In Ajaj's luggage, he carried a terrorist kit that included bomb-making manuals, among other things. After Yousef and Ajaj arrived at John F. Kennedy International Airport, inspectors of the INS discovered the terrorist kit in Ajaj's luggage and arrested him. Although Yousef was also stopped, he and Ajaj did not disclose their connection to one another, and INS officials allowed Yousef to enter the United States.

Once in New York, Yousef began to put together the manpower and supplies that he would need to carry out his plan to bomb the World Trade Center. Yousef assembled a group of co-conspirators to execute his plan, including convicted defendants Mohammad Salameh, Nidal Ayyad, Mahmud Abouhalima, and Abdul Rahman Yasin. Next, Yousef began accumulating the necessary ingredients for the bomb. He ordered the required chemicals, and his associates rented a shed in which to store them. Yousef and Salameh established their headquarters at an apartment they rented in Jersey City, New Jersey, an urban center located across the Hudson River from Manhattan. The apartment also functioned as their bomb-making factory.

In December 1992, Yousef contacted Ismoil, who was then living in Dallas, Texas. On February 22, 1993, Ismoil joined Yousef and the others in New York to help complete the bomb preparations. On February 26, 1993, Yousef and Ismoil were the ones who drove the bomb-laden van onto the B-2 level of the parking garage below the World Trade Center. Although the bombers had planned to use a timer, in the end they substituted an enormous fuse, which gave them time to escape.

Apparently not one to sit back on his laurels, a year and a half after the World Trade Center bombing, Yousef entered Manila, the capital of the Philippines, under an assumed name. By September 1994, he had devised a plan to attack U.S. airliners. According to the plan, five individuals would place bombs aboard 12 U.S.-registered aircraft that served routes in Southeast Asia. The conspirators would board an airliner in Southeast Asia, assemble a bomb on the plane, and then exit the plane during its first layover. As the planes continued on toward their next destinations, the time bombs would detonate. Eleven of the 12 flights targeted were ultimately destined for cities in the United States.

Yousef and his co-conspirators performed several tests in preparation for the airline bombings. In December 1994, Yousef and co-conspirator Wali Khan Amin Shah placed one of the bombs they had constructed in a Manila movie theater. The bomb exploded, injuring several patrons of the theater. Ten days later, Yousef planted another test bomb under a passenger's seat during the first leg of a Philippine Airlines flight from Manila to Japan. Yousef disembarked from the plane during the stopover and then made his way back to Manila. During the second leg of the flight, the bomb exploded, killing one passenger, a Japanese national, and injuring others.

The plot to bomb the U.S.-flagged airliners was uncovered in January 1995, only two weeks before the conspirators intended to carry it out. Yousef and Murad were burning chemicals in their Manila apartment and accidentally caused a fire. An apartment security guard saw the smoke coming from the apartment and called the fire department. After the firemen left, the Philippine police arrived at the apartment, where they discovered chemicals and bomb components, a laptop computer on which Yousef had set forth the aircraft bombing plans, and other incriminating evidence. Philippine authorities arrested Murad and Shah, though Shah escaped and was not recaptured until nearly a year later. Yousef fled the country, but was captured in Pakistan the next month.[38]

On February 21, 1996, a grand jury in the Southern District of New York filed a 20-count superseding indictment against the defendants and others. Counts 1 through 11 charged Yousef and Ismoil with various offenses arising from their participation in the February 26, 1993, bombing of the World Trade Center. Counts 12–19 charged Yousef, Murad, and Shah with various crimes relating to their conspiracy to bomb U.S. airliners in Southeast Asia in 1994 and 1995.[39]

The trial of Yousef, Murad, and Shah on the airline bombing charges began on May 29, 1996, and ended on September 5, 1996, when the jury found all three defendants guilty on all counts. Yousef and Ismoil's trial on charges relating to the World Trade Center bombing began on July 15, 1997, and concluded on November 12, 1997, when the jury found both defendants guilty on all counts.

Yousef was sentenced for both convictions on January 8, 1998. For the World Trade Center convictions, he was sentenced principally to a total of 240 years of imprisonment: 180 years on counts 1–8, plus two 30-year terms on counts 9–10 for violations of federal weapons charges. For the airline bombing convictions, Yousef was sentenced principally to a term of life imprisonment, to be served consecutively to his 240-year sentence for the World Trade Center bombing.[40]

On April 3, 1998, Ismoil was sentenced principally to 180 years of imprisonment on counts 1–6, 8, and 11. Additionally, Ismoil was sentenced to two 30-year terms on counts 9–10 to be served consecutively to each other and to the 180-year sentence, for a total of 240 years of imprisonment.[41]

This time around, in a 1,172-page opinion, the U.S. Court of Appeals for the Second Circuit, after sifting through the defendants' lengthy list of objections, held with regard to the World Trade Center convictions:

1. The District Court did not err in denying Yousef's motion to dismiss the indictment.

2. Yousef's Miranda waiver was not rendered invalid simply because his right to counsel had already attached.
3. Because Yousef did not invoke his right to counsel before any United States official, the admission of his post-arrest statements into evidence did not violate his Sixth Amendment right to counsel.
4. Yousef's Fifth Amendment right to due process was not violated by the United States Government's failure to provide him with counsel after taking him into custody.
5. Yousef waived any argument that his post-arrest statements were involuntary and coerced as a result of his alleged torture by foreign officials.
6. The District Court properly denied Ismoil's motions to suppress his post-arrest statements.
7. The District Court did not commit reversible error by requiring the defense to produce their experts at the Daubert hearing.
8. The District Court did not abuse its discretion in choosing to redact certain references to Yousef from Ismoil's written confession rather than granting Yousef's motion for severance, and neither Yousef nor Ismoil was significantly prejudiced by the joint trial.
9. The District Court did not abuse its discretion in denying Yousef's motion for a change of venue.
10. The District Court did not abuse its discretion by prohibiting Ismoil from introducing various items of evidence from the first World Trade Center bombing trial into evidence because these items were irrelevant and, therefore, inadmissible under Federal Rule of Evidence 402.
11. The District Court did not abuse its discretion by admitting into evidence comparisons made of Ismoil's latent fingerprints found on items at the Pamrapo Apartment with latent fingerprints found on personal documents that Ismoil was known to have handled.
12. The District Court properly instructed the jury on the element of knowledge with respect to Ismoil.
13. The District Court properly instructed the jury on the issue of "aiding and abetting."
14. The District Court did not commit plain error by declining to dismiss the alternate jurors once the jury had retired to deliberate.
15. Ismoil was not denied his due process right to a fair trial by the cumulative effect of the District Court's errors during the trial because the District Court committed no trial errors with respect to Ismoil.[42]

Meanwhile, Judge Duffy at the federal district court reviewed the original four defendants' motions on remand from the Second Circuit's 1998 decision. On remand, these defendants filed motions for new trials on grounds of newly discovered evidence and ineffective assistance of counsel. Judge Duffy held that: (1) counsels' decision not to seek testimony of experts on DNA, linguistics, explosives, computers, sociology, or voice analysis did not amount to ineffective assistance; (2) a government expert's allegedly perjured testimony as to the composition of the bomb did not warrant a new trial; and (3) the alleged torture of one defendant (Abouhalima) in Egypt did not preclude his prosecution in the United States.[43]

1.6 The Civil Trial

Victims of the 1993 bombing—obviously unable to recover a thin dime from the six incarcerated terrorists—sued the Port Authority of New York and New Jersey, alleging that the authority's negligence contributed to their injuries. A 2006 New York state court decision found the agency comparatively responsible at the level of 68%, amazingly assigning only 32% liability to the terrorists who actually did the dirty deed. In January 2008, stunned Port Authority officials asked a five-judge panel of the Appellate Division of the New York Supreme Court[44] to toss out the jury's verdict, which its brief branded as "bizarre."

Remarkably, on April 29, 2008, the appeals panel upheld the $5.5 million verdict.[45] In so holding, the appellate judges opined:

> To be clear, it is not defendant's position that it was prepared to prove that the World Trade Center bombing of February 26, 1993 would have occurred even if it had taken the precautions urged by plaintiff. Indeed, there is no indication that defendant possessed any evidence that the bombers, as they approached the World Trade Center on the morning of the attack, were prepared to do anything other than what they did and evidently planned after reconnoitering their target, namely, to drive into the subgrade public parking garage, park on the access ramp, set a fuse and leave—all without meeting a scintilla of resistance. Instead, defendant sought to prove that the recommended garage precautions would not have prevented the bombers from carrying out another "similar" attack. But, even if this had been shown, and it was not by the evidence adduced, showing no more than that the bombers executed with relative ease a plan specifically premised upon the absence of any impediment to their penetration of their target, it would not suffice to demonstrate the absence of a causal nexus between the defendant's failure to adopt its consultants' recommendations respecting the underground garage and the explosion that occurred there.[46]

1.7 Conspiracy Theories

As I noted in my Introduction, the celebrated terrorist trials of the past few decades have in common, among many things, their fertility for spawning conspiracy theories. The 1993 World Trade Center bombing is certainly not an exception.

On the ragged fringe of conspiracy theory is the notion that the bombers were going for a hydrogen bomb. The strapping of hydrogen cylinders around the core urea nitrate monster inspired this theory. Never mind that a hydrogen bomb does not use hydrogen gas; this theory postulates the presence of an atom bomb in the Big Apple, such as one of the shells that can be fired by the U.S. Army's Atomic Annie cannon in a tactical battlefield situation. Under this theory, what went wrong?

> If it was the bombers [sic] intent to create a hydrogen bomb and the atomic bombs were not synchronized to explode simultaneously the first to explode would blow the rest of the bomb to pieces without getting the desired effect.[47]

More credible, and thus more disturbing, are assorted allegations of government pre-attack knowledge or—worse yet—of instigation of the bombing. Such allegations are not uncommon in terrorism/conspiracy cases.

As noted in the Introduction, there exists much intriguing evidence that the Molly Maguires were not a terrorist organization in the Pennsylvania hard coal country in the 1870s. Rather, goes the counter-theory, Irish miners, politicians, and labor organizations, gaining strength enough to challenge the railroad and mining interests, were branded "Mollies." To make a case against them, agent provocateurs, notably one James McParland, infiltrated the Irish fraternal organization, the Ancient Order of Hibernians, and instigated or personally performed acts of murder, assault, and arson.[48]

Regarding the 1993 bombing, the FBI's relationship to an Egyptian informant, Emad Salem, points to the Bureau's advance knowledge of the pending attack. Salem has said that he thought he was participating in an FBI sting operation during which he would give the plotters harmless powder in lieu of deadly explosive ingredients.[49] Salem's claims are bolstered by hours of tapes he secretly recorded of conversations with his FBI handlers. Some of these tapes remain readily accessible today on YouTube.com. A key tape includes the following:[50]

FBI Special Agent John Anticev: But, uh, basically nothing has changed. I'm just telling you for my own sake that nothing, that this isn't a salary, that it's—you know. But you got paid regularly for good information. I mean, the expenses were a little bit out of the ordinary and it was really questioned. Don't tell Nancy I told you this.

[Nancy Floyd is another FBI special agent who worked with Emad A. Salem in his informant capacity.]

FBI undercover agent Emad A. Salem: Well, I have to tell her, of course.

Anticev: Well then, if you have to, you have to.

Salem: Yeah, I mean because the lady was being honest and I was being honest and everything was submitted with a receipt and now it's questionable.

Anticev: It's not questionable. It's like a little out of the ordinary.

Salem: OK. All right. I don't think it was. If that's what you think, guys, fine, but I don't think that because we was start already building the bomb which is went off in the World Trade Center. It was built by supervising supervision from the Bureau and the D.A. and we was all informed about it and we know that the bomb start to be built. By who? By your confidential informant. What a wonderful, great case!

Anticev: Well.

Salem: And then he put his head in the sand and said, "Oh, no, no, that's not true, he is son of a bitch." [Deep breath.] Okay. It's built with a different way in another place and that's it.

Anticev: No, don't make any rash decisions. I'm just trying to be as honest with you as I can.

Salem: Of course, I appreciate that.

Anticev: And as far as the payments go, and everything like that, they're there. I guarantee you that they are there.

Last, but not least, is the (inevitable?) allegation of an Iraqi connection. In an October 2001 PBS interview, former Central Intelligence Agency (CIA) director James Wooley made a claim that Ramzi Yousef worked for Iraqi intelligence.[51] However, while Yousef may have been in Iraq, extensive investigation by a number of agencies failed to make the connection between the bombing and Saddam Hussein's regime.

1.8 The Last Words

Let me give the last word to the authors of the *9/11 Commission Report*:

> Although the bombing heightened awareness of a new terrorist danger, [the] successful prosecutions contributed to widespread underestimation of the threat. The government's attorneys stressed the seriousness of the crimes, and put forward evidence of Yousef's technical ingenuity. Yet the public image that persisted was not of clever Yousef but of stupid Salameh going back again and again to reclaim his $400 rental deposit.[52]

On February 26, 2023–30 years later to the day—bombing survivor Tim Lang told new media: "I always knew they'd be back."[53]

Notes

1. Thomas Jefferson expressed his opinion of the Missouri Compromise in a letter to John Holms, dated April 22, 1820. Jefferson wrote, famously, that the Missouri question, "like a fire bell in the night, awakened and filled me with terror. I considered it at once as the knell of the Union." See http://www.loc.gov/rr/program/bib/ourdocs/Missouri.html.
2. See my discussion of two major examples from the late 19th and early 20th centuries—the Molly Maguires and the Black Tom Island explosion— in the Introduction.
3. Robert E. Precht, *Defending Mohammad: Justice on Trial* (Ithaca, New York: Cornell University Press, 2003), p. ix.
4. Ibid.
5. History Commons, "Profile: Meir Kahane," http://www.historycommons.org/entity.jsp?entity=meir_kahane.
6. Wikipedia, "El Sayyid Nosair," http://en.wikipedia.org/wiki/El_Sayyid_Nosair.
7. Precht called Kunstler "one of the country's most outrageous and effective defense lawyers" (Precht, supra, note 3, p. 43). Kunstler was best known for his defense of the so-called Chicago Seven, radicals accused of fomenting riots during the 1968 Chicago Democratic Convention. He was in his early 70s in 1993, nearing the end of his career and his life.
8. William M. Kunstler, *My Life as a Radical Lawyer* (New York: Birch Lane Press, 1994), p. 320.
9. Ibid., p. 321.
10. Jeffrey B. Abramson, *We, the Jury: The Jury System and the Ideal of Democracy* (Cambridge, MA: Harvard University Press, 2000), p. 144.
11. Wikipedia, "El Sayyid Nosair," http://en.wikipedia.org/wiki/El_Sayyid_Nosair.
12. For example, "after Kahane was shot, a crazy Jewish doctor jumped into the ambulance with the rabbi and prevented the EMS personnel from intubating him, a procedure that might have saved his life." Kunstler, p. 321.
13. Kunstler, p. 322.
14. Ibid., p. 323.
15. *Path to Paradise*, DVD, directed by Leslie Libman and Larry Williams, Time Warner Entertainment, 1997.
16. Federal Bureau of Investigation Press Room, "First Strike: Global Terror in America," http://www.fbi.gov/page2/feb08/tradebom_022608.html.
17. The background facts that follow are closely adapted from the court's statement of facts in *U.S. v. Salameh* (*Salameh I*), 152 F.3d 88 (2d Cir., 1998), cert. denied, *Abouhalima v. U.S.*, 525 U.S. 1112 (1999).
18. *The 9/11 Commission Report: Final Report of the National Commission on Terrorist Attacks upon the United States* (New York: W.W. Norton & Company, 2004), p. 71.
19. Precht, p. 1.
20. Ibid., p. 7.

21. *U.S. v. Salameh (Salameh I).*
22. Ibid.
23. Ibid.
24. Ibid.
25. Ibid.
26. Precht, p. 45.
27. There exists a vast body of academic and professional research on jurors. See, e.g., Jeffrey T. Frederick, *Mastering Voir Dire and Jury Selection: Gain an Edge in Selecting and Questioning Your Jury* (2nd ed.) (Chicago: ABA Publishing, 2005); Joel D. Lieberman et al., *Scientific Jury Selection* (Washington, DC: American Psychological Association 2006); Neil Kressel et al., *Stack and Sway: The New Science of Jury Consulting* (Oxford: Westview Press, 2004); V. Hale Starr et al., *Jury Selection* (New York: Aspen Law and Business, 2001); Stephanie Leonard Yarbrough, "The Jury Consultant: Friend or Foe of Justice?" *S.M.U. Law Review*, 54, 1885 (2001).
28. Precht, p. 46.
29. *United States v. Salameh*, 1993 WL 364486 (U.S.D.C., S.D.N.Y.). Note that two decades later, it was the prosecutors who proposed a jury selection questionnaire in the 9/11 trial of Zacarias Moussaoui, which is the subject of Chapter 3 of this book. That questionnaire is accessible at http://www.capitaldefense-weekly.com/library/moussaoui/1_01-cr-00455/docs/70927/0.pdf. Also note that much research was available to Judge Duffy and counsel for both sides at the time of jury selection. See, e.g., Geoffrey P. Kramer et al., "Pretrial Publicity, Judicial Remedies, and Jury Bias," Law and Human Behavior, 14, 5, 1990, pp. 409–438; Honorable Robert M. Tagasuki, "Jury Selection in a High Profile Case: *United States v. DeLorean*," American University Law Review, 40, 1990–1991, p. 837.
30. Precht, p. 47.
31. Precht, pp. 51–52.
32. Precht, p. 53.
33. *U.S. v. Salameh* (*Salameh I*), p. 122.
34. Ibid., p. 140.
35. Ibid.
36. Ibid., p. 161.
37. Ibid.
38. *U.S. v. Yousef*, 327 F.3d 56, 78 (2d Cir., 2003).
39. Ibid., p. 80.
40. Ibid.
41. Ibid.
42. Ibid., p. 172.
43. *U.S. v. Salameh*, 54 F.Supp.2d 236 (S.D.N.Y., 1999), cert. denied, *Salameh v. U.S.*, 526 U.S. 1028 (1999).
44. Note that, uniquely turning American nomenclature on its head, the Empire State's court system is labeled "the Supreme Court" at the trial level, while the state's highest court is called the Court of Appeals.

45. *Nash v. Port Authority of New York and New Jersey*, 51 A.D.3d 337, 856 N.Y.S.2d 583 (2008).
46. Ibid., p. 593.
47. Fatt Grudge, "Was 1993 WTC Bomb a Thermonuclear Dud?" *The Grudge Report*, http://www.ez-websites.com/grudge/index.php?article=thermonuclear.
48. See, e.g., Thomas Barrett, *The Mollies Were Men* (New York: Vantage Press, 1969) (2nd ed. by Thomas Barrett Jr., 2003) [http://www.coalregion.com/ amazon/molly.htm]:

    > [this pardon] "brings to closure a violent time in anthracite mining history. On January 12, 1979, one hundred years and thirty-five days after Jack Kehoe was hung, the Pennsylvania Board of Pardons, after full and public hearings, recommended, with written reasons that the arrests and trials were ridden with perjury, false accusations and unbelievable miscarriages of justice all condoned by the politicians of the era, that the pardon of John Kehoe be granted accordingly [posthumously].

49. Wikipedia, "1993 World Trade Center Bombing," http://en.wikipedia.org/wiki/1993_World_Trade_Center_bombing.
50. Accessed at http://www.youtube.com/watch?v=KmcidzFa4hg. With permission.
51. Public Broadcasting Service, "Interviews: R. James Wooley," http://www.pbs.org/wgbh/pages/frontline/shows/gunning/interviews/Woolsey.html.
52. *9/11 Commission Report*, p. 72.
53. Dan Barry, "Survivor of 1993, 9/11 Terror Attacks Is Still Procession Events," *New York Times*, February 26, 2023, https://buffalonews.com/survivor-of-1993-9-11-terror-attacks-is-still-processing-events/article_cebbad18-9fe2-5b66-adaf-53ff793efb35.html (accessed December 26, 2023).

Homegrown Terrorists Timothy McVeigh and Terry Nichols (1995)

2

> To . . . officials working the FBI command center, the questions were popping up as fast as leads on their massive charts. Could this be war? Was it the work of religious fanatics? Of Middle Eastern terrorists? But why in the world Oklahoma? The failed attempt at bringing down New York's World Trade Center two years earlier, yes. The plan to blow out the Holland and Lincoln tunnels and the conspiracy to take down the United Nations Building . . . it was understandable that terrorists might want to hit a recognizable national landmark. But in the middle of the country?[1]

> It is not my intention by these remarks tonight to magnify my office. But it is hardly possible, for the reasons I have stated tonight, to exaggerate the importance of this case and what it means to our country. Someday when you know what I know and what I have learned, and that day will come, you will never again think of the United States of America in the same way.[2]

The parallels to the 1993 World Trade Center bombing are striking: a huge, homemade bomb, concocted mainly from readily available ingredients such as fertilizer, driven in a rented truck to the site of the attack by a terrorist, who activates the fuse and then escapes; a subsequent arrest primarily due to the stupidity or carelessness of a prime suspect.

But the contrasts are even more stark: where the 1993 World Trade Center bombing was perpetrated by Islamic extremists, the April 19, 1995, destruction of the Murrah Federal Building in Oklahoma City was the hateful act of two young Americans, veterans of the U.S. Army, one of them a decorated Gulf War veteran. And, while the World Trade Center attack was destructive, it failed to topple the Twin Towers, as the terrorists had hoped; Timothy McVeigh and Terry Nichols utterly ruined their target, killing 168 fellow Americans in the process.

2.1 Background[3]

Timothy James McVeigh and Terry Nichols met during army basic training at Fort Benning, Georgia, in May 1988. Their paths crossed again at Fort Riley,

 DOI: 10.4324/9781003474104-2

Kansas. Nichols was honorably discharged from the military in May 1989. McVeigh stayed on to make sergeant and serve a four-month tour in the Persian Gulf War, receiving a commendation and brief notoriety as part of an honor guard for General Norman Schwarzkopf. He was accepted for Special Forces training, but he washed out and quit the Army in December 1991.

Now, McVeigh's vagabond days began. His "bible" was a book called *The Turner Diaries.* He had acquired and read it as early as 1988. Four years later, the underground novel was his handbook. The book was written by a white supremacist named William Luther Pierce in the late 1970s and published under the pen name Andrew Macdonald. The plot summary is as follows:

> The narrative starts with a foreword set in the year 2099, one hundred years after the events depicted in the book. The bulk of the book then quotes a recently discovered diary of a man named Earl Turner, an active member of the movement that caused these events. The book details a violent overthrow of the United States federal government by Turner and his militant comrades and a brutal contemporaneous race war that takes place first in North America, and then the rest of the world.
>
> The story starts soon after the federal government has confiscated all civilian firearms in the country under the Cohen Act, and the Organization to which Turner and his cohorts belong goes underground and engages in guerrilla war against the System, which is depicted as the totality of the government, media, and economy that is under Jewish control. The Organization starts with acts such as the bombing of FBI headquarters and continues to prosecute an ongoing, low-level campaign of terrorism, assassination and economic sabotage throughout the United States. Turner's exploits lead to his initiation into the Order, a quasi-religious inner cadre that directs the Organization and whose existence remains secret to both the System and ordinary Organization members.
>
> Eventually, the Organization seizes physical control of Southern California, including the nuclear weapons at Vandenberg Air Force Base, ethnically cleanses the area of all blacks and summarily executes all Jews and "race traitors." . . .
>
> The Organization then uses both the Southern California base of operations and their nuclear weapons to open a wider war in which they launch nuclear strikes against New York City and Israel, initiate a nuclear exchange between the US and the Soviet Union, and plant nuclear weapons and new terrorist cells throughout North America. The diary section ends with the protagonist flying an airplane equipped with an atomic bomb on a suicide mission to destroy the Pentagon, in order to eliminate the leadership of the remaining military government before it orders an assault to retake California. The novel ends with an epilogue summarizing how the Organization continued on to conquer the rest of the world and how all people of other races were eliminated.[4]

By 1992, McVeigh—at loose ends after leaving the Army—was suffering from depression, entertaining suicidal urges, and venting his growing hatred of the federal government in letters to newspapers and congressmen. During the summer of 1992, he stayed with Terry Nichols on the family farm in Michigan. There he found Terry and his brother James to be kindred spirits when it came to antigovernment vitriol. In late August, the trio followed with interest and growing anger the ten-day siege of survivalist Randy Weaver's Ruby Ridge, Idaho, homestead, a siege that ended with Weaver's son and a Federal Bureau of Investigation (FBI) agent dead.

During the succeeding autumn and early winter, McVeigh supported himself as a security guard and by buying and selling firearms at gun shows. Then, in February 1993, the U.S. Bureau of Alcohol, Tobacco and Firearms (ATF) spearheaded the siege of David Koresh's Branch Davidians religious commune near Waco, Texas. An initial assault on the compound left a total of ten dead and resulted in a 51-day standoff. McVeigh drove to Texas in an attempt to join the group but was blocked at a checkpoint some 3 miles away. There he gave an interview that appeared in the Southern Methodist University student newspaper, along with a photograph of the future bomber, seated on the hood of his car and wearing an Army fatigue cap.

McVeigh's nomadic existence continued for a time after Waco. Also a political nomad, he wandered farther and farther from the mainstream, submerging himself into the world of right-wing militias. Finally settling into a rented house in Kingman, Arizona, where he worked in a lumberyard, McVeigh began to learn the art of bomb building. Returning to Michigan, he stayed in close contact with Terry Nichols, who had settled down with a Filipino wife. By September 1994, McVeigh had settled on the Murrah Federal Building as the target by which he would ignite a second American Civil War. Between September 1994 and April 19, 1995, McVeigh executed his plans. Preparations involved renting storage facilities, accumulating the requisite quantity of ammonium nitrate fertilizer and nitromethane racing fuel, as well as dynamite and blasting caps which he stole from a Marion, Kansas quarry. He may have participated in bank robberies during this time period to raise necessary capital. He seems to have conferred with various like-minded rightist radicals. He certainly worked like a hand and a glove with Terry Nichols.

The upshot is that the McVeigh/Nichols bomb exploded at 9:02 a.m. on Wednesday, April 19, 1995, killing 168—including 19 children at play in the Murrah Building's day care center—and injuring more than 500 more. Less than 90 minutes later, a state trooper made a routine stop of McVeigh's car because it lacked a license plate. Having no registration papers, and armed with an illegal handgun, McVeigh was taken to the county jail in Perry, Oklahoma. A few days later, he very nearly was released on bail before the authorities realized whom in fact the local police were holding.

The first break for federal agents was discovering the rented truck's rear axle, which carried a vehicle identification number (VIN). From there, it was not hard to locate witnesses who could identify McVeigh as the man who had rented the truck. He was still in the Perry jail on April 21 when the FBI knew whom they were seeking. Terry Nichols was quickly implicated, interviewed, and—after spilling his guts—arrested as McVeigh's accomplice.

Then began the legal maneuvering that would climax in Timothy McVeigh's trial some two years later.

2.2 Pretrial Proceedings

After some other local lawyers initially tagged to represent McVeigh bowed out, Stephen Jones, a transplanted Texan who had represented oil and gas interests from his offices in Enid, was appointed by the federal court to represent McVeigh. Michael Tigar, a Texan, was appointed to defend Nichols. The defense team soon initiated a series of pretrial maneuvers to better their clients' chances. Shortly after a grand jury indicted the two on murder and conspiracy charges in August 1995, Jones and Tigar launched their challenges to the proceedings as planned by the U.S. District Court.

Federal Judge Wayne Alley had been selected to try the case in a courthouse situated less than 1,000 yards from ground zero. Alley's courtroom itself had suffered some (apparently only slight) damage from the blast. The two defendants were slated to be tried together.

First, Tigar and Jones contended that no Oklahoma judge could render unbiased justice:

> More than 33 of the dead had conducted regular business affairs in the courthouse, most prominently the eight federal law enforcement officers. Some of the judges attended as many as seven funerals. Other judges helped in the rescue effort. An employee in the court clerk's office had lost her baby"[5] in the blast.

A fundraiser had been run for the victims right inside the courthouse itself.

When Judge Alley refused to recuse himself, the defense attorneys appealed to the U.S. Court of Appeals for the Tenth Circuit. The three-judge panel described the case before them as follows:

> On April 19, 1995, a bomb exploded at the Alfred P. Murrah Federal Building in Oklahoma City. The explosion destroyed the Murrah Building, killed 168 people, injured many others, and caused extensive damage in the surrounding vicinity. The explosion inflicted massive damage (upwards of $1,000,000)

> to the United States Federal Courthouse, which is located one block south of the Murrah Building. Over one hundred windows shattered and were blown out. The explosion caused substantial damage to interior ceilings, walls, and fixtures. The explosion decimated the glass doors at the entrance to the courthouse. District Court chambers located on the third and fourth floors along the north side of the courthouse, including Judge Alley's third floor chambers and courtroom, were heavily damaged. Flying glass damaged woodwork and furniture in Judge Alley's courtroom. Parts of the ceiling collapsed in Judge Alley's chambers. Plaster ceiling tiles fell from the office ceilings and light fixtures were dislodged and 350 left hanging. The skylight in Judge Alley's courtroom shattered, covering the courtroom floor in an inch of broken glass. Although Judge Alley lost no family or friends in the bombing, the explosion slightly injured a member of his staff, and injured other court personnel. Some court personnel and employees had friends or relatives who were injured or killed in the Murrah Building explosion. It is likely that other court personnel and two judges would have been severely injured had they been at their desks.
>
> Timothy McVeigh and Terry Nichols were charged by grand jury indictment with the bombing. The indictment charges defendants with a total of 11 counts of violating the laws of the United States: one count of Conspiracy to Use a Weapon of Mass Destruction in violation of 18U.S.C.§2332a; one count of the Use of a Weapon of Mass Destruction in violation of 18U.S.C.§§2332a and 2(a)&(b); one count of Destruction by Explosive in violation of 18U.S.C.§§844(f) and 2(a)&(b); and eight counts of First Degree Murder in violation of 18U.S.C.§§1114, 1111 and 2(a)&(b).
>
> Mr. McVeigh filed a motion for recusal of the presiding judge, the Honorable Wayne E. Alley, who had been randomly assigned to the case. Thereafter, Mr. Nichols filed his own recusal motion, arguing additional bases for recusal not presented by Mr. McVeigh. By order dated September 14, 1995, Judge Alley denied both recusal motions. Mr. Nichols then filed a petition for writ of mandamus with this court, seeking disqualification of all judges of the Western District of Oklahoma (including Judge Alley) or, in the alternative, an order directing Judge Alley to permit discovery and hold an evidentiary hearing regarding the factual bases for disqualification issues raised in the recusal motion. Thus, this matter is before us as an original proceeding in the nature of mandamus.

On this characterization of the controversy, the court concluded that because his honor's impartiality might reasonably be questioned, recusal was required.[6] Although the decision stops short of embracing the defense contention that no federal judge in Oklahoma could render unbiased justice in the case, U.S. District Judge Richard P. Matsch of Denver was selected to take over the trial.

The defense's next move was to move for a change of venue, contending that no jury comprised of Oklahomans could render a fair and unbiased verdict for their clients. U.S. Attorney Patrick Ryan, newly appointed by President Bill Clinton to Oklahoma City, pleaded "eloquently, even tearfully" to keep the trial in Oklahoma. Do not make the victims suffer again, he argued, this time by depriving them of the opportunity to attend the trial in person. Judge Matsch moved the trial home to Denver anyway.

Now two for two, the defense team next sought to have McVeigh and Nichols receive separate trials. The advantage of separate trials in terrorism cases has long been appreciated by criminal defense lawyers. In this book's Introduction, I quoted from my novel concerning Clarence Darrow's defense of the Western Federation of Miners' (WFM) top officials in the murder/conspiracy trial for the bombing death of former Idaho governor Frank Steunenberg in 1905. WFM officers Haywood, Moyer, and Pettibone were forcibly kidnapped in Denver and hustled back to Idaho to stand trial for conspiring to have the ex-governor—despised by labor for having forcibly crushed a strike while in office—assassinated. Darrow understood the value of forcing the state to prosecute each defendant separately: if he won only one acquittal, the entire conspiracy theory would fall under a shadow of doubt, opening the way for successful appeals of any other "guilty" verdicts. In the event, the first trial—that of "Big Bill" Haywood, the union's treasurer and most prominent radical—ended in a verdict of not guilty. After that, the subsequent acquittal of union president George Pettibone was almost a foregone conclusion.[7]

As if taking a page from Darrow's 1907 trial notebook, Jones and Tigar contended that: (1) Terry Nichols's statements to the FBI during the marathon (nine-hour) interrogation immediately following his arrest were coerced and that he had not been properly apprised of his rights; and (2) for a jury to hear Nichols's words echoing from the basement of the police station, without McVeigh's lawyer being able to interrogate Nichols on the stand (thus violating Nichols's Fifth Amendment right against self-incrimination) would be unfair under any circumstances. The defense was on a roll. Judge Matsch ruled that not only would the two receive separate trials, but additionally, none of Nichols's police station statements could be heard by McVeigh's jury.[8]

He also set down McVeigh's trial for March 31, 1997.

2.3 McVeigh's Trial

Federal Prosecutor Joseph Hartzler, confined to a wheelchair by multiple sclerosis, opened for the prosecution on April 24, 1997. His audience included not only a packed Denver courtroom, but also victims and families watching on closed-circuit television (CCTV)—a first for any federal trial—back in Oklahoma City. He reached immediately for the heartstrings of the dozen jurors.

> Ladies and gentlemen of the jury, April 19th, 1995, was a beautiful day in Oklahoma City—at least it started out as a beautiful day. The sun was shining. Flowers were blooming. It was springtime in Oklahoma City. Sometime after six o'clock that morning, Tevin Garrett's mother woke him up to get him ready for the day. He was only 16 months old. He was a toddler; and as some of you know that have experience with toddlers, he had a keen eye for mischief. He would often pull on the cord of her curling iron in the morning, pull it off the counter top until it fell down, often till it fell down on him.
>
> That morning, she picked him up and wrestled with him on her bed before she got him dressed. She remembers this morning because that was the last morning of his life.
>
> That morning, Mrs. Garrett got Tevin and her daughter ready for school and they left the house at about 7:15 to go downtown to Oklahoma City. She had to be at work at eight o'clock. Tevin's sister went to kindergarten, and they dropped the little girl off at kindergarten first; and Helena Garrett and Tevin proceeded to downtown Oklahoma City.
>
> Usually she parked a little bit distant from her building; but this day, she was running a little bit late, so she decided that she would park in the Murrah Federal Building. She did not work in the Murrah Building. She wasn't even a federal employee. She worked across the street in the General Records Building.
>
> She pulled into the lot, the parking lot of the federal building, in order to make it into work on time; and she went upstairs to the second floor with Tevin, because Tevin attended the day-care center on the second floor of the federal building. When she went in, she saw that Chase and Colton Smith were already there, two year old and three year old. Dominique London was there already. He was just shy of his third birthday. So was Zack Chavez. He had already turned three.
>
> When she turned to leave to go to her work, Tevin, as so often, often happens with small children, cried and clung to her; and then, as you see with children so frequently, they try to help each other. Little—one of the little Coverdale boys—there were two of them, Elijah and Aaron. The youngest one was two and a half. Elijah came up to Tevin and patted him on the back and comforted him as his mother left.
>
> As Helena Garrett left the Murrah Federal Building to go to work across the street, she could look back up at the building; and there was a wall of plate glass windows on the second floor. You can look through those windows and see into the day-care center; and the children would run up to those windows and press their hands and faces to those windows to say goodbye to their parents. And standing on the sidewalk, it was almost as though you can reach up and touch the children there on the second floor. But none of the parents of any of the children that I just mentioned ever touched those children again while they were still alive.[9]

Hartzler then characterized the crime—and the criminal.

> In plain, simple language, it was an act of terror, violence, intend—intended to serve a selfish political purpose. The man who committed this act is sitting in this courtroom behind me, and he's the one that committed those murders. After he did so, he fled the scene; and he avoided even damaging his eardrums, because he had earplugs with him.[10]

Turning to motive, the federal prosecutor employed the T-shirt McVeigh was wearing, when apprehended some 75 minutes later, as a powerful metaphor.

> The T-shirt he was wearing virtually broadcast his intention. On its front was the image of Abraham Lincoln; and beneath the image was a phrase about tyrants, which is a phrase that John Wilkes Booth shouted in Ford's Theater to the audience when he murdered President Lincoln. And on the back of the T-shirt that McVeigh was wearing on that morning, the morning of the bombing, the morning that he was arrested, was this phrase: It said, "The tree of liberty must be refreshed from time to time with the blood of patriots and tyrants." And above those words was the image of a tree. You'll see that T-shirt; you'll see the tree; you'll see the words beneath the tree, and you'll notice that instead of fruit, the T-shirt—the tree on the T-shirt bears a depiction of droplets of scarlet-red blood.[11]

Then, in good workmanlike fashion, Hartzler laid out evidence he planned to present during the course of the government's case:

- A business card for a military supplies firm, found in McVeigh's car and carrying his prints, and in his handwriting a reminder to himself, "TNT at $5 a stick. Need more. Call after May 1."
- A sealed envelope, also in the car, containing pamphlets and news clippings that the prosecution contended were windows into McVeigh's mind. "And one of them was a quotation that—from a book that McVeigh had copied. And it was a book that he had read and believed in like the Bible. The book is entitled *The Turner Diaries*. It's a fictional account of an attack on the federal government that is carried out with a truck bomb blowing up a federal building and killing hundreds of people. And the clipping that McVeigh had with him on this day of the bombing talks about the value of killing innocent people for a cause. It reads—and he highlighted this—"The real value of our attacks today lies in the psychological impact, not in the immediate casualties."
- The truck axle with the crucial VIN and the witness who watched it land and bounce into the street.[12]

Hartzler talked about McVeigh's life, McVeigh's growing hatred for the government, the impact of Waco on McVeigh's mindset—how McVeigh and Nichols experimented with homemade bombs, educating themselves, preparing for action. Then he ticked off more of the key pieces of evidence the jurors should expect to see introduced:

- Receipts for bomb-making materials.
- Calling cards and phone records of transactions.
- The leases for three storage lockers.
- The anticipated testimony of Michael and Lori Fortier, like-minded Arizonans in whom McVeigh allegedly confided his plans.
- Correspondence with his sister Jennifer, in which his motives once again appeared to be plain.
- Records of the motel and truck rental proximate to the crime.
- Surveillance tape placing him in a MacDonald's near where the yellow getaway car was purchased.[13]

Now Hartzler had to deal with a bit of a problem. For many months, the FBI had pursued a so-called John Doe 2. This was not Terry Nichols. This was someone who the truck rental folks had said accompanied Timothy McVeigh when he picked up the 20-foot truck into which he built his bomb. The authorities had a sketch of JD 2.

Although Mr. Doe looked nothing like Terry Nichols, he did resemble lots of other suspects. The FBI and various other law enforcement agencies received hundreds of tips. One caller went so far as to say John Doe was "my wife."[14] Most likely, the rental clerks had seen a Fort Riley soldier, Private Todd Bunting, who had come into the Ryder agency near the military post at around the same time that McVeigh came by to claim his rental truck.[15] No matter, Defense Lawyer Jones had pushed the John Doe 2 angle to the hilt. Conspiracy theory enthusiasts also latched energetically onto Mr. Doe. Indeed, to this very day, websites devoted to this mystery man—who in reality was probably either Private Bunting or else was nonexistent—persist on the World Wide Web.[16] As speculation refused to die, post-9/11 events and actors were connected by conspiracy theorists to the 1995 bombing.[17] Anticipating the dust Jones would try to toss in the jurors' eyes, Hartzler cautioned:

> There is another face that Mr. Elliott does not remember as well as he remembers McVeigh's face. It's the face of a second man that Mr. Elliott believes he saw with McVeigh on that Monday afternoon, only once, not on the first occasion. The man—nobody was with McVeigh that time. This is when McVeigh came to pick up the truck.

> He saw that person just for a moment, glanced at him. His business, of course, was with McVeigh. That's who he was concentrating on.
> Now, whether Mr. Elliott was mistaken about the existence of another person and who that other person might possibly be, if there is such a person, doesn't change the fact that Mr. Elliott will say that this defendant rented the truck that blew up the Murrah Building.[18]

That same day, Stephen Jones opened for the defense, asserting:

> I have waited two years for this moment to outline the evidence to you that the Government will produce, that I will produce, both by direct and cross-examination, by exhibits, photographs, transcripts of telephone conversations, transcripts of conversations inside houses, videotapes, that will establish not a reasonable doubt but that my client is innocent of the crime that Mr. Hartzler has outlined to you.

[Remarkably, echoing his opponent, he began by highlighting the experience of a particular victim.]

> And like Mr. Hartzler, I begin where he began. As he said, it was a spring day in Oklahoma City. And inside the office of the Social Security Administration located in the Alfred P. Murrah Building, named after a distinguished chief judge of the United States Court of Appeals for the Tenth Circuit, a young black woman named Daina Bradley was feeling the atmosphere a little stuffy and warm; so she left her mother, her two children, and her sister in line and she wandered out into the lobby of the Alfred P. Murrah Building. And as she was looking out the plate glass window, a Ryder truck slowly pulled into a parking place and stopped. She didn't give it any particular attention until the door opened on the passenger side, and she saw a man get out.

[In the next breath, he unveiled his defense strategy.]

> Approximately three weeks later, she described the man to the Federal Bureau of Investigation agents, as indeed she did to us and to others, as short, stocky, olive-complected, wearing a puffy jacket, with black hair, a description that does not match my client. She did not see anyone else.[19]

Jones intended to raise a reasonable doubt in the jurors' minds. Jones intended to demonstrate that somebody else—anybody except his client—had killed all those innocent people.

The government bore the burden. Jones did not have to prove McVeigh's innocence. He did not have to prove who did it, if not his client. Consequently, while the prosecutors were required to shoot at McVeigh with a high-powered rifle, Jones could fire off shotgun blasts, hoping some of the pellets would hit his target: reasonable doubt.

But before firing those shotgun blasts at the jury, he tried to humanize his client. In fact, that was the threshold chore of the defense: to plant doubts about whether the young man seated beside Jones was the sort of person who would do such a dastardly deed, or if—and this was part 2, already begun with Jones's reference to a "short, stocky, olive-complected" man—only an alien terrorist would perpetrate such an atrocity.

> So let me begin first with Timothy McVeigh. The evidence in this case, probably from the Government as well as from the defense, will show that yesterday, he turned 29 years old, as I think Mr. Hartzler has already made some reference to; for he was born on April 23, 1968 in Lockport, New York, son of William and Mildred McVeigh; and as Mr. Hartzler has indicated to you, he has a sister, Jennifer, younger by six years, and an older sister, Patricia, older by two years. Tim's dad, Bill McVeigh, had been an autoworker since 1963 and his mother, Micki, worked at various jobs, including most frequently as a travel agent.
>
> There [sic] parents were separated in June of 1984, when Tim was 16 years old, and they were divorced in March of 1986. Tim continued to live in the family home with his father, Bill. He grew up in upstate New York. Witnesses will tell you that he started the first grade in September of 1974 in Lockport, New York, a small town just outside of Buffalo.
>
> He continued through all of his schooling at Lockport. He made good grades except perhaps in his senior year—in fact, well above average grades. He got an honor pass award, which is reserved for students who exhibited above average academic performance and initiative, in his senior year; and when he graduated from the Star Point High School in Lockport in June of 1986, he had a small regents' scholarship to a state university in New York; but he didn't go to college.
>
> He first started working at Burger King in the fall of 1986, until the spring of 1987. Then he switched jobs and went to work as an armored car driver for Burke's Security in Buffalo from the spring of 1987 to the spring of 1988. It was during that period of time that he knew and was well acquainted with some of the people that Mr. Hartzler mentioned to you, friends of his, like Mr. Darlak that he grew up with in upstate New York.
>
> Then he went to work at the Burns International Security Service, March of 1992. He had a supervisory position there, and he left it in January of 1993. He came to Arizona, where his friends Mike and Lori Fortier lived; and Tim worked at the TruValue Hardware store in Kingman beginning in 1993 and again as a security guard at State Security during the same period of time. And then he went to work, so to speak, on his own, buying and selling and trading weapons at the numerous gun shows held throughout the country, of which there are probably anywhere from 2 to 3,000 a year.

> But in May of 1988, he entered the armed services and stayed there until December of 1991, in the United States Army. After Fort Benning, his permanent station duty was Fort Riley, Kansas. And there he became a gunner for a Bradley fighting vehicle and repeatedly throughout his Army service, as his friends will testify here, he achieved a top gun ranking. In fact, first among 93 other Bradley gunners.
>
> He achieved extraordinary advancement in the enlisted ranks from a private E1 to a sergeant E5 in less than three years. And then when the Operation Desert Shield, which became Operation Desert Storm, started, he served in the front line assault, in the Kuwait/Iraq operations. He was literally on the front line and made one of the first invasions into the enemy area.
>
> During this service in the military, he earned one of our highest awards, the Bronze Star. He also earned the Army Commendation medal with an upgrade for valor. He received the Army Commendation medal, two Army Achievement medals, and several others. In fact, his unit was chosen to be the inner perimeter guard at the site where General Schwarzkopf and his opposite number in the Iraqi army arranged the terms of the armistice that ended the war.
>
> After the war, he returned to the United States. He came back initially to go into the Special Forces. He had been accepted into it, but he had been in the desert for several months, had lost a considerable amount of weight and frankly physically wasn't up to it; so he and a friend of his who came back with him and joined on the same day dropped out the second day, because they knew they weren't cut out for this physically. He went back to Fort Riley, stayed in the service and then eventually got out, went into the reserves in New York, and then went to work at some of the places that I have suggested to you here.
>
> That's basically his background, where he grew up, who his parents were, where he worked, and what his position was.[20]

Jones had struggled mightily during the months leading up to this day to work the media on behalf of his client. He had gotten himself reprimanded by the court early on for sneaking a *Newsweek* team into the jail, resulting in a cover story about McVeigh.[21]

But this campaign came crashing down around his ears as news media somehow got their hands on what purported to be internal defense memoranda, replete with damaging facts and opinions about McVeigh. These leaks had led the trial judge to seal inadmissible interview notes and other suppressed evidence. The Dallas Morning News, a prime beneficiary of the leaks, joined with other media in seeking a writ of mandamus to force his honor to unseal these documents. In the midst of the trial, the Tenth Circuit denied its motion, refusing to issue the writ.[22] However, the damage was already done. And McVeigh's cold, detached demeanor during the trial would support the portrait of a callous killer, already established in the media, as against the sympathetic portrait painted by Jones in his opening.

Jones droned on into the late afternoon and began again the next morning, first suggesting that his client's right-wing extremist views were more common and less incendiary than they might seem at first blush. Then he attacked the government's leading witnesses, McVeigh's former friends and alleged accomplices, the Fortiers and Nichols, and the physical evidence. He tried to cast a shadow over the competency and quality of the government's investigations.

However, the defense's only real hope was its conspiracy theory. This, too, Jones had been peddling relentlessly in the newspapers and on TV.[23] Following a mid-morning break on the second day of the trial, Jones at last returned to the theme with which he had begun his opening statement on the previous afternoon. He contended in great detail that someone—two someones, in fact—other than his client had rented the Ryder truck.

> Ladies and gentlemen of the jury, before the recess, I was describing to you what the three people at Elliott's remembered about the two men that came in to rent the Ryder truck that the FBI says carried the bomb.
>
> From both the standpoint of the Government's evidence and ours, this is the critical event; and that is why I'm spending the time to tell you now, because we won't put on our case until much later, what we believe the evidence will show.
>
> I have described for you what I believe the evidence will show Mr. Kessinger remembered as one of the people that was in the room the entire time Mr. Kling was. Mr. Elliott was not in the room except briefly.
>
> I left off by telling you Mr. Elliott's memory as I believe the evidence will show it. Mr. Elliott, as Ms. Beemer had said to Mr. Kling, was working at his body shop. And I should say parenthetically that the rental of Ryder trucks is incidental to his body shop. His principal business there is he's got a body shop; but he's also got the Ryder truck franchise, and it's hooked up by the computer system to the Ryder office, wherever the corporate headquarters are.
>
> In any event, be that as it may, he was working that Saturday morning, as he did most Saturday mornings, at his shop on April 15, 1995.
>
> This fellow Kling comes up to him, and they have a brief conversation about putting a deposit on the truck. This is about 8:45 Saturday morning.
>
> Kling paid the entire sum, which was exactly $280.32 to rent the Ryder truck.
>
> Elliott's memory was that Kling was approximately the same height as Elliott, and Elliott will testify that his height is about 5' 10".
>
> Kling on this Saturday morning was wearing a camouflage military T-shirt, and he had a wrinkle or a drawn-in mark on his chin.
>
> Kling came back to Elliott's Body Shop on Monday, April 17, 1995; and according to Mr. Elliott, this was about 4:20 P.M. Elliott asked Kling at that time if he had changed his mind about insurance and whether Kling wanted to inspect the truck with Elliott.
>
> Now, this was important to Mr. Elliott, because if Kling wanted insurance, Elliott didn't have to inspect the truck, because if there was any marks on it or damage, it was covered by insurance. But if Kling didn't want insurance, then

> Elliott had the obligation to take a form and go out and inspect the truck and mark on the form whatever damage was already on the truck so that presumably when Kling turned in the truck, he wouldn't be charged for damage that was already on the truck before he rented it.
> Elliott himself remembers that on that Monday afternoon, Kling was accompanied by John Doe 2, or another man. Elliott remembers that the second man had a hat with blue stripes or lightening [sic] on the side of it. He remembers that John Doe 2 talked to Robert Kling briefly and that John Doe 2 was a little shorter than Kling.
> Also, Elliott remembers that on April 17, Kling was wearing Army fatigues or military-type clothing when he was in picking up the truck.
> The individual with Kling on Monday was described by Elliott as being about 5' 7" to 5' 8", wearing a white cap with blue stripes.

[Jones then worked hard to plant the notion that the government obfuscated and ignored the eyewitness evidence that someone other than McVeigh had rented the Ryder truck.]

> In June of 1995, the Government attorneys showed Mr. Elliott a photograph of a cap worn by Todd Bunting on April 19—or actually, the next day, April 18, 1995, the Tuesday before the bomb went off on Wednesday.
> Mr. Elliott, like Mr. Kessinger, told the prosecutors that the cap was not the same one worn by John Doe 2.
> Mr. Elliott again told the prosecutors that Mr. Kling was with a John Doe 2 when Kling rented the truck.
> Mr. Elliott was interviewed on numerous occasions in late April: on the 20th, again on the 20th, on the 27th. He was not invited down to Oklahoma City. He wasn't shown a photographic lineup. He was contacted again by the FBI on May 8. He told them he had no new information. And on May 19, he was again interviewed, this time concerning the color of the Ryder truck.
> And on June 6, 1995, Mr. Elliott was served with a grand jury subpoena. On June 8, approximately fifty days after the Oklahoma City bombing, he was asked for the first time—in June—to look at a photo lineup. He had never been asked to participate in the lineup, he had never been asked to look at a photo spread or a photo lineup prior to June 8.
> Before that time, he had seen countless media depictions of Tim McVeigh coming out of the Noble County Jail. He admits himself that he saw some of them; but on that day, almost two months after the bombing, shown the spread, he identifies Tim McVeigh.
> The third person present was Vickie Beemer. She was the bookkeeper; and she worked the counter at Elliott's Body Shop. She was the one who actually handled the transaction. She stood directly across from Kling almost the entire time. Kessinger—he'll testify, he'll show you where he was sitting. He was kind of sitting over here. The counter goes like that; but Vickie Beemer is directly across the counter for ten, fifteen minutes with this man Kling.

> She starts the paperwork. A reservation has been made. It's been prepaid with cash. The truck is there.
> According to her, Kling tells her that his birthday is April 19; and Vickie Beemer states to Kling that she had been married longer than Kling had been alive.
> She remembered that Kling had telephoned her on April 14 to do a rate quote. He had provided to her Omaha, Nebraska, as an address. She told the FBI she could not remember his face. She could not remember what Robert Kling's face looked like, but she did remember that a second person accompanied him.
> While she could not remember Kling's face, she stated that he was approximately 5 feet, 10 inches tall, medium build. She was interviewed by the FBI on the 19th, the 20th, the 27th, the 28th, May 5, 8, June 6, June 9, June 28, November 14, 1996. In none of these interviews did she ever change her indication that Robert Kling was accompanied by John Doe 2.
> On August 1, 1995, the proof will show that Vickie Beemer came before the grand jury in Oklahoma City; and when asked by the prosecutor how certain she was that somebody was with Kling when he rented the truck, she responded, "Without a doubt, a hundred percent sure."
> She told the grand jury Kling was 5'10" to 5'11".
> On Tuesday, the 18th of April, at the same hour, approximately 4:30, two men entered Elliott's. One is about the same height as Tim McVeigh, about the same build, and about the same facial features, except he has a mustache, or at least he did then. The other gentleman who accompanied him is a shorter man with a kind of a tan complexion. He has black hair, has a tattoo, and he's a kind of a stocky fella.
> The taller man is Sergeant Michael Hertig. The shorter man is Todd Bunting. Todd Bunting has a hat that has stripes on it, like lightening [sic]. It's white and blue. He calls it his Carolina Panther hat.
> The proof will show that Mr. Elliott and Ms. Beemer and Mr. Kessinger are mistaken about two men being there on Monday and in their confusion described to the FBI—honestly, I'm sure—the people on Monday for the people on Tuesday, or the proof will show that the two people on Monday bear a striking resemblance to the two people on Tuesday, or it will show there was only one person on Monday; and our proof is if they're not even sure about whether there was a second one, how can they be sure what the first one looks like?

This was a somewhat subtle argument. Jones was not accusing the two soldiers, Hertig and Bunting. Rather, he was suggesting that the witnesses from the rental agency had confused two other customers from the day before with the two GIs. This went hand in hand with the "short, stocky, olive-complected" man Daina Bradley supposedly saw leave the truck bomb moments before it exploded, very nearly killing her.

Jones had planted his seeds. Now he had to wait weeks to see if they sprouted and bore fruit. Meanwhile, Hartzler and his team laid out a textbook prosecution case.

First, they presented a series of witnesses who painted a complete picture of the bombing, the devastation, and the subsequent arrest of McVeigh. Patrick Ryan, the U.S. Attorney assigned to Oklahoma City, was tasked to interrogate some of the survivors. One such witness was retired army captain Lawrence Martin, whose career had been cut short by the loss of an eye in the blast. He was assigned to the large Army recruiting office in the Murrah Building. That morning, Sgt. Bill Titsworth from Fort Riley was paying a social call. He had been reassigned to the federal building. He had brought his wife and two little daughters to introduce to his new colleagues. Some 20 Army staffers were present in the offices as Sergeant Titsworth made the rounds. The time was about 9 a.m. A moment or two later came the blast.

Ryan: Did you ever again see Sergeant Vickie Sohn alive?
Martin: No, I didn't.
Ryan: How about Dolores Stratton?
Martin: No.
Ryan: Wanda Walker?
Martin: No.
[Ryan ran down the list of victims. Then he asked the maimed captain what had happened to him when the bomb exploded.]
Martin: I ended up about 12 feet from my desk, went through a wall, and ended up in the next office.
Ryan: Did you hear anything?
Martin: No. I . . . I didn't hear a noise at all. When I looked up to what used to be my window, all I saw was fire and smoke.
Ryan: All right. What did you do now after you had found yourself in this position? You felt numb? What happened? What next occurred?
Martin: Well, two of my sergeants, female sergeants, were crying, and it wasn't like a normal cry. It was like a wailing sound and it was very eerie, and I knew something had really happened. And then I looked at myself and noticed that my wrist was damaged really badly and blood was pouring out.[24]

The tears were not confined to Captain Martin's testimony. Attorney Ryan was in tears himself, needing to pause to compose himself from time to time during Martin's testimony. Others in the courtroom cried, while the defense attorneys looked down at their feet. McVeigh simply stared straight ahead.[25] Lori Fortier out of Arizona was the bridge between this horror show and the defendant. Granted immunity, she had turned on her old friend, who had stayed with her and her husband many times on his travels back and forth around the South and Midwest. Referring to April 19, 1995, she recalled, "We turned the news on early that morning and seen what happened. We saw that the building had been blown up, and I knew right away that it was Tim."

Hartzler asked her if she felt any personal responsibility. "I could have stopped it," she conceded.

Hartzler: Why didn't you say anything?
Lori Fortier: Because I guess on some level, I—Tim was my friend and I thought that he wasn't capable of it at that time. I don't know.
Hartzler: He told you that he had the materials. Is that right?
Fortier: Yes.
Hartzler: He diagrammed the bomb. Is that right?
Fortier: Yes.
Hartzler: He told you what his target was. Is that correct?
Fortier: Yes.
Hartzler: He indicated he was capable, didn't he?
Fortier: Yes, he did.
Hartzler: Why did you think he wasn't?
Fortier: Because I guess at some level I was in denial that he really was capable of this.
Hartzler: [Rubbing it in] You recognize today that you could have stopped this from happening, do you not?
Fortier: Yes, I do.[26]

Lori Fortier's husband Michael, who received no immunity, and had hopes—caught on tape by FBI wiretaps—of achieving fortune and glory for his connection to the atrocity, but who ended up in prison for a batch of lesser federal offenses, corroborated his wife's testimony.

Hartzler: You realize that as you sit here today that you might have stopped this bombing, had you called someone?
Michael Fortier: Yes, sir. I live with that knowledge every day.
Hartzler: Why didn't you?
Mr. Fortier: There is really—there is no excuse that I could offer that would compensate for why I didn't. I think one would have to look at my lifestyle and my friendship with Tim. I . . . I had known Tim for a while, eight years up to that point, maybe less than that, six years.

He added, "But Tim—well, if you don't consider what happened in Oklahoma, Tim is a good person." Then, reminiscent of those who have contended that Hitler liked dogs, "He would stop . . . he would stop and help somebody that was broken down on the side of the road."[27]

Following a month of such testimony for the prosecution, Jones took up only a few days of the jury's time. As promised in the first few paragraphs of his opening statement, he presented victim Daina Bradley, who had had business in the Social Security office on April 19, 1995. Co-counsel Cheryl Ramsey, a soft-spoken interrogator, suggested to Bradley, "You don't want to be here, do you?" Bradley replied, "No."

Q: OK. When you got to the Social Security office—first of all, where is the Social Security office in the Murrah Building? Where was it on April the 19th?
A: It's on the first floor.
Q: Okay. When you went into the Murrah Building and went into the Social Security office, then what happened next?
A: I went in and signed the papers, and my mom was standing in line for—for us—for me. And I was doing the papers. I went to her and let her look over the papers.
Q: Okay. So she was actually holding your place in line?
A: Yes.
Q: While you were trying to get everything ready to present to the person you were going to talk to at Social Security; is that correct?
A: Yes.
Q: All right. You went over and talked to your mom about the papers that you had filled out; is that right?
A: Yes.
Q: And what happened next?
A: At this time, I turned around and looked out the window.
Q: Are there all—is the front part of the Social Security office windows?
A: Yes.
Q: OK. And so you looked out the window, and what did you see?
A: I seen the yellow Ryder truck drive up.
Q: And what did you think when you saw the Ryder truck pull up into the—pull up?
A: That it was very unusual that—downtown, they do not allow moving trucks as far as those kind of vehicles being parked down in that area.
Q: OK. And did the—what did the truck do when you saw it?
A: It . . . they stopped.
Q: Did it park?
A: Yes. It parked.
Q: OK. And did you see anything else at that time, or did you continue your conversation with your mother?
A: I went back and I looked up and I started talking to my mother again and I looked back out. I seen two men get out of the truck.
Q: All right. Did you say anything to your mother about the Ryder truck when it pulled in and parked, or did you just think it to yourself?
A: I—me and my sister and my mother, we both thought that it was unusual.

Q: OK. So there was something mentioned about it?
A: Yes.
Q: All right. Now, you saw the men get out, and then what happens next that you remember?
A: I seen the driver get out.
Q: I don't want to get into your—what happened at that point yet. What happened after you saw the Ryder truck park and the men get out? Did you go back to talking with your mother?
A: No. At this time, my mother had told me to go back to my sister to—for her to help me fill out the part that—that I did not fill out on the application. At this time that I was going back, that's when I was looking out the window.
Q: OK. You went over to your sister; is that correct?
A: Yes.
Q: You were talking with her?
A: Yes.
Q: Right? And then what happens next? Does the explosion occur shortly thereafter?
A: Yes.
Q: All right. How long were you in the Murrah Building, do you think, before the explosion occurred, if you remember?
A: I don't. All I know is that when I was talking to my sister, that a flash of light came over the desk, and that's—that's where I—I don't know how long that it was there.
Q: And what is it that you remember next?
A: That I was trapped.
Q: All right. How long were you trapped in the building?
A: Before rescue or completely out?
Q: Completely.
A: I was in there for five hours.
Q: All right. And during that time that you were trapped, you had to have your leg amputated, didn't you?
A: Yes.
Q: In order to be released from the building; is that correct?
A: Yes.
Q: And did your mother and your two children survive?
A: No.
Q: And your sister was severely injured, also, wasn't she?
A: Yes.
Q: And you were then taken to the hospital at some point after you were retrieved from the building; is that correct?
A: Right.

[Ramsey then directed Bradley's attention to her hospital interview with the FBI.]

Q: Did you tell them the Ryder truck came up and parked?
A: Yes.
Q: All right. Did you tell them that you observed an individual get out of the passenger side of the vehicle?
A: Yes.
Q: OK. And did you give them a description of the person?
A: Yeah.
Q: All right. And what did you tell them about the person that got out of the vehicle? Do you recall?
A: I recall telling them that—that it was an olive-complexion man with short hair, curly, clean-cut. He had on a blue Starter jacket, blue jeans, and tennis shoes and a white hat with purple flames.
Q: All right. And did you tell him that—or tell them that he was wearing a baseball cap?
A: Yes.
Q: And did you also tell them when you talked to them on May the 3rd and 4th that you observed him from a side view?
A: Yes.
Q: And did you also tell the FBI what this person did when he got out of the Ryder truck?
A: Yes.
Q: And what did you tell them?
A: I had told him that—I told them that he had got out of the truck, went to the back of the truck, and proceeded to walk very fast forward in front of the truck. He went back on the sidewalk and left.
Q: All right.
A: In a rapid speed.
Q: And he was walking very quickly?
A: Yes.
Q: And did that also call your attention to him?
A: Yes.
Q: OK. Did you also talk with the FBI on May the 3rd and 4th about the sketch that you had seen when you were in the hospital?
A: Yes.
Q: And what did you tell the FBI about that sketch?
A: That that man was familiar; that I had seen him get out of the truck.
Q: All right. And when had you seen that sketch? Did they show it to you or had you seen it when you were in the hospital?
A: I had seen it when I was in the hospital.

Q: When you saw the sketch when you were in the hospital, were you with someone or were you by yourself?
A: I was by myself.
Q: Now, on your screen, I have what's previously been admitted as Government's Exhibit 320. Is that the sketch that you saw on television?
A: Yes.
Q: All right. And when you saw this sketch, did you say to yourself—I believe you told the FBI that you were certain that this was the person that you had seen get out of the Ryder truck?
A: Yes.
Q: And I believe also, you told the FBI that when you saw him get out of the truck and walk down the sidewalk very quickly, the next thing that you recall was the explosion; is that correct?
A: Yes.
Q: Now, did the FBI also show you sketches on May the 3rd and 4th when you met with them?
A: Yes.
Q: And did you tell them that you had only seen one person—
Mr. Ryan: Your Honor, I'm going to object to leading.
Ms. Ramsey: I'll rephrase the question.
The Court: All right.
[Ramsey continues]
Q: Did you tell them about anyone else getting out of the vehicle?
A: No, I did not.
Q: Did they—did the FBI show you a sketch of the other person?
A: Yes.
Q: And you could not identify that; isn't that correct?
A: Right.
Q: Because you said you'd only seen one person; correct?
A: Yes.
Q: OK. Now, you also met with the FBI on May the 21st; isn't that correct?
A: Yes.
Q: When you met with them on May the 21st, had you been released from the hospital?
A: Yes.
Q: And you met with them where?
A: I met with them at my lawyer's office.
Q: At Ms. Wallace's office?
A: Yes.
Q: And is that in Oklahoma City?
A: Yes.

Q: And when you met with the FBI on May the 21st, did you tell them about the Ryder truck?
A: Yes.
Q: What did you tell them about the Ryder truck?
A: That it parked in front of the Social Security office.
Q: Did you also give them a description of the person you saw get out of the vehicle?
A: Yes, I did.
Q: And what was that description?
A: The olive-complexion man and the short hair—curly hair—with the Starter jacket, blue jeans, and tennis shoes, with the baseball hat with the flame—purple flame.
Q: Did you also tell them that the hat was white on one side with a purple flame on it?
A: I told him the hat was white with flames on it.
Q: OK. And did you also tell them that he—the person—left the vehicle and walked at a very rapid pace?
A: Yes.[28]

Jones also presented the testimony of Frederic William Whitehurst, an FBI forensics expert, subpoenaed as an adverse witness, in an effort to undermine the prosecution's physical evidence.[29] Then at the end of May, little more than a month after they opened, lead counsel closed their cases. And only a few days after that, the jury returned a verdict of guilty. They had deliberated about three days.

The next step was the sentencing hearing. A *Newsweek* poll, published within less than a week of the guilty verdict, found that 67% of Americans favored the death penalty.[30] The jury did not disappoint them.

2.4 Appeals and Execution

The U.S. Court of Appeals for the Tenth Circuit affirmed McVeigh's conviction and sentence, ruling:

> (1) defendant was not entitled to relief based on claims of presumed and actual prejudice due to pretrial publicity; (2) allowing juror who allegedly made statement prejudging case to remain seated was not abuse of discretion; (3) evidence of alternative perpetrators was properly excluded; (4) "knowingly" intent standard applied to offenses of use of and conspiracy to use weapon of mass destruction; (5) lesser-included offense instructions were not warranted; (6) admission of victim testimony during guilt phase of trial was proper; and (7) admission of victim impact testimony during sentencing phase of trial was proper.[31]

Six months later, the U.S. Supreme Court declined to review the Tenth Circuit's decision.[32]

Further appeals postponed the inevitable.[33] Then, in January 2001, McVeigh expedited the matter, dropping all pending appeals. Judge Matsch set May 16 as execution day. U.S. Attorney General John Ashcroft then released some 4,000 pages of government documents not previously provided to the defense. Angered, McVeigh at first threatened to seek reinstatement of his appeals. But on June 7, he renewed his request to die.

His wish was granted on June 10, 2001.

But, McVeigh's legacy lives on:

> The Proud Boys played a critical part in carrying out the January 6 [2021] attack, but the group is just one part of a trend of increased white supremacist and far-right violence. Top U.S. law enforcement officials say those extremist movements are the biggest domestic terrorism threat facing the country. [See Chapter 11][34]

Notes

1. Richard A. Serrano, *One of Ours: Timothy McVeigh and the Oklahoma City Bombing* (New York: W.W. Norton & Company 1998), p. 187.
2. Stephen Jones, McVeigh's lead counsel, in a speech given at the University of Oklahoma in the fall of 1995, as quoted by Serrano, p. 254.
3. Douglas O. Linder, "Oklahoma City Bombing Trial," Famous Trials (Chronology), http://www.law.umkc.edu/faculty/projects/ftrials/mcveigh/mcveighchrono.html.
4. Wikipedia, "The Turner Diaries," http://en.wikipedia.org/wiki/The_Turner_Diaries. With permission.
5. Serrano, p. 254.
6. *Nichols v. Alley*, 71 F.3d 347 (10th Cir., 1995).
7. See, generally, J. Anthony Lukas, *Big Trouble: A Murder in a Small Western Town Sets Off a Struggle for the Soul of America* (New York: Simon & Schuster, 1997), especially p. 729 (regarding the Pettibone acquittal). By contrast, in the 1924 Leopold and Loeb thrill killing case, another celebrated Darrow defense, the famed attorney realized that separate trials of his young, wealthy clients on kidnapping and murder charges (this time the state wished to separate the two offenses) would result in giving the prosecution "two bites at the apple," and that a conviction on either charge would carry the death penalty. Realizing, too, that no jury would accept that the privileged, well-educated Nathan Leopold and Dicky Loeb were criminally insane when they bludgeoned their cousin Bobby Franks to death in a coldly calculated thrill killing, Darrow persuaded his clients to plead guilty to both counts of the indictment and throw themselves on the mercy of the court in a lengthy sentencing hearing. His gamble paid off: the judge

sentenced the pair to life in prison. One, Leopold, eventually was paroled and went on to live an exemplary later life. See, generally, "Illinois v. Nathan Leopold and Richard Loeb," *Famous Trials*, http://www.law.umkc.edu/faculty/projects/ftrials/leoploeb/leopold.htm.

8. Serrano, pp. 256–257.
9. Accessed at http://www.law.umkc.edu/faculty/projects/ftrials/mcveigh/prosecutionopen.html.
10. Ibid.
11. Ibid.
12. Ibid.
13. Ibid.
14. Serrano, p. 282.
15. Ibid., p. 285.
16. See, e.g., James Ridgeway, "In Search of John Doe No. 2: The Story the Feds Never Told about the Oklahoma City Bombing," *Mother Jones*, July/August 2007, http://motherjones.com/politics/2007/07/search-john-doe-no-2-story-feds-never-told-about-oklahoma-city-bombing (accessed August 21, 2010); David Niewert, "The Mystery of John Doe No. 2," *Salon*, June 9, 2001, http://www.salon.com/news/feature/2001/06/09/john_doe (accessed August 21, 2010); Dee Finney, "John Doe #2—Who Is He?" http://www.greatdreams.com/john-doe-2.htm (accessed August 21, 2010).
17. See, e.g., "Is Jose Padilla 'John Doe Number 2' at the Oklahoma City Bombing?" http://whatreallyhappened.com/WRHARTICLES/padillaJD2.html?q=padillaJD2.html (accessed August 21, 2010).
18. "Opening Statement of Defense Attorney Steven Jones in the Timothy McVeigh Trial," April 24, 1997, http://www.law.umkc.edu/faculty/projects/ftrials/mcveigh/defenseopen.html.
19. Ibid.
20. Ibid.
21. Serrano, p. 247.
22. *U.S. v. McVeigh*, 119 F.3d 806 (10th Cir., 1997). In so holding, the appeals panel emphasized the restraint exercised by the court in sealing only so much of the record as seemed absolutely necessary for a fair trial. The judges noted, too, that a contrary decision might have required imposing on the jurors the hardship of sequestration, while at the same time nullifying the value to McVeigh of a separate trial for Terry Nichols.

    > Furthermore, we believe that the sealing orders were narrowly tailored to the compelling fair trial interests at stake. This is not a case where the district court has sealed entire documents or held closed pre-trial proceedings. Rather, the suppression and severance hearings were held in open court, and redacted versions of the documents at issue were made available to the public. Many of the other avenues often available to limit the prejudicial publicity that would arise from disclosure of these materials—such as a venue change, a continuance, extensive voir dire, and admonishments to the jury—had already been exhausted by the time the orders were entered

> or were ongoing processes utilized by the court to try to protect the defendants' right to a fair trial from the substantial publicity that was occurring. Further, we cannot say that the district court abused its discretion in electing not to sequester the jury during what was anticipated to be a several month long trial.
>
> Finally, we have conducted an *in camera* review of the sealed and redacted material. Based on that review we conclude that the district court properly sealed only those portions of the documents at issue necessary to protect, respectively, the integrity of suppressed evidence and the defendants' ability to argue effectively that separate trials were warranted. Furthermore, the court recognized that at some later point in the proceedings the balance of interests could change, and that further disclosures might be appropriate at such time.

23. Serrano, p. 257.
24. Ibid., pp. 281–282.
25. Ibid., p. 282.
26. Ibid., p. 285.
27. Ibid., pp. 286–287.
28. http://www.law.umkc.edu/faculty/projects/ftrials/mcveigh/bradleytestimony.html.
29. Dr. Whitehurst's testimony can be accessed at http://www.law.umkc.edu/faculty/projects/ftrials/mcveigh/whitehursttestimony.html.
30. Serrano, p. 295.
31. *U.S. v. McVeigh* (1998).
32. *McVeigh v. U.S.*, 526 U.S. 1007, 119 S. Ct. 1148, 143 L.Ed.2d 215, 67 USLW 3560 (2000).
33. See *U.S. v. McVeigh*, 118 F.Supp.2d 1137 (D.Colo., October 12, 2000) (post-conviction relief denied); *U.S. v. McVeigh*, 2001 WL 611163 (D.Colo., June 6, 2001) (stay denied), affirmed, 9 Fed. Appx. 980, 2001 DJCAR 2858 (10th Cir. (Colo.), June 7, 2001).
34. "Far-Right Violence a Growing Threat and Law Enforcement's Top Domestic Terrorism Concern," *PBS News Hour*, September 5, 2023, https://www.pbs.org/newshour/show/far-right-violence-a-growing-threat-and-law-enforcements-top-domestic-terrorism-concern (accessed December 27, 2023).

3 Should Zacarias Moussaoui Die for Usama Bin Laden's Sins? (2006)

Dr. Douglas Linder of the University of Missouri at Kansas City writes of the trial of Zacarias Moussaoui:

> On the horrific morning of September 11, 2001, when planes crashed into buildings and fell from the sky, Zacarias Moussaoui was sitting in a jail in Minnesota facing immigration charges. Even if he had not been arrested three weeks earlier, when he raised suspicion by paying large sums to a flight training school to learn to pilot a Boeing 747 despite his never having piloted a small plane, it seems unlikely that Moussaoui would have been "the twentieth hijacker" on one of the four doomed planes. Nonetheless, largely because of the convenient fact that he was alive and in custody, the French citizen of Moroccan descent became the only person tried in an American courtroom for involvement in the 9/11 tragedy. As such, his trial came to be much more than a proceeding to determine whether one would-be terrorist would live or die: it became an opportunity for survivors and relatives of 9/11 victims to seek that elusive "closure," and an occasion for evaluating—with the benefit of revealing documents released at the trial—whether thousands of innocent lives could have been saved if bureaucrats only focused more on protecting the country than advancing their careers.[1]

3.1 Background[2]

Starting sometime in 1989, a new international terrorist group existed on the world stage which was dedicated to opposing non-Islamic governments with force and violence. This organization grew out of the *mekhtab al khidemat* (the Services Office), which had maintained offices in various parts of the world, including Afghanistan, Pakistan (particularly in Peshawar), and the United States for some time prior to 1989. The group was founded by Usama (sometimes spelled Osama) bin Laden and Muhammad Atef, a.k.a. Abu Hafs al Masry, together with Abu Ubaidah al Banshiri and others. From its inception to the present, the group called itself al Qaeda (the Base). Until about 1991, the group was headquartered in Afghanistan and Peshawar. Its *emir* (or prince), Usama bin Laden, relocated to the Sudan. Al Qaeda was headquartered in the

DOI: 10.4324/9781003474104-3

Sudan from approximately 1991 until approximately 1996 but still maintained offices in various parts of the world. In 1996, bin Laden and other members of al Qaeda again relocated, this time to Afghanistan, where bin Laden had made a reputation as a warrior and financier in the decade-long jihad to expel the Russians. Members of al Qaeda pledged an oath of allegiance (called a *bayat*) to bin Laden and al Qaeda.

Bin Laden and al Qaeda explicitly stated that they violently opposed the United States for several reasons. First, the United States was regarded as an "infidel" because it was not governed in a manner consistent with the group's extremist interpretation of Islam. Second, the United States was viewed as providing essential support for other infidel governments and institutions, particularly the governments of Saudi Arabia and Egypt, the nation of Israel, and the United Nations organization, which all were regarded as enemies of the group. Third, al Qaeda opposed the involvement of the U.S. armed forces in the Gulf War in 1991 and in Operation Restore Hope in Somalia in 1992 and 1993. In particular, al Qaeda opposed the continued presence of American military forces in Saudi Arabia (and elsewhere on the Arabian Peninsula) following the Gulf War. Fourth, al Qaeda opposed the U.S. government because of the arrest, conviction, and imprisonment of persons belonging to al Qaeda or its affiliated terrorist groups, or those with whom it worked. For these and other reasons, bin Laden declared a jihad, or holy war, against the United States.

One of the principal goals of al Qaeda was to drive the American armed forces out of Saudi Arabia (and elsewhere on the Arabian Peninsula) and Somalia by force. Not only bin Laden, but also other al Qaeda members, issued fatwahs,[3] indicating that such attacks were both proper and necessary. "A decade of conflict in Afghanistan, from 1979 to 1989, gave Islamist extremists a rallying point and training field."[4] Although the departure of the Russian bear with its tail between its legs was arguably the CIA's greatest operational triumph of the Cold War, because the agency channeled its enormous river of weapons through Pakistani intelligence and military to the Afghan freedom fighters, "the miracle victory over the Soviets was all the work of Allah—not the billions of dollars that America and Saudi Arabia poured into the battle, not the ten year commitment of the CIA that turned an army of primitive tribesmen into techno-holy warriors."[5]

With the Soviets' departure, the communist puppet regime in Kabul soon fell to a group of Islamic hardliners, the Taliban, whose views were highly compatible with al Qaeda's. As this historic power shift was occurring in late 1991 and early 1992 it "was completely overshadowed by the historic events sweeping the world. In December 1991, the Soviet Union ceased to exist . . . . People everywhere were now referring to the United States as the world's lone superpower."[6]

> But that's not how history works. Inevitably, great events have unintended consequences. What no one anticipated was that it might be dangerous to awaken the dormant dreams and visions of Islam. Which, of course, is exactly what happened.[7]

At home in Afghanistan, al Qaeda functioned both on its own and through some of the terrorist organizations that operated under its umbrella, including Egyptian Islamic Jihad, which was led by Ayman al-Zawahiri, and at times, the Islamic Group (also known as el Gamaa Islamia or simply Gamaa't), and a number of jihad groups in other countries, including the Sudan, Egypt, Saudi Arabia, Yemen, Somalia, Eritrea, Djibouti, Afghanistan, Pakistan, Bosnia, Croatia, Albania, Algeria, Tunisia, Lebanon, the Philippines, Tajikistan, Azerbaijan, the Kashmiri region of India and the Chechnyan region of Russia. Al Qaeda also maintained cells and personnel in a number of countries to facilitate its activities, including in Kenya, Tanzania, the United Kingdom, Germany, Canada, Malaysia, and the United States.

Al Qaeda had a command and control structure that included a *majlis al shura* (or consultation council) that discussed and approved major undertakings, including terrorist operations, as well as a "military committee" that considered and approved military matters. Usama bin Laden and al Qaeda also forged alliances with the National Islamic Front in the Sudan and with representatives of the government of Iran—and its associated terrorist group, Hizballah—for the purpose of working together against their perceived common enemies in the West, particularly the United States.

However, it would be a mistake to view al Qaeda as a cohesive, vertically structured military organization. More accurately, in the words of one federal official,

> We talk about the bin Laden organization, but it is really a bin Laden alliance. It is unusual to find Palestinians and Yemenis, Sudanese and East Asians in the same alliance. He is the glue between groups that have little in common with each other, for instance the Kashmiris and Egypt's Islamic Jihad.[8]

Al Qaeda sponsored, managed, or financially supported training camps in Afghanistan, which were used to instruct members and associates of al Qaeda and its affiliated terrorist groups in the use of firearms, explosives, chemical weapons, and other weapons of mass destruction. In addition to providing training in the use of various weapons, these camps were used to conduct operational planning against U.S. targets around the world and experiments in the use of chemical and biological weapons. These camps were also used to train others in security and counterintelligence methods, such as the use of codes and passwords, and to teach members and associates of al Qaeda about traveling to perform operations. For example, al Qaeda instructed its members and associates to dress in Western attire and to use other methods to avoid detection by security officials. The group also taught its members and associates to monitor media reporting of its operations to determine the effectiveness of their terrorist activities.

3.2 Early al Qaeda Attacks

Chapter 1 details the 1993 World Trade Center bombing. The 9/11 Commission characterized bin Laden's personal involvement as "at best cloudy." The 2004 report came to the same conclusion concerning a related plot to attack other New York landmarks, such as the Holland and Lincoln tunnels and the Statue of Liberty, and a scheme to blow up U.S.-registered airliners in the Philippines.[9] The commission placed other terrorist strikes in al Qaeda's "win" column:

- December 1992: Two bombs exploded outside hotels in Aden, Somalia, where U.S. troops were billeted.
- February 1993: A massive bomb carved a seven-story hole in the World Trade Center parking garage (see Chapter 1).
- August 1994: Truck bombs exploded outside U.S. embassies in Nairobi and Dar es Salaam.
- November 1995: A car bomb exploded outside the joint Saudi-U.S. facility in Riyadh, used to train the Saudi National Guard.
- June 1996: An enormous truck bomb exploded in Dhahran's Khobar Towers, where U.S. Air Force personnel were housed.[10]

On October 12, 2000—less than a year before the 9/11 attacks—a Navy vessel, the *USS Cole*, was the target of a successful suicide attack while refueling at anchor off the Yemeni port of Aden. The toll of U.S. sailors was 17 dead and 39 wounded.

I entitled Chapter 1 "The Fire Bell in the Night." However, I noted the 9/11 Commission's observation that the successful capture and prosecution of the perpetrators of the 1993 World Trade Center attack led to complacency, among both responsible government officials and the American public at large.[11] The preceding list might be analogized to a periodically—if not constantly—clanging alarm bell. In an extensive exegesis, subtitled "Adaptation—and Nonadaptation—in the Law Enforcement Community,"[12] the Commission implies that the vast law enforcement, intelligence, and political array of federal, state, and local agencies—from the White House and Congress at the top, through the dizzying alphabet soup of intelligence services, to the FBI and the state and local police—was neither focused upon nor tactically prepared for what was coming.

What was coming arrived on September 11, 2001.

3.3 Planning and Execution[13]

In February 1998, Usama bin Laden endorsed a fatwah under the banner "International Islamic Front for Jihad on the Jews and Crusaders." This fatwah, published in the London-based *Al-Quds al-'Arabi* newspaper[14] on February 23, 1998, stated that Muslims should kill Americans—including civilians—anywhere in the world where they can be found.

That same year, if the grand jury indictment of Moussaoui got it right, the plot to attack the following major targets in the continental United States was set in motion.

THE GERMAN CELL

15. Beginning in and about 1998, Ramzi Bin al-Shibh, Mohammed Atta (#11), Marwan al-Shehhi (#175), and Ziad Jarrah (#93), and others, formed and maintained an al Qaeda terrorist cell in Germany.

HIJACKERS TRAVEL TO THE UNITED STATES

16. On or about January 15, 2000, Khalid al-Midhar (#77) and Nawaf al-Hazmi (#77) traveled from Bangkok, Thailand, to Los Angeles, California.

ATTA (#11) INQUIRES ABOUT AERIAL APPLICATION OF PESTICIDES

17. At various times in 2000 and 2001, in Florida, Mohammed Atta (#11) made inquiries regarding starting a crop dusting company.

HIJACKERS RECEIVE FLIGHT TRAINING

18. On or about June 3, 2000, Mohammed Atta (#11) traveled to the United States from Prague, Czech Republic.
19. In or about early July 2000, Mohammed Atta (#11) and Marwan al-Shehhi (#175) visited the Airman Flight School in Norman, Oklahoma.
20. Between in or about July 2000 and in or about December 2000, Mohamed Atta (#11) and Marwan al-Shehhi (#175) attended flight training classes at Huffman Aviation in Venice, Florida.

MONEY IS MOVED TO THE HIJACKERS

21. On or about June 29, 2000, $4,790 was wired from the United Arab Emirates (UAE) to Marwan al-Shehhi (#175) in Manhattan.
22. On or about July 19, 2000, $9,985 was wired from UAE into a Florida SunTrust bank account in the names of Mohammed Atta (#11) and Marwan al-Shehhi (#175).
23. On or about July 26, 2000, in Germany, Ramzi Bin al-Shibh wired money to Marwan al-Shehhi (#175) in Florida.
24. On or about August 7, 2000, $9,485 was wired from UAE into a Florida SunTrust bank account in the names of Mohammed Atta (#11) and Marwan al-Shehhi (#175).
25. On or about August 30, 2000, $19,985 was wired from UAE into a Florida SunTrust bank account in the names of Mohammed Atta (#11) and Marwan al-Shehhi (#175).
26. On or about September 18, 2000, $69,985 was wired from UAE into a Florida SunTrust bank account in the names of Mohamed Atta (#11) and Marwan al-Shehhi (#175).

JARRAH (#93) ATTEMPTS TO ENROLL BIN AL-SHIBH IN FLIGHT TRAINING COURSES

27. In or about August 2000, Ziad Jarrah (#93) attempted to enroll Ramzi Bin al-Shibh in a flight school in Florida.
28. On or about May 17, 2000, in Germany, Ramzi Bin al-Shibh applied for a visa to travel to the United States, listing a German telephone number ("German Telephone #1"). This visa application was denied.
29. On or about June 15, 2000, in Germany, Ramzi Bin al-Shibh applied for a visa to travel to the United States. This visa application was denied.
30. On or about August 14, 2000, in Yemen, Ramzi Bin al-Shibh arranged to wire money from his account in Germany to the account of a flight training school in Florida.
31. On or about September 15, 2000, in Yemen, Ramzi Bin al-Shibh applied for a visa to travel to the United States, listing a residence in Hamburg, Germany. This visa application was denied in September 2000.
32. On or about October 25, 2000, in Germany, Ramzi Bin al-Shibh applied for a visa to travel to the United States. This visa application was denied.

BIN AL-SHIBH SENDS MONEY TO AL-SHEHHI (#175)

33. On or about September 25, 2000, in Hamburg, Germany, Ramzi Bin al-Shibh sent money via wire transfer to Marwan al-Shehhi (#175) in Florida.

MOUSSAOUI INQUIRES ABOUT FLIGHT TRAINING

34. On or about September 29, 2000, Zacarias Moussaoui contacted Airman Flight School in Norman, Oklahoma using an email account he set up on September 6 with an Internet service provider in Malaysia.
35. In or about October 2000, Zacarias Moussaoui received letters from Infocus Tech, a Malaysian company, stating that Moussaoui was appointed Infocus Tech's marketing consultant in the United States, the United Kingdom, and Europe, and that he would receive, among other things, an allowance of $2500 per month.

ATTA (#11) PURCHASES FLIGHT TRAINING EQUIPMENT

36. On or about November 5, 2000, Mohammed Atta (#11) purchased flight deck videos for the Boeing 747 Model 200, Boeing 757 Model 200, and other items from a pilot store in Ohio ("Ohio Pilot Store").

BIN AL-SHIBH TRAVELS TO LONDON

37. Between on or about December 2 and December 9, 2000, Ramzi Bin al-Shibh traveled from Hamburg, Germany to London, England.

MOUSSAOUI TRAVELS FROM LONDON TO PAKISTAN

38. On or about December 9, 2000, Zacarias Moussaoui flew from London, England to Pakistan.

ATTA (#11) PURCHASES MORE FLIGHT TRAINING EQUIPMENT

39. On or about December 11, 2000, Mohammed Atta (#11) purchased flight deck videos for the Boeing 767 Model 300ER, and the Airbus A320 Model 200 from the Ohio Pilot Store.

FLIGHT TRAINING AND EXERCISE

40. Between in or about January 2001 and March 2001, Hani Hanjour (#77) attended pilot training courses in Phoenix, Arizona, including at Pan Am International Flight Academy.
41. Between on or about February 1, 2001, and on or about February 15, 2001, Mohammed Atta (#11) and Marwan al-Shehhi (#175) took a flight check ride around Decatur, Georgia.
42. In or about February 2001, Mohammed Atta (#11) and Marwan al-Shehhi (#175) attended a health club in Decatur, Georgia.

MOUSSAOUI COMES TO THE UNITED STATES

43. On or about February 7, 2001, Zacarias Moussaoui flew from Pakistan to London, England.
44. On or about February 23, 2001, Zacarias Moussaoui flew from London, England to Chicago, Illinois, declaring at least $35,000 cash on his Customs declaration, and then from Chicago to Oklahoma City, Oklahoma.
45. On or about February 26, 2001, Zacarias Moussaoui opened a bank account in Norman, Oklahoma, depositing approximately $32,000 cash.
46. Between on or about February 26, 2001, and on or about May 29, 2001, Zacarias Moussaoui attended the Airman Flight School in Norman, Oklahoma, ending his classes early.

NAWAF AL-HAZMI (#77) PURCHASES FLIGHT TRAINING EQUIPMENT

47. On or about March 19, 2001, Nawaf al-Hazmi (#77) purchased flight deck videos for the Boeing 747 Model 400, the Boeing 747 Model 200, and the Boeing 777 Model 200, and another video from the Ohio Pilot Store.

MOUSSAOUI JOINS A GYM

48. In or about March 2001, Zacarias Moussaoui joined a gym in Norman, Oklahoma.

HIJACKERS TRAVEL TO AND WITHIN THE UNITED STATES

49. On or about April 1, 2001, Nawaf al-Hazmi (#77) was in Oklahoma.
50. Between on or about April 23, 2001, and on or about June 29, 2001, Satam al-Suqami (#11), Waleed al-Shehri (#11), Ahmed al-Ghamdi (#175), Majed Moqed (#77), Marwan al-Shehhi (#175), Mohammed Atta (#11), Ahmed al-Nami (#93), Hamza al-Ghamdi (#175), Mohald al-Shehri (#175), Wail al-Shehri (#11), Ahmed al-Haznawi (#93), Fayez Ahmed (#175), and Salem al-Hazmi (#77) traveled from various points in the world to the United States.

MOUSSAOUI CONTACTS A COMMERCIAL FLIGHT SCHOOL

51. On or about May 23, 2001, Zacarias Moussaoui contacted an office of the Pan Am International Flight Academy in Miami, Florida via email.

HIJACKERS OPEN BANK ACCOUNTS

52. In Summer 2001, Fayez Ahmed (#175), Saeed al-Ghamdi (#93), Hamza al-Ghamdi (#175), Waleed al-Shehri (#11), Ziad Jarrah (#93), Satam al-Suqami (#11), Mohald al-Shehri (#175), Ahmed al-Nami (#93), and Ahmed al-Haznawi (#93) each opened a Florida SunTrust bank account with a cash deposit.

MOUSSAOUI INQUIRES ABOUT AERIAL APPLICATION OF PESTICIDES

53. In or about June 2001, in Norman, Oklahoma, Zacarias Moussaoui made inquiries about starting a crop dusting company.

OTHER HIJACKERS ATTEND GYM TRAINING

54. Between May and July 2001, in Florida, Ziad Jarrah (#93) joined a gym and took martial arts lessons, which included instruction in kickboxing and knife fighting.
55. In or about June 2001, in Florida, Waleed al-Shehri (#11), Marwan al-Shehhi (#175), and Satam al-Suqami (#11) joined a gym.

MOUSSAOUI PURCHASES FLIGHT TRAINING EQUIPMENT

56. On or about June 20, 2001, Zacarias Moussaoui purchased flight deck videos for the Boeing 747 Model 400, and the Boeing 747 Model 200 from the Ohio Pilot Store.

AL-HAWSAWI AND FAYEZ AHMED (#175) OPEN UAE BANK ACCOUNTS

57. On June 25, 2001, Mustafa Ahmed al-Hawsawi used a cash deposit to open a checking account at a Standard Chartered Bank branch in Dubai, UAE.
58. On June 25, 2001, at the same Standard Chartered Bank branch in Dubai, UAE, Fayez Ahmed (#175) used a cash deposit to open a savings account and also opened a checking account.

ATTA (#11) AND AL-SHEHHI (#175) PURCHASE A KNIFE

59. On or about July 8, 2001, Mohammed Atta (#11) purchased a knife in Zurich, Switzerland.

MOUSSAOUI PAYS FOR FLIGHT LESSONS

60. On or about July 10 and July 11, 2001, Zacarias Moussaoui made credit card payments to the Pan Am International Flight Academy for a simulator course in commercial flight training.

FAYEZ AHMED (#175) GIVES AL-HAWSAWI CONTROL OVER UAE ACCOUNT

61. On July 18, 2001, Fayez Ahmed (#175) gave power of attorney to Mustafa Ahmed al-Hawsawi for Fayez Ahmed's Standard Chartered Bank accounts in UAE.
62. On July 18, 2001, using his power of attorney, Al-Hawsawi picked up Fayez Ahmed's Visa and automated teller machine (ATM) cards in UAE.

63. Between July 18 and August 1, 2001, Mustafa Ahmed al-Hawsawi caused Fayez Ahmed's Visa and ATM cards to be shipped from UAE to Fayez Ahmed in Florida. (The Visa card was then used for the first time on August 1, 2001, in Florida.)

JARRAH (#93) TRAVELS TO GERMANY

64. On or about July 25, 2001, Ziad Jarrah (#93) traveled from the United States to Germany.

BIN AL-SHIBH MOVES MONEY TO MOUSSAOUI FROM UAE

65. Between on or about July 29 and August 2, 2001, in Norman, Oklahoma, Zacarias Moussaoui made several telephone calls from public telephones to a number in Düsseldorf, Germany ("German Telephone #2").
66. On or about July 30 and 31, 2001, in Hamburg, Germany, Ramzi Bin al-Shibh, using the name "Ahad Sabet," received two wire transfers, totaling approximately $15,000, from "Hashim Abdulrahman" in UAE.
67. On or about August 1 and 3, 2001, Ramzi Bin al-Shibh, using the name "Ahad Sabet," wired approximately $14,000 in money orders to Zacarias Moussaoui in Oklahoma from train stations in Dusseldorf and Hamburg, Germany.

MOUSSAOUI PURCHASES KNIVES

68. On or about August 3, 2001, Zacarias Moussaoui purchased two knives in Oklahoma City, Oklahoma.

JARRAH (#93) RETURNS TO THE UNITED STATES FROM GERMANY

69. On or about August 4, 2001, Ziad Jarrah (#93) traveled from Germany to the United States.

MOUSSAOUI TRAVELS FROM OKLAHOMA TO MINNESOTA

70. On or about August 9 and August 10, 2001, Zacarias Moussaoui was driven from Oklahoma to Minnesota.

MOUSSAOUI TAKES COMMERCIAL FLYING LESSONS IN MINNESOTA

71. On or about August 10, 2001, in Minneapolis, Minnesota, Zacarias Moussaoui paid approximately $6,300 in cash to the Pan Am International Flight Academy.

72. Between August 13 and August 15, 2001, Zacarias Moussaoui attended the Pan Am International Flight Academy in Minneapolis, Minnesota, for simulator training on the Boeing 747 Model 400.

MOUSSAOUI POSSESSES KNIVES AND OTHER ITEMS

73. On or about August 16, 2001, Zacarias Moussaoui possessed, among other things: two knives; a pair of binoculars; flight manuals for the Boeing 747 Model 400; a flight simulator computer program; fighting gloves and shin guards; a piece of paper referring to a handheld Global Positioning System receiver and a camcorder; software that could be used to review pilot procedures for the Boeing 747 Model 400; a notebook listing German Telephone #1, German Telephone #2, and the name "Ahad Sabet;" letters indicating that Moussaoui is a marketing consultant in the United States for Infocus Tech; a computer disk containing information related to the aerial application of pesticides; and a handheld aviation radio.

MOUSSAOUI LIES TO FEDERAL AGENTS

74. On or about August 17, 2001, Zacarias Moussaoui, while being interviewed by federal agents in Minneapolis, attempted to explain his presence in the United States by falsely stating that he was simply interested in learning to fly.

JARRAH (#93) UNDERTAKES "CHECK RIDE" AT FLIGHT SCHOOL

75. On or about August 17, 2001, Ziad Jarrah (#93) undertook a "check ride" at a flight school in Fort Lauderdale, Florida.

FINAL PREPARATIONS FOR THE COORDINATED AIR ATTACK

76. On or about August 22, 2001, Fayez Ahmed (#175) used his Visa card in Florida to obtain approximately $4,900 cash, which had been deposited into his Standard Chartered Bank account in UAE the day before.
77. On or about August 22, 2001, in Miami, Florida, Ziad Jarrah (#93) purchased an antenna for a global positioning system (GPS), other GPS-related equipment, and schematics for 757 cockpit instrument diagrams. (GPS allows an individual to navigate to a position using coordinates pre-programmed into the GPS unit.)
78. On or about August 25, 2001, Khalid al-Midhar and Majed Moqed purchased with cash tickets for American Airlines Flight 77, from Virginia to Los Angeles, California, scheduled for September 11, 2001.

79. On or about August 26, 2001, Waleed al-Shehri and Wail al-Shehri made reservations on American Airlines Flight 11, from Boston, Massachusetts, to Los Angeles, California, scheduled for September 11, 2001, listing a telephone number in Florida ("Florida Telephone #1") as a contact number.
80. On or about August 27, 2001, reservations for electronic, one-way tickets were made for Fayez Ahmed and Mohald al-Shehri, for United Airlines Flight 175, from Boston, Massachusetts, to Los Angeles, California, scheduled for September 11, 2001, listing Florida Telephone Number #1 as a contact number.
81. On or about August 27, 2001, Nawaf al-Hazmi and Salem al-Hazmi booked flights on American Airlines Flight 77.
82. On or about August 28, 2001, Satam al-Suqami purchased a ticket with cash for American Airlines Flight 11.
83. On or about August 28, 2001, Mohammed Atta and Abdulaziz Alomari reserved two seats on American Airlines Flight 11, listing Florida Telephone #1 as a contact number.
84. On or about August 29, 2001, Ahmed al-Ghamdi and Hamza al-Ghamdi reserved electronic, one-way tickets for United Airlines Flight 175.
85. On or about August 29, 2001, Ahmed al-Haznawi purchased a ticket on United Airlines Flight 93 from Newark, New Jersey, to San Francisco, California, scheduled for September 11, 2001.
86. On or about August 30, 2001, Mohammed Atta (#11) purchased a utility tool that contained a knife.

By August 30, the stage was set. A dozen days later, four commercial airliners were boarded in the early morning hours by a total of 19 terrorists. By lunchtime, all four planes had crashed, two of them succeeding where the 1993 bombers had failed in bringing down the Twin Towers of the World Trade Center, another doing significant damage to the Pentagon, and the fourth—which got off the ground late, so that passengers onboard became aware of what was transpiring and staged a revolt against the hijackers—crashing into a western Pennsylvania field. Including the 19 suicide attackers themselves, 2,995 people died. The losses in terms of property and economic disruption were staggering.[15]

Meanwhile, in mid-August, as noted previously, Moussaoui had been arrested on immigration charges. On September 14, he was moved from a jail in Minnesota to New York as a probable material witness with regard to the 9/11 attacks. He was indicted on December 11, and two days later he was moved to Alexandria, Virginia, to await trial.[16]

3.4 Pretrial Legal Maneuvers

Moussaoui's case was assigned to U.S. District Judge Leonie Brinkema.[17] Then, another four years elapsed before he actually came to trial. Extensive legal maneuvering was responsible for much of this delay.[18] Two issues were particularly time-consuming. One was the defendant's initial insistence on representing himself. In the end, her honor ordered that attorneys be appointed by the court to defend Moussaoui. Second was the refusal of the Department of Justice (DOJ) refusal to allow those court-appointed counsel to interview detained al Qaeda operatives as potential witnesses. Brinkema sanctioned the DOJ by eliminating the possibility of the death penalty from the case. This ruling was the subject of an interlocutory appeal[19] to the U.S. Court of Appeals for the Fourth Circuit, which sits in Richmond.[20] When in March 2005 the U.S. Supreme Court refused to review[21] the Fourth Circuit's most recent ruling—that enemy combatants in U.S. armed forces' custody outside the United States could be reached by the court's subpoena powers, but that summaries of their anticipated testimony could be substituted for deposition testimony for national security reasons—Moussaoui threw in the towel. He proposed in April 2005 to plead guilty. Pleading guilty to lying to federal agents,[22] Moussaoui left nothing for the jury to decide, except the nature of his punishment.[23]

Judge Brinkema bifurcated the trial into a hearing wherein the jury would decide if the government had proved beyond a reasonable doubt that the defendant's lies to federal agents prior to 9/11 were a cause of the subsequent carnage, and if so, if he deserved death or life in prison.

3.5 The Trial: Phase 1

In his opening statement, U.S. Attorney Robert Spencer told the jurors that Moussaoui "killed the 9/11 victims as surely as if he had been at the controls of one of the airplanes."[24]

Defense Counsel Edward MacMahon[25] retorted:

> What the Statement of Facts contains is mostly historical admissions of a general nature about al Qaeda and its training and other plans that Moussaoui, as an admitted al Qaeda member, was in a position to know, including, yes, the existence of a plane's operation. The reason Mr. Spencer declines to tell you that he is going to prove what role Moussaoui played in the 9/11 attacks is because there is no evidence to support it.
>
> There is no evidence as to what he did in these attacks, and the government would surely come forward with that evidence if it existed. And you will learn

> that before September 11th, al Qaeda was preparing many operations that involved killing Americans, and that many involved hijacking aircraft. And of those plots, the 9/11 plot was only one of them. The Statement of Facts that Moussaoui has signed contains no admission of involvement in or knowledge of the attacks that occurred on September 11. Moussaoui certainly wasn't sent over here to tell a lie, ladies and gentlemen.[26]

The key witness was FBI Special Agent Harry Samit.

Some observers of Samit's performance on the witness stand praised him. One commentator gushed about Samit:

> Samit is the real-life version of *24* Agent Jack Bauer. But real-life FBI agents have to deal with layers and layers of untalented, useless bureaucratic managers and superiors. And unlike Jack Bauer, those FBI bureaucrats usually succeed in foiling successful terrorism investigations.[27]

The implication is that FBI bureaucrats—and not Moussaoui's lies—prevented a prompt intervention prior to the launch of the 9/11 attacks. In this regard, Samit was honest but equivocal. Professor Douglas Linder of the University of Missouri states explicitly, "While Samit testified that Moussaoui's lies sent him 'on a wild goose chase' until September 11, he refused to say for sure that but for the defendant's lies, the 9/11 attacks could have been prevented."[28]

Key testimony by Samit involved mid-August 2001—a bit less than a month before the 9/11 attacks:[29]

Q: When you say obsession, could you tell us what do you mean by that?

A: I mean that on the basis of the interviews that Special Agent Weess and myself had done on the 16th and the 17th, we were convinced that Mr. Moussaoui was involved in some type of plot, and so all of our energies were directed at accumulating whatever was required, evidence or intelligence, to get into his belongings and search them for information as to what was going to happen.

Q: Now, at some point, your request to get a FISA search warrant[30] was denied by your headquarters; is that right?

A: Yes, sir.

Q: OK. Do you know approximately when that was?

A: Approximately August 28.

Q: All right. At the time that your request for a search warrant was denied, could you explain to us what was the extent of the information that you had available that connected you to a terrorist organization?

A: Yes, sir.

Q: Or Mr. Moussaoui, I'm sorry.

A: Yes, sir. We had information from our legat in Paris that Mr. Moussaoui had recruited this fighter for the Chechens who had since been killed in Chechnya, that that fighter, in fact, was connected to Ibn Khattab, who was the leader of the Chechen fighters. The CIA was able to confirm that information and also to provide information that Ibn Khattab and Usama bin Laden had a relationship.

Q: So to get to the proof of al Qaeda, you were trying to go through Moussaoui's friend to the leader of the Chechens, from the leader of the Chechens to al Qaeda; is that right?

A: Yes.

Q: If Mr. Moussaoui told you what was in paragraph 4 that we showed you, would you have needed to do that?

MacMahon: Your Honor, I'm going to object. It's a misleading question, that anybody at the government ever even looked at a warrant or even a warrant request along the lines that Mr. Novak just described.

The Court: Wait, wait, wait. It's more appropriate—I don't think that question got into that at all, but I think this is area for cross-examination, but this question is not objectionable.

MacMahon: OK.

The Court: Overruled.

MacMahon: All right.

[Novak continues questioning.]

Q: So had Mr. Moussaoui said, as he did before this Court, that he was a member of al Qaeda, would you have had to try that circuitous route in order to try to get to al Qaeda?

A: Absolutely not.

Q: The designated organization?

A: In fact, if he had answered our specific questions as to what group he was a member of, who his associates were, it would have met the foreign power standard immediately.

Q: Now, after the FISA request was denied by your headquarters, did they relay to you why it was that they were denying it?

A: They did.

Q: And what was that?

A: They informed that . . .

MacMahon: Objection, Your Honor, as to why—first of all, the question is misleading that a warrant was ever presented to anybody. If he wants to clarify that, he can, but then to get the hearsay about what happened to it is inappropriate.

The Court: I'm not going to permit the government to use hearsay in this case.

Novak: That's fine. I'll move on.

The Court: Sustained.
Novak: All right.
Q: Let me ask you this: At any point, were you able to satisfy your headquarters' demands as to the proof as to what the foreign power was?
A: No.

On cross, Samit's testimony was even more damaging to the government's case, as he conceded that his masters in Washington "took a calculated risk not to advance the investigation" and adding, "the wager was a national tragedy."[31]

But Samit also had stated strongly from the stand that a warning finally did go out to federal agencies on September 5, a warning that might have gone sooner and been stronger, had Moussaoui told him the truth:[32]

Q: And on September 5 of 2001, do you know if your headquarters did, in fact, make that notification?
A: They did. In fact, our headquarters issued a teletype, a message to a number of other government agencies, to include the FAA [Federal Aviation Administration].
Q: Now, in addition to what you requested your headquarters to do, were you so concerned about the FAA being notified that you took steps on your own as a local guy on the ground out in Minnesota to make sure the FAA knew what was going on with Mr. Moussaoui?
A: Yes, sir. Special Agent Weess and myself on September 5 went to the FAA investigators in the Twin Cities, in Minneapolis-St. Paul, and provided them a personal briefing on the contents of the teletype, as well as case agent perspective on what we believed was actually going on.
Q: And did that include the lies that he had told you on August 16 and August 17?
MacMahon: Your Honor, that's argumentative. If he's going to the Statement of Facts again, did it include what he told them? Did it include the lies? It couldn't have included the lies, Your Honor.
The Court: I'm going to overrule the objection, but be careful. I don't want questions being argumentative or overly . . .
Novak: That's fine, Judge. Yes.
Q: Did you tell the FAA the things that Mr. Moussaoui told you on August 16?
A: We did. We were only able to report what he told us.
Q: Had Mr. Moussaoui told you the things that in the Statement of Facts he admitted in front of this Court, for example, that he was part of a plot to fly planes into buildings, could you have supplied that information to the FAA on September 5, as well?
A: Absolutely. It would have gone much sooner, obviously, but yes, we would have been in a position to do that.

Q: Well, why would it have been smoother? What would you have done?
A: We would have notified them immediately, along with other members of the intelligence community, FBI headquarters, FBI New York. Within minutes of Mr. Moussaoui disclosing any of those—answering any of those questions truthfully, that information would have been forwarded to, to every member of the intelligence community, and especially the FAA.

The government's case hit a serious speed bump when the judge learned that some of the prosecution witnesses had been improperly coached. Brinkema chastised from the bench, "I've never seen a more egregious violation of the rule about witnesses." However, she declined to declare a mistrial or dismiss the case. When she ruled that the prosecutors could offer substitute witnesses, Moussaoui sang out, "The show must go on!"[33]

Beginning March 23, 2006, the defense presented its side. Besides its contention that Washington bureaucrats were responsible for the nation's failure to detect and prevent 9/11, MacMahon and team also contended that their client was "out of the loop." However, this aspect of the strategy was blown up, like the Twin Towers themselves, when their client insisted upon exercising his right to testify. Moussaoui, it seems, was more interested in making a political statement than saving his own neck. A representative example of his testimony (though actually taken from the second phase of the trial) is reproduced here in what follows.[34]

U.S. Attorney Robert Spencer: You told the jury that you have no regret for your part in any of this?
Moussaoui: I just wish it will happen on the 12th, the 13th, the 14th, the 15th, the 16th, the 17th, and I can go on and on.
Spencer: No remorse?
Moussaoui: There is no remorse for justice.
Spencer: You also enjoyed the testimony about the attack on the Pentagon?
Moussaoui: Definitely.
Spencer: You smiled at times during that testimony, didn't you?
Moussaoui: That's for sure. I would have even laughed if I didn't know that I would be kicked out of the court.
Spencer: Right. You enjoyed seeing the Pentagon on fire?
Moussaoui: My pleasure.
Spencer: And you remember hearing Lt. Col. John Thurman describe he had to crawl out with his face against the floor to save his life?
Moussaoui: He was pathetic.
Spencer: You enjoyed that, didn't you?
Moussaoui: I was regretful he didn't die.
Spencer: Well, here is somebody who did die. [A victim's picture is shown on the courtroom's screens.] Do you remember that gentleman?

Moussaoui: I remember his wife, the blonde-haired girl.
Spencer: That's Vince Tolbert, who worked for the United States Navy, right? He was killed on 9/11 in the Pentagon.
Moussaoui: Yes, the one that said to her children that some bad people have killed her husband. And she forgot to tell to her children that her husband was working classified, something about targeting.
Spencer: And it made you particularly happy that he was killed that day, correct?
Moussaoui: Make my day.
Spencer: Do you remember the testimony of Lt. McKeown?
Moussaoui: The woman like was talking about "Where are my boy? Where are my boy?"
Spencer: Right. Sobbing in that very chair because the people under her command were killed. Do you remember that?
Moussaoui: I think it was disgusting for a military person to pretend that they should not be killed as an act of war. She is military. She should expect that people who are at war with her will try to kill her. I will never, I will never cry because an American bombed my camp.
Spencer: And you were happy that her two men were killed that day?
Moussaoui: Make my day.
Spencer: All right. You were happy that every single person who came in here sad, telling about the effect that you and your brothers [had]. You were happy about all that, weren't you? No regret, no remorse—right, Mr. Moussaoui?
Moussaoui: No regret, no remorse.
Spencer: Like it to all happen again, right?
Moussaoui: Every day, until we get here to you.

Not surprisingly, after six days of deliberations, the jury found unanimously that Moussaoui's lies were a material contributing cause of 9/11's nearly 3,000 fatalities.

3.6 The Trial: Phase 2

In 1972, the U.S. Supreme Court held that the death penalty, as imposed by several state courts in a selection of consolidated cases, constituted cruel and unusual punishment under the Eighth Amendment.[35] The effect of the case was to cause all states still having a death penalty to suspend its imposition, while their legislatures went back to the drawing boards. An influential concurring opinion by Justice Hugo Black provided them with their blueprint:

> The test, then, will ordinarily be a cumulative one: if a punishment is unusually severe, if there is a strong probability that it is inflicted arbitrarily, if it is substantially rejected by contemporary society, and if there is no reason to believe that it serves any penal purpose more effectively than some less severe punishment, then the continued infliction of that punishment violates the command of the Clause that the State may not inflict inhuman and uncivilized punishments upon those convicted of crimes.[36]

One outcome of this revisionist trend was that between 1977 and 1997, no one was executed for any crime not involving homicide.[37] Furthermore, in virtually all states still imposing a death penalty for a select list of crimes, capital punishment is discretionary. Virtually all such statutes require a weighing of aggravating and mitigating circumstances.[38] And, as we saw in detail in Chapter 2, the same is true of the relevant federal statute.

In phase 2 of Moussaoui's trial, the jurors heard from a number of survivors and the families of deceased victims of 9/11. They had recounted to them the conversation between witness Lee Hanson of Easton, Connecticut, and his son Peter, who called him at just before 9 a.m. from United Flight 175. Hanson's son said, "I think they've taken over the cockpit—an attendant has been stabbed—and someone else up front may have been killed. The plane is making strange moves." Peter Hanson added, "Call United Airlines—tell them it's Flight 175, Boston to LA."[39]

At about 9 a.m. sharp, Peter called his dad again: "It's getting bad, Dad—A stewardess was stabbed—They seem to have knives and Mace—They said they have a bomb—It's getting very bad on the plane—Passengers are throwing up and getting sick—The plane is making jerky movements—I don't think the pilot is flying the plane—I think we are going down—I think they intend to go to Chicago or someplace and fly into a building."

Then, as many a good son (as my own son) might say, Peter added, "Don't worry, Dad—if it happens, it'll be very fast."

And then, "My God, my God."[40]

However, the defense was able to produce other survivors and family members who urged that we all needed to "move on."[41] Judge Brinkema sent the jurors to their deliberation room armed with 26 aggravating and 23 mitigating factors in total. And despite Moussaoui's testimony that, among many outrageous remarks, Timothy McVeigh was "the greatest American," the panel was unable to reach a unanimous verdict for the death penalty. Shortly after the foreman's report to the judge—"We the jury do not unanimously find that a sentence of death should be imposed on the defendant"—Moussaoui was transferred to Uncle Sam's "Supermax" facility in Florence, Colorado.

3.7 Aftermath

The Moussaoui case has been back before the courts periodically since he was sentenced to life in prison. In 2007, the Fourth Circuit reversed the federal district court, which would have allowed 9/11 survivors and families of deceased victims to access grand jury records in the case. Saying no, the appeals panel held the following.

1. District court's orders were immediately appealable under the collateral order doctrine;
2. Neither the Crime Victims Rights Act (CVRA) nor the Air Transportation Safety and System Stabilization Act (ATSSSA) authorized the district court's order;
3. The procedure for disclosure of grand jury minutes to private plaintiffs acts did not authorize such an order; and
4. The district court lacked the inherent authority to allow victims to intervene in a criminal process to obtain non-public discovery from Government.[42]

In February 2010, the Fourth Circuit rejected Moussaoui's attempt to withdraw his guilty plea and reopen his case, based upon classified information that became public information following his conviction and sentencing. The panel of judges held,

> Moussaoui has failed to demonstrate that the Government withheld exculpatory material that would have caused Moussaoui to forego his guilty plea and proceed to trial, much less evidence of his actual innocence. Should that change, as a result of the ongoing tapes investigation or otherwise, Moussaoui, like every other criminal defendant, has collateral avenues for raising such claims. In the meantime, the finality of the guilty plea, entered knowingly, intelligently, and with sufficient awareness of the relevant circumstances and likely consequences, stands.[43]

Last and probably least, the Fourth Circuit in March 2010, in a paltry one-page opinion, rejected Moussaoui's last-ditch effort at a reversal on the basis of what his counsel claimed was a faulty jury instruction.[44]

At this writing, Zacarias Moussaoui remains in a high-security federal penitentiary and is likely to die there. Unlike George Armstrong Custer, who is sometimes said to have died for the white man's sins against the American Indian,[45] an American jury decided that Moussaoui should not die for the sins of his 19 co-conspirators. In light of the defendant's vociferous praise for the deadly deeds of 9/11—deeds in which he clearly wished he had participated and apparently hoped his lying had protected, if not furthered—the verdict, I think, speaks well for the American federal justice system and the American jury in particular.

The verdict also demonstrates that Moussaoui received first-rate representation by counsel. Indeed, he seems to have had every reasonable avenue explored on his behalf by his attorneys, as my brief survey of the numerous appellate court decisions reinforces.

3.8 Conspiracy Theories

It comes as no surprise, of course, that the blogosphere is resplendent with conspiracy theories concerning the tragic events of 9/11.[46] Theories include the following.

- The World Trade Center towers were toppled by a controlled demolition.[47]
- The towers were brought down by a missile fired by "elements of the American state apparatus."[48]
- United Flight 93, which crashed in western Pennsylvania, was shot down by a missile.[49]
- The planes that hit the towers were remotely controlled.[50]
- Insider trading of United and American stock shortly before 9/11 is proof of advance knowledge of the attacks by sovereign state investment funds or others, perhaps Israeli intelligence.[51]
- Four thousand Jews failed to show up for work in the World Trade Center on September 11, 2001, demonstrating that Israel, not al Qaeda, was behind the attacks.[52]

Just as the theory persists that the Roosevelt administration, eager to join England in its war against the Third Reich, allowed Americans to be massacred at Pearl Harbor (the second most deadly attack on American soil, after 9/11),[53] the listed conspiracy theories all come down to one overarching "master theory," if you will. Namely, there are—and I suppose will always be—those who believe that the Bush administration or the Israelis, in order (like FDR) to motivate the American people to enthusiastically go to war, either allowed al Qaeda to go forward with its dastardly acts or (worse yet) did the dirty deeds and put the blame on international Islamic terrorism.

I leave it to you, the reader, to make your own judgment, hopeful that this chapter has helped.

Meanwhile, Moussaoui made this statement in 2020: "I denounce, repudiate Usama bin Laden as a useful idiot of the CIA/Saudi. I also proclaim unequivocally my opposition to any terrorist action, attack, propaganda against the U.S." Part of yet another of his seemingly endless court motions, it added that he wanted "to warn young Muslim[s] against the deception and the manipulation of these fake Jihadis."

> Moussaoui made his renunciation in a petition seeking relaxation of the special administrative measures under which he serves his sentence. In particular, he says he wants either Rudy Giuliani or Alan Dershowitz to represent him as a lawyer, so he can testify in a civil trial filed by victims of the Sept. 11 attacks.[54]

Rudy Giuliani seems an interesting choice. Known as "America's Mayor" following the 9/11 World Trade Center attack, his reputation has endured a steady decline in the 23 years that have followed. His antics in filing dozens of suits across the country challenging the outcome of the 2020 presidential election results—efforts that came to nothing—helped land him in legal hot water. That hot water boiled over in August of 2023.

> On Aug. 1, he was listed as an unindicted co-conspirator in former President Donald Trump's federal Jan. 6 indictment. On Aug. 14, he was indicted in Georgia for his actions in the same alleged plot. And last week, he was found liable for defaming two Georgia election workers in a particularly ugly episode of that whole saga.[55]

That awarded the plaintiffs $148 million, leading "America's Mayer" to file for bankruptcy. It's unlikely Moussaoui, or anyone else, will be choosing Giuliani for their counsel, even if in the wake of these legal disasters he retains his license to practice law. [See Chapter 11.]

Notes

1. Douglas O. Linder, "The Trial of Zacarias Moussaoui: An Account," Famous Trials, http://www.law.umkc.edu/faculty/projects/ftrials/moussaoui/zmac-count.html.
2. Adapted from the grand jury indictment of Zacarias Moussaoui, U.S. District Court for the Eastern District of Virginia, December 11, 2001, http://www.law.umkc.edu/faculty/projects/ftrials/moussaoui/indictment.html, except where otherwise indicated.
3. The term *fatwah* means, strictly speaking, "a legal opinion or ruling issued by an Islamic scholar" (http://www.thefreedictionary.com/fatwah).
4. *The 9/11 Commission Report: Final Report of the National Commission on Terrorist Attacks upon the United States (New York: W.W. Norton, 2004)*, p. 55.

5. George Crile, *Charlie Wilson's War* (New York: Grove Press, 2003), p. 521.
6. Crile, p. 520. Note: Americans were no more aware of the CIA's remarkable achievement at the time it was being executed than were the Afghan freedom fighters aware of the sources of their weaponry and other materiel. By way of example, let me cite *The Washington Post*'s Bob Woodward's *Veil: The Secret Wars of the CIA* (New York: Simon & Schuster, 1987), which was concerned primarily with the Iran-Contra scandal. Looking back at Woodward's best-seller, one finds about a dozen references to the CIA–Afghan connection in the index. Woodward comes to appreciating the impact of the CIA's covert Afghan intervention late in the book, when he paraphrases DCIA Casey's comment, "There was good news for the Afghanistan operation in particular. On the ground, in those mountains and in some of the most god-awful terrain in the world, the Russians were getting the tar beaten out of them, Casey thought, and CIA support was increasing" (p. 385). However, it's clear that Woodward was more interested in the inadvertent co-mingling of CIA Afghan and Iran-Contra funds (see p. 502).
7. Crile, p. 522.
8. Peter L. Bergen, *Holy War Inc.: Inside the Secret World of Osama Bin Laden* (New York: The Free Press, 2001), p. 195. There is evidence, about which more will be said in subsequent chapters, that al Qaeda has embraced to a significant extent the principle of "leaderless resistance," about which I have written in an earlier book (James Ottavio Castagnera, *Al-Qaeda Goes to College: Impact of the War on Terror on American Higher Education* [Westport, CT: Praeger, 2009], pp. 70–71):

    > Substantial evidence of Al Qaeda's reliance on leaderless resistance is extant. Incidents in the United States over the past 16 years or so, which are likely examples of leaderless-resistance actions, include:
    >
    > - January 25, 1992: Two CIA employees are shot and three others wounded outside the agency's Langley, Virginia headquarters by Mir Aimal Kasi.
    > - March 1, 1994: Rashid Baz boards a bus in Brooklyn and opens fire on Jewish Yeshiva students.
    > - February 25, 1997: Ali Hassan Abu Ali Kamal fires on tourists on the observation deck of the Empire State Building.
    > - July 31, 1997: Lafi Khalil and Ghazi Ibrahim Abu Mezer are arrested in their New York restaurant after police find five pipe bombs, which the pair planned to set off in the NYC subways.
    > - July 4, 2002: Hesham Mohamed Hadayet attacks the El Al ticket counter at Los Angeles International Airport, killing two and wounding four.
    > - September 6, 2002: German police arrest an American woman and her Turkish fiancé in Heidelberg, alleging they planned to detonate pipe bombs in the nearby U.S. military base.

9. *9/11 Commission Report*, p. 60.
10. Ibid., pp. 60–61 and 70–71.
11. Ibid., p. 73.
12. Ibid., pp. 73–107.

13. Excerpted from the Moussaoui indictment, supra note 2. Note: Since, as we shall see, Moussaoui pled guilty, no trial was held with regard to the substantive crimes with which he stood indicted. However, the lengthy hearings, discussed in detail in the second half of this chapter, concerning his punishment did deal in depth with many of the allegations of the indictment.
14. http://www.alquds.co.uk. See also http://en.wikipedia.org/wiki/Al-Quds_Al-Arabi.
15. One reasoned estimate puts the total loss at $2 trillion (Institute for Analysis of Global Security, http://www.iags.org/costof911.html). Other excellent sources on this subject are:

    - Gail Makinen et al., *The Economic Effects of 9/11: A Retrospective Assessment* (Washington, DC: U.S. Government Printing Office, September 27, 2002).
    - William C. Thompson Jr., One Year Later: The Fiscal Impact of 9/11 on New York City (New York: Comptroller of the City of New York, September 4, 2002).
    - Dick K. Nanto, *9/11 Terrorism: Global Economic Costs* (Washington, DC: U.S. Government Printing Office, October 5, 2004).

16. "Chronology Courtesy of Dr. Douglas O. Linder," *Famous Trials*, http://www.law.umkc.edu/faculty/projects/ftrials/moussaoui/zmchronology.html.
17. Some readers who are unfamiliar with American court systems may be interested in knowing that in the federal system, a case is assigned randomly to a trial judge by the clerk of the court soon after the complaint is filed. That judge then has responsibility for the case all the way through to a resolution, whether that resolution is a verdict or other final judgment, following a trial or some earlier disposition, such as a summary resolution based upon a motion filed by one side or the other. By contrast, in most state court systems, after a complaint is filed, the case remains with the court clerk's office. As the litigation progresses through the pretrial stages, motions are heard by a motion court judge, and not until the case is certified by counsel to be ripe for trial is it assigned to a particular judge, who then presides over the trial. Note: A biography of Judge Brinkema, current roughly to the time of trial, is accessible at http://www.techlawjournal.com/people/brinkema.htm.
18. Again for the benefit of readers unfamiliar with the American federal court system, let me note that after a complaint (in a civil trial) or an indictment/criminal complaint is filed and a judge assigned (as described in endnote 17), the case enters a pretrial phase which can include all manner of motions (requests to the judge to take action, e.g., exclude tainted evidence) and discovery (interviewing witnesses, retaining and prepping experts, etc.). Usually all this is accomplished in a year or less. However, in high-profile or highly complex cases, significantly more time may be required.
19. According to *Black's Law Dictionary*, "An interlocutory order or decree is one which does not finally determine a cause of action but only decides some intervening matter pertaining to the cause, and which requires further steps to be

taken in order to enable the court to adjudicate the cause on the merits." *Black's Law Dictionary* (6th ed.) (St. Paul, MN: West Publishing, 1991), p. 562. Interlocutory appeals are not favored by the appellate courts. However, where a trial judge's ruling is dispositive in some sense—as here, the jury's potential verdict of the death penalty was taken by Judge Brinkema out of their hands—review of the ruling will be entertained by the appeals court. (Sometimes, too, a significant question, which can substantially affect the final outcome of the case, will be "certified" to the U.S. or a state supreme court, if it calls for a "first impression" ruling in the jurisdiction.)

20. This issue, as well as a closely related one of media access to classified materials that might be admitted in the case, resulted in a whole string of opinions issued by the Fourth Circuit over a two-year span:

- *U.S. v. Moussaoui*, 43 Fed. Appx. 612 (4th Cir., 2002):

Zacarias Moussaoui appeals several pretrial orders entered by the district court in connection with the criminal proceedings against him. We conclude that we lack jurisdiction over these consolidated appeals and accordingly dismiss them.

- *In re Moussaoui*, 43 Fed. Appx. 672 (4th Cir., 2002):

Charles Freeman, on behalf of Zacarias Moussaoui, seeks rehearing and rehearing en banc of our order dated July 25, 2002, denying the issuance of extraordinary writs of mandamus, prohibition, and injunction, claiming that extraordinary writs should issue to direct Judge Brinkema to allow Moussaoui unfettered access to meet and consult with Freeman. This Court lacks jurisdiction to hear Freeman's and Moussaoui's petitions for extraordinary writs because the district court's order denying Moussaoui access to Freeman is reviewable on appeal if there is a conviction. Thus, Freeman and Moussaoui have not demonstrated that there are no other adequate means to attain the relief they desire.

- *U.S. v. Moussaoui*, 2003 WL 1889018 (4th Cir., 2003):

For reasons appearing to the court, this appeal is temporarily stayed and the cause remanded to the district court for a limited purpose. On remand, the Government is to be given an opportunity to propose substitutions for the classified information authorized to be disclosed by the district court in its order of January 31, 2003, and the defendant and standby counsel are to be given an opportunity to respond to any proposed substitutions.

- *U.S. v. Moussaoui*, 65 Fed. Appx. 881 (4th Cir., 2003):

Capital defendant, who was indicted on charges arising from his alleged participation in plot that culminated in terrorist attacks, was granted access to one of plot's captured leaders. After government appealed and also petitioned for writ of mandamus, members of media moved to intervene for limited purpose of obtaining access to certain portions of the record and oral argument on appeal. The Court of Appeals held that: (1) Classified Information Procedures Act (CIPA) could not, alone, justify sealing of oral arguments and documents; (2) all classified information filed with Court of Appeals would remain under seal; (3) procedure for handling defendant's unclassified, pro se pleadings filed in Court of Appeals would not be altered; (4) classified, ex parte appendices were properly kept under seal; (5) documents in remaining appendices had to be examined to determine whether disclosure was required; (6) sealing of government's certificate of confidentiality and motion to seal oral argument, and motion to seal certificate of confidentiality and motion to seal oral argument, was not justified; and (7) bifurcated oral argument was warranted.

- *U.S. v. Moussaoui*, 333 F.3d 509 (4th Cir., 2003):

In proceedings in a capital case, against an admitted member of al-Qaeda terrorist organization, indicted for being a part of planned 9/11 terrorist attacks, the United States District Court for the Eastern District of Virginia, Leonie M. Brinkema, J., ordered government to produce an enemy combatant witness for deposition. Government appealed and petitioned for writ of mandamus. The Court of Appeals, Wilkins, Chief Judge, held that (1) Court of Appeals lacked jurisdiction to hear appeal, and (2) government was not entitled to mandamus relief.

- *U.S. v. Moussaoui*, 365 F.3d 292 (4th Cir., 2004). The Court of Appeals, William W. Wilkins, Chief Judge, held that:

  1. enemy combatant witnesses, who were foreign nationals outside the boundaries of the United States, were not beyond the process power of the district court where witnesses were in the custody of the United States military;
  2. defendant had a Sixth Amendment right to testimony of enemy combatant witnesses;
  3. allowing defendant access to witness would not interfere with the Executive's power to make and conduct war in violation of violate separation of powers doctrine; and
  4. in order to remedy violation of defendant's Sixth Amendment right to compulsory process, Government would be required to produce an adequate substitute for the classified information in the form of a series of statements derived from summaries of reports accurately reflecting the witnesses' statements.

- *U.S. v. Moussaoui*, 382 F.3d 453 (4th Cir., 2004), cert. denied, 544 U.S. 931 (2005). The Court of Appeals, Wilkins, Chief Judge, held that:

  1. enemy combatant witnesses who were foreign nationals in military custody outside the boundaries of the United States were not beyond the process power of the district court;
  2. ordering production of enemy combatant witnesses did not infringe on the Executive's warmaking authority, in violation of separation of powers principles; and

3. government's rightful exercise of its prerogative to protect national security interests by refusing to produce the witnesses warranted use of written summaries of the witness' statements made over the course of several months in lieu of their deposition testimony.

21. *Moussaoui v. U.S.*, 544 U.S. 931, 125 S. Ct. 1670, 161 L.Ed.2d 496 (2005).
22. Readers will recall that the portion of the Moussaoui indictment excerpted above includes the following allegation No. 74: "On or about August 17, 2001, Zacarias Moussaoui, while being interviewed by federal agents in Minneapolis, attempted to explain his presence in the United States by falsely stating that he was simply interested in learning to fly."
23. In my Introduction, I deal briefly with one of Clarence Darrow's most famous cases, the terrorism trial of "Big Bill" Haywood, an officer of the Western Federation of Miners, for the bombing death of a former Idaho governor. Far more famous—and the subject of three major motion pictures and a Broadway play—is the Leopold and Loeb thrill killing case. In that case, realizing that his wealthy, bright young clients could never persuade a jury that they were either innocent or insane, Darrow had his clients plead guilty of kidnapping and murder and throw themselves on the mercy of the judge in a lengthy hearing, spanning several months (like Moussaoui's), on mitigation of punishment. Darrow's gamble succeeded and the judge spared the two defendants from the gallows. (Nathan Leopold ultimately won parole and lived an exemplary later life.) See http://www.law.umkc.edu/faculty/projects/ftrials/leoploeb/leopold.htm.
24. http://www.law.umkc.edu/faculty/projects/ftrials/moussaoui/zmspencer.html.
25. Moussaoui was extremely well represented (http://www.aclu.org/national-security/john-adams-project-lawyer-biographies#macmahon):

    > Edward MacMahon has been practicing criminal law since 1986, and has represented numerous clients charged with offenses related to national security as well as clients facing the death penalty. For example, in the 1980s, Mr. MacMahon represented one of the Army officers tried by Court Martial in the Iran-Contra case. More recently, he was lead counsel in the case of *United States v. al-Timimi*, who was charged with soliciting others to levy war against the United States and inducing others to use firearms in violation of federal law. Although that case is currently on appeal, it was recently sent back to the district court for further proceedings regarding claims that Dr. al-Timimi was subject to the warrantless wiretapping.

    Marindale-Hubble, the leading reference source on U.S. Attorneys, in August 2010 stated of MacMahon's "Profile Visibility," "#11 in weekly profile views out of 25,524 lawyers in Washington, District of Columbia[;] #378 in weekly profile views out of 1,008,836 total lawyers" (http://www.martindale.com/Edward-B-MacMahon-Jr/369616-lawyer.htm).
26. http://www.law.umkc.edu/faculty/projects/ftrials/moussaoui/zmmacmahon.html.
27. Debbie Schlussel, "Special Agent Harry Samit: This American Hero Is the Real Jack Bauer," http://www.debbieschlussel.com/1121/special-agent-harry—samit-this-american-hero-is-the-real-jack-bauer.

28. Linder, "The Trial of Zacarias Moussaoui."
29. http://www.law.umkc.edu/faculty/projects/ftrials/moussaoui/zmsamit.html.
30. The reference is to the Foreign Intelligence Surveillance Court, created by the Foreign Intelligence Surveillance Act of 1978, accessible at http://www.fas.org/irp/agency/doj/fisa.
31. http://www.law.umkc.edu/faculty/projects/ftrials/moussaoui/zmsamit.html.
32. Ibid.
33. Linder, "The Trial of Zacarias Moussaoui."
34. http://www.law.umkc.edu/faculty/projects/ftrials/moussaoui/zmzm.html.
35. The three consolidated cases are styled *Furman v. Georgia*, 408 U.S. 238, 92 S. Ct. 2726 (1972).
36. 408 U.S., at 282.
37. Hugo Adam Bedau (ed.), *The Death Penalty in America: Current Controversies* (Oxford: Oxford University Press, 1997), p. 6.
38. Ibid., p. 26.
39. *9/11 Commission Report*, p. 7.
40. Ibid., p. 8. The 9/11 report cites an FBI interview of the elder Hanson taken the very day of the attacks. (See endnote 49 of Chapter 1.) However, Hanson recited essentially the same conversation again in court. (See note 1.)
41. Linder, "The Trial of Zacarias Moussaoui."
42. *United States v. Moussaoui*, 483 F.3d 220 (4th Cir., 2007).
43. *U.S. v. Moussaoui*, 591 F.3d 263, 307 (4th Cir., 2010).
44. U.S. v. Moussaoui, 368 Fed. Appx. 970 (4th Cir., 2010).
45. Vine Deloria Jr., *Custer Died for Your Sins: An Indian Manifesto* (Norman, OK: Oklahoma University Press, 1988), http://www.akpress.org/2004/items/custerdiedforyoursins.
46. A Google search entitled "9/11 conspiracy theories" on August 15, 2010, resulted in 5,160,000 hits.
47. See Brent Blanchard, "A Critical Analysis of the Collapse of WTC Towers 1, 2 and 7 from an Explosives and Conventional Demolition Industry Viewpoint," August 8, 2006, http://www.implosionworld.com/Article-WTC%20STUDY%208-06%20w%20clarif%20as%20of%209-8-06%20.pdf.
48. See Thierrry Meyssan, *9/11: The Big Lie* (L'Effroyable Imposture) (London: Carnot Publishing, 2002).
49. See http://www.america.gov/st/webchat-english/2009/May/20060828133846esnamfuaK0.2676355.html.
50. Ibid.
51. Ibid. Note: This theory was acknowledged and debunked by the 9/11 Commission in its report.
52. See "The 4,000 Jews Rumor," April 28, 2009, http://www.america.gov/st/webchat-english/2009/April/20090430132244atlahtnevel4.020327e-02.html.
53. See, e.g., Robert B. Stinnett et al., "Do Freedom of Information Act Files Prove FDR Had Foreknowledge of Pearl Harbor?" *The Independent Institute*, March 11, 2002, http://www.independent.org/newsroom/article.asp?id=408.

54. Matthew Barakat, "September 11 Convict Now Says He renounces Terrorism, Bin Laden," *Associated Press*, May 20, 2020, https://apnews.com/article/terrorism-us-news-ap-top-news-co-state-wire-nj-state-wire-ee171bf63cd9436953ed0b1edbefb5cc (last accessed December 27, 2023).
55. Aaron Blake, "Rudy Giuliani's Stunning Fall from Grace, in One Chart," *Washington Post*, September 5, 2023, https://www.washingtonpost.com/politics/2023/09/05/giuliani-popularity-fall/ (last accessed December 27, 2023).

It Shouldn't Happen to a Dog?
The Trial of the SHAC 7 (2006)

4

4.1 The Roots of the Animal Rights Movement

In his novel of 17th-century England, *Quicksilver*, author Neal Stephenson has members of the Royal Society "starving a toad in a jar to see if new toads would grow out of it,"[1] draining "all the blood out of a large dog and putting it into a smaller dog minutes later,"[2] and removing "the rib cage from a living mongrel."[3] Since Stephenson's representations appear to be historically accurate, little wonder that the "first significant animal rights movement began in 19th-century England, where the impetus was opposition to the use of un-anaesthetized animals in scientific research."[4] The only wonder is that it took so long for social mores to rise to the level of repugnance for this practice that the "movement inspired protests, legislative reforms in the United Kingdom, and the birth of numerous animal protection organizations."[5]

The rise of such sentiments paralleled the changing views of England's leading philosophers (including so-called natural philosophers) toward animals. While Rene Descartes considered animals to be "organic machines,"[6] David Hume wrote in the 18th century,

> Next to the ridicule of denying an evident truth, is that of taking much pains to defend it; and no truth appears to me more evident, than that beasts are endow'd with thought and reason as well as men. The arguments are in this case so obvious, that they never escape the most stupid and ignorant.[7]

Jeremy Bentham, the early 19th-century father of Utilitarianism, added,

> Other animals . . . , on account of their interests having been neglected by the insensibility of the ancient jurists, stand degraded into the class of things . . . . The day has been, I grieve it to say in many places it is not yet past, in which the greater part of the species, under the denomination of slaves, have been treated . . . upon the same footing as . . . animals are still. The day may come, when the rest of the animal creation may acquire those rights which never could

DOI: 10.4324/9781003474104-4

> have been withholden from them but by the hand of tyranny. The French have already discovered that the blackness of skin is no reason why a human being should be abandoned without redress to the caprice of a tormentor. It may come one day to be recognized, that the number of legs, the villosity of the skin, or the termination of the os sacrum, are reasons equally insufficient for abandoning a sensitive being to the same fate. What else is it that should trace the insuperable line? Is it the faculty of reason, or perhaps, the faculty for discourse? . . . The question is not, Can they reason? nor, Can they talk? but, Can they suffer? Why should the law refuse its protection to any sensitive being? . . . The time will come when humanity will extend its mantle over everything which breathes.[8]

Although the antivivisection movement was birthed in the early 19th century alongside the significant scientific activity that characterized that period, and despite its long history of opposition to animal research, the movement cannot be credited with stopping a single scientific experiment until 1977,[9] when the movement's outcries ended National Institutes of Health (NIH) funding of certain grizzly and notorious cat experiments that the federal agency had funded for some 17 years at New York's Museum of Natural History.[10]

In fact, not until the 1960s did a robust animal rights movement emerge in the United States, part and parcel of the socio-cultural revolution that swept through American society in such varied forms as the hippy movement, the antiwar protests, the sexual revolution, and the drug culture.[11] An early victory was the 1966 Laboratory Animal Welfare Act.[12] In 1971, NIH issued its policy "Care and Treatment of Laboratory Animals." This was replaced in 1973 by Public Health Service Regulations.[13]

In 1981, Johns Hopkins University established its Center for Alternatives to Animal Testing, which describes itself as follows:

> The Johns Hopkins Center for Alternatives to Animal Testing (CAAT) has worked with scientists since 1981 to find new methods to replace the use of laboratory animals in experiments, reduce the number of animals tested, and refine necessary tests to eliminate pain and distress.[14]

The Center for Alternatives to Animal Testing is affiliated with the Johns Hopkins University Bloomberg School of Public Health, and is "an academic, science-based center" that believes "the best science is humane science." In addition to programs that seek alternatives to animal testing, the center also awards grants to scientists who endeavor to do the same. Finally, it manages Altweb, a website that gathers news and resources on alternatives to animal testing.

Despite these pioneering efforts and all the subsequent advances in the regulation and humane treatment of laboratory animals, animal rights activists' targeting of scientific—including university—laboratories has increased in recent years. To understand why, it is worth noting the several levels of animal activists in terms of philosophical orientation.

4.2 Animal Activist Philosophy and Tactics

David DeGrazia[15] identifies three gradations of standards subscribed by activists:

- Sliding scale model: "Animals may be used in research only where their use is consistent with giving their interests appropriate moral weight in view of the animals' cognitive, emotional, and social complexity."
- Utilitarianism: "Animals may be used in research only where their use is likely to maximize the overall balance of benefits—factoring in likelihood of success—over harms, where all parties' (including animals') interests are impartially considered."
- Strong animal rights view:

  > Animals may be used in research only where (1) their involvement does not harm them or (2) their involvement is in their overall best interests (therapeutic research). This view might also permit animals to be used in research where (3) their involvement poses only minimal risk to them.[16]

Clearly, the third level is the most demanding. Indeed, the definition proffered by DeGrazia masks the extreme nature of this last position. The devil, as they say, is in the details. For example, whether what a scientist does to the animals harms them or not depends entirely on the definition of the word harm. If one includes under harm the mere caging of an animal, then it is virtually impossible for a research scientist to work with animals in the lab. Similarly, if one deems the anxiety caused to an animal by the mere handling of that animal to be harm, then once again, the definition would make it well-nigh impossible for researchers to work with any such animals.

If these interpretations seem far-fetched, then consider the website for People for the Ethical Treatment of Animals (PETA), circa 2013, which stated:

> Every day in countries around the world, animals are fighting for their lives. They are enslaved, beaten, and kept in chains to make them perform for humans' "entertainment" . . . they are burned, blinded, poisoned, and cut up alive in the name of "science" . . . and worse.[17]

The website went on to explain that animals deserve responsible homes whose owners will not "parade" them around for entertainment, eat them, or wear their skin as clothing, and that they are "counting on a compassionate human like you" to ensure that happens.

Those who subscribe to such anthropomorphic sentiments, as those reflected in this statement, also tend to deny that—to borrow from George Orwell's *Animal Farm*—some animals are more equal than others. Thus, for example, an essay by two biologists rejected all of the following arguments for distinguishing among phyla and species in according animals rights:

- The evolutionary argument.
- Variations in awareness of self.
- Variations in memory and planning skills.
- Animal intentionality.

These writers concluded that:

> [G]iven our present state of knowledge of the needs and capabilities of classes of animals, let alone individual species, we feel, as biologists, that we first and foremost ought to guard against, or at least be very cautious about, the temptations of creating a scale of lesser or greater value of one species over another.[18]

The distance from such philosophical/ethical tenets to radical tactics is short.

Consider the Animal Liberation Front website, circa 2013: "The Animal Liberation Front (ALF) carries out direct action against animal abuse in the form of rescuing animals and causing financial loss to animal exploiters, usually through the damage and destruction of property.[19]

The ALF's short-term aim is to save as many animals as possible and directly disrupt the practice of animal abuse. Their long-term aim is to end all animal suffering by forcing animal abuse companies out of business. It is a nonviolent campaign, activists taking all precautions not to harm any animal (human or otherwise). Because ALF actions may be against the law, activists work anonymously, either in small groups or individually, and do not have any centralized organization or coordination. The ALF consists of small autonomous groups of people all over the world who carry out direct action according to the ALF guidelines. Any group of people who are vegetarians or vegans and who carry out actions according to ALF guidelines have the right to regard themselves as part of the ALF.[20]

The last paragraph of this credo springs from the broader radical tradition of "leaderless resistance."

> Leaderless resistance (or phantom cell structure) is a political resistance strategy in which small, independent groups (covert cells) challenge an established adversary such as a government. Leaderless resistance can encompass anything from nonviolent disruption and civil disobedience to bombings, assassinations and other violent agitation. Leaderless cells lack bidirectional, vertical command links and operate without hierarchal command.[21]

The term *leaderless resistance* was popularized by the white supremacist Louis Beam, who published an essay on leaderless resistance in 1983 and again in 1992. Beam advocated leaderless resistance as a technique for fighting an incumbent government using self-organizing clandestine cells; he attributed the strategy to Col. Ulius Louis Amoss, allegedly a U.S. intelligence officer who was fearful that Communists were about to seize control of the United States in the early 1960s.

In his essay, Beam argued that traditional liberation armies employing pyramid-style organization are "extremely dangerous for the participants when [they are] utilized in a resistance movement against state tyranny":

> Especially is this so in technologically advanced societies where electronic surveillance can often penetrate the structure revealing its chain of command. Experience has revealed over and over again that anti-state, political organizations utilizing this method of command and control are easy prey for government infiltration, entrapment, and destruction of the personnel involved. This has been seen repeatedly in the United States where pro-government infiltrators or agent provocateurs weasel their way into patriotic groups and destroy them from within.

A more workable approach, argued Beam, is to convince like-minded individuals to form independent cells that will commit acts of sabotage or terrorism without coordination from above, and while minimizing communication with other cells:

> The so-called "phantom cell" mode of organization, developed by Col. Amoss, or Leaderless Resistance, is based upon the cell organization but does not have any central control or direction. In the Leaderless Resistance concept, cells operate independently of each other, but they do not report to a central headquarters or top chief, as do the communist cells . . . .
>
> Participants in a program of Leaderless Resistance through phantom cell organization must know exactly what they are doing and how to do it. This is by no means as impractical as it appears, because it is certainly true that in any movement, all persons involved have the same general outlook, are acquainted with the same philosophy, and generally react to given situations in similar ways. As the entire purpose of Leaderless Resistance is to defeat the enemy by whatever means possible, all members of phantom cells will tend to react to objective events in the same way, usually through tactics of resistance and sabotage.

Despite exhorting the adoption of a resistance without a leader, it is likely that Beam was advocating leaderless resistance in an attempt to cement his position as a leader and thinker in the white separatist movement. Indeed, leaderless resistance is taken by some to be a technique of splitting an organization into an aboveground wing that primarily deals in propaganda and an underground wing that actually carries out terrorist attacks.[22]

The Oklahoma City bombing (Chapter 2) is a textbook example of leaderless resistance. Stop Huntington Animal Cruelty (SHAC) sought to apply this principle to its activities in an effort to avoid criminal liability for the illegal acts of its adherents.

As we shall see, SHAC failed.

4.2.1 Federal Legislation to Protect Scientists Using Animals

Congress acted to protect researchers who use animals in their experiments in 1992 with the following legislation.

Animal Enterprise Protection Act of 1992 (AEPA)

Public Law 102–346—Aug. 26, 1992
102nd Congress
An Act To Protect Animal Enterprises.
Be it enacted by the Senate and House of Representatives of the United States of America in Congress assembled,

SECTION 1. SHORT TILE

This Act may be cited as the "Animal Enterprise Protection Act of 1992".

SEC. 2. ANIMAL ENTERPRISE TERRORISM

(a) IN GENERAL.—Title 18, United States Code, is amended by inserting after section 42 the following:

§ 43. Animal enterprise terrorism

(a) OFFENSE.—Whoever—
  (1) travels in interstate or foreign commerce, or uses or causes to be used the mail or any facility in interstate or foreign commerce, for the purpose of causing physical disruption to the functioning of an animal enterprise; and
  (2) intentionally causes physical disruption to the functioning of an animal enterprise by intentionally stealing, damaging, or causing the loss of, any property (including animals or records) used

by the animal enterprise, and thereby causes economic damage exceeding $10,000 to that enterprise, or conspires to do so; shall be fined under this title or imprisoned not more than one year, or both.

(b) AGGRAVATED OFFENSE.—
  (1) SERIOUS BODILY INJURY.—Whoever in the course of a violation of subsection (a) causes serious bodily injury to another individual shall be fined under this title or imprisoned not more than 10 years, or both.
  (2) DEATH.—Whoever in the course of a violation of subsection (a) causes the death of an individual shall be fined under this title and imprisoned for life or for any term of years.

(c) RESTITUTION.—An order of restitution under section 3663 of this title with respect to a violation of this section may also include restitution—
  (1) for the reasonable cost of repeating any experimentation that was interrupted or invalidated as a result of the offense; and
  (2) the loss of food production or farm income reasonably attributable to the offense.

(d) DEFINITIONS.—As used in this section—
  (1) the term 'animal enterprise' means—
    (A) a commercial or academic enterprise that uses animals for food or fiber production, agriculture, research, or testing;
    (B) a zoo, aquarium, circus, rodeo, or lawful competitive animal event; or
    (C) any fair or similar event intended to advance agricultural arts and sciences[.]
  (2) the term 'physical disruption' does not include any lawful disruption that results from lawful public, governmental, or animal enterprise employee reaction to the disclosure of information about an animal enterprise;
  (3) the term 'economic damage' means the replacement costs of lost or damaged property or records, the costs of repeating an interrupted or invalidated experiment, or the loss of profits; and
  (4) the term 'serious bodily injury' has the meaning given that term in section 1365 of this title.

(e) NON-PREEMPTION.—Nothing in this section preempts any State law.

(f) CLERICAL AMENDMENT.—The item relating to section 43 in table of sections at the beginning of Chapter 3 of title, United States Code, is amended to read as follows:

43. Animal enterprise terrorism.

Sec. 3. STUDY OF EFFECT OF TERRORISM ON CERTAIN ANIMAL ENTERPRISES

(a) STUDY.—The Attorney General and the Secretary of Agriculture shall jointly conduct a study on the extent and effects of domestic and international terrorism on enterprises using animals for food or fiber production, agriculture, research, or testing.

(b) SUBMISSION OF STUDY.—Not later than 1 year after the date of enactment of this Act, the Attorney General and the Secretary of Agriculture shall submit a report that describes the results of the study conducted under subsection (a) together with any appropriate recommendations and legislation to the Congress.

Approved August 26, 1992.

What was the effect of this federal statute? In the words of one scientist, who said that he himself had been victimized by animal rights activists:

> After accepting the responsibility to write this article, I immediately plowed into the subject expecting to find myself awash in information about the Act on the internet. Having been detoured there on many occasions, I was nervous about the task of ferreting the relevant from the extraneous, so I fired up my favorite search engine and browsed the web for information on two items, the "Animal Enterprise Protection Act" and the "Animal Welfare Act," fully anticipating both searches to yield the standard mega-response that typically goes with such unsophisticated search strategies. To my amazement, the phrase "Animal Enterprise Protection Act" yielded less than 40 hits. This simple test set the stage for a remarkable discovery. Unlike the Animal Welfare Act, a topic that yielded more than 1,600 hits on my global search of the internet, no one seemed to care very much about the Act that offered such hope for so many just seven years ago.
>
> I immediately picked up the phone and began calling colleagues who I knew could help me understand how this potentially important piece of legislation, written to protect honest users of animals from animal rights terrorists, had suffered such undignified rejection at the hands of the federal prosecutors it was designed to energize. I was then stunned to learn that no one has been prosecuted under the provisions of the Act. No one. Not a single soul since the Animal Enterprise Protection Act became the law of the land.
>
> While there may be many explanations for the dormancy of prosecutors in the use of this legal tool, we can all be certain that the failure to exercise the Act in the courts is unrelated to the level of animal rights activity during the period

> since its enactment. On the contrary, a strong case can be made that the overall level of animal enterprise terrorism in the US has dramatically increased since 1992. Numerous laboratory break-ins have occurred during this time frame, violence and vandalism at fur farms are on the rise, as are animal releases from research and animal husbandry facilities around the world. During this period, death and bomb threats have continued to flow from activists as freely as small talk at the local tavern, and animal rights leaders continue to egg on their foot soldiers with inflammatory talk of revolution.[23]

This commentator criticized the act for carrying penalties that are too light to deter, as well as for failing to forbid or punish the many minor acts of humiliation, such as "pies in the face," that fall short of anything a federal prosecutor would care to handle. He noted that two attempts to pursue private actions fell flat, dismissed because the courts held that the act was a purely criminal statute that accorded no such right to a civil suit.[24] The writer concluded,

> The question that I pose as central to this discussion and the one that I had to grapple with as I wondered about my decision to write this essay is, "Can the handful of philosophers, lawyers, and political activists among us who are promoting the idea that ethical distinctions cannot be made among members of the animal kingdom ever truly hope to win this extreme argument that they wage?" I seriously doubt it. But if they were successful, those other human tragedies to which I refer would be compounded by the *Alice in Wonderland* atmosphere that would have consumed us.[25]

Dr. Walsh's article was published in 2000. With the September 11, 2001, terrorist attacks, it was not only Uncle Sam's attitude toward Islamic terrorists that changed. However, it would be another five years until the Department of Justice would bring a group of cyber-terrorists from the radical animal rights movement into a federal court to test whether their brand of leaderless resistance was protected by the First Amendment or, conversely, if it could be punished under this long-ignored federal law.

4.3 Stop Huntington Animal Cruelty (SHAC)[26]

Huntingdon Life Sciences was a research corporation that performed testing for companies seeking to bring their products to market.[27] The testing that Huntingdon provided to its clients was mandated by the laws and regulations of the United States and Europe to ensure the safety and efficacy of pharmaceuticals, agricultural products, veterinary products, and medical implants.[28] Huntingdon had three laboratories, two in the United Kingdom and one in New Jersey. All Huntingdon laboratories used animals as test subjects. Approximately 85% of the animals used by Huntingdon were rats and mice, and the remaining 15% composed of other species, including fish, dogs, monkeys, and guinea pigs.[29]

In the late 1990s, an individual posing as a laboratory technician recorded the conditions inside a Huntingdon laboratory in the United Kingdom.[30] The footage, which depicted animal abuse, became public when it was used in a television program, igniting protests against Huntingdon by a number of animal rights organizations. At about the same time, Stop Huntingdon Animal Cruelty was formed in the United Kingdom (SHAC-UK). The organization's mission was to close Huntingdon laboratories.

Immediately after SHAC-UK formed in November 1999, the organization published a newsletter that listed the names and addresses of the Huntingdon directors in the UK. Following the publication of the newsletter, animal rights protestors subjected the Huntingdon directors to an ongoing campaign of harassment, including vandalizing their homes and cars.

In February 2001, the chief operating officer and managing director of Huntingdon, Brian Cass, was physically assaulted by three masked individuals in front of his home in England. Cass suffered cracked ribs, several lacerations, and a 4-inch gash on his head that required nine stitches. David Blinkinsopp, who had been identified in video footage of SHAC-UK protests in front of Huntingdon, was convicted of the assault.[31] The remaining two assailants were never identified.

SHAC-UK's campaign evolved to include companies and individuals who were associated with Huntingdon, such as suppliers and customers. In addition, SHAC-UK began to target Huntingdon's shareholders, demanding that the shareholders sell their stock in Huntingdon or face 24-hour demonstrations at their homes. Because the laws in the UK require companies to publish the names and addresses of their shareholders, Huntingdon relocated its financial base to the United States in an effort to protect its shareholders. SHAC then formed a branch in the United States to target the New Jersey-based branch of Huntingdon. The New Jersey branch of SHAC was one of the defendants in this action, along with six individuals—thus "the SHAC 7."[32]

4.4 SHAC's Website[33]

SHAC's primary organizing tool was its website, through which members coordinated future protests. It also published information about protests that had previously taken place. The website included a page dedicated to the concept of direct action, which all parties to the 2006 criminal prosecution and subsequent appeal conceded was a type of protest that included the illegal activities that ended in a grand jury indictment. With regard to its position on the use of direct action, SHAC stated the following on its website:

> We operate within the boundaries of the law, but recognize and support those who choose to operate outside the confines of the legal system.
> Big business has shown time and time again their lack of concern for eics, instead focusing their attention on their profit. Often, simply targeting said business proves fruitless. However, as above ground activists have successfully targeted [Huntingdon's] financial pillars of support, underground activists have too targeted [Huntingdon's] pocketbooks. Unidentified individuals as well as underground cells of the Animal Liberation Front and the Earth Liberation Front have engaged in economic sabotage of [Huntingdon] and their associates. They have also spent their time directly intervening and liberating the animals who are slated to die inside of [Huntingdon]. Animals have been liberated from breeders as well as the laboratories themselves.
> SHAC does not organize any such actions or have any knowledge of who is doing them or when they will happen, but [SHAC] encourage[s] people to support direct action when it happens and those who may participate in it.[34]

The website often posted the organization's "accomplishments," which lauded both legal and illegal protest activities. The illegal activities included, among other things:

- A break-in at the Huntingdon lab in New Jersey, during which protestors broke windows and "liberated 14 beagles," in addition to overturning a worker's car.
- Detonating a "stink bomb" in the Seattle office of a Huntingdon investor.
- Destroying Bank of New York ATMs, windows, and other property.
- Sinking a yacht owned by the Bank of New York's president.
- Launching repeated "paint attacks" in the New York offices of a Huntingdon investor.
- "Rescuing" dogs and ferrets from a Huntingdon breeder farm.

The website also posted anonymous bulletins of successful, but illegal, protest activities. In this capacity the site postured as a mere conduit of information, roughly analogous to a news medium's website. One such anonymous bulletin stated:

> Late last night, August 30th, we paid a visit to the home of Rodney Armstead, MD and took out two of his front windows . . . gave him something to labor over this Labor Day weekend. Rodney serves as an officer and agent of service

> for "Medical Diagnostic Management, Inc.," a scummy little company [associated with Huntingdon]. Any ties with [Huntingdon] or its executives will yield only headaches and a mess to clean up.[35]

The name and home address of Dr. Armstead followed. However, shedding the mask of neutrality, this bulletin was prefaced by SHAC's statement that it was "excited to see such an upswing in action against Huntingdon and their cohorts. From the unsolicited direct action to the phone calls, emails, faxes and protests. Keep up the good work!" Similar bulletins included photographs of extensive vandalism of the homes of people indirectly affiliated with Huntingdon, such as employees of Bank of New York.[36] These bulletins almost always contained a disclaimer that "all illegal activity is done by anonymous activists who have no relation with SHAC."[37]

The SHAC website also posted a piece called the "Top 20 Terror Tactics" that was originally published by an organization that denounced the use of animals in medical research and testing.[38] With its standard disclaimer about SHAC not organizing illegal activity, SHAC republished the list on its website. Some of the tactics included abusive graffiti, posters, and stickers on houses, cars, and in neighborhoods of targeted individuals; invading offices, damaging property, and stealing documents; chaining gates shut or blocking gates with old cars to trap staff on-site; physical assaults against the targeted individuals, as well as their partners, including spraying cleaning fluid into their eyes; smashing windows in houses when the occupants were home; flooding houses with a hose attached to an outside tap inserted through a letterbox or window while the home was unoccupied; vandalizing personal vehicles by gluing locks, slashing tires, and pouring paint on the exterior; smashing personal vehicles with a sledgehammer while the targeted individual was inside; firebombing cars, sheds, and garages; bomb threats to instigate evacuations; threatening telephone calls and letters, including threats to injure or kill the targeted individual, as well their children and partners; abusive telephone calls and letters; ordering goods and services in the targeted individual's name and address; and arranging for an undertaker to collect the target's body. Following the list, the SHAC website stated, "Now don't go getting any funny ideas!"[39]

The website had a series of links dedicated to educating activists on how to evade investigators. These links were entitled "Ears and Eyes Everywhere," "Dealing with Interrogation," "When an Agent Knocks," and "Illegal Activity." In these sections of the website, SHAC advised its protestors to

> never say anything over the phone, email or in your house or car that you wouldn't want the authorities to hear. If you need to discuss sensitive information, do it in a remote location. Burn anything with sensitive information on it. . . . Visit www.pgp.com and download an email encryption program to protect your email conversations.[40]

PGP stands for "pretty good privacy," an encryption device generally effective at protecting email conversations from outside monitoring.[41] PGP is also used to erase data from hard drives. The software was found on eight of the nine computers at SHAC's de facto headquarters, which three of the defendants also called home.

Through its website, SHAC also invited its supporters to engage in electronic civil disobedience against Huntingdon and various companies associated with Huntingdon. Electronic civil disobedience involved a coordinated campaign by a large number of individuals to inundate websites, email servers, and the telephone service of a targeted company. Electronic civil disobedience also included the use of "black faxes," repeatedly faxing a black piece of paper to the same fax machine to exhaust the toner or ink supply. SHAC sponsored electronic civil disobedience campaigns on the first Monday of every month. It reminded its supporters that electronic civil disobedience was illegal, and therefore supporters should only participate if they "are like Martin Luther King and are ready to suffer the consequences . . . or if [the supporters] want to live to fight another day, do the electronic civil disobedience from a public computer that cannot be traced."[42]

Another way that SHAC encouraged the use of electronic civil disobedience was through its "Investor of the Week" feature, which highlighted a company associated with Huntingdon by publishing the company's contact information. SHAC told its supporters to "take advantage of pay phones! Especially with toll free numbers!"[43]

The website also provided a link to a black fax for their personal use. Alternatively, the website noted that supporters could just use black paper to "give your target's fax machine a run for its money . . . or ink!"[44] The website explained how a supporter could block a phone number so that it would not appear on the fax or telephone line's caller identification. In addition, the website explained how to prevent the targeted company's servers from blocking emails and provided a link to encryption devices that ostensibly masked the sender.

One specific example of SHAC's coordination of electronic civil disobedience, cited by the U.S. Court of Appeals in its 2009 review of the case,[45] is an email from shacuse@envirolink.org that was disseminated on October 26, 2003. The subject line of the email was "Electronic Civil Disobedience," and it advised SHAC supporters that on the following day, SHAC's website would provide a link to the SHAC-Moscow website where "electronic civil disobedience will be taking place." The email stated that "participation is mandatory," and that by taking part in the coordinated electronic civil disobedience, supporters would "help . . . halt the ever important web medium for particular companies sponsoring Huntingdon." Participation would also "send a loud message that no silly injunctions or crooked politicians can derail the campaign to close Huntingdon."[46]

4.5 Indictments and Trial

An indictment was filed against the SHAC 7 in the U.S. District Court of New Jersey in its Trenton courthouse on May 20, 2004.[47] On September 16, 2004, the government filed a superseding indictment.[48] That day, SHAC, Kjonaas, Gazzola, Conroy, Harper, Stepanian, and Fullmer were charged in that superseding indictment. Count 1 of the indictment charged that all six individual defendants conspired to violate the Animal Enterprise Protection Act, 18 U.S.C. §43. Count 3 charged SHAC, Kjonaas, Gazzola, and Conroy with conspiring to commit interstate stalking in violation of 18 U.S.C. §2261A(2) and 18 U.S.C. §371. Counts 3–5 charged SHAC, Kjonaas, Gazzola, and Conroy with substantive interstate stalking of Sally Dillenback, Marion Harlos, and Robert Harper, respectively. Count 6 charged SHAC, Kjonaas, Gazzola, Conroy, and Harper of conspiring to use a telecommunications device to abuse, threaten, and harass in violation of 18 U.S.C. §371 and 47 U.S.C. §223(a)(1)(c).

The three-week trial began in early February 2006. The government presented a parade of corporate witnesses who described in graphic detail the patterns of harassment to which they had been subjected. SHAC did not confine its campaign to Huntingdon's New Jersey employees. It targeted the management of service providers, shareholders of corporations holding a block of Huntingdon's stock, and anyone else who seemed to be supporting its *bête noire.*

4.5.1 Andrew Baker

SHAC's website said of Andrew Baker, chairman of Life Sciences Research,[49] a Huntingdon holding company,

> If there is one man on whom you could place the most blame for [Huntingdon's] crimes since 1998, it is him. For the last four years since he watched little dogs getting punched in the face, Baker has put his all into keeping Huntingdon afloat. Not an easy job. As a trained chartered accountant Baker is skilled at pulling the financial strings of companies he is in charge of.... He currently works out of a NJ office called Focused HealthCare Partners LLC—which acts as a general partner for healthcare startups ... or failing labs like Huntingdon .... Baker has been essentially reduced to scrambling full time to save Huntingdon.

He has nothing else going for him. If [Focused HealthCare Partners] is the vehicle he uses to support Huntingdon, [Focused HealthCare Partners] is the company we must dismantle.[50]

Placed into evidence was this posting from the SHAC website:

Despite driving winds, rain, and cold weather 75+ activists gathered at [address redacted by the court] to protest the home of Andrew Baker CEO to Huntingdon. Andrew Baker is at the top of our "SH&)%;!" list for his lead in trying to save Huntingdon from certain closure. This was the largest and angriest of the 3 days of protest . . . . Andrew you and all your senior management and "science" staff have no idea what we have in store for you! Murderers, lairs [*sic*], thieves, and perverts deserve to be treated as such. In the near future when we see you in the gutter stripped of all your riches and fabricated respect, the only handout you will get is our spit![51]

Baker himself testified that protestors also targeted his daughter's New York apartment. He stated that vandals "plastered" the front door of her apartment "with posters and pictures . . . depicting [his] death."[52]

The website added,

So, apparently Andy is bi-coastal (as if you couldn't tell). In addition to the 2 million dollar penthouse apartment he owns on NYC's upper Westside ([address redacted by the court]), Baker also has a sunny California home in Los Angeles. This choice location on Sunset Plaza Drive should be the number one attraction on any animal rights activist's Hollywood star-map.[53]

Baker went on to testify that the house in Los Angeles had been attacked three times. He stated that during the first attack, the protestors kicked in the gate at the street entrance, broke the front door, and broke two windows. During the second attack, the protestors broke a window in the garage and threw a smoke bomb inside. During the third attack, the protestors threw rocks and tile over the wall, hitting the top and sides of the house, including windows and doors.[54]

4.5.2 Sally Dillenback

Dillenback was a senior executive in the Dallas offices of Marsh, Inc., the huge international insurance broker.[55] She testified that in early 2002, she learned that SHAC had targeted Marsh. In March 2002, Dillenback checked the SHAC website after learning that personal information about employees had been posted there. When she viewed the website, she saw that her personal information had been posted, including the names of her husband and her children, as well as their home address; the name of her children's school; the make, model, and license plate of their personal vehicle; the name of their church; and the name of the country club where they were members.[56]

Shortly after the information appeared on the SHAC website, Dillenback testified that her family began receiving phone calls, often "angry and belligerent," day and night, as well as a "tremendous" volume of mail. Dillenback testified that one morning, her family awoke to find that pictures of mutilated animals had been glued to the sidewalk in front of her home, as well as the exterior side wall of her home. At the same time, the following was posted on the SHAC website:

> Received anonymously on March 10:
>
> > Last night the homes of Dallas Marsh employees Michael Rogan and Sally Dillenback were visited by activists. Mr. Rogan's garage was plastered with stickers of mutilated puppies such as those his company insures. Mrs. Dillenback's side wall was covered in stickers, as was her mailbox. Let the stickers serve to remind Marsh employees and their neighbors that their homes are paid for in blood, the blood of innocent animals that are killed in labs like Huntingdon. Every day that Marsh insures Huntingdon, they insure death.[57]

Dillenback testified that after this incident, she was "sickened and terrified," and that her children were scared, especially the youngest child, who was 7 years old at the time. Marsh provided 24-hour security at her home following this incident.

Dillenback also received an email that she perceived as a direct threat to her youngest son. She testified that the email asked how she would feel "if they cut open my son . . . and filled him with poison the way that [Huntingdon] was doing to animals."[58] She testified that this email "devastated" her. She further testified that during this period of time, her husband purchased a semi-automatic weapon and that her 7-year-old son twice brandished a kitchen knife while inside the house in an effort to protect himself and the family.

After Dillenback initially testified regarding her son's use of the knife at her deposition, the following posting, attributed to "TX activists," appeared on the SHAC website:

> On Saturday, December 14, activists paid a holiday visit to Sally Dillenback, head of Dallas Marsh office. She was surprised, finding her working on her Christmas tree with her family . . . . Contrary to Sally's sworn testimony at her deposition, her son did not run for a kitchen knife and to hide when he saw the activists. Instead, he and his sister seemed quite interested in the signs and appeared to be trying to read them from across the street.

> Merry Christmas, Sally. Take a moment to think of all the dogs, like the one who shares your home, who will be spending Christmas in their own congealed blood and feces at Huntingdon, thanks in part [to] your company's insurance.[59]

Dillenback testified that the protests stopped in early 2003, when Marsh stopped providing insurance brokerage services to Huntingdon. Notably, the SHAC website quoted a *Financial Times* article explaining that Marsh had dropped Huntingdon as a client on December 18, 2002.[60]

4.5.3 Marion Harlos

Harlos headed up the San Antonio offices of Seabury & Smith, a Marsh subsidiary.[61] Like Dillenback, she learned from corporate headquarters that she had been targeted for protests on the SHAC website, which listed her home address and phone number. Within a week, there was a protest at Harlos's office. Protestors "bashed" in the door and threw pamphlets across the office while screaming, "You have the blood of death on your fingers," "We know where you live," "You cannot sleep at night," and "We will find you." Seabury & Smith subsequently hired security guards for the San Antonio office.[62]

Harlos testified that the protestors returned to the office a few weeks later. Although the security guard stopped most of the protestors, one made it inside, throwing pamphlets and screaming, "Puppy killer" and "We know where you live." This protest was memorialized on the SHAC website as follows:

> Today around 11:30 am, 5 activists visited the San Antonio Marsh office . . . and gained access to the lobby. They rang the bell and a security guard answered, one activist made an attempt to get in past the guard and got half way in. It was enough to throw two or three dozen anti Huntingdon flyers into the air scattering and landing into the cubicles. All of the activist[s] screamed "puppy killer" and "we won't stop [until] you drop Huntingdon." As they left they banged on the windows and promised "next time we will be at your HOME."[63]

Harlos testified that after this protest, she began receiving phone calls at her home late at night. She stated that sometimes the caller asked, "Are you scared? Do you think the puppies should be scared?"[64] Protestors, wearing bandannas and masks to conceal their faces, often sat in a car outside her residence between 4 a.m. and 6 a.m., watching her house. Then, protests began. One morning, nine activists were arrested outside Harlos's home and were charged with third-degree stalking. The SHAC website announced the arrests and urged its protestors to call the local police department in Texas to demand the protestors' release.

Harlos also testified that she was "petrified" and frightened for her children, who were no longer permitted to play outside.[65] She also testified that her fear stemmed, in part, from her knowledge of what had happened to others who had been targeted by SHAC, including physical attacks. The activists continued to trespass on her property, despite an injunction that was intended to limit the permissible bounds of the protests. Harlos testified that the protests had a profound effect on her life, and the lives of her family members, ultimately forcing her to move to a new home. As with Dillenback, Harlos testified that the protests ceased when Marsh ended its business relationship with Huntingdon.

4.5.4 Robert Harper

Harper was a property broker in Marsh's Boston office. SHAC's website posted the following missive to Mr. Harper:

> Received anonymously:
>
> Happy Father[']s [D]ay Rob Harper. I hope you liked our gift[.]
> In the wee hours of the mourning [*sic*] on June 15, Marsh Boston Employee, Rob Harper [home address redacted] received an early Father[']s Day gift that he will never forget. A few gallons of red paint were thrown all over Harper's front steps and door. This left the front of his house caked in a huge pool of red paint.
> Rob Harper is responsible for 500 animals dying within [Huntingdon] today and as long as Marsh has ties with [Huntingdon], Marsh will be a target. This also goes for any other company or business that has times [*sic*] with Huntingdon—they will pay for it. [*sic*]
> There will be no rest for these murders. [Huntingdon] will be closed.
> This action is dedicated to the 500 animals that were murdered inside of [Huntingdon] today.
>
> Love,
>
> The Animal Liberation Front[66]

Harper testified that after these protests began, his workday was "consumed" with checking the SHAC website. He testified that he became aware of other protests and other targets, including the physical assault of Brian Cass in the UK, as well as protestors destroying vehicles. He stated that this made him feel "vulnerable" and "concerned for his family," as well as angry and helpless because his life was so profoundly disrupted.[67]

On August 9, 2002, Harper added, he was at work when a protest occurred at his home. His wife called him, crying and frantic. He arrived home to find his wife and 2-year-old son upset. The protestors outside were screaming "puppy killer" and threatening to burn the house down. A video played at trial showed that Lauren Gazzola, a defendant in this case, was present at this demonstration, shouting into a bullhorn,

> Where were the police when a [Huntingdon] worker's car got flipped over in his driveway? Where were the police when a Marsh executive had all his windows smashed in and his house covered in red paint in Chicago? And where were the police when your house was covered in red paint a few weeks ago? They can't protect you. Your injunctions can't stop us. We'll always find a way around whatever they throw at us.[68]

Harper testified that this was "one of the worst days of [his] life."[69] He feared that someone would "throw a Molotov cocktail" into the house, or that someone would physically assault him or his family.[70] He contemplated moving and quitting his job, but yet again the protests stopped when Marsh ended its business relationship with Huntingdon.

4.6 Conviction and Appeal

The jury convicted all the defendants on all counts. On September 12, 2006, the district judge sentenced SHAC to five years' probation, Kjonaas to 72 months' imprisonment, Gazzola to 52 months' imprisonment, Conroy to 48 months' imprisonment, Harper to 36 months' imprisonment, Stepanian to 36 months' imprisonment, and Fullmer to 12 months' imprisonment. Defendants filed a timely notice of appeal in the U.S. Court of Appeals for the Third Circuit, which calls Philadelphia home, challenging both their underlying convictions and the sentences.[71]

In 2009, the Third Circuit affirmed the convictions and the sentences, holding: (1) the AEPA was not unconstitutionally vague; (2) conduct defendants were convicted of was not protected by the First Amendment; (3) the government provided sufficient evidence to prove defendants conspired to violate the AEPA; and (4) the government produced sufficient evidence to convict the defendants of interstate stalking offenses.[72]

4.7 Aftermath

Since the successful prosecution of the SHAC 7, radical animal activists have not eased their activities. Even a cursory survey of stories published in *The Chronicle of Higher Education* in succeeding years drives home the severity of the threat posed to higher education by animal rights activists.

Animal-Rights Groups Fight Colleges over Access to Research Records

By Jeffrey Brainard

The Ohio Supreme Court has ruled that Ohio State University is not required to release videotapes of animal research sought under the state's open-records law by an advocacy group opposed to such studies.[73]

UCLA Professor Halts Monkey Research

By Samantha Henig

Responding to pressure from animal-rights activists, Dario Ringach, an associate professor of neurobiology at the University of California at Los Angeles, has abandoned his research on monkeys. In an email message with the subject line "You win," Mr. Ringach wrote to a news office for animal-rights groups that he would no longer conduct animal research, and asked that the groups leave him and his family alone.[74]

UCLA's Acting Chancellor Takes Steps against Animal-Rights Extremists

By Paul Fain

The acting chancellor of the University of California at Los Angeles has announced plans to push back at animal-rights groups, which he says have recently stepped up harassment of faculty members.

In a letter to the campus, Norman Abrams, who became acting chancellor on July 1, said "illegal and often violent" acts by activists, who are protesting research conducted by university scientists on nonhuman primates and other animals, had "culminated this summer in an incident involving a powerful incendiary device placed on the doorstep of a neighbor of one of our faculty members."[75]

The Growing Field of Animal Law Is Attracting Activists and Pragmatists Alike

By Peter Monaghan

Portland, Ore.

In the Pacific Northwest, many young people say they want to liberate animals from human subjection, so much so that defending activists who break into research laboratories to set loose animals is now a cottage industry.

Here at Lewis & Clark College School of Law, students of "animal law" are learning another way to change social practices that involve animals. They are just as passionate as animal-liberation advocates. And they may become more influential.

Animal law is the study of all laws relating to animals, whether they enable harsh treatment of animals or encourage kind treatment. "It's a lot like where environmental law was in the 1970s," says Laura Ireland Moore, founder and executive director of the National Center for Animal Law, based at Lewis & Clark.[76]

Animal Researchers' Homes Are Attacked: As Protests Intensify, Colleges Take Steps to Protect Scientists

By Richard Monastersky

When six masked people pounded on the front door of a scientist's home in Santa Cruz, Calif., and allegedly struck her husband late last month, the echo was heard by biomedical researchers and universities around the country. The intrusion represents an apparent escalation in the level of violence used by animal-rights protesters, who until now have not physically attacked academic scientists.

"We're facing a national movement," says George Blumenthal, chancellor of the University of California at Santa Cruz, where the biologist works. Other universities, he says, are going to have to face "individuals who are prepared to use potentially violent tactics that have a terrorizing effect on researchers."[77]

New Front in Battle over Studies of Animals: Activists Take Aim at Non-Research Colleges

By Jeffrey Brainard

Far from the front lines of the nasty fight over laboratory-animal experiments at large research universities, activists are strategically drawing some teaching-oriented institutions into the same battle.

Amherst College, Fairfield University, Francis Marion University, and 10 other institutions, none of which are known for conducting animal experiments, recently signed a pledge not to subject any research animals to "severe" unrelieved pain or distress. The pledge was written by the Humane Society of the United States, which has sent it to a total of 301 presidents at similar institutions.[78]

New Attacks on Animal Researchers Provoke Anger and Worry

By Lila Guterman

After firebomb attacks this month set the home of a neuroscientist at the University of California at Santa Cruz aflame and destroyed a car parked in the driveway of another university researcher's home, researchers and academic leaders were shaken. The attacks are believed to be the work of animal-rights protesters.[79]

It was of little wonder then that the New Jersey Department of Homeland Security and Preparedness issued the following alert in mid-2008.

Escalation of West Coast Animal Rights Extremist Activity and Implications for New Jersey

Key Findings

- There has been an increase in the intensity and overall number of violent criminal acts perpetrated by animal rights extremist groups against university researchers on the West Coast.
- Animal rights extremist groups represent the most active, single-issue domestic terrorism group in New Jersey.
- Given the apparent connectivity between animal rights groups and the extent of their travel between coasts, the use of violence and intimidation against university researchers on the West Coast is likely to spread to New Jersey.

Threat Overview

Over the past ten months, there has been an increase in the number of violent criminal incidents perpetrated by animal rights extremists against university researchers on the West Coast. The majority of the violent incidents have occurred in California, with a limited number also occurring in Oregon. In roughly eighty percent of the incidents the targets were university researchers involved in primate research.

Historically, animal rights extremist groups in the United States have carried out direct actions against university laboratories and not individual researchers. Such actions have included criminal trespassing, vandalism and the release of laboratory animals. However, since approximately June 2007, extremists have begun escalating the violence and using more intimidating tactics against individual university researchers, including: death threats, bomb threats, the mailing of suspicious packages and letters stuffed with razor blades, attempted home invasions, attempted arson, intentional flooding of a home, and the placement of incendiary devices under cars and at residences. These incidents have been carried out by ALF (Animal Liberation Front), Animal Liberation Brigade, UCLA Primate Freedom Project, SHAC (Stop Huntingdon Animal Cruelty) and their affiliates. This shift in tactics coincides with an overall increase in threats and acts of violence by the animal rights extremist movement against a wide variety of targets, including biotech, life sciences, pharmaceutical and biomedical research companies.

While animal rights extremist groups have not publicly announced a change in their targeting tactics, there are several reasons for such a shift. Targeting individual researchers at their residences results in greater fear and intimidation, as extremists "personalize" their attacks by directly threatening the individuals and their families. In addition, by targeting individuals at their homes extremists avoid having to deal with security impediments that might exist at the university laboratory or employment facility. This change in modus operandi enables the extremists to carry out their attacks with fewer resources. Animal rights groups are also increasingly using the Internet to access public records and identify university researchers, and then posting their names and addresses online.

This shift in targeting tactics coincides with a growing sentiment among members of the animal rights movement that researchers, businesses, and the general public have been sufficiently warned and violence can now be rationalized in order to permanently end animal abuse. Violent rhetoric is expressed in extremist communiqués, literature and threat letters. For example, in a June 2007 communiqué, the Animal Liberation Brigade alluded to the need for more violent tactics, asserting that "demonstrators need to realize that just demonstrating won't stop this kind of evil." Similarly, Jerry Vlasak, co-founder of the North American Animal Liberation Press Office and leader in the US animal rights movement has stated on several occasions that the notion of murdering medical researchers in order to save laboratory animals is a "morally justifiable solution." While these statements may simply be aimed at motivating followers, it might also portend a shift toward greater violence.

Outlook for New Jersey

Animal rights extremist groups represent the most active, single-issue, domestic terrorism group in New Jersey where they have historically focused their campaigns on biotech, life-sciences and pharmaceutical companies. However, since 2003, these groups have branched out, conducting direct actions against "tertiary targets," including financial and technology-based companies and attacking the employees of targeted companies at their residences. Looking forward, the increased use of violence and intimidation perpetrated against university researchers on the West Coast is likely to be emulated on the East Coast, especially given the apparent connectivity between animal rights groups throughout the country and the extent of their travel between coasts. This type of connectivity has been exemplified in New Jersey through "Days of Action," direct action campaigns organized by animal rights groups which are attended by supporters from across the US. These events reveal a willingness to travel long distances to protest and target businesses, laboratories and individuals in New Jersey. While there is currently no intelligence indicating that animal rights extremists are planning to target university researchers or other New Jersey facilities involved in animal research, the nature of this threat warrants ongoing situational awareness within university, private sector and law enforcement communities.

For additional information and GIS mapping of New Jersey companies targeted by animal rights groups, please refer to the December 2007 OHSP Assessment: Animal Rights Extremism: Current Trends and Implications for New Jersey, available on the OHSP secure Web site, through http://www.state.nj.us/.

Suspicious activity involving animal rights extremist groups should be treated as having a possible nexus to terrorism, and should be reported immediately to the New Jersey Office of Homeland Security and Preparedness (OHSP) at 866–4-SAFE-NJ and to local law enforcement authorities.

Author of Report:
Caroline Vassallo, Intelligence Analyst: Caroline.Vassallo@ohsp.state. nj.us (609–588–0996)

For further information on this document or other OHSP analytical products, please contact the OHSP Intelligence Bureau at OHSPINTEL@ohsp.state. nj.us or 609-588-4000, ext. 7.

In September 2010, the *Jersey Journal* reported, "A gathering of citizens and activists in front of the Liberty Humane Society animal shelter last night to protest its use of euthanasia and later held a candlelight vigil for the animals that have been put down." The story eerily continued, "In other developments, a week ago, board members of the animal shelter say they started receiving alarming phone calls and spotting threats posted on Facebook, the social networking site."[80]

Meanwhile, arrest and prosecution of animal-rights radicals has also intensified, as the following December 3, 2012 ALF press release admits:

The largest eco-terrorism case in U.S. history may be closing in on its final chapters.

After a decade on the run, Canadian citizen and animal rights activist Rebecca Jeanette Rubin turned herself in to authorities at the border in Blaine, Washington. Rubin is the 11th of 13 people wanted by the FBI as part of Operation Backfire, a conspiracy investigation into the Earth Liberation Front and the ALF. The cell called itself "The Family."

"The alleged leader of The Family, William C. Rodgers, committed suicide in a jail in Arizona after being indicted in 2006. Along with another member of The Family, Rodgers is believed to have been the author of the ALF manual, *Setting Fires With Electrical Timers: An Earth Liberation Front Guide*," reports the Southern Poverty Law Center:

> Rubin and 12 others were charged with 20 acts of arson across five states from 1996–2001, according to a press release distributed by the FBI last week.
> In 2007, 10 other members plead guilty and received prison terms from 37 to 156 months.
> Authorities say Rubin was a participant in a 1997 arson that targeted a U.S. Bureau of Land Management facility in Oregon, an attempted arson in 1998 in Colorado, and conspiracy and other charges for her role in a 2001 fire in California.
> The FBI says only Joseph Mahmoud Dibee and Josephine Sunshine Overaker remain at large as "international fugitives."[81]

4.8 Current Status of the Radical Animal Rights Movement

According to a February 2023 report released by the Federation of American Societies for Experimental Biology,

> While some organizations continue to employ extreme tactics, many animal rights groups have predominantly shifted their strategies over the last decade. They are increasingly using policy, legislative, regulatory, and public relations maneuvers to achieve their goals and thwart life-saving animal research. These actions represent a significant burden for the scientific community that could jeopardize biomedical progress as well as human and animal health.[82]

Apparently, vigorous law enforcement and prosecutorial efforts, such as those successfully carried out against the SHAC 7, have paid off.

> Since 2008, there has been a rapid decline in animal rights extremism, which is now at an all-time low. Occasionally one may hear about a verbal threat or some graffiti, but large-scale property damage or attacks on individuals are now unheard of. The extremism of the early 2000s resulted in a public backlash that has made illegal direct action unpopular among even the most committed activists.[83]

Notes

1. Neal Stephenson, *Quicksilver* (New York, NY: Harper/Collins, 2003), p. 129. See also Umberto Eco, *The Island of the Day Before* (New York: Harcourt Brace, 1995) (Quotation accessed at http://www.readinggroupguides.com/guides_I/island_of_the_day_before1.asp):

   > No wonder the French court was so eager to steal longitude secrets from state enemies. Coerced by Cardinal Richelieu, Roberto sails aboard a Dutch ship to spy on a British scientist who, navigating unknown waters by the cries of a wounded dog, seems to have unlocked the secret of the longitude. Although this technique of navigation by canine vivisection may sound like the purest fiction, it was actually proposed as a solution in London in 1688—whether in desperation or in jest is not known. The anonymous author relied on the same Powder of Sympathy that dusts Eco's pages. This quack cure, brought to England from France by Sir Kenelm Digby, was a powder that could purportedly heal at a distance when applied to some article from an injured person. As Roberto learned at the siege of Casale and later during his sojourn in Paris, the treatment was not painless: Patients jumped or swooned when practitioners powdered the swords that had cut them or the cloths that had dressed their wounds.

2. Stephenson, p. 129. See also Eco, p. 138.
3. Stephenson, p. 129. See also Eco, p. 187.
4. David DeGrazia, *Animal Rights: A Very Short Introduction* (Oxford: Oxford University Press, 2002), p. 7.
5. Ibid., pp. 7–8.
6. Ibid., p. 4.
7. David Hume, *Of the Reason of Animals*, http://www.animal-rights-library.com/texts-c/hume01.htm (accessed July 15, 2008).
8. Jeremy Bentham, *Introduction to the Principles of Morals and Legislation*, http://utilitarianism.com/jeremybentham.html (accessed July 15, 2008).
9. DeGrazia, p. 102.
10. Ibid., p. 98.
11. Ibid., p. 99.
12. Public Law, pp. 89–544.
13. Office of Laboratory Animal Welfare, NIH, *Institutional Animal Care and Use Committee Guidebook* (2nd ed.). (Washington, DC: U.S. Government Printing Office, 2002).
14. http://caat.jhsph.edu.
15. Professor of Philosophy, George Washington University, webpage accessible at http://www.gwu.edu/~philosop/faculty/DeGrazia.cfm.
16. DeGrazia, p. 110.
17. http://www.peta.org/issues/default.aspx; see also "Humane Alert: Chimps Deserve Better," *Humane Society of the United States*, https://secure.humanesociety.org/site/Advocacy?cmd=display&page=UserAction&id=4660 (accessed September 12, 2010):

   > Please halt the National Center for Research Resources' plans to transfer 202 chimpanzees from the Alamogordo Primate Facility to the Southwest National Primate Research Center. These animals have had long and difficult decades in laboratories and deserve better. Their care was taken over by the National Institutes of Health in 2001 when the laboratory that previously managed them was charged with serious violations of the Animal Welfare Act, Public Health Service Policy, and Food and Drug Administration regulations. Most of the 202 chimpanzees are considered elderly and none have been used in research for the past nine years. It is simply not necessary to use them in further research. If these chimpanzees are retired in place, they will receive superior care at significant cost savings to taxpayers and they will be able to live out the remainder of their lives in peace.

18. Lesley J. Rogers and Gisela Kaplan, "All Animals Are *Not* Equal: The Interface between Scientific Knowledge and Legislation for Animal Rights," in Cass R. Sunstein and Martha C. Nussbaum (eds.), *Animal Rights: Current Debates and New Directions* (Oxford: Oxford University Press, 2004), p. 196.
19. Animal Liberation Front, http://www.animalliberationfront.com (accessed July 17, 2008); see also Animal Liberation Frontline, https://animalliberationfrontline.com/ (accessed December 27, 2023) (This homepage indicates that the

organization's philosophy and tactics have not changed significantly from when the *First Edition* of this book was published a decade ago. See, e.g., "New Book: ALF—Complete Diary of Actions Every ALF raid, in one place: New 130 page book chronicling over 40 years of the Animal Liberation Front. Just back from the printer: The first assembled timeline of the Animal Liberation Front's 40+ year history—from broken windows to lab raids. In 2009, I released the first timeline of the ALF's (then-)30-year history. After selling over 1,000 copies, the book went out of print in 2012. Now, 10 years later, I gave the 'A.L.F. Diary of Actions' a thorough update and all new layout, bringing it up to date for 2022. It is now available in two formats: Free PDF download, or paperback. Wikipedia, "Leaderless Resistance," http://en.wikipedia.org/wiki/Leaderless_resistance (accessed July 18, 2008).

20. Louis Beam, "Leaderless Resistance," *The Seditionist*, February 1992, http://www.louisbeam.com/leaderless.htm (accessed December 13, 2012).
21. Simson L. Gafinkel, "Leaderless Resistance Today," *First Monday Peer-Reviewed Journal on the Internet*, http://www.firstmonday.org/issues/issue8_3/garfinkel/index.html (accessed July 18, 2008).
22. Ibid., *see also* Beam, op. cit., Note 20.
23. Edward J. Walsh, "The Animal Enterprise Protection Act: A Scientist's Perspective Brings the Law into Focus," *Lab Animal*, 29, 2, February 2000, http://www.naiaonline.org/articles/archives/animalenterprise.htm (accessed May 6, 2024).
24. Ibid.
25. Ibid.
26. The bulk of this material is drawn from *United States v. Fullmer*, 584 F.3d 182 (3d Cir., 2009), in particular the joint appendix filed by the appellants and appellees and cited extensively by the appeals panel in its published opinion.
27. Huntingdon Life Sciences website is accessible at http://www.huntingdon.com. (With regard to animal welfare, the company states:

> We live in remarkable times. Many of us experience a standard of living and healthcare that would be inconceivable to our great grandparents. Moreover we enjoy and expect the right to high standards of quality and safety in the products we use.
>
> But this level of expectation demands a high level of safety assessment, particularly when it concerns products with the potential to cause personal harm or injury. On a daily basis we have contact with an astonishing variety of such substances, for example:
>
> - Medicines
> - Food additives
> - Food packaging
> - Adhesives
> - Clothes dyes
> - Veterinary products
>
> As consumers we strive for a 'no-risk' guarantee. In response, government regulatory bodies insist upon stringent and comprehensive safety testing for these products, including testing on animals. Huntingdon Life Sciences provides this essential service for a wide variety of customers including

> governmental agencies. "It is our job to ensure that these tests are performed to strict scientific criteria, provide reliable results that can be reproduced, and with leading standards of animal care and welfare.
>
> This places an important burden of responsibility upon us, one which we do not take lightly. We have to respect the needs of the animals and be fully aware of the welfare issues involved. We are committed to providing the highest levels of animal husbandry and welfare.
>
> In May 2003 Huntingdon Life sciences was awarded an Achievement of Accreditation by the Association For Assessment and Accreditation of Laboratory Animal Care, AAALAC (aaalac.org). We are one of only a few Contract Research Organisations in the world to be accredited.
>
> (http://www.huntingdon.com/index.php?currentNumber=3&currentIsExpanded=0, accessed September 11, 2010)

See generally http://en.wikipedia.org/wiki/Animal_testing (accessed September 12, 2010); see also Society of Cosmetic Chemists, http://www.scconline.org/website/referrals/testing_labs.shtml; U.S. Food and Drug Administration, http://www.fda.gov; Code of Federal Regulations, Title 21, Parts 1–1499, http://www.accessdata.fda.gov/scripts/cdrh/cfdocs/cfcfr/cfrsearch.cfm (a searchable version of the relevant federal regulations, administered by the FDA).

28. See generally http://en.wikipedia.org/wiki/Animal_testing (accessed September 12, 2010); see also Society of Cosmetic Chemists, http://www.scconline.org/website/referrals/testing_labs.shtml; U.S. Food and Drug Administration, http://www.fda.gov; Code of Federal Regulations, Title 21, Parts 1–1499, http://www.accessdata.fda.gov/scripts/cdrh/cfdocs/cfcfr/cfrsearch.cfm (a searchable version of the relevant federal regulations, administered by the FDA).
29. Huntingdon justifies its use of animals as follows:

> There are stages in any research programme when it is not enough to know how individual molecules, cells or tissues behave. The living body is much more than just a collection of these parts, and the need to understand how they interact or how they are controlled is essential. There are ethical limits to the experiments that we can perform in people, so the only alternative is to use the most suitable animal to study a particular disease or biological function.

(See http://www.huntingdon.com/index.php?currentNumber=4&currentIsExpanded=0 [accessed September 12, 2010].)

30. Numerous videos critical of Huntingdon remain readily available. See, e.g., http://www.youtube.com/results?search_query=huntingdon+labs&aq=f (accessed September 12, 2010).
31. "Jail for Lab Boss Attacker," *BBC News*, August 16, 2001, http://news.bbc.co.uk/2/hi/uk_news/1494924.stm (accessed September 12, 2010).
32. See the SHAC 7 website, http://www.shac7.com/case.htm:

> The SHAC 7 are 6 animal rights activists and the organization Stop Huntingdon Animal Cruelty USA (SHAC USA) who were convicted on March 2, 2006, under the controversial Federal Animal Enterprise Protection Act.

> The Act punishes anyone who 'physically disrupts' an animal enterprise. The charges stem from these activists' alleged participation in an international campaign to close the notorious product testing lab Huntingdon Life Sciences. Specifically, these activists are alleged to have operated a website that reported on and expressed ideological support for protest activity against Huntingdon and its business affiliates. For this they are charged with 'terrorism' and face an aggregate of 23 years in Federal Prison.
>
> The SHAC 7 case is the latest in an onslaught of attacks against domestic dissidents under the guise of fighting terrorism. Animal rights is a 'fringe' issue and the government is banking on the broader social justice movement to turn a blind eye to those focusing on the 'less important' issue of animals and expressing 'extremist' views. But make no mistake—these activists are the canaries in the mine. This case is intended to pave the way for further silencing of activists involved in all issues. It is imperative that the broader social justice movement stand behind these activists in our communal defense of free speech, press, and association. Support the SHAC 7 and support your right to free expression!)

Note: This website was no longer active in 2024, as this Second Edition went to press.

33. The current version can be accessed at https://shacjustice.com (accessed December 27, 2023).
34. *United States v. Fullmer*, 584 F.3d 182 (3d Cir., 2009), Joint Appendix, p. 775.
35. Ibid., Joint Appendix, p. 935.
36. This tactic—putting pressure on third parties in order to induce them to pressure the real target of the campaign—is well known in the world of organized labor. Prior to the passage of the Taft-Hartley Act in 1947, secondary boycotts were a common feature of labor disputes. Today, while striking third parties who have no direct involvement in the labor dispute are illegal, other tactics implicating third parties remain available in organized labor's quiver. See, e.g., Rik Kirkland, "The New Face of Labor," *Fortune*, October 10, 2006, http://money.cnn.com/magazines/fortune/fortune_archive/2006/10/16/8390290. ("That's why, though the SEIU has no stake in organizing workers at Wal-Mart, Stern nonetheless cooked up the idea for the grass-roots pressure group Wal-Mart Watch, and is now spending nearly $4 million a year to support it.") See also Mark R. Filip and James Ottavio Castagnera, *Employment Law Answer Book* (7th ed.) (New York: Aspen Law and Business, 2010), pp. 15–63:

    An organization called Union Network International (UNI) announced at its August 2005 Chicago convention that signing global agreements with targeted companies will be that organization's focus going forward. In 2007, UNI expanded its attention to monitoring private equity funds. In a March 2007 press release, UNI stated: "In the furor that has enveloped private equity these past weeks, one of the criticisms of their way of doing business is the absence of any regard to corporate social responsibility (CSR) . . . . In the weeks to come, we will be keeping a close watch on whether there will be a shift toward more transparency, disclosure or any commitment to CSR principles."

37. *United States v. Fullmer*, Joint Appendix, p. 1233.
38. When the SHAC 7 were indicted, this was the aspect of the indictment that caught the news media's attention the most. See, e.g., John Cook, "Thugs for Puppies," *Salon*, February 7, 2007, http://www.salon.com/life/feature/2006/02/07/thugs_puppies:

    The indictment's pièce de résistance is a lengthy quote from the "Top 20 terror tactics" posted on the SHAC USA site, which, in addition to listing several perfectly lawful practices, suggests "physical assault including spraying cleaning fluid into one's eyes"; "smashing the windows of one's house while the individual's family was at home"; and "threats to kill or injure one's partner or children."
39. *United States v. Fullmer*, Joint Appendix, p. 780.
40. Ibid., Joint Appendix, p. 1512.
41. Ibid., Joint Appendix, p. 3095–3099.
42. Ibid., Joint Appendix, p. 835. See also Henry David Thoreau, "On the Duty of Civil Disobedience," http://www.transcendentalists.com/civil_disobedience.htm:

    Unjust laws exist: shall we be content to obey them, or shall we endeavor to amend them, and obey them until we have succeeded, or shall we transgress them at once? Men, generally, under such a government as this, think that they ought to wait until they have persuaded the majority to alter them. They think that, if they should resist, the remedy would be worse than the evil. But it is the fault of the government itself that the remedy is worse than the evil. It makes it worse. Why is it not more apt to anticipate and provide for reform? Why does it not cherish its wise minority? Why does it cry and resist before it is hurt? Why does it not encourage its citizens to put out its faults, and do better than it would have them? Why does it always crucify Christ and excommunicate Copernicus and Luther, and pronounce Washington and Franklin rebels?"
43. *United States v. Fullmer*, Joint Appendix, p. 788.
44. Ibid.
45. Ibid.
46. Ibid., Joint Appendix, p. 2615.
47. *United States v. Stop Huntington Animal Cruelty, Inc., Kevin Kjonaas, a/k/a "Kevin Jonas," a/k/a "Steve Shore," a/k/a "Jim Fareer," Lauren Gazzola, a/k/a "Angela Jackson," a/k/a "Danielle Matthews," Jacob Conroy, Joshua Harper, Andrew Stepanian, Darius Fullmer, and John Mcgee*, Criminal 04-373 (MLC), under 18 U.S.C. Sections 2, 43, 371, and 2261A.
48. The new indictment added 47 U.S.C. 223(a)(1)(C) to its statutory bases. (Note: The indictments were signed by U.S. Attorney Christopher Christie, at this writing the governor of New Jersey.) See also contemporary commentary on the indictments, e.g., the official Justice Department press release, accessible at www.justice.gov/usao/nj/press/files/pdffiles/shac0912rel.pdf; "The British Terror Invasion," The Scientist, http://www.the-scientist.com/yr2004/jul/upfront_040705.html, article accessed at http://www.mitosyfraudes.org/Polit/Terror.html, September 12, 2010; Catherine E. Smith, "Threats.com," *Southern Poverty Law Center Intelligence Report*, Summer 2005, http://www.splcenter.org/get-informed/intelligence-report/browse-all-issues/2005/summer/threatscom.

49. The corporation's website, accessible at http://www.lsrinc.net, describes the company as follows:

    > Life Sciences Research is one of the world's leading Contract Research Organizations (CROs), providing pre-clinical and non-clinical biological safety evaluation research services to most of the world's leading pharmaceutical, biotechnology, agrochemical and industrial chemical companies. LSR's services are designed to meet the regulatory requirements of governments around the world, and are an indispensable part of safely developing new drugs to manage and improve mankind's health.

    The Company is based in the United States, with a professional and support staff of over 1,400 working in facilities near Princeton (NJ), and Huntingdon and Eye, England.
50. *United States v. Fullmer*, Joint Appendix, p. 937.
51. Ibid., Joint Appendix, p. 922.
52. Ibid., Joint Appendix, p. 2834.
53. Ibid., Joint Appendix, p. 924.
54. Ibid., Joint Appendix, p. 927.
55. Accessible at http://global.marsh.com, Marsh describes itself as "the world's leading insurance broker and risk adviser, has over 23,000 employees and provides advice and transactional capabilities to clients in over 100 countries."
56. *United States v. Fullmer*, Joint Appendix, p. 144.
57. Ibid., Joint Appendix, p. 1292.
58. Ibid., Joint Appendix, p. 3004.
59. Ibid., Joint Appendix, p. 1271.
60. Ibid., Joint Appendix, p. 145.
61. At its website, http://www.seaburyandsmith.com, Seabury & Smith says, "For over 27 years, Seabury & Smith, Inc., has been FINRA's insurance program administrator, proudly serving the securities industry with excellent customer service, comprehensive products designed specifically for broker-dealers, and affordable premiums." The home page goes on to explain,

    FINRA is a registered trademark of the Financial Industry Regulatory Authority, Inc. Seabury & Smith, Inc. FINRA's insurance program administrator, is a third-party provider of insurance products. It is in no way owned or managed by FINRA. FINRA seeks to assist firms' compliance efforts by finding, reviewing and making third-party tools and services available at discounted prices or with additional features. These tools and services are provided as a convenience to firms. Firms are not obligated to use them, and their use does not ensure compliance with FINRA rules or other regulations or laws.
62. *United States v. Fullmer*, Joint Appendix, p. 2993.
63. Ibid., Joint Appendix, p. 1282.
64. Ibid., Joint Appendix, p. 2994.
65. Ibid., Joint Appendix, p. 2995.
66. Ibid., Joint Appendix, p. 1225.
67. Ibid., Joint Appendix, pp. 2979–2980.

68. Ibid., Joint Appendix, pp. 2980, 2985; Appellee's Brief, pp. 65–66.
69. Ibid., Joint Appendix, p. 2980.
70. Ibid., Joint Appendix, p. 2981.
71. Ibid., Opinion, p. 151.
72. Ibid., 584 F.3d at 182.
73. *Chronicle of Higher Education*, May 31, 2006, http://chronicle.com/weekly/v52/i30/30a02901.htm (accessed June 23, 2008).
74. *Chronicle of Higher Education*, 53, 2, September 1, 2006, p. A22.
75. *Chronicle of Higher Education*, 53, 3, September 8, 2006, p. A19.
76. *Chronicle of Higher Education*, 53, 43, June 29, 2007, p. A6.
77. *Chronicle of Higher Education*, 54, 26, March 7, 2008, p. A1.
78. *Chronicle of Higher Education*, 54, 42, June 27, 2008, p. A1.
79. Lila Guterman, "New Attacks on Animal Researchers Provoke Anger and Worry," *Chronicle of Higher Education*, 54, 49, August 15, 2008, p. A6.
80. "'No-kill' Animal Activists Hold Vigil; Death Threats Reported against Board Members of Jersey City Animal Shelter," *Jersey Journal*, September 3, 2010, http://www.nj.com/hudson/index.ssf/2010/09/no-kill_animal_activists_hold.html.
81. Carlton Purvis, "Operation Backfire: Eleven Down, Two to Go," *North American Animal Liberation Press Office*, December 3, 2012, http://animalliberationpressoffice.org/NAALPO/2012/12/03/operation-backfire-eleven-down-two-to-go/ (accessed December 13, 2012).
82. "Federation of American Societies for Experimental Biology," *Animal Research Activism,* February 2023, https://www.faseb.org/getmedia/d6fdf327-982f-435e-8ac3-a48552ea57b0/Animal-Research-Activism-Report-2023-1-23-v2.pdf (accessed December 27, 2023).
83. "Animal Rights Extremism," *Understanding Animal Research,* https://www.understandinganimalresearch.org.uk/regulation/animal-rights-extremism (accessed December 27, 2023).

All My Trials Soon be Over? Sami Al-Arian (2005–2010)

5

> THIS MATTER is before the court on the Motion of The Tribune Company to Intervene and Petition for Access. The Tribune Company, publisher of the *Tampa Tribune*, (hereinafter, "*Tribune*"), is seeking to obtain from the above files, a copy of the sealed search warrants, the probable cause affidavits, and the court's orders sealing these documents. The Government has not filed a response in opposition, however, the United States Attorney's Office orally presented its objections at the January 5, 1996 hearing on this matter. Dr. Al-Arian's counsel appeared and objected on his behalf.[1]

This is an excerpt from the first reported opinion, way back in 1996, in which appeared the name of Dr. Sami Al-Arian, a professor in the Computer Sciences Department of the University of South Florida (USF). The case involved a search by federal agents of his home and office. Thus began the courtroom trials and tribulations of the man who was arguably the second most controversial, post-9/11 academic (after Ward Churchill[2]).

Al-Arian was born in Kuwait in 1958.[3] He relocated with his family to Egypt in 1966 and at the age of 17 came to the United States to commence his college education in 1975. A 1978 degree in electrical engineering was followed by an M.A. and a Ph.D. in computer engineering. He was hired, a newly minted Ph.D., by USF in 1986. Meanwhile, during the 1980s, Al-Arian became one of the most active lecturers in North America concerning the Palestinian cause, the Arab-Israeli conflict, and more generally, Islam's relationship to the West. He co-founded an organization known as the Islamic Committee for Palestine[4] and another styled the World and Islam Studies Enterprise.[5] A third organization he is credited with helping to birth was the Islamic Association for Palestine, better known by its subsidiary, Holy Land Foundation for Relief and Development, which grew into the largest Islamic charitable organization in the United States.[6]

Al-Arian was also involved in local community organizations, such as Tampa's Islamic Community Center and the Florida Islamic Academy,[7] and as an imam in his local mosque. Until 9/11, Al-Arian retained an air of respectability. In fact, he enjoyed a certain cachet in the lower tiers of national politics. For example, in March 2000 he met soon-to-be U.S. President George W. and Laura Bush, who posed for a photo with the Al-Arian family.[8] He also

DOI: 10.4324/9781003474104-5

reportedly lobbied Congress on civil liberties issues, donated funds to Congressional campaigns, and was one of about 150 prominent Muslim-Americans to attend a White House briefing conducted by Karl Rove in June 2001.[9]

But in the years leading up to 9/11, a Mr. Hyde had begun to emerge alongside this Dr. Jekyll persona. In the mid-1990s, Al-Arian dodged a very large bullet.

> The FBI, in affidavits, accused World and Islam Studies Enterprises of raising money for terrorist organizations and shut it down in 1995. Mr. Al-Arian was placed on paid leave from 1996 to 1998 while the agency investigated whether he was connected to terrorist organizations in the Middle East. South Florida's own investigation turned up no evidence of wrongdoing.[10]

Like Ward Churchill's "Chickens" essay, Al-Arian's brush with fire during the mid-1990s remained low profile, as his ability to engage in legitimate national political activities attests, until in the wake of the 9/11 attacks he accepted an invitation to appear on Fox Network's *The O'Reilly Factor* in October 2001.

The major topic of Al-Arian's TV appearance was the World and Islam Studies Enterprise, by then defunct for some six years. "During a heated discussion with the show's host, Bill O'Reilly, Mr. Al-Arian said he was 'shocked' that two former colleagues from WISE were apparently involved in terrorist activities."[11] Yet again USF, which was identified as Al-Arian's employer during the volatile interview, placed the controversial professor on a paid leave of absence.

From that interview onward, the vise began to close on Sami Al-Arian. As 2002, like the American army in Afghanistan, marched forward, the USF Board of Trustees proceeded cautiously toward terminating the controversial Muslim faculty member. In early September, the board sought a declaratory judgment in a Florida state court that its planned firing of Al-Arian would not violate his constitutional rights.[12] While the case was pending, Al-Arian was indicted.

> In announcing the indictment of Mr. Al-Arian and seven other defendants on racketeering charges, Attorney General John Ashcroft called the organization—the Palestinian Islamic Jihad—"one of the most violent terrorist organizations in the world." The fifty-count indictment charged that Mr. Al-Arian was the head of the group in this country and that, for years, he directed many of the financial transactions that supported terrorist activities around the world.[13]

With that government action, USF felt free to lower its own boom on Al-Arian. Stated President Judy L. Genshaft,

> We have determined that USF must sever all ties to Sami Al-Arian once and for all. His use of this educational institution for improper, non-educational purposes will not be tolerated. No longer will he be able to hide behind the shield of academic freedom.[14]

Within the year, the American Association of University Professors condemned the canning of Al-Arian:

> On February 26, University of South Florida [P]resident Judy Genshaft notified professor Sami Al-Arian of his immediate dismissal. She based her action on proposed grounds for termination, issued last August after Al-Arian had been kept on paid leave for nearly a year, that accused him of using his academic position to support terrorists.
>
> The dismissal occurred six days after Al-Arian was arrested by the Federal Bureau of Investigation (FBI) following the return of a fifty-count grand jury indictment. The indictment charges that Al-Arian was a key official in the Palestinian Islamic Jihad, designated by the U.S. government as a terrorist organization. It charges him with having managed money for the organization, helped develop its policy, maintained contact with its leaders abroad, and claimed responsibility for bombings in Israel. Genshaft stated that she dismissed Al-Arian because he had used USF "for improper, non-educational purposes" rather than because of the criminal charges, but also said that the activities specified in the indictment "confirm" the administration's position that dismissal is justified.
>
> In a previous development, a federal district court judge in December dismissed the university board's request for a declaratory judgment on whether it could discharge Al-Arian without violating his constitutional rights. The administration stated that it needed this judgment partly to avoid AAUP censure. The court called the claim to be an inappropriate use of judicial resources and stated that a court ruling on the professor's First Amendment rights "would have no binding effect on the AAUP and would serve only as an advisory opinion that the AAUP could ignore in its totality."
>
> Joan Wallach Scott, chair of the AAUP's Committee A on Academic Freedom and Tenure, points out that the FBI's charges against Al-Arian, while manifestly very serious, remain to be proven in a court of law. She decries his dismissal before he had any opportunity to defend himself against the administration's charges. It is especially unfortunate, she says, when the adage of "innocent until proven guilty" is disregarded at an institution of higher learning.[15]

5.1 Al-Arian's Terrorism Trial

Another three years of legal maneuvers and media finger pointing elapsed before Al-Arian finally came to trial in June 2005. He came to trial with three co-defendants in the U.S. District Court for the Middle District of Florida, which, like USF, calls Tampa its home. The trial was a courtroom soap opera rivaling in its length some of the more notorious trials of the modern era, such as the O.J. Simpson murder case. It extended across six months, featured some 80 witnesses and 400 transcripts of intercepted telephone conversations and faxes, and ended with a whimper rather than a bang as the disgraced college professor's defense team declined to put on a counter presentation. This proved to be a wise tactic. Following 13 days of deliberations, the jury acquitted Al-Arian on eight of 17 counts and deadlocked on all of the other nine. None of the defendants was convicted of anything.[16]

Following the stunning verdict, *Time* magazine commented, "According to U.S. court documents, Sami Al-Arian, a Palestinian computer-science professor at USF in Tampa, wrote a letter to an associate in Kuwait bragging that the Beit Lid carnage was 'an example of what P.I.J. could do' and soliciting funds for the bombers' families."[17] The magazine noted that a year earlier, Al-Arian had sent a fax to Islamic Jihad bosses in England and the Middle East, suggesting he be in charge of the group's finances, and he was well known to have urged audiences to " 'damn' the U.S. and Israel 'until death.' " Despite the evidence, however,

> [the] Tampa jury has made it joltingly clear to the Bush administration that praising terrorist acts, raising money for terrorists' widows or making an unaccepted offer to manage a terrorist group's money does not make a man a terrorist in a U.S. court of law.[18]

Of course, double jeopardy prevented the government from further pursuing Al-Arian and his co-defendants with regard to the acquittals. But the nine deadlocked accusations remained a sword over Al-Arian's head. Consequently, on March 2, 2006, he entered a plea bargain with Uncle Sam in which he pleaded guilty to one conspiracy count, viz., "to make or receive contributions of funds, goods or services to or for the benefit of the Palestinian Islamic Jihad, a Specially Designated Terrorist [sic], in violation of U.S.C. 371." At the plea agreement hearing, he told the federal magistrate that he had raised money for the Islamic Jihad and conspired to conceal the identity of his contacts. The government reciprocated, agreeing that Al-Arian's activities were all nonviolent.[19]

The federal judge sentenced him to 57 months in prison, plus deportation. With credit for time served, Al-Arian faced a 19-month prison term. His honor, Judge James Moody, in passing the sentence, said, "You lifted not one finger. To the contrary, you laughed when you heard of the bombings. You are a master manipulator. The evidence is clear in this case. You were the leader of the PIJ."[20]

Judge Moody added,

> You looked your neighbors in the eyes and said you had nothing to do with the Palestinian Islamic Jihad. This trial exposed that as a lie. Your back-up claim is that your efforts were only to provide charities for widows and orphans. That, too, is a lie. The evidence was clear in this case that you were a leader of the Palestinian Islamic Jihad. You were on the board of directors and an officer, the secretary. Directors control the actions of an organization, even the PIJ; and you were an active leader.[21]

5.2 Al-Arian's Civil Contempt Case

Al-Arian's story hardly ended with his incarceration. Less than a month after Al-Arian was sentenced, in May 2006, the U.S. District Court for the Eastern District of Virginia issued to Al-Arian a grand jury subpoena ad testificandum. The subpoena was served on Al-Arian in early October 2006, and he filed a motion to quash the subpoena in the Virginia district court. Al-Arian argued that his plea agreement in the Florida district court prevented the government from forcing him to testify before the grand jury in Virginia. The government responded that the Florida district court, not the Virginia district court, was the proper court to adjudicate Al-Arian's motion and suggested that the Virginia district court should direct Al-Arian to file his motion in the Florida district court. The Virginia district court agreed and granted Al-Arian leave to file a motion to enforce the plea agreement in the Florida district court on or before October 26, 2006.

Al-Arian filed his motion in the Florida district court and argued that he and the government agreed that he would not be required to cooperate with the government in any manner. That agreement, however, is not documented in the plea agreement; Al-Arian asserted that the government purposefully omitted the standard cooperation provisions from the plea agreement because the government acquiesced to his refusal to cooperate. According to Al-Arian, the absence of a cooperation provision in the plea agreement demonstrated that the government agreed not to seek further testimony from him. Al-Arian contended that, in light of this agreement, his constitutional due process rights would be violated if he were compelled to testify before the grand jury in Virginia. Al-Arian requested that the Florida district court enforce the plea agreement and order specific performance of the non-cooperation aspect of that agreement, which would bar the government from compelling his testimony. The government responded that the Florida district court lacked jurisdiction to consider the motion and that the plea agreement did not immunize Al-Arian from the grand jury subpoena.

The Florida district court subsequently conducted a hearing on Al-Arian's motion. The district judge found that he had jurisdiction over the motion because Al-Arian sought "protection from the United States government" and that it did not matter in which judicial district the dispute over the grand jury subpoena took place. In a subsequent written order, the court held that Al-Arian's plea agreement was not ambiguous and did not prevent the government from issuing a subpoena compelling him to testify. Further, the court found that "cooperation" is not the equivalent of compelled testimony, so that even if the plea agreement provided that Al-Arian would not have to cooperate, that would not necessarily have meant that he could not be compelled to testify pursuant to a subpoena.

Al-Arian appealed the Florida district court's order to the U.S. Court of Appeals for the Eleventh Circuit. Subsequently, the Virginia district court found that Al-Arian had no legal basis on which to refuse to comply with the subpoena, granted the government's motion to hold Al-Arian in civil contempt, denied Al-Arian's motion to stay the contempt proceedings during the pendency of his appeal, and ordered Al-Arian's criminal sentence to be tolled until he testified before the grand jury. Al-Arian appealed his contempt citation to the U.S. Court of Appeals for the Fourth Circuit, which affirmed the Virginia district court's order. In May 2007, Al-Arian filed an unopposed motion for expedited consideration and resolution of his appeal with the Eleventh Circuit. Oral argument was held in the case in 2007—rather ironically, on September 11. On December 14, 2007, the Virginia district court vacated its contempt order. The Eleventh Circuit issued its ruling on January 25, 2008:[22]

> Al-Arian argues that, in exchange for his guilty plea, the government agreed never to seek his cooperation in any future matter, and that the government breached this agreement by subpoenaing him to testify before a grand jury in the Eastern District of Virginia. Whether the government has breached a plea agreement is a question of law that we review de novo. United States v. Mahique, 150 F.3d 1330, 1332 (11th Cir., 1998) (per curiam). However, the district court's factual findings regarding the scope of the agreement will be set aside only if they are clearly erroneous. Raulerson v. United States, 901 F.2d 1009, 1012 (11th Cir., 1990). "The court must decide whether the government's actions are inconsistent with what the defendant reasonably understood when he entered his guilty plea." Arnett, 804 F.2d at 1202–03. The court must use objective standards to resolve a dispute over the meaning of terms in a plea agreement. Id. at 1202. Parol evidence may be considered only where the language of the agreement is ambiguous or government overreaching is alleged. Raulerson, 901 F.2d at 1012.
>
> In In re Grand Jury Proceedings (Perdue), 819 F.2d 984 (11th Cir., 1987) (per curiam), we decided a case presenting very similar facts. After Perdue pled guilty pursuant to a written plea agreement, the government subpoenaed him

to testify before a grand jury and granted him immunity from prosecution based on his testimony. Perdue refused to testify and the district court held him in contempt. Id. at 985. Perdue appealed to this court, arguing that the government agreed that, in exchange for his guilty plea and acceptance of a longer sentence, the government would not require him to testify in other matters. Id. at 986. Because we decided that Perdue's plea "agreement simply [did] not contain any mention of future testimony, whether voluntary or compelled," we concluded that we would "not rewrite the agreement to include a bar on attempts by the government to compel testimony by Perdue." Id. at 987. Accordingly, we held that the plea agreement did not preclude the government from attempting to compel testimony from Perdue, and we so held even though we recognized that the government may have misled Perdue and that Perdue may have misunderstood the plea agreement. Id. at 986–87.

The Second Circuit reached the same result in a nearly identical case. In In re Grand Jury Witness (Altro), 180 F.3d 372 (2d Cir., 1999), a defendant refused to comply with a grand jury subpoena based upon his belief that his plea agreement afforded him immunity from the government's subpoena. The plea agreement contained no reference to future testimony, and the defendant did not establish that the government affirmatively made a "no-cooperation promise" (Id. at 376). Instead, the defendant relied upon his understanding that the plea agreement contained an "implicit" promise that he would not have to give grand jury testimony, based upon his course of dealing with the government. Id. at 375. The plea agreement contained an integration clause, providing that there were no other promises or under- standings between the parties other than those written in the agreement. Id. at 373. On those facts, the Second Circuit concluded that the defendant could not rely on an "implicit understanding" that was not reflected in the plea agreement to demonstrate that the government had breached the plea agreement and affirmed the district court's order holding him in contempt. Id. at 376–77.

This case falls squarely within Perdue and Altro. Al-Arian's plea agreement contains no mention of whether he could be compelled to testify before a grand jury in the future. It also contains an integration clause, providing that the plea agreement reflects all of the promises and agreements between Al-Arian and the government. Notwithstanding the integration clause, Al-Arian argues that the plea agreement's lack of any provision related to future testimony is actually affirmative evidence that the government agreed, as part of the plea agreement, not to seek future testimony from him. According to Al-Arian, the government agreed to omit the "standard cooperation provision"* from the plea agreement because Al-Arian conditioned his guilty plea on his refusal to cooperate. Appellant's Br. 16. Thus, Al-Arian contends that removing that language from the plea agreement achieved the same result as including a provision immunizing him from having to give any future testimony. We disagree. The exclusion of a standard plea agreement provision requiring a defendant to cooperate with the government, whether voluntarily or under subpoena, does not establish that the government immunized Al-Arian from future grand jury subpoenas. This contention is especially dubious where, as here, the plea agreement contains an integration clause stating that there are no other promises, agreements, or representations except those set forth in the agreement, and Al-Arian denied at his plea hearing that he pled guilty in reliance on any promises or inducements except for those found in the agreement. In addition, the United States Attorney's Office for the Eastern District of Virginia only agreed to be bound by the plea agreement such that it would not prosecute Al-Arian for crimes known to that office at the time of the agreement; that office did not agree to immunize Al-Arian from any future grand jury subpoenas.** Given these aspects of the plea agreement and plea hearing, we cannot conclude that Al-Arian reasonably believed that he would forever be immune from all grand jury subpoenas originating from any federal prosecutor's office.

> * The government filed a letter brief and attached the plea agreement provisions at issue in response to our request at oral argument. We note that the cooperation provisions are drafted such that cooperation includes testimony both provided voluntarily and compelled by a subpoena. However, because it is not necessary for us to decide in this appeal whether "cooperation" encompasses compelled testimony, we express no opinion as to whether the district court correctly found that "cooperation" does not include testimony compelled by a subpoena.
> ** Al-Arian also argues that the United States Attorney's Office for the Eastern District of Virginia is bound by the plea agreement. We address this additional issue in further detail to explain that, even if the government had immunized Al-Arian from future grand jury subpoenas, neither the plea agreement itself nor the modification of that agreement made during the plea hearing in the district court extended any such immunity to subpoenas issued from the Eastern District of Virginia. The plea agreement expressly binds only the United States Attorney's Office for the Middle District of Florida and the Counterterrorism Section of the Department of Justice. At the plea hearing, the agreement was orally modified to "further bind the Eastern District of Virginia such that, if the [c]ourt accepts the plea agreement, the United States Attorney's Office for the Eastern District of Virginia likewise will not charge [Al-Arian] with committing any other federal crimes known to that United States Attorney's Office at the time of the agreement." R124 at 18–19. This modification of the plea agreement binds the United States Attorney's Office Eastern District of Virginia only insofar as that office agreed not to prosecute Al-Arian for crimes known to that office at the time of the plea; it does not extend any purported immunity to Al-Arian from grand jury subpoenas.

In this case, like Perdue, there is a clear conflict between Al-Arian's understanding of the plea agreement versus the government's understanding of it. Also like Perdue, Al-Arian alleges that he was at least unintentionally misled by the government into believing that he would not have to give any further testimony, and the government did not present any evidence to render Al-Arian's misunderstanding implausible. Perdue, 819 F.2d at 986. However, as we stated in Perdue, even "where the government arguably misled [Al-Arian], and where [Al-Arian] plausibly misunderstood the plea agreement, we cannot enforce an agreement that was never agreed on with specificity." Id. at 987. As we have explained, the plea agreement reflects no agreement between Al-Arian and the government that Al-Arian could not be compelled to give grand jury testimony. Consequently, we hold that the written plea agreement between Al-Arian and the government does not prevent the government from issuing a subpoena to Al-Arian requiring him to testify before a grand jury.

III. Conclusion

Al-Arian appeals the district court's denial of his motion to enforce the plea agreement, in which he argued that his plea agreement in the Middle District of Florida precluded the United States Attorney's Office for the Eastern District of Virginia from compelling him to testify before a grand jury. Al-Arian argues that, as consideration for his guilty plea, the government agreed never to seek his testimony on any other matters, whether provided voluntarily or compelled. Upon review, we hold that the district court had jurisdiction over Al-Arian's motion pursuant to § 2255. The plea agreement is clear, unambiguous, and does not grant Al-Arian immunity from a future grand jury subpoena. Therefore, we hold that the government did not breach the plea agreement by issuing a subpoena commanding Al-Arian to testify before a grand jury.

AFFIRMED.[23]

5.3 Al-Arian's Criminal Contempt Case

While Al-Arian's challenge to the civil contempt case worked its way to the Eleventh Circuit's January 2008 decision, the government also acted to indict Al-Arian for criminal contempt.

A grand jury was impaneled in Virginia, and on January 17, 2007, the government obtained an immunity order from federal District Judge Gerald Bruce Lee. On January 22, 2007, instead of appearing before the grand jury, Al-Arian appeared before federal Judge Lee and advised the court that he would not answer any questions before the new grand jury. This is when Judge Lee held Al-Arian in civil contempt and ordered that his criminal sentence again be tolled.

In an unpublished per curiam opinion, the Fourth Circuit held that Judge Lee's contempt order was properly supported by the record and holdings of the district court in the Middle District of Florida.[24] Al-Arian's petition for rehearing en banc was denied on May 10, 2007, and he did not seek further review of the civil contempt finding.

On June 26, 2008, after pre-indictment negotiations failed, Al-Arian was charged in this district with two counts of criminal contempt under 18 U.S.C. §401(3), arising out of his refusal to testify before the grand jury on October 16, 2007, and March 20, 2008, in violation of Judge Lee's orders.[25]

In January 2007, Al-Arian commenced a hunger strike, which ultimately spanned some 60 days and cost him 53 of his 202 pounds.[26] Al-Arian eventually provided the government with two lengthy affidavits concerning his knowledge of the International Institute for Islamic Thought (IIIT), the target of the grand jury probe. His attorneys then moved to have him released on bail.[27]

On July 10, 2008 Al-Arian, whose litigation over testifying in the IIIT case had cost him something on the order of an extra year in jail, was released on bail, but with the government's criminal contempt indictment still pending, and with the government threatening to have the immigration authorities deport him, should he beat the contempt rap.[28] He was placed under house arrest in his daughter's Northern Virginia residence.

In March 2009, Al-Arian's lawyers moved to dismiss the indictment.[29] The supporting memorandum of law carried with it a number of the same affidavits that had failed to persuade the courts in the civil contempt proceedings. These included affidavits executed by Al-Arian himself, as well as his lawyers in the original criminal case, all asserting their mutual understanding of the plea agreement; to wit, Al-Arian was not required to testify in any other case.

While this motion was pending, the Muslim Public Affairs Council (MPAC)[30] filed a complaint against the federal prosecutor. In a related public statement, the MPAC contended:

> Gordon Kromberg, Assistant U.S. Attorney for the Eastern District of Virginia, has made repugnant statements about Muslim women, has suggested to a jury that Muslims believe it's religiously acceptable to lie, and has promoted the notion that Muslims are killers due to their nature.[31]

The MPAC filed a complaint that day with the Office of Professional Responsibility, demanding that the Department of Justice investigate Kromberg's remarks.

Meanwhile, U.S. District Judge Leoni Brinkema first scheduled and then postponed an April 2009 hearing on the motion. At least one commentator claimed, "In a February 20, 2009, hearing, Brinkema harrumphed about the government's contempt case . . . . But a year later she has never ruled. Why?" This writer continued to comment that Judge Brinkema backed away from dismissal when "Kromberg filed a response that demolished the defense argument. He cited the transcript of Al-Arian's 2006 plea hearing before a federal magistrate judge in Tampa, Thomas B. McCoun III."[32] The transcript failed to reflect any knowledge by Al-Arian that at the time he copped his plea he understood that the quid pro quo was freedom from all obligations to testify in other cases. The strength of Kromberg's responsive brief, bolstered as it was by Al-Arian's own testimony—or, more accurately, the lack thereof—apparently persuaded her honor to exercise a sort of "pocket veto" by sitting on the pending motion for more than a year.

Meanwhile, in late April 2009, William B. Moffitt, lead counsel in Al-Arian's criminal trial, died at age 60. He was eulogized on the blog of the professor's current counsel, Jonathan Turley of George Washington University Law School.[33] Turley, who has a distinguished resume as an attorney,[34] professor, and legal scholar, wrote a blog titled "Res ipsa loquitur," a legal term meaning "the thing speaks for itself." Unfortunately, where the Al-Arian litigation is concerned, Turley apparently could not speak for himself, as an August 2008 entry explained. While attending the trial of Al-Arian, the prosecution objected to the existence of Turley's blog, in particular the comments left by visitors. Therefore, the entry explained:

> While attorney blogs are allowed under local and federal rules to give updates on filings, we have decided to remove the Al-Arian entries to avoid this issue from being cited in the future as a distraction from the important issues in the case.[35]

Thus, during the second half of 2009 and the first half of 2010, Sami Al-Arian suffered—or perhaps enjoyed—a year of relative quiet. He remained under house arrest.

5.4 The Final Chapter?

Finally, in August 2010, the government returned to court, filing a one-page notice with Judge Brinkema in which it stated, "The United States Department of Justice and the United States Attorney have reviewed the status of the prosecution, and urge the Court to rule on the outstanding motions so that the prosecution can proceed." On September 7, 2010, her honor set October 29 for a hearing on the March motion, as well as an earlier filed government motion, also still in litigation limbo.[36]

However, when October 29, 2010, rolled around, the judge canceled the hearing.[37] Her order may be viewed as admirable or suspicious in its brevity:

> The government has filed a Notice, which scheduled a hearing on October 29, 2010, in which it advises that it will move the Court to deny defendant's Motion to Dismiss and grant a pending government Motion for Reconsideration. The Court finds that a hearing on these issues is not necessary. The parties have fully

> briefed their positions and the Court is working on an opinion which addresses all relevant issues. Accordingly, it is hereby ORDERED that the hearing scheduled for October 29, 2010 be and is cancelled.
> The Clerk is directed to forward copies of this Order to counsel of record, United States Pretrial Services, and the United States Marshals Service.[38]

The judge could now sit on the case indefinitely if she—or someone else with adequate influence over her—so desired. On February 28, 2012, a letter was posted on the "Free Sami Al-Arian" website, claiming that for ten years, Al-Arian dealt with persecution as "a voice of conscience for freedom in Palestine, and equal justice for all in America." The letter went on to detail the purported "innocent casualties" of the U.S. government's War on Terror, including American Muslim individuals who were supposedly framed due to religious beliefs or "thought crimes." The letter closed with the following statement:

> Our pledge of "Justice and Liberty for all" is not a cliché but the principle under which our country was founded, and our system of justice has endured. We must live up to it for the sake of the future of our Republic.[39]

On February 4, 2015, Al-Arian was deported to Turkey. In 2017, he founded the Center for Islam and Global Affairs at Istanbul Sabahattin Zaim University. He currently directs the center.[40] In 2024, he also maintains a presence on social media. On Facebook, he has approximately 2,600 "followers". A November 22, 2023 post is entitled, "A Conversation with Dr. Sami Al-Arian about the Israel Genocidal War in Gaza."[41] He also can be found on YouTube.[42]

Notes

1. Matter of Search of Office Suites for World and Islam Studies Enterprise, 925 F.Supp. 738 (M.D.Fla., 1996).
2. Ward Churchill, head of the ethnic studies program at the University of Colorado at Boulder, penned what was arguably the most controversial comments on the 9/11 tragedies, comments that ultimately cost him his job (Ward Churchill, " 'Some People Push Back': On the Justice of Roosting Chickens," *Pockets of Resistance*, September 12, 2001, p. 20):

   > As for those in the World Trade Center . . . . Well, really, let's get a grip here, shall we? True enough, they were civilians of a sort. But innocent? Gimme a break. They formed a technocratic corps at the very heart of America's global financial empire—the 'mighty engine of profit' to which the military dimension of U.S. policy has always been enslaved—and they did so both willingly and knowingly. Recourse to 'ignorance'—a derivative, after all,

> of the word 'ignore'—counts as less than an excuse among this relatively well-educated elite. To the extent that any of them were unaware of the costs and consequences to others of what they were involved in—and in many cases excelling at—it was because of their absolute refusal to see. More likely, it was because they were too busy braying, incessantly and self-importantly, into their cell phones, arranging power lunches and stock transactions, each of which translated, conveniently out of sight, mind and smelling distance, into the starved and rotting flesh of infants. If there was a better, more effective, or in fact any other way of visiting some penalty befitting their participation upon the little Eichmanns inhabiting the sterile sanctuary of the twin towers, I'd really be interested in hearing about it."

For a detailed discussion of Churchill's case, see James Ottavio Castagnera, *Al-Qaeda Goes to College: Impact of the War on Terror on American Higher Education* (Westport, CT: Praeger, 2009), pp. 13–27.

3. The basic biographical facts on Sami Al-Arian are drawn from Wikipedia, where they are available at http:en.wikipedia.org/wiki/Sami_Al-Arian (accessed July 24, 2008).
4. See, http://www.discoverthenetworks.org/groupProfile.asp?grpid=6385:

> Established in 1986 by Sami Al-Arian and Hussam Jubara, the Islamic Committee for Palestine (ICP) was promoted as a philanthropic advocacy group devoted to alleviating the suffering of Palestinian women and children. In reality, the organization served as an American front for the terrorist organization Palestinian Islamic Jihad. At a 1991 conference in Cleveland, Ohio, a lecturer introducing Al-Arian as the ICP President candidly called the Committee "the active arm of the Jihad movement in Palestine." "We like to call it the Islamic Committee for Palestine here for security reasons," he added. Shortly after being introduced that evening, Al-Arian declared, "Let us continue the protests. Let us damn America. Let us damn Israel. Let us damn their allies until death."

5. See http://www.discoverthenetworks.org/groupProfile.asp?grpid=6445:

> The World Islam Study Enterprise (WISE) was established as an "Islamic think tank" in 1991 by four professors at the University of South Florida (USF): Sami Al-Arian, his brother-in-law Mazen al Najjar, Khalil Shikaki, and Ramadan Abdullah Shallah. Abdullah left WISE (before it was shut down by federal authorities in 1995) to become head of the terrorist organization Palestinian Islamic Jihad (PIJ). Khalil Shikaki is the brother of Fathi Shikaki, the founder of PIJ. When Fahti Shikaki was assassinated, his replacement as PIJ's military head was Ramadan Abdullah Shallah.

6. See http://www.discoverthenetworks.org/groupProfile.asp?grpid=6181:

> Established in 1988 (under the name "Occupied Land Fund") by Shukri Abu Baker, Mohammad El-Mezain and Ghassan Elashi, the Holy Land Foundation for Relief and Development (HLF) was a non-profit,

tax-exempt, charitable trust headquartered in Richardson, Texas. It also maintained branch offices in New Jersey, California, and Illinois. Its name change took place in 1992. Calling itself America's largest Islamic charity, HLF purported to be a source of help for needy Palestinian Muslims in Israel, Jordan, Lebanon, and the Palestinian Authority. "Our mission," stated its website, "is to find and implement practical solutions for human suffering through humanitarian programs that impact the lives of the disadvantaged, disinherited, and displaced peoples suffering from man-made and natural disasters." In reality, however, the Foundation was a major financier of the terrorist organization Hamas.

7. See http://schools.privateschoolsreport.com/Florida/Tampa/IslamicAcademyOfFlorida.html.
8. Michael Isikoff, "Hiding in Plain Sight: Did a Muslim Professor Use Activism as a Cloak for Terror?" *Newsweek*, March 3, 2003, p. 27.
9. Ibid.
10. Dana Mulhauser, "Professor Linked to Terrorist Groups Is Placed on Leave by University of South Florida," *Chronicle of Higher Education*, October 26, 2001, http://chronicle.com/weekly/v48/i09/09a01901.htm (accessed July 24, 2008).
11. Ibid.
12. Sharon Walsh, "University Seeks Court Approval to Fire Professor It Accuses of Terrorism," *Chronicle of Higher Education*, September 6, 2002, http://chronicle.com/weekly/v49/i02/02a02201.htm (accessed July 25, 2008).
13. Sharon Walsh, "University of South Florida Professor Indicted of Aiding Terrorists," *Chronicle of Higher Education*, February 28, 2003, http://chronicle.com/weekly/v49/i25/25a01201.htm (accessed July 25, 2008).
14. Scott Smallwood, "University of South Florida Fires Professor Accused of Terrorism," *Chronicle of Higher Education*, March 7, 2003, http://chronicle.com/weekly/v49/i26/26a01201.htm (accessed July 25, 2008).
15. "Al-Arian Indicted, Arrested, and Dismissed," *Academe Online*, March–April 2003, http://www.aaup.org/AAUP/pubsres/academe/2003/MA/NB/AlArian.htm (accessed September 18, 2010). With permission.
16. Meg Laughlin, Jennifer Liberto, and Justin George, "Eight Times, Al-Arian Hears 'Not Guilty,'" *St. Petersburg Times*, December 7, 2005, http://www.sptimes.com/2005/12/07/Tampabay/8_time_Al_Arian_hea.shtml (accessed July 25, 2008).
17. "When Terror Charges Just Won't Stick," *TIME*, December 12, 2005, http://www.time.com/time/magazine/article/0,9171,1139813,00.html (accessed September 18, 2010). With permission.
18. Ibid.
19. Elaine Silvestrini, "Al-Arian Admits His Role in Jidad," *Tampa Tribune*, April 18, 2006, p. A1.
20. Reuters, "Ex-Professor Gets over 4 Years in Florida Jihad Case," May 1, 2006.
21. Ibid. See also Steve Emerson, "The Inexplicable Freeze on Sami Al-Arian's Contempt Case," *Family Security Matters*, March 24, 2010, http://www.family-securitymatters.org/publications/id.5807/pub_detail.asp (accessed September 18, 2010).

22. *United States v. Al-Arian*, 514 F.3d 1184, 21 Fla. Weekly Fed. C358 (11th Cir., 2008).
23. Ibid.
24. See *In re Grand Jury Subpoena*, No. 07-1155, 2007 WL 870380 (4th Cir., March 23, 2007).
25. See *U.S. v. Al-Arian*, 2008 WL 3843464 (E.D. Va.).
26. Meg Laughlin, "Gaunt Al-Arian Shocks Family," *St. Petersburg Times*, March 20, 2007, http://www.sptimes.com/2007/03/20/Hillsborough/Gaunt_Al_Arian_shocks.html (accessed July 25, 2008).
27. http://www.freesamialarian.com/home.htm.
28. American Muslim Association of America, "Dr. Sami Al-Arian Granted Bail," http://al-amana.net/home/2008/07/11/dr-sami-al-arian-granted-bail (accessed July 25, 2008).
29. "Defendant Dr. Sami Amin Al-Arian's Motion to Dismiss the Indictment," *U.S. v. Al-Arian*, Case No. 1:08cr131, http://www.freesamialarian.com (accessed September 18, 2010).
30. The Muslim Public Affairs Council's website can be accessed at http://www.mpac.org. It states:

    > The Muslim Public Affairs Council is a public service agency working for the civil rights of American Muslims, for the integration of Islam into American pluralism, and for a positive, constructive relationship between American Muslims and their representatives.
    > Since 1988, MPAC has worked diligently to promote a vibrant American Muslim community and enrich American society through exemplifying the Islamic values of Mercy, Justice, Peace, Human Dignity, Freedom, and Equality for all. Over the years, MPAC has built a reputation as a consistent and reliable resource for government and media, and is trusted by American Muslims as an authentic, experienced voice.
    > In all its actions, MPAC works diligently to offer the public a portrayal that goes beyond stereotypes in order to elucidate that Muslims worship God, abhor global terrorism, stand against oppression, and are part of a vibrant American pluralism. MPAC operates on the core belief that change in U.S. policy requires more from our community than attending meetings. It requires organized, sustained efforts in coalition with like-minded groups both at the grassroots and national levels. It requires a strong voice in the media, thoughtful analysis and authentic dialogue.

31. The statement presented a laundry list of alleged improper pronouncements about Muslims by the prosecutor, including:

    - Representing the U.S. government, Kromberg argued before a district judge last fall that Dr. Sami Al-Arian should not be released in to his daughter's custody because, "in this particular culture," a woman could not prevent her father from fleeing.
    - When Al-Arian's Tampa attorney, Jack Fernandez, asked Kromberg to delay the defendant's transfer 30 days until after the Islamic religious holidays of Ramadan, Kromberg responded: "If they can kill each other

during Ramadan, they can appear before the grand jury. All they can't do is eat before sunset. I believe Mr. Al-Arian's request is part of the attempted Islamization of the American Justice System. I am not going to put off Dr. Al-Arian's grand jury appearance just to assist in what is becoming the Islamization of America."

- In the trial of Virginia cancer researcher and Muslim religious leader Ali al-Timimi, who was accused of exhorting others to wage war against America by joining the Taliban, Kromberg said, "If you are a kaffir, Timimi believes in time of war, he's supposed to lie to you."

Accessed at http://www.mpac.org/article.php?id=809, September 18, 2010. With permission.

32. Mary Jabobi, "Commentary: Brinkema's Pocket Veto," *Main Justice*, July 8, 2010, http://www.mainjustice.com/2010/07/08/commentary-brinkemas-pocket-veto (accessed September 19, 2010).
33. Turley wrote of Moffitt (accessed at http://jonathanturley.org/2009/05/02/farewell-to-bill-moffitt/#more-10495, September 19, 2010):

> Today, William B. Moffitt will be buried in Washington, D.C. Bill was a friend and one of the greatest trial attorneys of his generation. He was only 60. He will be deeply missed.
> Bill was the former president of the National Association of Criminal Defense Lawyers and handled some of the greatest criminal cases of the last three decades. One of those cases was his incredible victory in securing acquittals for Dr. Sami Al-Arian in Tampa, Florida. I currently represent Dr. Al-Arian and I worked closely with Bill in the case where he offered important evidence and was expected to be called as a witness. Bill was an inspiration to many in my generation. Like the 1968 Mustang, he was a classic and genuine item. He was a master in the courtroom where his booming voice famously resonated with jurors across the country. He was a natural in the courtroom and assembled a career that could only be envied by his colleagues. The bar lost one of its greatest voices for justice and equality. Bill was the best of us and will remain the gold standard for trial attorneys for years to come. A memorial service is scheduled for Saturday, May 2, at Howard University Law School's Dunbarton Chapel, 2900 Van Ness Street N.W., Washington, D.C.

Jonathan Turley describes himself as follows (accessed at http://jona-thanturley.org/about/, September 19, 2010):

> Professor Jonathan Turley is a nationally recognized legal scholar who has written extensively in areas ranging from constitutional law to legal theory to tort law. He has written over three dozen academic articles that have appeared in a variety of leading law journals at Cornell, Duke, Georgetown, Harvard, Northwestern, and other schools. After a stint at Tulane Law School, Professor Turley joined the George Washington faculty in 1990 and, in 1998, was given the prestigious Shapiro Chair for Public Interest Law, the youngest chaired professor in the school's history. In addition to his extensive publications, Professor Turley has served as counsel in

some of the most notable cases in the last two decades, representing whistleblowers, military personnel, and a wide range of other clients.

34. Wikipedia offers the following summary of Turley's major cases (accessed at http://en.wikipedia.org/wiki/Jonathan_Turley, September 19, 2010.):

    Some of Turley's most notable non-academic work is his representation of the Area 51 workers at a secret air base in Nevada; the nuclear couriers at Oak Ridge, Tennessee; the Rocky Flats grand jury in Colorado; Dr. Eric Foretich, the husband in the famous Elizabeth Morgan custody controversy. He challenged Black Bag Operations authorized under the Foreign Intelligence Surveillance Act (FISA) in espionage cases against former CIA officer Harold Nicholson; and four former United States Attorneys General during the Clinton impeachment litigation. He has also represented defendants in terrorism cases including Dr. Ali Al-Timimi (the alleged head of the Virginia Jihad/Paintball conspiracy) and Dr. Sami Al-Arian (in a criminal contempt case). He also represented Larry Hanauer, a House Intelligence Committee staff member falsely accused of leaking classified information to the New York Times and David Faulk, a whistleblower who revealed abuses at NSA's Fort Gordon surveillance programs. He is also lead counsel in the litigation over the mass arrests at the World Bank/IMF protests in Washington. He testified on the Clinton impeachment as one of the constitutional experts on the standards and merits of the case. The conceptual thread running through many of the cases taken on by Turley is that they involve claims of Executive Privilege and national security exceptions to fundamental constitutional rights.

35. http://jonathanturley.org/2008/08/08/dr-sami-al-arian-update/ (accessed September 19, 2010).
36. Mary Jacoby, "Brinkema Sets Hearing in Terrorism-Related Case after Government Forces Her Hand," *Main Justice*, September 9, 2010, http://www.mainjustice.com/2010/09/09/brinkema-sets-hearing-after-government-forces-her-hand/ (accessed September 19, 2010).
37. "Judge Cancels Hearing in Dr. Al-Arian's Case," http://www.freesamialarian.com/index.php?option=com_content&view=article&id=740:judge-cancels-hearing-in-dr-al-arians-case-&catid=36:2010&Itemid=88 (accessed November 13, 2010).
38. Order dated October 28, 2010, *United States v. Sami Amin Al-Arian*, Case 1:8cr131 (U.S.D.C., N.D.Va.), http://www.investigativeproject.org/documents/case_docs/1407.pdf (accessed November 13, 2010).
39. http://freesamialarian.com/index.php?option=com_content&view=article&id=776:ninth-commemoration-of-the-political-persecution-of-professor-sami-al-arian&catid=43:2012&Itemid=100 (accessed June 30, 2012).
40. "Sami Al-Arian," *Wikipedia*, https://en.wikipedia.org/wiki/Sami_Al-Arian (accessed December 28, 2023).
41. "Sami Al-Arian," *Facebook*, https://www.facebook.com/ProfSamiAlArian/ (accessed December 28, 2023).
42. "The Israeli Genocide of Gaza; Featuring Prof. Sami Al-Arian," *YouTube*, https://www.youtube.com/live/puEVdyUJqH4?app=desktop&si=g8UxXfwVbWUBoG-9 (accessed December 28, 2023).

Victims Fight Back
The Persian Antiquities Cases (2001–2018)

6

In the 1981 film *Raiders of the Lost Ark*, professor of archaeology Indiana Jones has the following conversation with "Marcus," representative of an unidentified American museum, following Professor Jones's abortive expedition into Central America:

> "I had it, Marcus. I had it in my hand. Want to hear about it?"
> "Not at all. I'm sure everything you do for the museum conforms to the international treaties on antiquities."
> "It's beautiful, Marcus. I can get it. I've got it all figured out. There's only one place he can sell it . . . Marakesh. I need $2,000."
> Dr. Jones opens a drawer in his lab table and extracts a cloth containing several small statuettes.
> "Look," he urges them on Marcus. "They're good pieces, Marcus," he says. "They're worth at least a ticket to Marakesh."
> "Yes," Marcus replies, "the museum will buy them as usual. No questions asked." Pocketing them in his suit coat, he smiles wryly. "Yes, they are nice."

Raiders is set in the mid-1930s. Fast-forward some 60 years. On September 4, 1997, five American citizens were injured in a triple suicide bombing in a jammed pedestrian mall in Jerusalem. Joined by four family members claiming emotional harm, these terror victims in 2001 sued Iran, alleging that the perp—Hamas[1]—had received training and support from the nation formerly known as Persia.[2] Iran declined to defend itself. Six months after the suit was started, a U.S. district judge entered a default judgment in favor of the plaintiffs for $71.5 million in actual damages, plus an additional $37.5 million in punishment damages.[3]

Armed with this $109 million final judgment and faced with a defendant that was essentially judgment-proof in the United States, Jenny Rubin and eight co-plaintiffs—who, like her, had actually been injured in the blast—and their counsels began casting about for someone who could make good on the massive award. Their initial target was a fund belonging to the former Iranian embassy in Washington, safeguarded since its closing by the U.S. Treasury Department. The federal government resisted. The plaintiffs prevailed, but

DOI: 10.4324/9781003474104-6

subsequently discovered to their chagrin that an earlier judgment creditor possessed a superior lien on the money.[4]

Nothing if not persistent, the plaintiffs next went after three Iranian bank accounts in the Bank of New York.[5] The district judge awarded ownership to the Iranian banks involved in the action. The last of these initial attempts to make good their judgment was an attachment action against a piece of Iranian property near Lubbock, Texas. This was a home owned and occupied by an Iranian prince while he received fighter jet training at Reese Air Force Base. This time, the plaintiffs hit paydirt, if only a modest vein. The district judge in Amarillo issued an order directing sale of the property on the plaintiffs' behalf. On January 4, 2004, the U.S. Marshal auctioned the property for $390,000.[6] This was a start, but hardly a great victory.

Remarkably, where others might have quit, the plaintiffs came up with a list of prestigious universities and museums in Chicago, Detroit, and Boston which they hoped to raid for their winnings. Registering their judgment in federal district courts in Illinois, Massachusetts, and Michigan, they pleaded "on information and belief" that museums located in these jurisdictions held antiquities that still belonged to Persia (a.k.a. Iran).

Concentrating their attack in the Northern District of Illinois and the District of Massachusetts, the plaintiffs' primary targets included the Fields Museum of Natural History in Chicago, the Oriental Institute of the University of Chicago,[7] Boston's Museum of Fine Arts, as well as no fewer than five Harvard museums. In Massachusetts, the plaintiffs moved for an order of attachment covering "all objects . . . that are the property of the Islamic Republic of Iran" held in Harvard's Arthur M. Sackler Museum, Busch-Reisinger Museum, Fogg Art Museum, Semitic Museum, and Peabody Museum of Archaeology and Ethnology.[8]

When I first wrote about these cases in 2007,[9] none of the parties or their legal counsels was willing to talk to me, except on background. A typical response to my inquiries came from Attorney Bill Iverson of Washington (D.C.)'s Covington & Burling, co-counsel for the defendants in the case styled *Rubin v. Islamic Republic of Iran v. Museum of Fine Arts and Harvard University*.[10] "I'm sorry," Iverson responded to my email, "but because the MFA's policy is not to comment on pending litigation matters, they would prefer that I not speak to you."

Iverson, however, was kind enough to send me the MFA's official statement, which was representative of the defendants' collective stance in the matter. Originally released in March 2006, it reads,

> The Museum of Fine Arts, Boston has objects in its collection from what is modern day Iran. Most were excavated during official expeditions in the 1930s. Although sympathetic to the plaintiffs, the Museum is firmly of the conviction that these objects are the property of the museum, not Iran, and are therefore not subject to the claim asserted by the plaintiffs.

Full stop.

A 2005 story in the *Harvard Crimson*, obligingly provided by the director of Harvard's news office, Joe Wrinn—who likewise declined to speak for the record, reported, "The plaintiffs' [sic] only specifically identify a set of six limestone relief fragments from the site of Persepolis in southwestern Iran, on display on the third floor of the Sackler." The *Crimson* piece continues, "In court filings, Harvard's lawyers contend that none of the antiquities in its collections—including the six fragments in the Sackler, which were a gift from Grenville L. Winthrop, Class of 1886—are owned by Iran."[11]

The article adds that objects at the University of Pennsylvania Museum, the Philadelphia Museum of Art, the Detroit Institute of Arts, and the University of Michigan are also ultimately in the plaintiffs' gun sights.

The "current position" was not one of much comfort to the defendants. Harvard and the MFA reacted to the plaintiffs' move on their antiquities with a motion to quash the summonses and dissolve the attachments. Since these motions were based purely on the pleadings, no discovering occurred to actually determine which, if any, antiquities in any of the defendants' facilities belonged to Iran. Rather, District Judge O'Toole's September 30, 2006, decision turned upon complex issues of international law. Judge O'Toole's analysis began with the Foreign Sovereign Immunities Act (FSIA), which "defines the parameters of a foreign state's immunity in the courts of the United States." His honor concluded that any property of the state of Iran in the defendants' possession was "immune from execution and attachment unless one of the exceptions in" the FSIA applied. No such exceptions pertained here, he found. So far, so good for the museums. Ah, but that was not the end of it. The judge had more to say: "The property's immunity under the FSIA notwithstanding, the plaintiffs may still be able to obtain the antiquities pursuant to . . . the Terrorism Risk Insurance Act of 2002 [TRIA]."

Aye, there's the rub. Iran had been designated "a state sponsor of terrorism, and was therefore a 'terrorist party' as defined" under the TRIA. In that capacity, Iran's FSIA immunity evaporated. Following a winding path, which required the parsing of related executive orders that successively blocked and unblocked Iranian assets around the 1980–1981 U.S. embassy hostage crisis, Judge O'Toole decided that "if the plaintiffs are able to establish that the antiquities are indeed the property of Iran, those assets will be subject to attachment and execution pursuant to [the] TRIA."

Denying the defendants' motions, the judge added, "The other reason the . . . defendants say the summonses should be quashed is that the property in question does not belong to Iran." This, he cautioned, "is a disputed question of fact that remains to be resolved." He ordered the parties to reappear before him on October 31. Instead, the defendants responded with a motion for reconsideration by Judge O'Toole of his decision or, in the alternative, his certification of the issue up to the U.S. Court of Appeals for the Second

Circuit. The judge revisited his decision and concluded that he had been correct: the antiquities were subject to attachment.[12]

This reaffirmation of his ruling moved the case into the discovery phase. Just what Persian artifacts did the defendants hold—and who actually owned them?

6.1 The Museum of Fine Arts

Boston's MFA is one of America's oldest museums. Founded in 1870, it is surpassed only by New York City's Met in sheer size of its total collection. Writes Director Malcolm Rogers,

> If the heart of a great museum is its collections, then the MFA is truly one of the greatest in the world. The Museum offers not only outstanding art, but also innovative and exciting ways for you to interact with these masterpieces and with fellow art lovers.[13]

For more information, see "Overview of Art in the Ancient World."[14]

Drilling down into the MFA website, one can find such specific artifacts cataloged as the following.

- Mirror with paired sphinxes.
  Probably Persian, 12th–13th century Khorasan, Iran (eastern)
  Cast bronze Classification: Metalwork
  Accession number: 72.4482
- Candlestick.
  Persian, Safavid or Qajar Iran
  Steel, cut and inlaid with gold Classification: Metalwork Accession number: 77.45
- Fragment of trim from a coat.
  Persian or Mesopotamian, Sasanian, 6th to 7th century A.D. Find spot: Antinoe (excavation site), Egypt
  Place of manufacture: Iran or Mesopotamia
  Silk, twill weave with complementary wefts and inner warps (samite) Classification: Textiles
  Accession number: 04.1620[15]

6.2 The Arthur M. Sackler Museum of Harvard University

The plaintiffs had been rather particular in targeting the Sackler. Their focus was upon donations of a Harvard alumnus named Grenville L. Winthrop, who died in 1943. Perhaps ironically, Winthrop was not best known, nor is he best remembered, for the antiquities in his vast private collection. In a press release issued in 2002, when a selection of his 19th-century paintings became a traveling exhibition from Harvard's Fogg Museum, the university wrote,

> Grenville L. Winthrop (1864–1943) assembled a collection of more than 4,000 works of art that was commensurate in stature to other New York collections such as those of Pierpont Morgan, Benjamin Altman, H.O. Havermeyer, Henry Clay Frick, George and Florence Blumenthal, and Robert Lehman. Although Winthrop's interests as a collector ranged from Chinese Buddhist sculpture, to Peruvian gold, to prints by Dürer, the collection's areas of exceptional strength and depth include early Chinese works of art and 18th- and 19th-century British and French drawings, ceramics, and clocks. The Winthrop Collection's holdings of 19th-century Western works of art include 700 British, French, and American drawings, as well as 180 paintings pre-dominantly by French and British 19th-century masters as well as more than 100 sculptures. The collection's holdings of early Chinese art include one of the largest, finest, and most comprehensive collections of archaic Chinese jades, as well as bronze ritual vessels that rank among the finest in the world. Winthrop rarely loaned these works during his lifetime.[16]

Like Boston's MFA, Harvard's Sackler Museum boasts a significant collection of ancient artifacts:

> The collection of ancient art is comprised of over 24,000 works of Greek, Roman, Etruscan, Egyptian, and Near Eastern art, and includes vases, sculpture in stone, metalwork, terracottas, glass, glyptics, some wood, ivory, and bone, and a very large collection of ancient coins.[17]

Concerning the Winthrop legacy itself, the following note can be found in the July–September 1944 issue of the *American Journal of Archaeology*.

The *Journal* article indicates that one of the major events of 1943 in American archaeology was the bequest by Winthrop to Harvard's Fogg Museum. Singled out for special mention in the piece are the "Reliefs of Persepolis." Winthrop left the Fogg a total of five reliefs. These are large, elaborately carved stone slabs. They date from 359–338 BC and probably decorated a staircase. The author of the article speculates that they may date "from the time of Darius himself." He adds that they may have been a part of the décor of the "Hall of a Hundred Columns."[18]

The Indiana Jones movies may have gotten it just right. Apparently, the 1930s—despite, or perhaps because of, the global Great Depression—were an era of tomb raiders and freebooting adventurers who obtained antiquities by methods both fair and foul. Their booty found willing buyers among the wealthy, whose dollars and pounds stretched farther than ever during the severe economic downturn. Whether Winthrop's Persian reliefs fell into this category of "liberated" treasures was unclear. Crystal clear was the pinning of the plaintiffs' hopes on artifacts such as these, which are "priceless," and thus would go a long way toward satisfying their judgment if but one such trove could be connected back to modern-day Iran.

Note that while this 1944 article indicates that the reliefs were a small part of the total bequest to Harvard's Fogg Museum, the plaintiffs' pleadings place them in the Sackler. More recently, however, in conjunction with architectural alterations, the university grouped the Fogg, the Sackler, and the Busch-Reisinger Museum under the umbrella of "The Harvard Art Museum."[19]

6.3 The Field Museum

The Field Museum was incorporated by the state of Illinois on September 16, 1893, at the time of the great exhibition, as the Columbian Museum of Chicago with its stated purpose being the "accumulation and dissemination of knowledge, and the preservation and exhibition of objects illustrating art, archaeology, science and history." As such, it shares in the luster of America's first "world's fair" and the fair's cultural influences, which persist to the present day.

> The fair had a powerful and lasting impact on the nation's psyche, in ways both large and small. Walt Disney's father, Elias, helped build the White City; Walt's Magic Kingdom may well be a descendant . . . . The writer L. Frank Baum and his artist-partner William Wallace Denslow visited the fair; its grandeur informed their creation of Oz . . . . Even the Lincoln memorial in Washington can trace its heritage to the fair.
>
> The fair's greatest impact lay in the way Americans perceived their cities and their architects . . . . Other cities came to [city planner and architect] Daniel Burnham for citywide plans, . . . but he turned them down to concentrate on his last plan, for the city of Chicago. Over the years many aspects of his Chicago plan were adopted, among them the creation of the city's lovely ribbon of lakefront parks and Michigan Avenue's "Magnificent Mile." One portion of the lakefront, named Burnham Park in his honor, contains Soldier Field and the Field Museum, which he designed.[20]

It was not until 1905 that the name was changed to Field Museum of Natural History, the first half of the new moniker in honor of its first major benefactor, department store magnate Marshall Field, and the second half to better reflect its focus on the natural sciences. And it was not until 1921 that the museum moved from its original location in the Columbian Exposition's Jackson Park to its present site, as described in the preceding quotation. Today it is an important part of a lakefront "Museum Campus" that also includes the John G. Shedd Aquarium and the Adler Planetarium. These three institutions are regarded as among the finest of their kind in the world and together attract more visits annually than any rival site in Chicago.[21]

Biological and anthropological collections assembled for the Columbian Exposition form the core of the museum's collections, but these core collections have grown through worldwide expeditions, exchange, purchase, and gifts to more than 20 million specimens: "The collections form the foundation of the museum's exhibition, research and education programs, which are further informed by a world-class natural history library of more than 250,000 volumes."[22]

6.4 The Oriental Institute

The Oriental Institute

> is a research organization and museum devoted to the study of the ancient Near East. Founded in 1919 by James Henry Breasted, the Institute, a part of the University of Chicago, is an internationally recognized pioneer in the archaeology, philology, and history of early Near Eastern civilizations.[23]

Interestingly, the institute was the only defendant institution to admit early in the litigations that Iran actually did own the items at issue.

> It acknowledged the Persepolis Fortification archives and the Choga Mish materials were only on loan to the U.S. for cataloging and studying; ownership remained with the National Museum in Iran .... Thus, while the MFA could put forth a joint defense, based upon shared factual assertions, the Oriental Institute and the Field Museum found themselves arguing different positions.[24]

In May 2008, the federal district court issued the following ruling in the case involving these latter two institutions:

> Rubin is not seeking general discovery about every conceivable asset of Iran's in the United States. The only discovery requests that Iran has identified in its objection to the Magistrate Judge's order are requests for information about Persian artifacts in the possession of the Field Museum and the University of Chicago, and any disputes over the ownership of those artifacts. Thus, Iran's concerns that subjecting it to "broad-based discovery" about its assets in the United States will cause "other states worldwide ... to ignore long-standing principles of comity and sovereign immunity and issue broad assets discovery against the United States and other nations in the name of whatever policies

> the states wish to pursue" appears to be overblown. Rubin is not seeking "broad assets discovery," but rather has limited its requests to information about a discrete collection of artifacts that it believes falls within an exception to the immunity otherwise afforded a foreign sovereign's assets.
> Accordingly, Iran has identified no basis for concluding that the Magistrate Judge's order was clearly erroneous or contrary to law, and its objection is therefore overruled. Iran shall produce the requested materials no later than June 27, 2008.[25]

Following the issuance of this court order, the plaintiffs petitioned the court to amend the order, arguing that the judge had misapprehended their motion, which sought broad discovery rights with regard to Iran's U.S. assets. District Judge Blanche M. Manning responded favorably on June 23, 2008, ordering, "The remainder of the order is unaffected and Iran remains obligated to respond to the requests for discovery that were the subject of its objection, including discovery relating to its assets in the United States."[26]

Mention of Ernst Herzfeld in the judge's May 23 decision is intriguing.

> Herzfeld was born in Celle, Province of Hanover. He studied architecture in Munich and Berlin, while also taking classes in Assyriology, ancient history and art history.
> 1903–05 he was assistant to Walter Andrae in the acclaimed excavations of Assur, and later traveled widely in Iraq and Iran at the beginning of the twentieth century. He surveyed and documented many historical sites in Turkey, Syria, Persia (later Iran) and most importantly in Iraq (e.g. Baghdad, Ctesiphon). At Samara he carried out the first excavations of an Islamic period site in 1911–13. After military service during World War I he was appointed full professor for "Landes- und Altertumskunde des Orients" in Berlin in 1920. This was the first professorship for Near/Middle Eastern archaeology in the world. 1923–25 he started explorations in Persia and described many of the countries' most important ruins for the first time. In 1925 he moved to Tehran and stayed there most of the time until 1934. He was instrumental in creating a Persian law of antiquities and excavated in the Achaemenid capitals Pasargadae and Persepolis.[27]

Forced to flee Nazi Germany in 1935, this real-life Indiana Jones landed at Princeton's Institute for Advanced Study from 1936–1944. Just prior to Herzfeld's departure from Berlin to escape the Third Reich's harsh race laws, he went on an expedition on behalf of the University of Chicago. The Oriental Institute recalls it as follows:

> From the time of its barbaric destruction until A.D. 1620, when its site was first identified, Persepolis lay buried under its own ruins. During the following centuries many people traveled to and described Persepolis and the ruins of its Achaemenid palaces. Many of their observations were later condensed and

> published by George N. Curzon in *Persia and the Persian Question* (London and New York, 1892). But scholarly and scientifically planned work was not undertaken until 1931. Then Ernst Herzfeld, at that time Professor of Oriental Archaeology in Berlin, was commissioned by James H. Breasted, Director of the Oriental Institute of the University of Chicago, to undertake a thorough exploration, excavation and, if possible, restoration of the remains of Persepolis. Thus, Herzfeld, in 1931 became the first field director of the Oriental Institute's Persepolis Expeditions. In 1931–34, assisted by his architect, Fritz Krefter, he uncovered on the Persepolis Terrace the beautiful Eastern Stairway of the Apadana and the small stairs of the Council Hall. He also excavated the Harem of Xerxes. When Herzfeld left in 1934, Erich F. Schmidt took charge. He continued the large-scale excavations of the Persepolis complex and its environs until the end of 1939, when the onset of the war in Europe put an end to his archaeological work in Iran. During the last years of excavating, the University Museum in Philadelphia and the Museum of Fine Arts in Boston had joined the Oriental Institute in order to cope with the tremendous work at hand.[28]

The statement on the institute's web page that "Herzfeld left in 1934" is a classic understatement. In fact, his contract was canceled amid allegations that he had stolen some of the artifacts unearthed at Persepolis.[29] In 1944, as he planned his retirement from Princeton, Herzfeld sold artifacts. These artifacts have since been held by private parties, and Iran has proven itself vigilant in contesting their further sales. For example, in 2005, the 85-year-old alleged owner of a stone carving of a guardsman, a Frenchwoman named Denyse Berend, attempted to auction a piece through Christie's in London. Madame Berend claimed to have obtained the artifact at auction in 1974 in New York City. Iran initiated a legal action in Britain to block the sale and recover the piece.[30]

On February 1, 2007, the British judge ruled in favor of the defendant Berend.[31] After engaging in a complicated analysis of "conflict of laws" principles (not unlike what the Rubin judges had been required to do, as the decisions excerpted previously reflect) and deciding that French law ought to apply to determine ownership, Justice Eady stated,

> Naturally, if someone has obtained an artifact knowing it to have been stolen from a particular source, or suspecting it, there may well be policy reasons for placing obstacles in the way of his acquiring a good title by secret possession. Here, by contrast, the Defendant's good faith having been conceded, she had no reason to keep the fragment she had bought under wraps, nor yet even to suspect that the then government of Iran had a claim to repossess it. There was obviously no question of dissimulation on her part or of any intention to deceive. It makes no sense that innocent purchasers of such objects should be required to go on for up to 30 years advertising the fact of their possession—just in case a third party at some stage decides to assert a claim.[32]

To the extent that the U.S. district courts might have accorded any weight to Justice Eady's decision, the *Berand* case did not bode well for the Rubin plaintiffs, for even the Oriental Institute contends that Iran is not the sole owner of the artifacts at issue.[33]

6.5 2010 Developments

However, the next turn in the fortunes of their decade-long litigation roller coaster ride occurred on June 3, 2008, when the U.S. District Court in Washington (D.C.) issued an order authorizing the plaintiffs to attach Iranian property in pursuit of their massive judgment.[34] Perhaps the museums' counsels were asleep at the switch. At any rate, they fatally delayed filing a motion to intervene in the case. On September 8, 2010, District Judge Ricardo M. Urbina ruled that they were Johnny-come-latelies and that their motion was denied.[35]

III. Analysis

A. Legal Standard for a Motion to Intervene

> Federal Rule of Civil Procedure 24 sets forth the requirements for intervention as of right and permissive intervention. FED. R. CIV. P. 24; Fund for Animals, Inc. v. Norton, 322 F.3d 728, 731 (D.C. Cir., 2003). Rule 24(a) provides for intervention as of right, stating that: [o]n timely motion, the court must permit anyone to intervene who: (1) is given an unconditional right to intervene by a federal statute; or (2) claims an interest relating to the property or transaction that is the subject of the action, and is so situated that disposing of the action may as a practical matter impair or impede the movant's ability to protect its interest, unless existing parties adequately represent that interest.
>
> FED. R. CIV. P. 24(a).
>
> This Circuit has identified "four prerequisites to intervene as of right: '(1) the application to intervene must be timely; (2) the applicant must demonstrate a legally protected interest in the action; (3) the action must threaten to impair that interest; and (4) no party to the action can be an adequate representative of the applicant's interests.'" Karsner v. Lothian, 532 F.3d 876, 885 (D.C. Cir., 2008) (quoting Sec. Exch. Comm'n v. Prudential Sec. Inc., 136 F.3d 153, 156 (D.C. Cir., 1998)). In addition, an applicant must demonstrate that it has standing. Jones v. Prince George's County, Md., 348 F.3d 1014, 1017–18 (D.C. Cir., 2003).
>
> Alternatively, Rule 24(b) authorizes permissive intervention for an applicant who timely files a motion when a federal statute confers a conditional right to intervene or the applicant's claim or defense has a question of law or fact in common with the main action. FED. R. CIV. P. 24(b). In considering a motion for permissive intervention, a court must determine whether the proposed

intervention "will unduly delay or prejudice the adjudication of the rights of the original parties." *Id.*

Timeliness is a threshold question for both permissive intervention and intervention as of right. NAACP v. New York, 413 U.S. 345, 365 (1973). "Whether intervention be claimed of right or as permissive, it is at once apparent, from the initial words of both Rule 24(a) and Rule 24(b), that the application must be 'timely.' If it is untimely, intervention must be denied." Id.; see also *United States v. British Am. Tobacco Austl. Servs., Ltd.*, 437 F.3d 1235, 1238 (D.C. Cir., 2006) (holding that "[a]s a threshold matter . . . Rule 24 requires prospective intervenors to file a 'timely application'"); *Acree v. Republic of Iraq*, 370 F.3d 41, 49 (D.C. Cir., 2004) (noting that "[u]nder either [Rule 24(a) or Rule 24(b)], the prospective intervenors' motion must be 'timely'"), *abrogated on other grounds sub nom., Republic of Iraq v. Beaty*, 129 S. Ct. 2183 (2009); *Mass. Sch. of Law v. United States*, 118 F.3d 776, 783 n. 5 (D.C. Cir., 1997) (noting that "untimeliness in seeking intervention may justify its denial without consideration of the merits").

B. The Court Denies the Museums' Motion to Intervene as Untimely

The Museums assert that their motion to intervene is timely because it was filed "within the 10 business days for filing a motion for reconsideration under 59(e) and well within the 30 days permitted for filing a notice of appeal." Museums' Mot. at 6–9. The plaintiffs respond that the Museums' motion to intervene is untimely because the Museums had the opportunity to file it before the court granted the plaintiffs' motion but chose not to do so, instead submitting a letter opposing the plaintiffs' § 1083(c)(2) motion and waiting until after the motion was granted to move to intervene. Pls.' Opp'n at 17–18. They also assert that sending the letter was improper and sanctionable. Id. The Museums respond by asserting that they decided to send the letter instead of moving to intervene because they were "driven by a desire to present important arguments to the Court in as timely a fashion as possible." Museums' Reply at 5–6. They also state that they sent the letter as soon as they determined that the plaintiffs had misconstrued the NDAA because they "feared that the Court might soon rule on Plaintiffs' request . . . without the benefit of adversarial briefing." *Id.*

The timeliness of a motion to intervene "is to be judged in consideration of all the circumstances, especially weighing the factors of time elapsed since the inception of the suit, the purpose for which intervention is sought, the need for intervention as a means of preserving the applicant's rights, and the probability of prejudice to those already parties in the case." British Am. Tobacco Austl. Servs., 437 F.3d at 1238 (quoting United States v. Am. Tel. & Tel. Co., 642 F.2d 1285, 1295 (D.C. Cir., 1980)). This Circuit has, however, made clear that "[a] motion for 'intervention after judgment will usually be denied where a clear opportunity for pre-judgment intervention was not taken.'"

Associated Builders & Contractors, Inc. v. Herman, 166 F.3d 1248, 1257 (D.C. Cir., 1999) (quoting Dimond v. Dist. of Columbia, 792 F.2d 179, 193 (D.C. Cir., 1986)

In *Associated Builders*, the proposed intervenor filed a motion to intervene several weeks after the district court had ruled on the parties' cross-motions for summary judgment. 166 F.3d at 1254. In reviewing the district court's denial of the motion, the Circuit noted that the proposed intervenor "offered no reason, and no reason [was] apparent from the record, why it could not have sought intervention prior to judgment." Id. at 1257. In light of this failure, and "given the presumption that post-judgment motions to intervene will be denied," the Circuit affirmed the district court's denial of the motion, observing that "any motion for intervention must be 'timely.'" *Id.* (citing FED. R. CIV. P. 25) (emphasis added); see also *Mass. Sch. of Law*, 118 F.3d at 783 n. 5 (denying permissive intervention and holding that when "would-be intervenors . . . inexcusably neglect to try to enter the proceedings before judgment, at a time when notice of their arguments would have enabled the district court to avert the alleged errors . . . post-judgment intervention for the purpose of challenging those supposed defects on appeal would rightly be denied as untimely" (citing NAACP, 413 U.S. at 366–68)); Moten v. Bricklayers & Plasterers, 543 F.2d 224, 227–28 (D.C. Cir., 1976) (denying a motion to intervene as of right and holding that "cases in this Circuit permitting post-judgment intervention should not be controlling where clear opportunity for pre-judgment intervention . . . was not taken").

In this case, the Museums were aware long before the court granted the plaintiffs' motion in June 2008 that their interests were implicated in these proceedings. See *Catanzano v. Wing*, 103 F.3d 223, 232 (2d Cir., 1996) (noting that the relevant inquiry for determining timeliness of a motion to intervene is the point at which the proposed intervenor knew or should have known that an action could affect his interests). By February 2005, the plaintiffs had initiated attachment proceedings against the Museums in both the Northern District of Illinois and the District of Massachusetts seeking to enforce the default judgment issued in this case. See Museums' Mot. at 11; Pls.' Opp'n at 5–10. The Museums must have been aware early in the course of those proceedings that their interests were implicated in this action.

Moreover, the Museums had reason to intervene beginning on March 28, 2008, when the plaintiffs filed their motion for retroactive application of the NDAA. The Museums, however, did not move to intervene at that point, and indeed, took no action for two full months, when, instead of moving to intervene, they sent a letter to the court expressing their views on the merits of the plaintiffs' motion. See Museums' Reply at 5 n. 1. Although the Museums assert that they sent the letter as soon as they determined that the plaintiffs had misconstrued the NDAA, Museums' Reply at 5–6, they offer no explanation for why they waited two months after the plaintiffs filed their motion regarding the NDAA to raise their arguments to the court. See *generally* Museums' Mot.; Museums' Reply. Moreover, the Museums offer no explanation for why they chose to submit a letter rather than filing a motion to intervene, in which they could have referenced their substantive grounds for opposing the plaintiffs' motion and requested that the court delay ruling on the plaintiffs' motion pending resolution of the motion to intervene. See generally Museums' Mot.; Museums' Reply.

Instead, the Museums submitted a letter, with the apparent hope that the court would consider arguments submitted by a non-party to the litigation. This hope, however, was unfounded and does not justify their failure to seek formal intervention in a timely fashion. Thus, the Museums had a clear opportunity to intervene in this action prior to the resolution of the plaintiffs' motion but chose not to do so.

The Museums rely on United Airlines, Inc. v. McDonald, 432 U.S. 385, 394 (1977), to assert that motions to intervene are timely as long as they are filed within the time period for filing an appeal or seeking reconsideration. See Museums' Mot. at 6. Yet in McDonald, the post-judgment motion for permissive intervention was granted because "there was no reason for the [intervenor] to suppose that [the named plaintiffs] would not take an appeal until . . .after the trial court had entered its final judgment." McDonald, 432 U.S. at 394. Indeed, the Court noted "the critical fact" that "as soon as it became clear to the [intervenor] that the interests of the [nonparties] would no longer be protected by the named [parties], she promptly moved to intervene." Id.

In construing the holding of *McDonald*, this Circuit has required that motions to intervene be filed before the entry of judgment unless the proposed intervenor does not know until after judgment is entered that the named parties will not protect its interests. See *Smoke v. Norton*, 252 F.3d 468, 471 (D.C. Cir., 2001) (granting a post-judgment motion to intervene as of right because "the potential inadequacy of representation came into existence only at the appellate stage" [quoting Dimond, 792 F.2d at 193]); *Associated Builders*, 166 F.3d at 1257 (noting that in *McDonald*, "the necessity of intervention did not arise until after judgment had been entered" (citing *McDonald*, 432 U.S. at 393–94)). In this case, the Museums knew that intervention would be needed to protect their interests long before the plaintiffs' motion was granted, given the defendants' failure to participate at any point in this action. At the very least, the Museums must have been aware of the need for intervention when the deadline for opposing the plaintiffs' NDAA motion passed without any action from the defendants. Accordingly, the exception for post-judgment intervention set forth in *McDonald* does not apply. See *Associated Builders*, 166 F.3d at 1257 (citing *McDonald*, 432 U.S. at 393–94); *Moten*, 543 F.2d at 227–28.

The Museums also rely on *Acree v. Republic of Iraq*, 370 F.3d 41 (D.C. Cir., 2004), in which this Circuit held that the district court abused its discretion in denying a post-judgment motion to intervene. Museums' Mot. at 6. In *Acree*, however, the Circuit stated that it was making an exception to the established rule due to the "unique circumstances of [the] case,"—namely, that it was "a case with undeniable impact on the Government's conduct of foreign policy." *Acree*, 370 F.3d at 50. Indeed, the Circuit explicitly grounded its holding on the foreign policy implications of the case, stating that although "[c]ourts are generally reluctant to permit intervention after a suit has proceeded to final judgment, particularly where the applicant had the opportunity to intervene prior to judgment . . . in light of its clear foreign policy interests, the United States was entitled to intervene as of right." Id. at 49–50 *

The motion to intervene now before the court has not been brought by the United States based on its foreign policy interests in the action, but instead by a group of museums. See generally *Museums' Mot.* Moreover, the United States has already intervened in this action to assert its foreign policy interests. See *Minute Order* (July 15, 2004); see generally *United States' Motion to Quash Pls.' Writ of Attachment* (August 2, 2004). The Museums' motion to intervene, therefore, does not merit the exception that was applied in *Acree*. In short, the Museums have offered no explanation for their failure to seek intervention prior to the court's resolution of the plaintiffs' motion, despite the fact that they had a clear opportunity to do so. Accordingly, their motion to intervene is untimely and must be denied.

> * The Museums also rely on Benzman v. Whitman, 2006 WL 3771014 (S.D.N.Y., December 15, 2006). Museums' Mot. at 6. Yet *Benzman* concerned a case in which the motion to intervene had already been denied, and the motion to *reconsider* that denial was found to be timely. 2006 WL 37710014, at *1, 3. Accordingly, the Museums' reliance on *Benzman* is misplaced.

6.6 Conclusion

For the foregoing reasons, the court denies the Museums' motion to intervene and denies as moot the Museums' motion for an extension of time to appeal. An Order consistent with this Memorandum Opinion is separately and contemporaneously issued this 8th day of September, 2010.

Contemporaneously, two distinguished scholars commented:

Congress has passed ineffectual, "sound bite" antiterrorism legislation that has foisted conflicting jurisdictional mandates upon the federal courts, sucked terrorist victims into a vacuous, exhausting drama with no chance for justice, and interfered with the President's ability to conduct diplomatic relations in the Middle East. One group of victims is mired in multiple jurisdictions trying to enforce an exorbitant default judgment against the Islamic Republic of Iran by forcing auctions of antiquities collections housed in Harvard University, the Oriental Institute at the University of Chicago, the Field Museum of Natural History (Chicago), and the Museum of Fine Arts (Boston), among others. Congress in this political posturing has triggered the Department of Justice to participate in the litigation counter to the victims' interest. The victims likely feel ignored and maligned by their own President, while Congress all along was the master puppeteer of their false hopes.[36]

The case and the commentaries on it beg a much broader question.

6.6 Who Does Own Antiquity?

A more profound obstacle to the Rubin plaintiffs than the complex issues of entangled ownership of the artifacts upon which they hoped to levy their massive judgment was the weight of historical trends. A heated debate has been raging in the academy, in the art world, and in the international community of nations. On one side are those who contend that antiquities are the national heritage of the modern nations descended from the ancient empires that created the artifacts. Acquiescing to one such claim, Yale University in September 2007 agreed to return to Peru thousands of artifacts excavated at Machu Picchu in 1912. However, the transfer agreement is complicated, implicating aspects of the other side of the debate about who owns antiquity. Under the preliminary agreement, some objects were to remain at Yale's Peabody Museum of Natural History, on loan for continued study, and Yale would create a program of scholarly exchanges for at least three years' time. Furthermore, Yale and Peru would together organize a traveling exhibition of any excavated articles, and proceeds from the exhibition would go toward building a museum and research center in Cuzco. Yale would serve as the advisor.[37]

At the time, Yale president Richard C. Levin claimed, "We aim to create a world model for resolving competing interests in cultural property. This can best be achieved by building a collaborative relationship—one which involves scholars and researchers from Yale and Peru—that serves science and human understanding." [38] But then, the government of Peru changed and the incumbents accused Yale of possessing some 40,000 Machu Picchu artifacts, ten times the original estimate under discussion in 2006–2007. Peru's former first lady, Elaine Karp-Toledo, weighed in with: "I fail to understand the rationale for Yale to have any historical claim to the artifacts." The preliminary agreement, she carped, "reflects a colonial way of thinking not expected from a modern academic institution."[39] Peru changed its stance, demanding accounting for and return of all artifacts.

The problem for the Rubin plaintiffs was that they were the odd folks out. Whether one subscribes to Yale's view—i.e., antiquity is part of our human heritage—or with Peru's position that modern sovereign nations and their particular peoples are entitled to their particular pieces of the human heritage, individual tort claimants have no place in the equation.

As should be apparent, particularly from the May 2008 order reproduced in full in this chapter, the legal issues involved in these cases, as well as the evidentiary issues posed by the convoluted histories of the numerous expeditions, many remote in time, permit a court—notably the U.S. Supreme Court—to fashion whatever ruling it deems just.

6.7 Three Postscripts

As the Persian antiquity cases dragged on, in another part of the nation, another group of academic institutions was assisting the federal government in returning other antiquities to their country of origin:

ICE Returns More Than 60 Pre-Columbian Artifacts, Gold Pieces and Emeralds to Colombian Government

July 8, 2008

MIAMI—U.S. Immigration and Customs Enforcement (ICE) officials today returned more than 60 pre-Columbian artifacts to the Colombian government that were seized in 2005 following a joint investigation between ICE and the Broward Sheriff's Office (BSO).

The pre-Columbian era refers to a period preceding the exploration of the Americas by Christopher Columbus. The artifacts date as far back as 500 B.C.

ICE agents and BSO officers discovered the artifacts during the execution of three federal search warrants at various South Florida locations. The artifacts, which include ancient pottery, gold pieces and emeralds, were stolen from Colombia and illegally smuggled into the United States.

All of the artifacts were examined and authenticated by Florida International University (FIU) professor Dr. Carol Damian.

The emerald pieces, which were recovered from the Gemological Institute of America in San Diego, CA, were also studied by the University of Maine's Physics Department. The study was conducted to establish a baseline of the characteristics of the trace elements in the emeralds as measured by X-ray fluorescence to assist in the study of future pre-Columbian finds. The study determined that the measured emeralds were from the same source. Each emerald has tiny holes, which would indicate that they were drilled in order to create a necklace.

"Those who think that they can rob a nation of its cultural heritage to line their pockets are mistaken," said Anthony V. Mangione, ICE special agent-in-charge of the Office of Investigations in Miami. "We will continue working closely with our law enforcement partners and the U.S. Attorney's Office to bring these criminals to justice. Our message: These priceless items are not for sale."

"The U.S. Attorney's Office is pleased to have been involved in returning these precious artifacts to the people of Colombia," said U.S. Attorney R. Alexander Acosta. "These rare treasures of past civilizations should be enjoyed by everyone, not by a few who can pay to create private illegal collections."

"This should send a message to international criminals and looters that federal and local authorities in this country work together, whether the crimes are foreign or domestic," Sheriff Al Lamberti said.

"Colombia is proud of the cooperation that we have with the United States government and we are very happy with the repatriation of these important

> artifacts that are part of our cultural heritage," said Consul General Luis Ignacio Guzman. "We aim to keep working closely with the Department of State as well as with ICE to stop the illegal trafficking of pre-Columbian objects."
>
> ICE agents arrested and charged 66-year-old Italian national Ugo Bagnato. The U.S. Attorney's Office for the Southern District of Florida handled the prosecution of the case. Bagnato pleaded guilty to the sale and receipt of stolen goods and served 17 months in federal prison.
>
> Banato entered the country under the Visa Waiver Program, under which citizens of selected countries—including Italy—are allowed to enter the United States using a passport in lieu of a non-immigrant visa. He was deported to Italy in July 2007.[40]

My second postscript concerns the fate of the thousands of antiquities pilfered in Baghdad following the American conquest of the city in 2003. Some 7,000 pieces were believed to have been looted, while the occupying forces focused on more pressing security matters in the fallen capital. In April 2008, some 700 items—roughly 10% of what was taken—were recovered in Syria and returned to the Iraq National Museum. "This was a positive initiative taken by Syria, and we wish the same initiative to be taken by all neighboring countries," Mohammad Abbas al-Oreibi, Iraq's acting state minister of tourism and archaeology, was quoted as saying by the media. Al-Oreibi led the negotiations with Syria that led to the works' return.[41]

What does a win for Rubin and her co-plaintiffs portend? I will let the March 2010 words of one knowledgeable observer of the case close this second postscript:

> In addition to depriving Iranians of their cultural property, a decision to turn over the artifacts to the Rubin plaintiffs would have grave effects for the museums involved and cultural institutions in general. Four American institutions could be divested of objects currently in their collections and unable to use them for research purposes. In the case of the Oriental Institute, an opportunity to complete a ground-breaking research project that has been in process for over 70 years would be lost. The fallout from this case will also politicize art pieces and perhaps make countries think twice before sending their national treasures abroad for the purpose of scholarship—a potential problem for the entire museum and university community.
>
> The use of the Iranian antiquities to satisfy the Rubin judgment could also put American cultural property at risk and cause foreign policy complications for the United States. The U.S. Government has filed several statements of interest with the court expressing these concerns. On June 6, 2006 Abbas Salimi-Namin, the former head of Iran's Cultural Heritage and Tourism Organization, sent a letter to the United Nations that illustrates the potential for problems. The missive demanded the immediate return of the tablets. While the Oriental Institute had previously enjoyed a good relationship with Iran based on a shared interest

in gleaning knowledge from the tablets, the letter accused the museum of keeping the objects "on various grounds and pre-texts" and ominously suggested that if the antiquities are turned over to the terror victims, American museums with objects in Iran would "face a similar measure from Tehran."[42]

6.8 The Supreme Court Declined, Then Agreed to Intervene

In 2011, the U.S. Court of Appeals for the Seventh Circuit, sitting in Chicago, reversed the lower court's order compelling commencement of discovery regarding the ownership of the relics at issue in that particular case. The appellate panel stated,

> We now join these courts in concluding that under § 1609 of the FSIA, the property of a foreign state in the United States is presumed immune from attachment and execution. The immunity inheres in the property and does not depend on an appearance and special pleading by the foreign state itself. The party in possession of the property may raise the immunity or the court may address it sua sponte. Either way, the court must independently satisfy itself that an exception to § 1609 immunity applies before ordering attachment or other execution on foreign-state property in the United States.
> For the foregoing reasons, we REVERSE the district court's general-asset discovery order and its earlier order requiring Iran to appear and affirmatively plead § 1609 immunity, and REMAND for further proceedings consistent with this opinion.[43]

On June 25, 2012, the U.S. Supreme Court denied the plaintiffs' petition for certiorari in this case, effectively allowing the Seventh Circuit's ruling to stand.[44] The court's decision most likely was influenced by the U.S. government's position against permitting the lawsuits to proceed.[45]

In fact, it would be another six years before the Supreme Court finally put paid to the hopes of Jenny Rubin and the other plaintiffs. In 2018, the high court at long last held,

> For the foregoing reasons, we conclude that 28 U.S.C. § 1610(g) does not provide a freestanding basis for parties holding a judgment under § 1605A to attach and execute against the property of a foreign state, where the immunity of the property is not otherwise rescinded under a separate provision within § 1610. The judgment of the Seventh Circuit is affirmed.[46]

My third postscript does not concern antiquities at all. Quite the contrary, it involves the most modern of issues: whether social media platforms that permit terrorists to have access can be held liable for the dastardly deeds subsequently perpetrated by these bad actors. In 2023, the U.S. Supreme Court weighed in on this issue. The opinion being mercifully brief, I have reproduced it in its entirety.

I have included this decision here as the most recent example of the desperate—albeit creative—efforts of the victims of terrorism to obtain compensation for their and their loved ones' injuries at the hands of perpetrators who are either beyond the reach of the law's long arm or are judgment-proof (often because they died in the performance of their deadly acts of terrorism). In that broader context, this decision is appropriately included in this chapter of the book.

Reynaldo GONZALEZ, et al., Petitioners

v.

GOOGLE LLC

143 S. Ct. 1191

May 18, 2023

PER CURIAM. In 2015, ISIS terrorists unleashed a set of coordinated attacks across Paris, France, killing 130 victims, including Nohemi Gonzalez, a 23-year-old U. S. citizen. Gonzalez's parents and brothers then sued Google, LLC, under 18 U.S.C. §§ 2333(a) and (d)(2), alleging that Google was both directly and secondarily liable for the terrorist attack that killed Gonzalez. For their secondary-liability claims, plaintiffs alleged that Google aided and abetted and conspired with ISIS. All of their claims broadly center on the use of YouTube, which Google owns and operates, by ISIS and ISIS supporters.

The District Court dismissed plaintiffs' complaint for failure to state a claim, though it offered plaintiffs leave to amend their complaint. Instead, plaintiffs stood on their complaint and appealed, and the Ninth Circuit affirmed in a consolidated opinion that also addressed *Twitter, Inc.* v. *Taamneh*, --- U. S. ----, 143 S. Ct. 1206, --- L.Ed.2d ---- (2023). 2 F.4th 871 (2021). With respect to this case, the Ninth Circuit held that most of the plaintiffs' claims were barred by § 230 of the Communications Decency Act of 1996, 110 Stat. 137, 47 U.S.C. § 230(c)(1). The sole exceptions were plaintiffs' direct- and secondary-liability claims based on allegations that Google approved ISIS videos for advertisements and then shared proceeds with ISIS through YouTube's revenue-sharing system. The Ninth Circuit held that these potential claims were not barred by § 230, but that plaintiffs' allegations failed to state a viable claim in any event.

We granted certiorari to review the Ninth Circuit's application of § 230. See 598 U. S. ----, 143 S. Ct. 80, 214 L.Ed.2d 12 (2022). Plaintiffs did not seek review of the Ninth Circuit's holdings regarding their revenue-sharing claims. In light of those unchallenged holdings and our disposition of _Twitter_, on which we also granted certiorari and in which we today reverse the Ninth Circuit's judgment, it has become clear that plaintiffs' complaint—independent of § 230—states little if any claim for relief. As plaintiffs concede, the allegations underlying their secondary-liability claims are materially identical to those at issue in _Twitter_. See Tr. of Oral Arg. 58. Since we hold that the complaint in that case fails to state a claim for aiding and abetting under § 2333(d)(2), it appears to follow that the complaint here likewise fails to state such a claim. And, in discussing plaintiffs' revenue-sharing claims, the Ninth Circuit held that plaintiffs plausibly alleged neither that "Google reached an agreement with ISIS," as required for conspiracy liability, nor that Google's acts were "intended to intimidate or coerce a civilian population, or to influence or affect a government," as required for a direct-liability claim under § 2333(a). 2 F.4th at 901, 907. Perhaps for that reason, at oral argument, plaintiffs only suggested that they should receive leave to amend their complaint if we were to reverse and remand in _Twitter_. Tr. of Oral Arg. 58, 163.

We need not resolve either the viability of plaintiffs' claims as a whole or whether plaintiffs should receive further leave to amend. Rather, we think it sufficient to acknowledge that much (if not all) of plaintiffs' complaint seems to fail under either our decision in _Twitter_ or the Ninth Circuit's unchallenged holdings below. We therefore decline to address the application of § 230 to a complaint that appears to state little, if any, plausible claim for relief. Instead, we vacate the judgment below and remand the case for the Ninth Circuit to consider plaintiffs' complaint in light of our decision in _Twitter_.

It is so ordered.

Notes

1. Some plaintiffs also sued Hamas. See *Rubin v. Hamas—The Islamic Resistance Movement*, 2004 U.S. Dist. LEIX 20883. However, this action was filed only after a judgment had already been obtained against Iran. This chapter will focus on the actions against Iran.

2. *Campuzano v. Islamic Republic of Iran*, 281 F.Supp.2d 258 (D.D.C., 2003).
3. Ibid., pp. 274–277.
4. *Rubin v. Islamic Republic of Iran*, 2005 WL 670770 (D.D.C.).
5. *Bank of New York v. Rubin*, 2006 U.S. Dist. LEXIS 10215 (S.D.N.Y.), aff'd in part, vaca. in part, 484 F.3d 149 (2nd Cir., 2007). To be precise, as the case name suggests, Bank of New York initiated this action in order to resolve the competing claims to these Iranian accounts.
6. James A. Wawrzyniak Jr., "Rubin v. the Islamic Republic of Iran: A Struggle for Control of Persian Antiquities in America," *Unpublished Paper*, http://works.bepress.com/james_wawrzyniak/1/ (accessed June 8, 2008), p. 7.
7. By way of illustration, the institute is said to hold the largest collection of Persian pottery shards in America. Peggy Horton Grant, "Iranian Pottery in the Oriental Institute," *Oriental Institute News and Notes*, 142, Summer 1994, http://oi.uchicago.edu/research/pubs/nn/sum94_grant.html (accessed June 8, 2008).
8. See, e.g., Brian Boucher, "Terrorism Victims Sue for Museum Artifacts," *Art in America*, 94, September 1, 2006, p. 39; Robin Pogrebin, "An Unlikely Suit Linking Iran and a U.S. Museum Moves Forward," *New York Times*, July 18, 2006, p. E-1; Jim Castagnera, "Terror Victims Then, Museum Raiders Now," *Greentree Gazette*, January 2007, pp. 48, 74.
9. Castagnera, pp. 48, 74.
10. 456 F.Supp.2d 228, 66 Fed.R.Serv.3d 487, 214 Ed. Law Rep. 618, D. Mass., September 30, 2006 (No. Civ.A.06 11053 GAO).
11. "Bombing Victims Seek Iranian Antiquities," *Harvard Crimson*, December 19, 2005, http://www.thecrimson.com/article.aspx?ref=510726 (accessed June 8, 2005).
12. *Rubin v. Islamic Republic of Iran*, 541 F.Supp.2d 416 (D. Mass., 2008).
13. Malcolm Rogers, "Director's Welcome," *Museum of Fine Arts, Boston*, http://www.mfa.org/about/index.asp?key=4146 (accessed June 8, 2008).
14. "Overview of Art in the Ancient World," *Museum of Fine Arts, Boston*, http://www.mfa.org/collections/index.asp?key=19 (accessed June 8, 2008).
15. *Museum of Fine Arts, Boston*, http://www.mfa.org/collections/search_art.asp?coll_keywords=iran&submit.x=0&submit.y=0&coll_start=11 (accessed June 8, 2008). (This more or less random sample is reproduced here merely to provide the reader with some sense of the range of artifacts in the MFA's collection. Obviously, I offer no opinion here about whether any such artifacts or any others belong to the Republic of Iran or to the MFA or to anyone else.)
16. "Masterpieces of the 19th-Century Western Art from Harvard's Winthrop Collection to Tour London, New York, Lyon," *Press Release, Harvard University*, July 15, 2002, http://www.artmuseums.harvard.edu/press/released2002/winthrop.html (accessed June 8, 2008). With permission.
17. "Ancient and Byzantine Art and Numismatics," *Arthur M. Sackler Museum, Harvard University*, http://www.artmuseums.harvard.edu/sackler/ancient.html (accessed June 8, 2008).
18. Stephen B. Luce, "Archaeological News and Discussions," *American Journal of Archaeology*, 48, 3, July–September 1944, pp. 276, 281. With permission.

19. See http://www.artmuseums.harvard.edu/home/index.html (accessed June 8, 2008):

> Our transformation begins. After many years of academic and facilities planning, our organization is poised to undergo a major architectural transformation. This physical shift provides a rare opportunity to enact a conceptual shift as well: to clarify and create a new institutional name . . . Harvard Art Museum.

20. Erik Larson, *The Devil in the White City* (New York: Vintage Books, 2003), pp. 373–374. With permission.
21. The Field Museum, http://www.fieldmuseum.org/museum_info/default.htm.
22. Ibid.
23. The Oriental Institute of the University of Chicago, http://oi.uchicago.edu.
24. Wawrzyniak, p. 13.
25. *Rubin v. Islamic Republic of Iran*, 2008 WL 2501996 (N.D. Ill., May 23, 2008). Having previously obtained a judgment against defendant Iran in the district court for the District of Columbia, the plaintiffs ("Rubin") filed this suit seeking to execute or attach certain Iranian artifacts under Federal Rule of Civil Procedure 69. Rubin and Iran were engaged in discovery. In response to some of the requests served upon it by Rubin, Iran sought a protective order from the magistrate judge. The magistrate judge denied Iran's request for a protective order, which led Iran to file the instant objection.

    To succeed with its objection, Iran had to establish that the magistrate judge's order was "clearly erroneous or contrary to law." See Fed. R. Civ. P. 72(a). Iran identifies four points on which it contends the magistrate judge's order was clearly erroneous or contrary to law, which the court considers in turn:

    Discovery Is Not Available Under Federal Rule of Civil Procedure 69(a)

    First, Iran contends that discovery is not available under Federal Rule of Civil Procedure 69(a) because Rubin is attempting to execute a judgment under federal statutes rather than state law. Rule 69(a) reads as follows:

    > (1) Money Judgment; Applicable Procedure. A money judgment is enforcement by a writ of execution, unless the court directs otherwise. The procedure on execution—and in proceedings supplementary to and in aid of judgment or execution—must accord with the procedure of the state where the court is located, but a federal statute governs to the extent it applies.
    > (2) Obtaining Discovery. In aid of the judgment or execution, the judgment creditor or a successor in interest whose interest appears of record may obtain discovery from any person—including the judgment creditor—as provided in these rules or by the procedure of the state where the court is located. Fed. R. Civ. P. 69(a).

    According to Iran's interpretation, subsection 1 states that the procedure for executing a money judgment is provided either by (a) the law of the state where the court sits, or (b) if a federal statute applies, then the procedure for executing a money judgment is provided exclusively by the federal statute. Consistent with that interpretation, Iran contends that subsection 2 applies only if the parties are proceeding under state procedural law because if subsection 1 requires parties to proceed under a federal statute, discovery is available only if the federal statute provides for it.

The parties agree that two federal statutes apply to Rubin's attempts to execute its judgment against Iran—the Foreign Sovereign Immunities Act, see 28 U.S.C. § 1602; and the Terrorism Risk Insurance Act, see 28 U.S.C. § 1610. The FSIA places limits on executing judgment against property owned by foreign sovereigns, while the TRIA creates exceptions to the limitations imposed by the FSIA. Neither statute contains any provision that discusses a party's entitlement to discovery.

Because the FSIA and TRIA are both silent on the issue of discovery, Iran contends that Rubin is not entitled to discovery. But the FSIA and TRIA also lack any procedures for executing a judgment. Therefore, under Iran's interpretation, litigants could never execute judgments against foreign sovereigns. But such an interpretation would render meaningless those provisions of the FSIA and TRIA that make some properties subject to execution: there would be no reason to make some properties subject to execution if, in fact, nothing was subject to execution. See *McClain v. Retail Food Employers Joint Pension Plan*, 413 F.3d 582, 587 (7th Cir., 2005) (statutes should be interpreted so as not to render one part meaningless).

Iran's interpretation not only violates the rules of statutory interpretation, but is also unsupported by the text of the rule itself. Subsection 2 permits discovery in "aid of the judgment or execution." The text does not limit the availability of discovery only to those cases in which execution is proceeding under state law. Moreover, Iran has cited no authority stating that discovery is available only in cases proceeding under state law, and unavailable in cases when a federal statute limits what is subject to execution.

The court has carefully reviewed the Magistrate Judge's order, the parties' briefs, and the authorities cited in each. Based upon its review and for the reasons stated above, the court agrees with the Magistrate Judge's interpretation of Rule 69(a) and his conclusion that discovery is available in aid of execution, whether the execution proceedings are governed by state or federal law.

Discovery Regarding Chogha Mish Collection (Document Request 4 and Deposition Topic 2[a])

Next, Iran objects to the Magistrate Judge's order allowing Rubin to obtain information about the terms, conditions, nature and purpose of Iran's loan to the University of Chicago of Persian artifacts that comprise the Chogha Mish collection. Presumably, Rubin believes that details about the loan may reveal that Iran's ownership of the collection is contested, in which event the collection may be considered a "blocked asset" subject to execution under § 201 of the TRIA.

Iran identifies two reasons why the Magistrate Judge's decision was clearly erroneous or contrary to law. First, it contends that information about Iran's loan of artifacts to the University of Chicago is irrelevant because a "title contest could exist with or without a loan and regardless of the purpose and terms of that loan." (R.317 at 4.) While it is possible that Iran's loan is unrelated to any title contest, it is equally possible that the loan was the genesis of any title dispute. As Rubin pointed out in her response brief, presumably the Chogha Mish collection is in the United States rather than Iran as a result of the loan, so if a title dispute does exist, the loan would be at the heart of the dispute. Because discovery is permissible if there is "any possibility" that the information sought is relevant, the Magistrate Judge correctly concluded that Rubin is entitled to the information it requested about Iran's loan to the University of Chicago of the artifacts in the Chogha Mish collection. See Smith v. Aon Corp., No. 04 CV 6875, 2007 WL 495306, at *2 (N.D. Ill., February 14, 2007) [*internal quotation marks and cite omitted*].

Second, Iran contends that the Magistrate Judge erred by denying its request for a protective order because, at first, Rubin sought information about the loan to support its theory that the University of Chicago acted as Iran's agent, but now seeks the information to support its theory that a title dispute may exist over Iran's ownership of the collection. Iran argues that this "moving-target style of arguing should not be permitted." (R.317 at 4.) However, it offers no authority to support its argument that a discovery request should be denied if the reasons given to justify the request change. Nor has it identified any prejudice it would suffer as a result of the change in reason. Accordingly, Iran has forfeited this argument. See United States v. Useni, 516 F.3d 634, 658 (7th Cir., 2008) (undeveloped arguments unsupported by citations to authority are forfeited).

Discovery Regarding Alleged Theft of Artifacts from Iran (Documents Requests 8 & 9)

Next, Iran contends that the Magistrate Judge's order was clearly erroneous or contrary to law because it rejected Iran's request for a protective order regarding information about the University of Chicago's termination of Ernst Herzfeld, the alleged result of Herzfeld's theft of artifacts from Iran while working for the university. Iran objects to the Magistrate Judge's ruling on what appears to be two bases.

First, it contends that the requested discovery is irrelevant to the pending motion for summary judgment. However, general discovery has not been stayed pending the resolution of the motion for summary judgment. Therefore, nothing stands in Rubin's way of obtaining discovery about information relevant to the case, even if that information is not relevant to the pending motion for summary judgment.

Second, Iran contends that Rubin should direct its request about Herzfeld's termination to the University of Chicago since the university, not Iran, fired Herzfeld. However, the university's termination of Herzfeld was apparently at the behest of Iran. It is therefore conceivable that Iran has information about Herzfeld's termination and, if it does, Rubin is entitled to obtain that information.

The FSIA, the Algiers Accords, and Principles of International Comity Prohibit Discovery Regarding Iran's Assets

In addition to the arguments about specific discovery requests previously raised, Iran also argues that Rubin is generally prohibited from seeking discovery about Iran's assets. According to Iran, by ordering Iran to disclose information about its assets, the Magistrate Judge's order violates the Foreign Sovereign Immunity Act, the Algiers Accords, and principles of international comity.

Service Under the FSIA

Iran contends that discovery is prohibited under the FSIA because Rubin has not complied with the statute's terms. Specifically, Iran contends that in the District Court of Columbia, Rubin failed to properly serve it with a copy of the default judgment she obtained, the judgment upon which Rubin is now attempting to collect through the instant proceeding. Under 28 U.S.C. § 1610(c), execution of a default judgment against a foreign state may proceed only if the judgment was served in accordance with § 1608(e). Section § 1608(e) requires a default judgment to be served in the manner prescribed for service of summons and complaint as set out in § 1608(a). Section § 1608(a) sets out four methods of service in order of preference. In other words, service under the second method is available only "if service through the first method is unavailable or has proven unsuccessful." *Doe v. State of Israel*, 400 F.Supp.2d 86, 101 (D.D.C., 2005). Rubin initiated her suit against Iran in 2001 by attempting to serve Iran. The parties agree that service under the first two methods set out in § 1608(a) are unavailable because there are no agreements or treaties between the United States and Iran governing service. Therefore, Rubin first attempted service of summons and complaint through the third method under § 1608(a), service by mail, but that method did not work. As a result, Rubin relied on the fourth method, service through diplomatic channels, which succeeded.

When the time came to serve Iran with a copy of the default judgment Rubin obtained, the district court permitted Rubin to serve the judgment upon Iran through diplomatic means without first requiring it to attempt service by mail, which had previously proven unsuccessful. (R.1 at 4.) Service through diplomatic means again succeeded. See *Campuzano v. Islamic Republic of Iran*, No. 01 CV 1655, Docket Entry # 35 (D.D.C., September 13, 2004).

Iran now contends that because the methods of service in § 1608(a) are set out in order of preference, Rubin was required to attempt to serve the default judgment by mail before resorting to service through diplomatic means. However, a less preferred method of service becomes available once the more preferred method "has proven unsuccessful." Iran does not take issue with the Magistrate Judge's conclusion that service by mail was attempted but failed. Because service by mail had already "proven unsuccessful," service through diplomatic means was an acceptable alternative. In other words, Rubin was not required to engage in a futile attempt to serve by mail when service by mail had already proven to be unsuccessful, and therefore service through diplomatic means was proper.

The Algiers Accords

Next, Iran argues that the Algiers Accords prohibit the court from allowing Rubin to request discovery about any property that is the subject of a claim before the Iran–United States Claims Tribunal. Therefore, Iran contends, the Magistrate Judge erred in permitting general asset discovery, which could conceivably require Iran to disclose information about assets subject to claims before the Tribunal.

As the Magistrate Judge noted, Rubin's discovery requests merely seek information in order to segregate those assets that are subject to execution from those that are not because they are the subjects of a claim before the Tribunal. As the Supreme Court noted, the pendency of a claim before the Tribunal does not divest federal courts of jurisdiction, but rather provides to defendants a substantive defense. *Dames & Moore v. Regan*, 453 U.S. 654, 664–65, 101 S. Ct. 2972, 69 L.Ed.2d 918 (1981). Accordingly, the court may allow Rubin to obtain discovery about Iran's assets, though Iran may ultimately assert a defense based upon the Algiers Accords should Rubin attempt to pursue assets that are the subject of a claim before the Tribunal.

International Comity

Finally, Iran argues that under the FSIA, the TRIA, and principles of international comity, many of its assets are immune from attachment and, therefore, the court must guard Iran's rights as a foreign sovereign by permitting discovery about only those assets that are not immune. In support, Iran cites *Autotech Techs. LP v. Integral Research & Dev. Corp.*, 499 F.3d 737, 740 (7th Cir., 2007), in which the Seventh Circuit held that a plaintiff "must identify specific property upon which it is trying to act," and vacated a writ of execution issued by the district court that allowed the plaintiffs to seize the foreign state's assets generally. However, *Autotech* prohibits only the attachment or execution of assets described only generally; it does not purport to place similar restrictions on discovery into what assets are and are not immune from attachment or execution. In fact, it places the burden on the plaintiff to identify which assets are immune and which are amenable to attachment or execution, see id. at 750, presumably a burden that can be met only after reaping the benefits of discovery.

Moreover, Rubin is not seeking general discovery about every conceivable asset of Iran's in the United States. The only discovery requests that Iran has identified in its objection to the Magistrate Judge's order are requests for information about Persian artifacts in the possession of the Field Museum and the University of Chicago, and any disputes over the ownership of those artifacts. Thus, Iran's concerns that subjecting it to "broad-based discovery" about its assets in the United States will cause "other states worldwide . . . to ignore long-standing principles of comity and sovereign immunity and issue broad assets discovery against the United States and other nations in the name of whatever policies the states wish to pursue" appears to be overblown. Rubin is not seeking "broad assets discovery," but rather has limited its requests to information about a discrete collection of artifacts that it believes falls within an exception to the immunity otherwise afforded a foreign sovereign's assets.

Accordingly, Iran has identified no basis for concluding that the Magistrate Judge's order was clearly erroneous or contrary to law, and its objection is therefore overruled. Iran shall produce the requested materials no later than June 27, 2008.

26. *Rubin v. Islamic Republic of Iran*, 2008 WL 2502039 (N.D. Ill., June 23, 2008).
27. Wikipedia, "Ernst Herzfeld," http://en.wikipedia.org/wiki/Ernst_Herzfeld.
28. "Persepolis Terrace: Architecture, Reliefs, and Finds," *Oriental Institute of the University of Chicago*, http://oi.uchicago.edu/museum/collections/pa/persepo-lis/persepolis.html (accessed July 4, 2008). With permission.

29. Josh Gerstein, "Judge Gives Terror Victims a Victory Over Iran," *New York Sun*, May 28, 2008, http://www.nysun.com/foreign/judge-gives-terror-victims-a-victory-over-iran/78754 (accessed July 4, 2008).
30. Stephanie Condron, "Museums Face Fallout in Fight Over Carving," *Daily Telegraph*, January 17, 2007, http://www.telegraph.co.uk/news/uknews/1539637/Museums-face-fallout-in-fight-over-carving.html (accessed July 4, 2008).
31. See "Rejecting Revoi: Iran v. Berend," *Conflictoflaws.net*, http://www.conflictoflaws.net/2007/cases/rejecting-renvoi-iran-v-berend (accessed July 4, 2008).
32. *Iran v. Berend*, [2007] EWHC 132 (QB), http://www.bailii.org/ew/cases/EWHC/QB/2007/132.html (accessed July 4, 2008).
33. Wawrzyniak, *op. cit.*, note 159, p. 34.
34. *Rubin v. the Islamic Republic of Iran*, 563 F.Supp.2d 38 (D.D.C., 2008).
35. *Rubin v. Islamic Republic of Iran*, 2010 WL 3501554 (U.S.D.C., D.C., 2010); decision is accessible at http://www.leagle.com/unsecure/page.htm?shortname=infdco20100908980 and http://docs.justia.com/cases/federal/district-courts/district-of-columbia/dcdce/1:2001cv01655/14315/98/0.pdf?1284017171.
36. Kimberly DeGraaf and Jennifer Anglim Kreder, "Museums in the Crosshairs: Unintended Consequences of the War on Terror," *Duke Journal of Comparative and International Law*, http://papers.ssrn.com/sol3/papers.cfm?abstract_id=1648929 (accessed September 19, 2010). The article was forthcoming as this manuscript was being prepared. The journal can be accessed at http://www.law.duke.edu/journals/djcil. With permission.
37. James Cuno, "Antiquity Belongs to the World: Archaeology Must Be Shielded from Nationalistic Laws and Politics," *Chronicle of Higher Education*, July 4, 2008, p. B-6.
38. "Yale to Return Peruvian Artifacts," *BBC News*, September 17, 2007, http://news.bbc.co.uk/1/hi/world/americas/6998408.stm (accessed July 12, 2008).
39. Elaine Karp-Toledo, "The Lost Treasure of Machu Picchu," *New York Times*, February 23, 2008, http://www.nytimes.com/2008/02/23/opinion/23karp-toledo.html?n=Top/Reference/Times%20Topics/Organizations/N/National%20Geographic%20Society (accessed July 12, 2008).
40. Available at http://www.ice.gov/pi/nr/0807/080708miami.htm?searchstring=SEVIS%20AND%20enforcement%20OR%20prosecution (accessed August 10, 2008).
41. "Looted Antiquities Found in Syria Returned to Baghdad Museum," *CBC News*, April 27, 2008, http://www.cbc.ca/arts/artdesign/story/2008/04/27/iraq-museum.html (accessed October 12, 2008).
42. Alix McKenna, "Iran's Cultural Heritage under Threat," *California Literary Review*, March 22, 2010, http://calitreview.com/7851 (accessed November 13, 2010). With permission.
43. *Rubin v. Islamic Republic of Iran*, 637 F.3d 783 (7th Cir., 2011).
44. *Rubin v. Iran*, — S. Ct. —, 2012 WL 2368717 (U.S. 2012).
45. The Obama administration's amicus brief is accessible at http://sblog.s3.amazonaws.com/wp-content/uploads/2012/05/11-431-CVSG.pdf.
46. *Rubin v. Islamic Republic of Iran*, 583 U.S. 202, 138 S.Ct. 816 (2018).

At the Tipping Point on the Scales of Justice

7

National Security vs. Civil Liberties (When a U.S. Citizen is Declared an Unlawful Enemy Combatant)

7.1 Introduction: The Laws of War, War Crime Trials, and Combatants' Rights

Within a month of the 9/11 terrorist attacks, America was in Afghanistan. As Kabul was cleared and al Qaeda/Taliban forces driven into the vast, rocky hinterlands, or across the ambiguous border between Afghanistan and Pakistan—the so-called tribal regions—U.S. forces netted a motley mass of Arabs, Afghans, and even the odd American or other Western freebooter. What to do with this motley crew?

The rules of warfare are old, but not ancient.

> Constraints on war as we have experienced them in our own societies have been largely shaped by Christian ethic defined by leading teachers in the Catholic church of the Middle Ages and the Renaissance, an ethic transformed in the seventeenth and eighteenth centuries into something more rationalistic and utilitarian by such early international lawyers as the Dutchman Hugo Grotius and the Swiss Emerich de Vattel, and made increasingly specific by international agreements such as the Hague and Geneva Conventions in the nineteenth and twentieth centuries.[1]

The Allied victory in 1945, and the subsequent discovery of death camps in Germany, Poland, and other Nazi-controlled territories, resulted in an unprecedented series of trials at Nuremburg and, less notably, elsewhere. Article 1 of the Charter of the International Military Tribunal stated,

> In pursuance of the Agreement signed on the eighth day of August 1945 by the Government of the United States of America, the Provisional Government of the French Republic, the Government of the United Kingdom of Great Britain and Northern Ireland, and the Government of the Union of Soviet Socialist

DOI: 10.4324/9781003474104-7

> Republics, there shall be established an International Military Tribunal (hereafter called "the Tribunal") for the just and prompt trial and punishment of major war criminals of the European Axis.[2]

Who were these criminals? In the words of Professor Douglas O. Linder of the University of Missouri,

> Those who come to the trials expecting to find sadistic monsters are generally disappointed. What is shocking about Nuremberg is the ordinariness of the defendants: men who may be good fathers, kind to animals, even unassuming—yet committed unspeakable crimes. Years later, reporting on the trial of Adolf Eichmann, Hannah Arendt wrote of "the banality of evil." Like Eichmann, most Nuremberg defendants never aspired to be villains. Rather, they either over identified with an ideological cause or suffered from a lack of imagination: they couldn't fully appreciate the human consequences of their career-motivated decisions.[3]

Doctors, judges, even artists and entertainers were tried, along with the leading military and political leaders of the Third Reich. Indictments included such counts as the following.

- Conspiracy to wage aggressive war.
- Waging aggressive war.
- Traditional war crimes, such as mistreatment of prisoners and unleashing of outlawed weapons.
- Crimes against humanity (most radical of all).[4]

Some 25 of the worst Nazis were found guilty and sentenced to death. Dozens of lesser lights from in and around the Thousand-Year Reich received varying prison terms. Some, such as the controversial filmmaker Leni Riefenstahl, were detained but released or acquitted.

Meanwhile, selected Japanese leaders also were tried for war crimes. Though these cases have never commanded the same attention as Nuremberg,[5] the Japanese trials resulted in a seminal U.S. Supreme Court decision.[6]

General Tomoyuki Yamashita was the commanding general of the Fourteenth Army Group of the Imperial Japanese Army in the Philippine Islands, until September 3, 1945. On that date, he surrendered to and became a prisoner of war of the U.S. Army forces in Baguio, Philippine Islands. On September 25, by order of Lt. Gen. Wilhelm D. Styer, commanding general of the U.S. Army forces, Western Pacific, whose command embraced the Philippine Islands, Yamashita was served with a charge prepared by the Judge Advocate General's Department of the Army, purporting to charge him with a violation of the laws of war. On October 8, 1945, Yamashita, after pleading not guilty to the charge, was held for trial before a military commission of five army officers appointed by order of Lt. Gen. Styer. The order appointed six army officers, all lawyers, as defense counsel.

On the same date, the prosecution filed a bill of particulars and the commission heard a motion made on Yamashita's behalf to dismiss the charge on the ground that it failed to state a violation of the laws of war. On October 29, the commission was reconvened, a supplemental bill of particulars was filed, and the motion to dismiss was denied. The trial then proceeded until its conclusion on (perhaps ominously for the defendant) December 7, 1945. The commission heard 286 witnesses, who gave more than 3,000 pages of testimony. On that date, Yamashita was found guilty as charged and sentenced to death by hanging.[7] Yamashita challenged the military tribunal's power to impose this fate upon him. His appeal reached America's highest court.

The Supreme Court's majority opinion characterized Yamashita's habeas corpus claims as follows:

> The petitions for habeas corpus set up that the detention of petitioner for the purpose of the trial was unlawful for reasons which are now urged as showing that the military commission was without lawful authority or jurisdiction to place petitioner on trial, as follows:
>
> (a) That the military commission which tried and convicted petitioner was not lawfully created, and that no military commission to try petitioner for violations of the law of war could lawfully be convened after the cessation of hostilities between the armed forces of the United States and Japan;
> (b) that the charge proffered against petitioner fails to charge him with a violation of the law of war;
> (c) that the commission was without authority and jurisdiction to try and convict petitioner because the order governing the procedure of the commission permitted the admission in evidence of depositions, affidavits and hearsay and opinion evidence, and because the com- mission's rulings admitting such evidence were in violation of the 25th and 38th Articles of War (10 U.S.C. ss 1496, 1509, 10 U.S.C.A. ss 1496, 1509) and the Geneva Convention (47 Stat. 2021), and deprived petitioner of a fair trial in violation of the due process clause of the Fifth Amendment;
> (d) that the commission was without authority and jurisdiction in the premises because of the failure to give advance notice of petitioner's trial to the neutral power representing the interests of Japan as a belligerent as required by Article 60 of the Geneva Convention, 47 Stat. 2021, 2051.[8]

Writing for the majority, Chief Justice Stone denied Yamashita's petition, holding,

> It . . . appears that the order convening the commission was a lawful order, that the commission was lawfully constituted, that petitioner was charged with violation of the law of war, and that the commission had authority to proceed with the trial, and in doing so did not violate any military, statutory or constitutional command. We have considered, but find it unnecessary to discuss other contentions that we find to be without merit. We therefore conclude that the detention of petitioner for trial and his detention upon his conviction, subject to the prescribed review by the military authorities were lawful, and that the petition for certiorari, and leave to file in this Court petitions for writs of habeas corpus and prohibition should be, and they are.[9]

Writing eloquently and (presciently) in dissent, Justice Murphy predicted,

> In my opinion, such a procedure is unworthy of the traditions of our people or of the immense sacrifices that they have made to advance the common ideals of mankind. The high feelings of the moment doubtless will be satisfied. But in the sober afterglow will come the realization of the boundless and dangerous implications of the procedure sanctioned today. No one in a position of command in an army, from sergeant to general, can escape this future. Indeed, the fate of some future President of the United States and his chiefs of staff and military advisers may well have been sealed by this decision. But even more significant will be the hatred and ill-will growing out of the application of this unprecedented procedure. That has been the inevitable effect of every method of punishment disregarding the element of personal culpability. The effect in this instance, unfortunately, will be magnified infinitely for here we are dealing with the rights of man on an international level. To subject an enemy belligerent to an unfair trial, to charge him with an unrecognized crime, or to vent on him our retributive emotions only antagonizes the enemy nation and hinders the reconciliation necessary to a peaceful world.[10]

In fact, two decades later, a U.S. Army lieutenant's trial fulfilled Justice Murphy's prophecy. Lt. William L. Calley Jr. was charged on September 5, 1969, under the Uniform Code of Military Justice,[11] with the premeditated murder on March 16, 1968, of no fewer than 102 Vietnamese civilians at My Lai hamlet, Song My village, Quang Ngai province, Republic of South Vietnam. His trial by general court-martial began on November 12, 1970, at Fort Benning, Georgia, and the court members received the case on March 16, 1971. (The function of court members in a military court-martial is substantially equivalent to that of jurors in a civil court.) On March 29, the court-martial, whose members consisted of six Army officers, found Calley guilty of the premeditated murder of no fewer than 22 Vietnamese civilians of undetermined age and sex, and of assault with intent to murder one Vietnamese child. Two days later, on March 31, the court members sentenced Calley to dismissal from the service, forfeiture of all pay and allowances, and confinement at hard labor for life. On August 20, the convening authority, the commanding general of Fort Benning, Georgia, approved the findings and sentence, except as to the confinement period that was reduced to 20 years. The Army Court of Military Review then affirmed the conviction and sentence.[12] The U.S. Court of Military Appeals granted a petition for review as to certain of the assignments of error, and then affirmed the decision of the Court of Military Review.[13] The Secretary of the Army reviewed the sentence as required by Article 71(b), U.C.M.J., 10 U.S.C. s. 871(b), approved the findings and sentence, but in a separate clemency action commuted the confinement portion of the sentence to ten years. On May 3, 1974, President Richard Nixon notified the Secretary of the Army that he had reviewed the case and determined that he would take no further action in the matter. At this state of his case, Calley, like Yamashita 25 years earlier, launched a habeas corpus attack on his conviction. The case worked its way up the federal court system to the U.S. Court of Appeals for the Fifth Circuit.[14] The Fifth Circuit ruled:

- Court-martial convictions are subject to review by the federal civil courts on petitions for habeas corpus when it is asserted that the court-martial acted without jurisdiction, or that substantial constitutional rights have been violated, or that there was a fundamental error resulting in miscarriage of justice.
- Pretrial publicity in the case at hand did not deprive the defendant of a fair trial.
- There was no error in failing to subpoena the Secretaries of Defense and the Army, or the Army Chief of Staff, in the absence of a colorable showing in support of the defense team's speculation that such persons might have influenced the outcome of the case.
- In light of the extensive discovery available to the defendant, there was no denial of due process in the failure of Congress to provide him with testimony that various witnesses gave before a congressional subcommittee and which was equally unavailable to the prosecution.
- Any violation of the Jencks Act[15] with respect to such testimony was not of constitutional dimension.
- The court-martial specifications against the defendant, as amplified in the bill of particulars, met constitutional requirements with respect to notice and double jeopardy.

It is in the context of this history that the fate of the combatants captured in Afghanistan, and less than two years later in Iraq, must be viewed.

7.2 Children of a Lesser God? Second-Class Citizens and Unlawful Enemy Combatants

The rights of American citizens in the face of international and domestic terrorism present issues more complex than many of us would have anticipated 20 or so years go. The Fourteenth Amendment to the U.S. Constitution[16] was adopted on July 9, 1868. A natural corollary to the Thirteenth Amendment, which abolished slavery, the Fourteenth accorded U.S. citizenship under extremely generous terms: "All persons born or naturalized in the United States, and subject to the jurisdiction thereof, are citizens of the United States and of the State wherein they reside." The Congressional purpose was to ensure the citizenship of the newly emancipated African slaves. In the century and a half since it was adopted, the amendment's first sentence has had unintended consequences. For example, children born to illegal immigrants have all the rights of U.S. citizens, a reality that stands at the center of a divisive national debate.[17]

Section 1 goes on to state, "No State shall make or enforce any law which shall abridge the privileges or immunities of citizens of the United States; nor shall any State deprive any person of life, liberty, or property, without due process of law; nor deny to any person within its jurisdiction the equal protection of the laws." These words may well be among the most important, after the first ten amendments (the Bill of Rights) of the Constitution, insofar as civil liberties are concerned. They also are among the most heavily litigated.

Although a plain reading of the "equal protection" and "due process" clauses of the amendment may seem straightforward, in fact not all U.S. citizens have been treated equally under either state or federal law, nor have all persons always been accorded due process of law. For a century after the Civil War freed the slaves, African-Americans were denied de jure their civil rights, and even in the 60 years since the passage of the 1963 Voting Rights Act and the 1964 Civil Rights Act, African-Americans continue to confront inequality, especially in the economic arena.

Citizens by default, such as children of illegal aliens, are viewed by many to be citizens of a lesser god.

> Republicans are pushing for congressional hearings to consider changing the nation's 14th Amendment to deny such children the automatic citizenship the Constitution guarantees. They say [some alien] women are taking advantage of the constitutional amendment and paint a picture of pregnant women rushing across the border to give birth.[18]

Concurrent with this urge to curb citizenship by chance or convenience came, in our post-9/11 nation, a rediscovery of the concept of unlawful enemy combatant. While some incorrectly ascribe this term to the Patriot

Act or other post-9/11 legislation, in fact it dates back to a 1942 U.S. Supreme Court decision, *ex parte Quirin*,[19] a case involving German sabateurs.[20] The high court held:

> The law of war draws a distinction between the armed forces and the peaceful populations of belligerent nations and also between those who are lawful and unlawful combatants. Lawful combatants are subject to capture and detention as prisoners of war by opposing military forces. Unlawful combatants are likewise subject to capture and detention, but in addition they are subject to trial and punishment by military tribunals for acts which render their belligerency unlawful. The spy who secretly and without uniform passes the military lines of a belligerent in time of war, seeking to gather military information and communicate it to the enemy, or an enemy combatant who without uniform comes secretly through the lines for the purpose of waging war by destruction of life or property, are familiar examples of belligerents who are generally deemed not to be entitled to the status of prisoners of war, but to be offenders against the law of war subject to trial and punishment by military tribunals.

7.3 Enter Jose Padilla

Brooklyn-born Jose Padilla grew up in Chicago, where he joined a Latino gang, the Latin Disciples, and accrued an arrest record. Convictions included aggravated assault and manslaughter as a juvenile, when a rival gang member kicked in the head by Padilla subsequently died.[21]

In 1991, after the 21-year-old Padilla and his family relocated to South Florida, he was arrested for discharging a pistol at another driver in a road rage incident. The crime was just one of a lengthening list, and it landed Padilla back in jail that October. This time, however, his incarceration had a profound impact on the young Latino. In prison, he discovered Islam. Released, he sought out Muslims, who were relatively plentiful in South Florida. In 1994, he formally converted, legally changing his name to Ibrahim. In 1998, Padilla suddenly left his wife and moved to a suburb of Cairo, Egypt, ostensibly to learn Arabic. For years he had worn a red and white kaffiyeh, or headdress, expensive clothing, and jewelry, and he claimed that "friends" interested in his education sponsored his traveling. Once in Egypt, and using the name Abdullah al-Muhajir, he immersed himself in the extremist underground. He eventually moved to Pakistan for further study and, like so many other militants, married the widow of a jihadist. In 2001, he met with Abu Zubaydah for the first time. Padilla met with him again in the spring of 2002, at which time he allegedly proposed his nuclear bomb idea.[22] In March 2002, Zubaydah was captured in Pakistan. Cross-referencing information he provided with other intelligence data, the CIA came up with Padilla. FBI agents trailed Padilla on a connecting flight from Zurich to Chicago, and when he landed in Chicago, they took him to a secondary screening room and arrested him. The FBI attempted and failed to build a case against him for a month, and one day before he was to be released under laws protecting U.S. citizens against indefinite detention, President George W. Bush approved Padilla's reclassification as an enemy combatant. He was then transferred to a South Carolina naval base.[23]

Padilla obtained counsel, who challenged his indefinite incarceration. The case could hardly have been more significant, given that, unlike the detainees in the Iraqi and Cuban facilities, Padilla was a U.S. citizen. Was it possible in our brave new post-9/11 world that an American could be detained indefinitely without a trial, without a conviction, without a sentence?

Padilla's attorneys filed a habeas corpus petition with the U.S. District Court for the Southern District of New York, sitting in Manhattan. Judge Michael Mukasey denied the government's motion to dismiss the petition[24] and subsequently declined to reconsider his determination.[25] He finally certified the controversy as ripe for an interlocutory appeal[26] on the following half a dozen questions.

1. Is the Secretary of Defense, Donald Rumsfeld, a proper respondent in this case?
2. Does this court have personal jurisdiction over Secretary Rumsfeld?
3. Does the President have the authority to designate as an enemy combatant an American citizen captured within the United States, and, through the Secretary of Defense, to detain him for the duration of armed conflict with al Qaeda?
4. What burden must the government meet to detain petitioner as an enemy combatant?
5. Does petitioner have the right to present facts in support of his habeas corpus petition?
6. Was it a proper exercise of this court's discretion and its authority under the All Writs Act to direct that petitioner be afforded access to counsel for the purpose of presenting facts in support of his petition?[27]

The U.S. Court of Appeals handed the Bush administration a significant defeat. First, the appeals panel ruled that lead counsel Donna R. Newman had sufficient ties to the plaintiff to justify her standing to come into court and represent him, notwithstanding his being held incommunicado at the time. The judges applied the following two-pronged test enunciated by the Supreme Court for just such habeas corpus cases when the plaintiff is unavailable.

> Decisions applying the habeas corpus statute have adhered to at least two firmly rooted prerequisites for "next friend" standing. First, a "next friend" must provide an adequate explanation—such as inaccessibility, mental incompetence, or other disability—why the real party in interest cannot appear on his own behalf to prosecute the action. Second, the "next friend" must be truly dedicated to the best interests of the person on whose behalf he seeks to litigate, and it has been further suggested that a "next friend" must have some significant relationship with the real party in interest. The burden is on the "next friend" clearly to establish the propriety of his status and thereby justify the jurisdiction of the court.[28]

In this instance, concluded the court,

> There is no dispute that Padilla is unable to file a petition on his own behalf—he is being held incommunicado. Similarly, there is no issue as to Newman's professional relationship with Padilla. As a member of the bar, she is, of course, duty-bound to represent Padilla and to protect his interests zealously and within the bounds of the law. See N.Y. Code Prof. Resp. DR 7–101. Newman was assigned to represent Padilla when he was first brought into the Southern District and, before his transfer to military custody, she had begun to advise Padilla about the legal implications of his apprehension and confinement. From May 15 to June 9, 2002, she met with him in an effort to vacate the material witness warrant and to secure his release. She filed motions on his behalf that attacked the legal basis of his confinement, met with his family and appeared in court with him. Moreover, she was perhaps the only person aware of his wishes when he was taken into custody by the DOD, and nothing in the record before us has called into question her suitability to pursue those wishes. Finally, she has continued ably to represent him and indeed she, with others, argued this appeal on his behalf. We find this relationship to be a significant one, notwithstanding its duration. We also find it one in which Newman is neither an "intruder" nor an "uninvited meddler," Whitmore, 495 U.S. at 164, 110 S.Ct. 1717, and, consequently, we conclude that the District Court properly approved Newman as Padilla's next friend.[29]

Absent this determination, American citizens in Padilla's predicament might have been left with a right (to counsel) without a remedy when they have been dropped into deep, dark holes, as was he.

The Second Circuit then considered the significance to the case of the Non-Detention Act, which states, "No citizen shall be imprisoned or otherwise detained by the United States except pursuant to an Act of Congress."[30] Determining at the threshold that the act applies to military detentions, the judges went on to review the relevant Congressional history surrounding the various forms of authority it had accorded President George W. Bush following the 9/11 attacks. The court concluded,

> The War Powers Resolution requires the President to cease military operations within 60 days unless Congress has declared war or specifically authorized the use of the armed forces. 50 U.S.C. §1544(b). It is unlikely—indeed, inconceivable—that Congress would expressly provide in the Joint Resolution an authorization required by the War Powers Resolution but, at the same time, leave unstated and to inference something so significant and unprecedented as authorization to detain American citizens under the Non-Detention Act.[31]

The court advised the administration,

> The offenses Padilla is alleged to have committed are heinous crimes severely punishable under the criminal laws. Further, under those laws the Executive has the power to protect national security and the classified information upon which it depends. See, e.g., 18 U.S.C. app. § 3. And if the President believes this authority to be insufficient, he can ask Congress—which has shown its responsiveness—to authorize additional powers. To reiterate, we remand to the District Court with instructions to issue a writ of habeas corpus directing the Secretary of Defense to release Padilla from military custody within 30 days. The government can transfer Padilla to appropriate civilian authorities who can bring criminal charges against him. Also, if appropriate, Padilla can be held as a material witness in connection with grand jury proceedings. In any case, Padilla will be entitled to the constitutional protections extended to other citizens.[32]

The government appealed and the Supreme Court agreed to review the case.[33] In mid-2004, the Court rendered its decision.[34] The majority held that the proper defendant in the case was the commanding officer of the Navy brig where Padilla was being held. On its way to this holding, the court recited the relevant facts as follows:

> Respondent Padilla, a United States citizen, was brought to New York for detention in federal criminal custody after federal agents apprehended him while executing a material witness warrant issued by the District Court for the Southern District of New York (Southern District) in connection with its grand jury investigation into the September 11, 2001, al Qaeda terrorist attacks. While his motion to vacate the warrant was pending, the President issued an order to Secretary of Defense Rumsfeld designating Padilla an "enemy combatant" and directing that he be detained in military custody. Padilla was later moved to a Navy brig in Charleston, S.C., where he has been held ever since. His counsel then filed in the Southern District a habeas petition under 28 U.S.C. §2241, which, as amended, alleged that Padilla's military detention violates the Constitution, and named as respondents the President, the Secretary, and Melanie Marr, the brig's commander. The Government moved to dismiss, arguing, inter alia, that Commander Marr, as Padilla's immediate custodian, was the only proper respondent, and that the District Court lacked jurisdiction over her because she is located outside the

> Southern District. That court held that the Secretary's personal involvement in Padilla's military custody rendered him a proper respondent, and that it could assert jurisdiction over the Secretary under New York's long-arm statute, notwithstanding his absence from the District. On the merits, the court accepted the Government's contention that the President has authority as Commander in Chief to detain as enemy combatants citizens captured on American soil during a time of war. The Second Circuit agreed that the Secretary was a proper respondent and that the Southern District had jurisdiction over the Secretary under New York's long-arm statute. The appeals court reversed on the merits, however, holding that the President lacks authority to detain Padilla militarily.[35]

Holding that Padilla and Newman had named the wrong defendant, the court reversed without ever reaching the substantive issue of whether the president had the power to put Padilla in the pokey in the first place!

7.4 The Litigation Carnival Moves South

Padilla's indefatigable attorneys refiled their case in South Carolina, where the U.S. District Court came down in their favor, holding in February 2005, "(1) Congress did not authorize prisoner's indefinite detention without trial, and (2) President's inherent constitutional powers did not allow him to subject prisoner to indefinite military detention."[36] Keeping the litigation roller coaster ride in motion, the Fourth Circuit held that the president possessed authority, pursuant to Authorization for Use of Military Force (AUMF), to detain an enemy combatant. In so holding, the court concluded,

> The Congress of the United States, in the Authorization for Use of Military Force Joint Resolution, provided the President all powers necessary and appropriate to protect American citizens from terrorist acts by those who attacked the United States on September 11, 2001. As would be expected, and as the Supreme Court has held, those powers include the power to detain identified and committed enemies such as Padilla, who associated with al Qaeda and the Taliban regime, who took up arms against this Nation in its war against these enemies, and who entered the United States for the avowed purpose of further prosecuting that war by attacking American citizens and targets on our own soil—a power without which, Congress understood, the President could well be unable to protect American citizens from the very kind of savage attack that occurred four years ago almost to the day.[37]

In January 2006, responding to petitions filed by both sides, the Supreme Court ordered Padilla to be transferred from the Navy brig to a federal prison in Florida.[38] Padilla was indicted on three criminal counts. The indictment was the starting bell for months of pretrial motions and maneuvers.

7.5 Padilla's Pretrial Perambulations

For starters, Padilla's attorneys challenged the counts in the indictment. Initially, they experienced success with the trial judge. The first of the three counts, conspiracy to murder, was dismissed on August 16, 2006, on the grounds that it was duplicative of the other two counts pending against him. The second count was conspiracy to materially aid terrorists under 18 U.S.C. §371. The third was providing material support to terrorists, 18 U.S.C. §2339A. The trial court ordered that the government elect a single criminal statute in its second count of the indictment. The government appealed.

The U.S. Court of Appeals for the Eleventh Circuit—becoming the third federal appeals court to play a part in Padilla's unending case—reviewed the trial judge's decision and held that, as to Padilla and four co-defendants in his criminal case, the indictment's three counts were not duplicative and therefore did not violate the Constitution's double-jeopardy prohibition.[39]

The Eleventh Circuit announced this decision on January 30, 2007. Less than a month later, in February, on the defendant's motion, the trial court held a competency hearing. Dr. Angela Hagerty, a psychiatrist hired by defense counsel, testified that 22 hours of interviews with Padilla had persuaded her that he was not competent to stand trial. Her diagnosis included post-traumatic stress disorder[40] and Stockholm syndrome, both resulting from his long incarceration and lengthy interrogations. Dr. Hagerty concluded, "It's my opinion that he lacks the capacity to assist counsel. He has a great deal of difficulty talking about the current case before him."[41]

Dr. Hagerty's testimony did not hold up well on cross-examination, and it was contradicted by the government's own expert. At long last, on May 15, 2007—some five years following his arrest—Jose Padilla's three-month-long trial began.

7.6 Padilla's Trial and Post-Trial Proceedings

In contrast to several of the preceding chapters, where I've delved in some depth into the trial proceedings, Padilla's criminal trial, though protracted, came as an anticlimax to the five years of litigation and appellate practice preceding it. The district, appellate, and Supreme Court decisions discussed in some detail in this chapter wrote the latest—and perhaps most significant—chapter in the rapidly developing legal principles regarding war, war crimes, and enemy combatants in U.S. jurisprudence.

Padilla and his alleged co-conspirators—Islamic extremists with whom he was accused of conspiring to commit such crimes as murder and kidnapping—were all found guilty by the federal jury. His four co-conspirators received sentences, ranging from 15 years at the high end to a paltry eight months at the low. Padilla got the brass ring: He was sentenced on January 22, 2008, to 17 years and four months in federal prison.[42]

Without missing a beat, some two weeks prior to his sentencing, Padilla and his mother filed a civil action in the U.S. District Court for Northern California, claiming damages for his alleged subjection to torture. Creatively, Padilla named as the sole defendant John Yoo, the former official in the U.S. Department of Justice who became known for his leading role in providing legal guidance to the George W. Bush administration on the use of torture techniques.[43] Padilla contended that Yoo's infamous torture memorandum was a cause of the alleged acts of torture to which Padilla claimed to have been subjected. On January 12, 2009, the federal judge denied Yoo's motion to dismiss, allowing the civil case to continue.[44]

Commenting on the court's ruling, Attorney Jonathan Turley, who represented Sami Al-Arian (see Chapter 5), blogged that the ruling made it possible for Padilla to:

> sue University of California Professor John Yoo for the violation of his rights due to his physical abuse as a detainee. It is a relatively novel ruling that holds that government lawyers must be treated as other officials in participating in illegal programs or policies.[45]

In another scathing blog, Turley wrote: "Jose Padilla's case remains one of the most disturbing in U.S. history. After President Bush stripped him of his constitutional rights and held him without charge, he was subjected to cruel conditions and denied access to the courts and counsel." Turley contended that this abuse had gone on for years with the public's knowledge, with Padilla's freedom being thwarted at every turn and his rights illegally denied. Finally:

> Ultimately, the Justice Department charged Padilla on crimes entirely unrelated to the original alleged crime: planning a possible nuclear attack on a major city. That was the sensational allegation trumped by John Ashcroft at an infamous press conference—forcing the White House to later retract Ashcroft's statements.[46]

In yet another blog—December 9, 2009—Attorney Turley's comments bring this chapter full circle. The title of his article was "Nuremberg Revisited: Obama Administration Files to Dismiss Case against John Yoo." Commenting on the administration's filing with the Ninth Circuit, Turley said that the Obama administration had "gutted the victories in Nuremberg, where lawyers and judges were often guilty of war crimes in their legal advice and opinions."[47] Turley explained that one of the 12 trials for war crimes involved 16 German jurists and lawyers, nine of whom were officials of the Reich Ministry of Justice, and the others prosecutors and judges of the Special

Courts and People's Courts of Nazi Germany. He also noted that two lawyers, Adolf Georg Thierack and Carl Westphal, committed suicide before the trial could even commence.

7.7 Conspiracy Theories

As in some of the earlier chapters of this book, let me conclude with a passing nod to the ubiquitous conspiracy theorists. In this instance, the leading theory harked back to Chapter 2 and the Oklahoma City bombing of 1995. You will recall from that chapter that the existence—and, if he existed, the identity—of John Doe 2 became a hallmark of Timothy McVeigh's defense. It also became the source of wild speculation.

I suppose it was inevitable that Jose Padilla's name would surface in that sea of speculation, swirling in the blogosphere. One blogger, on a site aptly entitled whatreallyhappened.com, opined at the height of the litigation to get Padilla a trial in open court:

> OK City happened between the time Jose was released from prison but before he left the country. If Jose is the operative that the FBI worked so hard to persuade everyone did not exist, then this would explain why the Government has backed off from the 'Dirty bomb' story so quickly, why Jose is being held in secret and not even his attorney is allowed to speak with him.[48]

The "logic" of this theory runs as follows:

> Padilla is an American citizen, he OBVIOUSLY speaks 'American', he gets hooked up with a gang in South Florida so he MUST have 'learned' a Hispanic dialect, he BECOMES a Muslim and goes overseas to one of the 'Terror States', etc and is befriended by the folks there so he MUST have 'learned' Pushtun, Urdu or one of the other dialects mixed in with 'American'. Just how many languages does this man speak? Are we being duped again into thinking this is another 'under-educated minority' who just happens to know how to search the net and find enough data to build a so-called 'Dirty Bomb' and then set it off at the behest of his handlers? There is more to this than meets the eye as anyone who knows languages can tell you that Pushtun, Urdu and the other dialects spoken overseas are not easily picked up in the ghettos of Chicago or South Florida in a few weeks or months, it takes years.[49]

Shades of Lee Harvey Oswald, the conclusion here is, "Jose has 'spook' written all over him."[50]

The speculation lingers in cyberspace that this Latino gang member and wannabe Islamic terrorist was all along a government agent. Meanwhile, on

May 2, 2012, the U.S. Court of Appeals for the Ninth Circuit held that John Yoo was entitled to immunity.[51]

Fast-forward a dozen years: the name "Jose Padilla" was back in the news in connection with an attempt to subvert the government of the United States. According to NBC News:

> WASHINGTON—A Trump supporter who engaged in a battle with law enforcement officers at the Capitol on Jan. 6 and then bragged about his conduct on the pro-Trump forum "The Donald," was sentenced Wednesday to 6½ years in federal prison.
> Jose Padilla was sentenced to 78 months by U.S. District Judge John Bates, who convicted Padilla, 43, a disabled Army veteran, on ten counts at a bench trial in May.
> Federal prosecutors sought just over 14 years in prison, which would have been among the ten longest sentences given to Jan. 6 rioters.
> Padilla will get credit for time served in pretrial custody. He was arrested in early 2021.[52]

No, it was not the same "Jose Padilla", but a January 6, 2021 rioter of the same name. We will revisit his case and other similar convictions in Chapter 11.

Notes

1. Michael Howard, George J. Andreopoulis, and Mark R. Shulman (eds.), *The Laws of War: Constraints on Warfare in the Western World* (New Haven, CT: Yale University Press, 1994), p. 2.
2. "Charter of the International Military Tribunal," *Article 1*, http://www.law.umkc.edu/faculty/projects/ftrials/nuremberg/NurembergIndictments.html.
3. Douglas O. Linder, "Nuremberg Trials 1945–1949: A Trial Account," *Famous Trials*, http://www.law.umkc.edu/faculty/projects/ftrials/nuremberg/nurem-berg.htm.
4. Ibid.
5. In addition to the innumerable books about the Nuremberg trials, a succession of feature films, from 1961's *Judgment at Nuremberg* through 2000's *Nuremberg*, have kept the story in the public consciousness.
6. *Application of Yamashita*, 327 U.S. 1, 66 S. Ct. 340 (1946).
7. Ibid., p. 5.
8. Ibid., p. 7.
9. Ibid., p. 25.
10. Ibid., pp. 28–29.
11. 10 U.S.C. s. 801 et seq.
12. *United States v. Calley*, 46 C.M.R. 1131 (1973).
13. *United States v. Calley*, 22 U.S.C.M.A. 534, 48 C.M.R. 19 (1973); see Art. 67(b)(3), U.C.M.J., 10 U.S.C. s. 867(b)(3).

14. *Calley v. Callaway*, 519 F.2d 184 (5th Cir., 1975), *cert. den.*, *Calley v. Hoffman*, 405 U.S. 911, 96 S. Ct. 1505 (1976).
15. The Jencks Act, 18 U.S.C. s. 5000, states, among other things,

> In any criminal prosecution brought by the United States, no statement or report in the possession of the United States which was made by a Government witness or prospective Government witness (other than the defendant) shall be the subject of subpoena, discovery, or inspection until said witness has testified on direct examination in the trial of the case.

16. The Fourteenth Amendment reads in full:

> Section 1. All persons born or naturalized in the United States, and subject to the jurisdiction thereof, are citizens of the United States and of the State wherein they reside. No State shall make or enforce any law which shall abridge the privileges or immunities of citizens of the United States; nor shall any State deprive any person of life, liberty, or property, without due process of law; nor deny to any person within its jurisdiction the equal protection of the laws.
> Section 2. Representatives shall be apportioned among the several States according to their respective numbers, counting the whole number of persons in each State, excluding Indians not taxed. But when the right to vote at any election for the choice of electors for President and Vice President of the United States, Representatives in Congress, the Executive and Judicial officers of a State, or the members of the Legislature thereof, is denied to any of the male inhabitants of such State, being twenty-one years of age, and citizens of the United States, or in any way abridged, except for participation in rebellion, or other crime, the basis of representation therein shall be reduced in the proportion which the number of such male citizens shall bear to the whole number of male citizens twenty-one years of age in such State. Section 3. No person shall be a Senator or Representative in Congress, or elector of President and Vice President, or hold any office, civil or military, under the United States, or under any State, who, having previously taken an oath, as a member of Congress, or as an officer of the United States, or as a member of any State legislature, or as an executive or judicial officer of any State, to support the Constitution of the United States, shall have engaged in insurrection or rebellion against the same, or given aid or comfort to the enemies thereof. But Congress may, by a vote of two-thirds of each House, remove such disability.
> Section 4. The validity of the public debt of the United States, authorized by law, including debts incurred for payment of pensions and bounties for services in suppressing insurrection or rebellion, shall not be questioned. But neither the United States nor any State shall assume or pay any debt or obligation incurred in aid of insurrection or rebellion against the United States, or any claim for the loss or emancipation of any slave; but all such debts, obligations and claims shall be held illegal and void.
> Section 5. The Congress shall have power to enforce, by appropriate legislation, the provisions of this article.

17. Associated Press, "'Birth Tourism' Makes up a Tiny Portion of Immigrant Babies in the U.S.," September 11, 2010, http://www.syracuse.com/have-you-heard/index.ssf/2010/09/birth_tourism_makes_up_a_tiny.html.
18. Ibid.
19. *Ex parte Quirin*, 317 U.S. 1 (1942).
20. German saboteurs, during the two world wars of the 20th century, wrote a colorful, if largely ineffectual, chapter in the history of those two global conflicts. During World War II, they accomplished very little. In World War I, they enjoyed one great triumph on U.S. soil, the Black Tom Island attack, which is covered in detail in the Introduction.
21. Amanda Ripley, "The Case of the Dirty Bomber," *TIME*, June 16, 2002, http://www.time.com/time/nation/article/0,8599,262917,00.html.
22. Ibid.
23. Ibid.
24. *Padilla ex. rel. Newman v. Rumsfeld*, 233 F.Supp.2d 564 (S.D.N.Y., 2002).
25. *Padilla ex. rel. Newman v. Rumsfeld*, 243 F.Supp.2d 42 (A.D.N.Y., 2003).
26. The federal Interlocutory Appeals Act, 28 U.S.C.A. s. 1292(b) (*Black's Law Dictionary* [St. Paul, MN: West Publishing Co., 1991], p. 563):

    > grants discretion to the courts of appeals to review any interlocutory order . . . if the [trial judge], in making the order, has stated in writing that the order involves a controlling question of law as to which there is substantial ground for difference of opinion and that an immediate appeal from the order may materially advance the ultimate termination of litigation.

    This rule is an exception from the usual one that a case is not ripe for an appeal until a final judgment or other dispositive order has ended the proceedings at the trial court level.
27. *Padilla ex. rel. Newman v. Rumsfeld*, 256 F.Supp.2d 218 (S.D.N.Y., 2003).
28. *Whitmore v. Arkansas*, 495 U.S. 149, 163–63, 110 S. Ct. 1717 (1990).
29. *Padilla v. Rumsfeld*, 352 F.3d 695, 703–04 (2d Cir., 2003).
30. 18 U.S.C. s. 4001(a).
31. *Padilla v. Rumsfeld*, 352 F.3d 695, 703–04 (2d Cir., 2003), p. 723.
32. Ibid., p. 724.
33. *Rumsfeld v. Padilla*, 540 U.S. 1173, 124 S. Ct. 1353, 157 L.Ed.2d 1226, 72 USLW 3488, 72 USLW 3521, 72 USLW 3533, 2004 Daily Journal D.A.R. 2273 (U.S., February 20, 2004).
34. *Rumsfeld v. Padilla*, 542 U.S. 426, 124 S. Ct. 2711, 159 L.Ed.2d 513, 72 USLW 4584, 04 Cal. Daily Op. Serv. 5701, 2004 Daily Journal D.A.R. 7765, 17 Fla. L. Weekly Fed. S 466 (U.S., June 28, 2004).
35. 124 S. Ct., *supra*, pp. 2713–2714.
36. *Padilla v. Hanft*, 389 F.Supp.2d 678 (D.S.C., 2005), reversed, 423 F.3d 386 (4th Cir., 2005).
37. *Padilla v. Hanft*, 423 F.3d 386, 397 (4th Cir., 2005).
38. *Hanft v. Padilla*, 546 U.S. 1084, 126 S. Ct. 978 (2006).
39. *U.S. v. Hassoun*, 476 F.3d 1181 (11th Cir., 2007).

40. Post-traumatic stress disorder (PTSD) has been defined as "a severe anxiety disorder that can develop after exposure to any event that results in psychological trauma" (http://en.wikipedia.org/wiki/Post-traumatic_stress_disorder). Stockholm syndrome (http://en.wikipedia.org/wiki/Stockholm_syndrome):

> is a term used to describe a paradoxical psychological phenomenon wherein hostages express adulation and have positive feelings towards their captors that appear irrational in light of the danger or risk endured by the victims, essentially mistaking a lack of abuse from their captors as an act of kindness.

41. Quoted by Jay Weaver, "Terror Suspect Hearing Gets Underway," *Miami Herald*, February 22, 2007, http://www.bradenton.com/mld/bradenton/news/nation/16760156.htm.
42. See "Jose Padilla Sentenced on Terrorism Charges," *MSNBC*, http://www.msnbc.msn.com/id/22784470; David Oscar Markus, "Jose Padilla to the Supermax," April 18, 2008, http://sdfla.blogspot.com/2008/04/jose-padilla-to-supermax.html; Kiely Lewandowski, "Padilla Sent to Colorado 'Supermax' Prison to Serve out Terrorism Conspiracy Sentence," Jurist, April 19, 2008, http://jurist.law.pitt.edu/paperchase/2008/04/padilla-sent-to-colorado-supermax.php.
43. See http://en.wikipedia.org/wiki/John_Yoo.
44. *Padilla v. Yoo*, 633 F.Supp.2d 1005 (N.D. Cal., 2009).
45. Jonathan Turley, "Judge Rules That Jose Padilla Can Sue John Yoo," http://jona-thanturley.org/2009/06/15/judge-rules-that-jose-padilla-can-sue-john-yoo/.
46. Jonathan Turley, "Accused Terrorist Jose Padilla Sues Law Professor John Yoo," http://jonathanturley.org/2008/01/06/accused-terrorist-jose-padilla-sues-law—professor-john-yoo/.
47. Jonathan Turley, "Nuremberg Revisited: Obama Administration Files to Dismiss Case against John Yoo," http://jonathanturley.org/2009/12/09/obama-administration-files-to-dismiss-case-against-john-yoo/.
48. "Is Jose Padilla 'John Doe Number 2' at the Oklahoma City Bombing?" http://whatreallyhappened.com/WRHARTICLES/padillaJD2.html?q=padillaJD2.html (accessed October 10, 2010).
49. Ibid.
50. Ibid.
51. *Padilla v. Yoo*, 678 F.3d 748 (9th Cir., 2012).
52. Gary Grumback and Ryan J. Reilly, "'The Donald Forum' User Gets More Than Six Years in Prison for Battling Officers at Capitol Riot," *NBC News*, September 28, 2023, https://www.nbcnews.com/politics/justice-department/-donald-forum-user-gets-6-years-prison-battling-officers-capitol-riot-rcna104656 (accessed December 28, 2023).

Of Wannabes and Bumblers
The Fort Dix Conspirators and the Underwear Bomber

8

During the decade after 9/11, no new terrorist attack took place on U.S. soil (unless one counts the 2009 Fort Hood massacre by the insane psychiatrist Nidal Malik Hasan as such an attack, which I believe would be a stretch[1]). However, a number of attempts, which conceivably could have been devastating, were thwarted or ran amok. One such foiled plot involved Fort Dix in southern New Jersey.

8.1 The Fort Dix Wannabes

Hollywood often portrays terrorists as evil geniuses.[2] Some real-life terrorists apparently approach this mythic image. Notably, Osama bin Laden evaded capture for nearly the entire decade, not being located and killed until 2011. He has become the stuff of myth and legend. In 2006, in my then-weekly column "Attorney at Large," I wrote this about him:

Osama bin Laden Is Our Sci-Fi Nightmare[3]

> The future is now. We live in a Sci-Fi world: supersonic flight and space travel; cloning and organ transplants; computers and artificial intelligence; weapons of mass destruction and stealth bombers. The best evidence of our having entered the realms of fantasy and science fiction is Osama bin Laden.
>
> Our Western world imagined Osama bin Laden long before he was born. He is Conan Doyle's Professor Moriarty. He is Sax Rohmer's Fu Manchu. He would have liked to become Marvel Comic's Ming the Merciless.
>
> Professor Moriarty is described by his chief antagonist, Sherlock Holmes, as "the Napoleon of Crime." Moriarty lurks in the shadows, masterminding murder and mayhem, and even influencing world affairs. In The Final Solution the two opponents finally meet face to face atop Switzerland's 200-foot Reisenbach Falls, apparently falling together to their deaths. The U.S. armed forces hoped for such a final solution for Osama among the craggy peaks of Afghanistan, but so far our modern-day Napoleon of Crime has apparently not obliged.
>
> Fu Manchu prefigures Osama. A villain out of the mysterious East—albeit Far, not Middle, East—he is described in The Insidious Fu Manchu as "a person, tall, lean and feline, high shouldered, with a brow like Shakespeare and a face like

DOI: 10.4324/9781003474104-8

Satan, a close-shaven skull, magnetic eyes of the true cat-green. Invest him with the cruel cunning of an entire Eastern race, accumulated in one giant intellect, with all the resources of science past and present . . . . Imagine that awful being, and you have a mental picture of Dr. Fu Manchu, the yellow peril incarnate in one man." I don't know about Shakespeare's brow or the cat-green eyes, but otherwise, couldn't this fit our image of bin Laden?

Last is Ming. Flash Gordon's nemesis is our worst nightmare . . . . Osama bin Laden triumphant, the leader of a fundamentalist-Islamic empire arrayed in undying enmity against our "decadent" West. Ming's empire, "Mingo," intent upon enslaving the galaxy, is armed with rocket ships, robots and death rays. Ming, whose name sounds Asian, resembles Fu Manchu. In the 1980 movie "Flash Gordon," Max Von Sydow (of all people) captures the Asian-super-villain look perfectly: shaved head, angular jet-black eyebrows and goatee, slanting eyes that stare right through you.

Where the heck is Osama bin Laden and what exactly is al-Qaeda? And the biggest question of them all: With all our computers, and supersonic aircraft, and satellites and even a space station, plus our nukes and other assorted weapons of mass destruction . . . with all our sci-fi gadgets, why can't America catch and kill this guy? Perhaps he's no longer human.

Sure, laugh at me if you must. But I say that in a world where Google can give me 25,700,000 hits on "Osama bin Laden" in .07 seconds (try it yourself); where airliners travel at 600 miles per hour, seven miles high, in air temperatures of 50 to 60 degrees below zero to deliver me from Philly to London in some six hours; and where a futuristic stealth bomber can deliver a nuclear device capable of killing millions in a millisecond and never even be detected by the victims' radar . . . in a world like this, our worst recurring nightmares can become reality.

If you can't buy that hypothesis, then try this one on for size: If Osama bin Laden and al Qaeda didn't exist, someone would have invented them. This theory has plenty of precedents. In the hard-coal fields of eastern Pennsylvania in the 1870s, every murder and act of arson was blamed on the "Molly Maguires," an alleged secret society of Irish terrorists. Throughout much of the 20th century organized crime was equated to the "Mafia." Yet, as Italian writer Luigi Barzini once said, "Almost everything is known about the Mafia except whether or not it really exists." During the 19th and early 20th centuries, Anarchists assassinated half a dozen western leaders including our own President McKinley. Yet Anarchism is an idea that eschews formal organization. We seem to need labels like these to make some sense of our violent world. The plot foiled by the Brits last week is a 21st century case on point. The plan was to blow up airliners. The method was seriously sci-fi. Bombs were to be assembled from harmless-looking carry-on items ignited by digital cameras. The culprits are British citizens. None carried an al Qaeda membership card when captured.

In our sci-fi world, Osama bin Laden no longer needs to be alive at all. Digital technology can produce tapes of the legendary terrorist leader talking to his admirers. The messages can be beamed around the globe at the speed of light. Like Moriarty, Fu Manchu, and Ming the Merciless, an imaginary bin Laden can be as effective an enemy of the West as any flesh-and-blood human being . . . maybe more so. Perhaps he really still exists, but he no longer needs to.

Other terrorists present us with more of a mixed bag. The 1993 World Trade Center attackers succeeded in setting off their truck bomb. They failed to bring down the towers, and most were quickly caught when one of their number repeatedly returned to the rental agency, demanding back the deposit he had made on the van.[4] Timothy McVeigh, too, succeeded. And he, too, was quickly caught, because his escape car lacked a license plate.[5]

At the other extreme of the spectrum are the would-be terrorists, who plotted together to attack New Jersey's Fort Dix.

8.2 The Target[6]

Located in Burlington County, in relatively rural South New Jersey, Fort Dix is named for Major General John Adams Dix, a veteran of the War of 1812 and the Civil War. During his career, Dix was a U.S. senator, Secretary of the Treasury, minister to France, and governor of New York. Construction began in June 1917, and on July 18, the War Department named the cantonment Camp Dix. During World War I, Camp Dix was the training and staging ground for the 34th, 78th, and 87th Divisions. Camp Dix grew quickly and became the largest military reservation in the northeastern United States. After the November 11, 1918, armistice, the camp became a demobilization center.

During the inter-war period, Camp Dix was a training facility for active-duty Army, Army Reserve, and National Guard units. From 1933–1941, Camp Dix was also a reception, training, and discharge center for the Civilian Conservation Corps. On March 8, 1939, Camp Dix became Fort Dix, acknowledging that it was a permanent Army installation. The fort served as a reception and training center for men inducted under the draft of 1939. Ten divisions and many smaller units trained and staged there before entering the battlefields of World War II. At the end of the war, the reception center became the separation center, returning more than 1.2 million soldiers to civilian life.

On July 15, 1947, Fort Dix became a basic training center and the home of the 9th Infantry Division. In April 1954, the 9th Division was transferred to Europe and the 69th Infantry Division moved into Fort Dix. The 69th Division's stay was short-lived; it was deactivated on March 16, 1956. On that date, Fort Dix became the U.S. Army Training Center, Infantry.

Fort Dix expanded rapidly during the Vietnam War. A mock Vietnam village was constructed and future "grunts" received Southeast Asian-specific training before being deployed. In July 1973, Fort Dix became a part of the newly formed U.S. Army Training and Doctrine Command. In 1988 the fort, which is cheek-to-jowl with McGuire Air Force Base, began training Air Force Security Police in ground combat skills. Air Base Ground Defense Command trained enlisted, non-commissioned officer (NCO), and officer security police to better defend air force installations around the world.

In August 1990, Fort Dix began around-the-clock operations deploying troops for Operation Desert Shield and Operation Desert Storm. In January 1991, Fort Dix was chosen to train selected Kuwaiti civilians in basic military skills. After a brief course, they boarded planes to take part in the liberation of their country. As a result of Base Realignment and Closure Commission recommendations of 1988, Fort Dix again ended its active Army training mission.

On October 1, 1992, Fort Dix transferred from Training and Doctrine Command to Forces Command. In December 1995, Fort Dix began mobilizing and deploying troops for the Bosnia Peace Missions. On October 1, 1997, Fort Dix transferred from Forces Command to the U.S. Army Reserve Command. During the succeeding decade, with the so-called War on Terror raging in Afghanistan and Iraq, Fort Dix was yet again a major training and mobilization center for the Army Reserve and National Guard. As such, it was an attractive target for aspiring jihadists.

8.3 The Plotters

Shortly after the criminal complaints were filed in the U.S. District Court for New Jersey on May 7, 2007, by then-U.S. Attorney (later New Jersey Gov.) Christopher J. Christie, *The Washington Post* reported that a group of five foreign-born radical Islamists were arrested for conspiring to attack Fort Dix after they attempted to copy videos for jihad training onto DVD. A sixth man was also charged for helping to obtain illegal weapons for the would be terrorists.[7] The men had trained at a shooting range in the Pocono Mountains of Pennsylvania, with plans to kill as many soldiers as possible during their attack on the Army base.

But almost immediately, questions were raised about whether the six were real terrorists or just kids playing at global jihad. In one article, *The Philadelphia Inquirer* raised the issue by interviewing friends and relatives of the men, painting a picture of normal young men, the well-mannered sons of hard-working immigrants.[8] Could they possibly be terrorists?

The first reported decision, issued by the federal trial court on May 24, denied a motion for bail by one of the six. In announcing his decision, U.S.

Magistrate Judge Joel Schneider offered this description of the evidence against the defendants:

> On May 7, 2007, this Court signed a Complaint [Doc. No. 1] and Arrest Warrant [Doc. No. 2] naming defendant. The Complaint charges defendant with violating 18U.S.C.§922(g) and 2. Contemporaneously with the issuance of these documents the Court also signed five related Complaints and Arrest Warrants naming Eljvir Duka (07-2047(JS)), Mohamad Ibrahim Shnewer (07-2045(JS)), Dritan Duka (07-2046(JS)), Shain Duka (07-2048(JS)) and Serdar Tatar (07-2049(JS)). (These five (5) individuals will hereinafter be referred to as the "other charged individuals.") Defendant [Agron Abdullahu] and the other charged individuals were arrested on May 7, 2007 and pursuant to Fed.R.Crim.P.5, appeared before this Court for an initial appearance on May 8, 2007. On that date an Order of Temporary Detention was entered and a detention hearing was scheduled for May 11, 2007. [Doc. No. 7]. On May 11, 2007, defendant's counsel requested and was granted an extension for the date of the detention hearing until May 17, 2007.[9]

Magistrate Schneider continued:

> The charges against defendant arise in the context of the government's claim that the five other charged individuals conspired to attack soldiers or other personnel at the United States Army Base in Fort Dix, Burlington County, New Jersey. The government's investigation started after it learned that an individual brought to a local store a video to be duplicated onto a digital video disk ("DVD"). The video depicted conduct that was recorded as having occurred on January 3, 2006. The government describes the video as showing "men shooting assault weapons at a firing range in a militia-like style while calling for jihad and shouting in Arabic "Allahu Akbar" ("God is Great"). . . .
>
> Although the government did not proffer direct evidence that the defendant specifically knew the other charged individuals were planning to attack Fort Dix, defendant was in their company on several occasions when plans for the attack were more likely than not discussed or preparations for the attack took place. For example, defendant appeared in the shooting video at the Pocono Mountain firing range that was taken on January 3, 2006. Further, approximately one (1) year later, between January 31 to February 1, 2007, defendant was also observed (via video and photographic surveillance) carrying "dark colored rifle style bags" into Dritan Duka's residence. An informant also reported that defendant brought two firearms, a 9[-]millimeter handgun and a Yugoslavian semi-automatic rifle, to Dritan Duka's residence. Law enforcement officers also observed Shain Duka transfer a green rifle style soft case from Dritan Duka's residence to defendant who then loaded it into his vehicle. CW-2 also reported that defendant loaded a shotgun and Beretta rifle into his car. Id. at ¶¶ 47, 48. This informant, defendant and most of the other charged individuals drove

> to the Pocono Mountain home the Duka brothers rented. Law enforcement officers continued their surveillance and observed defendant participating in shooting practice on February 2, 2007 and "teaching" several individuals where to place a shotgun when firing it. Id. at ¶ 50. The weapons used included an SKS semi-automatic rifle, a Beretta storm semi-automatic rifle, a Mossberg 12 gauge pump shotgun and a 9-millimeter Beretta handgun. Defendant admitted he bought ammunition used in the Pocono training.[10]

Chief Inspector Joseph E. O'Connor, head of the Philadelphia Police Department's counterterrorism unit, opined, "These were young people who came to this country but who developed an empathy toward the ideology of al-Qaida."[11] By contrast, a 23-year-old neighborhood girl who new brothers Shain and Eljvir Duka from their days as pizza parlor employees claimed, "They were just regular boys flirting with girls."[12]

The left-leaning magazine *Mother Jones* became perhaps the most vocal critic of the arrest and conviction of the so-called Fort Dix Six. Said the magazine on June 6, 2010:

> Informers have by now become our first line of defense in our battles with the evildoers, the go-to guys in the never-ending domestic War on Terror. They regularly do the dirty work—suggesting and encouraging the plots, laboring as bagmen to move the money, fashioning the bombs, and eliciting the flamboyant dialogue, even while following the scripts of their handlers to the letter. They have attended to all the little details that make for the successful and now familiar arrests, criminal complaints, trials, and (for the most part) convictions in the ever-distracting war against . . . what? Al-Qaeda? Terror? Muslims? The inept? The poor?[13]

Referring specifically to the Fort Dix Six, the article commented sarcastically, "A cell of New Jersey roofers, handymen, and cab drivers was scheming to use a laminated pizza delivery map to guide them through a devastating attack on Fort Dix, the enormous military base in Burlington County, south of Trenton."[14]

Concluded Stephen Salisbury, the author of the *Mother Jones* article, "It remains to be asked: How expansive will the stage become for creative informers and their government directors now working the theater of the Great Recession?"[15]

So, were the Fort Dix Six a dedicated band of jihadists intent upon killing "as many soldiers as possible" or a group of "good boys," whose circle was infiltrated by an FBI informant-provocateur?[16]

In his opening address to the federal jury on October 19, 2008, Assistant U.S. Attorney William Fitzpatrick said: "Their motive was to defend Islam.

Their inspiration was al-Qaeda and Osama Bin Laden. Their intention was to attack the US."[17]

The prosecution went on to offer evidence of the following chronology of incriminating events:

- January 31, 2006: An individual brought a tape to a Circuit City in New Jersey for duplication and transfer to DVD. The video features ten young men conducting militia-style assault training shooting their weapons at a firing range while shouting, "God is great." The Circuit City employee, Brian Morgenstern, who saw the video, contacted the Mount Laurel Police Department, which in turn contacted the FBI.
- April 2006: The FBI hired informant Mahmoud Omar to approach the accused.
- August 11, 2006: Ibrahim Shnewer traveled to Fort Dix and Fort Monmouth to conduct surveillance.
- August 13, 2006: Shnewer traveled to Dover Air Force Base, Delaware, to conduct surveillance.
- August 13, 2006: Shnewer traveled to the U.S. Coast Guard building in Philadelphia, Pennsylvania, to conduct surveillance.
- August 16, 2006: Shnewer traveled to Naval Air Engineering Station Lakehurst to conduct surveillance.
- November 28, 2006: Serdar Tatar, who had delivered pizza to Fort Dix before, obtained a map of the Fort Dix military installation through his employer's pizza delivery restaurant, which serviced the military base.
- February 2, 2007: Dritan Duka, Eljvir Duka, and Sulayman Shain Duka conducted weapons training in Gouldsboro, Pennsylvania.
- February 4, 2007: Mohamad Ibrahim Shnewer, Dritan Duka, Eljvir Duka, and Sulayman Shain Duka reviewed terrorist training materials.
- February 26, 2007: Dritan Duka and Eljvir Duka conducted weapons training in Cherry Hill, New Jersey.
- March 15, 2007: Dritan Duka and Sulayman Shain Duka conducted weapons training in Cherry Hill, New Jersey.
- April 16, 2007: Dritan Duka contacted an arms dealer (an FBI informant) for weaponry.
- May 7, 2007: The FBI arrested six members of the group.

On December 22, 2008, the jury found five of the six defendants guilty. Of course, their attorneys appealed the convictions. Their unsuccessful efforts to overturn the verdicts ended on June 11, 2012, when the U.S. Supreme Court declined to review their case.[18]

8.4 The Underwear Bomber

If the Fort Dix Six were terrorist wannabes who took their fantasies too far and are now paying a heavy price, poor Umar Farouk Abdulmutallab most likely will go down in the history of international terrorism as something of a buffoon and the butt (no pun intended) of unnumbered jokes.

Abdulmutallab smuggled a homemade bomb, sewn into his underwear, onto Northwest Airlines Flight 253 on Christmas Day, of all days, December 25, 2009. The flight departed from Amsterdam and was headed for Detroit, Michigan. Other passengers on the plane heard a loud pop, like a firecracker, and saw smoke rising from the hapless wannabe's seat. According to reports, the 23-year-old Nigerian's underwear contained 80 grams of Pentaerytritol tetranitrate (PETN), which was more than enough to blow a hole in the airliner. The detonator that he tried to use was acid in a syringe. Instead of detonating the bomb, the acid melted the syringe and caused a fire. Taken into custody on landing, he was indicted on January 6, 2010, and arraigned two days later at the U.S. District Court in Detroit. His charges included trying to use a weapon of mass destruction, attempted murder, willful attempt to destroy an aircraft, placing a bomb on a plane, and possession of a destructive device.[19]

When Abdulmutallab shuffled into court on January 8, observers speculated whether his shuffling gait was solely the result of the shackles on his ankles, or if the burns he suffered when his bomb fizzled were a contributing factor. One defense attorney quipped, "All my clients walk that way." Another commentator added that if Abdulmutallab's underwear and genitalia did not count as carry-on luggage, they may well have qualified as "carry-offs." New Yorker Magazine columnist Calvin Trillin accomplished the ultimate put-on just ten days after Abdulmutallab's arraignment. Claiming credit for having predicted the underwear bomber, Trillin posited a jihadist named Khalid the Drole. Wrote Trillin, tongue firmly planted in his cheek, "That's right: I predicted the Underwear Bomber in 2006. You could look it up."[20] Trillin went on to ask whimsically why no one ever followed up on his "underwear tip," and that perhaps Khalid the Droll was simply part of a great scheme to embarrass us all.

However, when the laughter subsided, other pundits turned their attention to the serious side of the threat posed by what was also an innovative effort to circumvent the enhanced security systems implemented and steadily refined since 9/11. Two main debates emerged from the Noel 2009 incident. First came questions about why the intelligence/law enforcement community was unable to "connect the dots," leading to a conclusion that Abdulmutallab posed a threat and ought not to be allowed on a plane. Analyzing this issue in the *Harvard Business Review*, writer Tom Davenport argued that the criticism might have been unwarranted. Although there were warning signs of Abdulmutallab's intentions, Davenport contended that it would have been difficult to connect the dots before the flight, comparing the pieces of information at the disposal of law enforcement and intelligence to a jigsaw puzzle. They knew he was the president of University College London's Islamic Society and that his father had warned the CIA he might be radical and might have traveled to Yemen. They knew he had a two-year, multiple-entry visa into the United States, that he paid cash for a plane ticket from Nigeria to the United States, and that the UK government denied renewal of his student visa because part of his application was faked. Only a couple of those facts were at all notable.[21]

Equally controversial were the efforts to place full-body scanners in airports. The first such devices proved to be so revealing that wails of protest arose from civil libertarians and privacy proponents across the country. In the words of one such opponent, "After an alleged terrorist unsuccessfully tried to detonate his explosive underwear on a Christmas Day flight to Detroit, current and former American officials are now using the failed attack to push for more airport scanners to spot such explosives—and a lot more." He contended, "The problem, privacy advocates say, is that a zap from one of the devices amounts to a 'digital strip search' from a system 'designed to capture, record, and store detailed images of individuals undressed.' "[22]

The Transportation Security Administration in 2010–2012 did in fact install such scanners in major airports across the country. In most cases, passengers have been permitted to opt for a pat-down search instead. This remains the case in most major American airports in 2024.

"You've got to find some way of detecting things in parts of the body that aren't easy to get at," former Homeland Security chief Michael Chertoff reportedly said back in the day. "It's either pat-downs or imaging."

Photographic samples accompanying these comments were worth more than 1,000 words, graphically illustrating the intrusive nature of the technology. Airports have attempted to meet such critiques by making the images "fuzzier," and allowing passengers a choice between such a scan and an alternative pat-down. When the devices debuted at the Philadelphia International Airport in October 2010, some passengers actually embraced them.

> "Hey, you've got to try everything new, no?" said Antonio DiMaria, who was flying home to Montreal after a business trip to Philadelphia. "It's better. You won't have these planes falling into buildings anymore, so why not[?]"[23]

Meanwhile, the instigator of all this argument and activity reappeared in court on October 14, 2010. In his pretrial hearing, Abdulmutallab asked to be allowed to represent himself. Attorney Anthony Chambers, who appeared beside the defendant, was described as "standby counsel". District Judge Nancy

Edmunds ordered that Chambers be given full access to all the evidence by the federal prosecutors.[24]

Most remarkable, however, may be the fact that Abdulmutallab managed to become the plaintiff in a federal case during the brief time between his arraignment and his pretrial hearing. In a legal action that would seem utterly absurd if offered in a novel or feature film as fiction, Abdulmutallab joined with a fellow prisoner in suing none other than the 2010 Times Square bomber (see Chapter 10). In the words of an incredulous federal judge,

> Plaintiff Jonathan Lee Riches, a well-known frequent filer of frivolous lawsuits throughout the federal court system, brings this action as a "Preliminary Injunction, Temporary Restraining Order, TRO 28USC1331." Riches allegedly brings this suit along with Umar Farouk Abdulmutallab, the Nigerian man charged with attempting to detonate an explosive device hidden in his underwear while on an airplane on Christmas Day 2009, and Hakimullah Mehsud, a Pakistan Taliban leader. In the handwritten document, Riches sues Faisal Shahzad, the suspect in the May 1, 2010, Times Square Car Bomb plot, and Huma Asif Mian, Shahzad's wife. In the complaint, Riches raises ridiculous, outrageous, and wholly frivolous allegations against Defendants.[25]

Despite Chief Judge Thomas B. Russell's excoriation of the apparently meritless lawsuit, the gist of his order was merely to require the plaintiff Riches to pay the $350 filing fee. In issuing his order, his honor noted that a computer search uncovered some 2,100 suits filed by Riches across the country since his incarceration. The judge also questioned the authenticity of the other two plaintiffs' signatures on the complaint.

So be it. But one might speculate that the underwear bomber was gaining quite a law school education while awaiting his own trial date.

If so, it did not help him. On February 16, 2012, Abdulmutallab was sentenced to life in prison without possibility of parole.[26]

Notes

1. See Chapter 9.
2. See, e.g., *Nighthawks* (1981), starring Sylvester Stallone and Rutger Hauer, accessible at http://en.wikipedia.org/wiki/Nighthawks_(film); *Arlington Road* (1999), starring Jeff Bridges and Tim Robbins, accessible at http://www.imdb.com/title/tt0137363/.
3. James Castagnera, "Osama bin Laden is Our Sci-Fi Nightmare," *News of Delaware County*, August 18, 2006, and *Carbon County Times News*, August 14, 2006, accessible at History News Network, http://hnn.us/roundup/entries/29216.html.
4. See Chapter 1.
5. See Chapter 2.

6. The background facts that follow are closely adapted from "John Adams Dix and the History of Fort Dix," http://www.dix.army.mil/history/history.htm (accessed October 16, 2010).
7. Dale Russakoff and Dan Eggen, "Six Charged in Plot to Attack Fort Dix," *Washington Post*, May 9, 2007, http://www.washingtonpost.com/wp-dyn/con-tent/article/2007/05/08/AR2007050800465.html (accessed October 16, 2010).
8. George Anastasia, "Fort Dix 6: 'Good Boys' or Terrorists?" *Seattle Times*, May 13, 2007, http://seattletimes.nwsource.com/html/nation-world/2003704914_dixprofiles13.html (accessed October 16, 2010).
9. *U.S. v. Abdullahu*, 488 F.Supp.2d 433, 435 (D.N.J., 2007).
10. Ibid., pp. 435–436.
11. Anastasia.
12. Ibid.
13. "Stage-Managing the War on Terror," *Mother Jones*, June 6, 2010, http://motherjones. com/politics/2010/07/stage-managing-war-terror (accessed October 16, 2010). The quoted portion was reprinted by *Mother Jones* from an article by Stephen Salisbury, originally posted on the TomDispatch, accessible at http://www. tomdispatch. com/archive/175270. Salisbury, described as a cultural writer for *The Philadelphia Inquirer*, expanded on this argument in his book *Mohamed's Ghosts: An American Story of Love and Fear in the Homeland* (New York: Nation Books, 2010). Stephen Salisbury, "Stage-Managing the War on Terror," Mother Jones, June 6, 2010, http://motherjones.com/politics/2010/07/stage-managing-war-terror (accessed October 16, 2010).
14. Ibid.
15. Ibid.
16. As I noted in my Introduction, those who suspect the government of provoking criminal activities can point to the Molly Maguires of Pennsylvania's 19th-century coal fields, as well as the trial of the Western Federation of Miners' "Big Bill" Haywood for the murder of former Idaho governor Frank Steunenberg a century ago, as evidence that such behavior allegedly has happened in the American past.
17. "U.S. Base Accused 'Plotted Jihad,'" *BBC News*, October 20, 2008, http://news.bbc.co.uk/2/hi/americas/7680988.stm (accessed October 30, 2010).
18. *Shnewer v. United States*, — S. Ct. —, 2012 WL 1643034 (U.S., June 11, 2012).
19. "Underwear Bomber," *Muhalo.com*, http://www.mahalo.com/underwear-bomber (accessed October 30, 2010).
20. Calvin Trillin, "Crystal Ball," *New Yorker*, January 18, 2010, http://www.newyorker.com/talk/2010/01/18/100118ta_talk_trillin (accessed October 30, 2010). With permission.
21. Tom Davenport, "The Underwear Bomber: Why They Didn't 'Connect the Dots,'" *Harvard Business Review*, January 8, 2010, http://blogs.hbr.org/davenport/2010/01/why_they_didnt_connect_the_dot.html (accessed October 30, 2010).
22. Noah Shachtman, "Underwear Bomber Renews Calls for 'Naked Scanners,'" *Danger Room*, December 28, 2009, http://www.wired.com/danger-room/2009/12/

underwear-bomber-renews-calls-for-naked-scanners (accessed October 30, 2010). With permission.

23. Linda Loyd, "Full-Body Scanners Debut at Phila. Int'l Airport," *Philadelphia Inquirer*, October 28, 2010, http://www.philly.com/inquirer/breaking/business_breaking/20101028_Whole-body_scans_begin_at_Philadelphia_airport.html (accessed October 30, 2010).
24. Hugh Collins, "Alleged Underwear Bomber Represents Himself in Court," *AOL-News*, October 14, 2010, http://www.aolnews.com/crime/article/alleged-underwear-bomber-represents-himself-in-court/19674657 (accessed October 30, 2010).
25. *Abdulmutallab v. Shahzad*, 2010 WL 3119500 (U.S.D.C., W.D.Ky., August 6, 2010).
26. Associated Press, "'Unrepentant Would-Be Mass Murderer': Underwear Bomber Jailed for Life without Parole for Failed Christmas Day Plane Attack," February 17, 2012, http://www.dailymail.co.uk/news/article-2102254/Underwear-bomber-Umar-Farouk-Abdulmutallab-sentenced-life-prison.html (accessed July 1, 2012).

Lone Madman or Freelance Jihadist?

Nidal Malik Hasan and the Fort Hood Shootings (2009)

9

On November 5, 2009, a lone gunman opened fire in the crowded Soldier Readiness Center at Fort Hood, where deploying soldiers were receiving vaccines. The gunman wore a combat uniform and shouted "Allahu Akbar!"—or, "God is greatest!"—as he fired rapidly at unarmed, startled soldiers. Within ten minutes, 13 were dead and more than 30 injured. SWAT team markswoman Kimberly Munley managed to shoot the lone gunman in the chest; he was handcuffed as he lay unconscious from the wound that, although not fatal, paralyzed him from the chest down. The gunman was quickly identified as U.S. Army Maj. Nidal Malik Hasan.

Hasan, a devout Muslim and a psychiatrist at Fort Hood, had been deeply distressed about his deployment to Afghanistan, scheduled for November 28, because he believed, "You're not supposed to have alliances with Jews or Christian[s] or others, and if you are killed in the military fighting against Muslims, you will go to hell."[1] Over the previous five years, Hasan had begun to openly oppose the War on Terror because of his religion.

What was unclear in this case, however, was whether or not Hasan expected to wake up in a martyr's paradise rather than a hospital bed. Considering the fact that Hasan gave away most of his possessions, including his furniture and copies of the Koran, on the morning of the shooting, it seems doubtful that he planned on surviving that fateful day. Whether or not he considered himself a religious martyr, however, was unclear. Was the shooting simply yet another case of workplace violence? Or of mental illness manifesting itself, unfortunately but arbitrarily, in the workplace? Or did Hasan feel backed into a corner, convinced he could not avoid deployment and equally unable to bring himself to fight fellow Muslims in Afghanistan? Or were Hasan's actions part of some larger conspiracy or operation? Specifically, were they an act of terrorism? And to that point, does it make any difference in terms of how we deal with such incidents?

DOI: 10.4324/9781003474104-9

9.1 Background[2]

Hasan was born on September 8, 1970, in Virginia to Palestinian parents who had emigrated from the West Bank in the 1960s. Hasan's parents ran small businesses—a convenience store and two restaurants—which Hasan and his two brothers helped with until they left home for college and professional schools. Hasan was not a devout Muslim growing up, and so immediately after graduating high school, against the wishes of his parents, Hasan enlisted in the U.S. Army Reserve Officers' Training Corps (ROTC) while attending Virginia Tech. According to a cousin, Hasan stated, "I was born and raised here, I'm going to do my duty to my country."[3] An aunt also said that the military "was his life." In 1995, Hasan graduated from college with a bachelor's degree in biochemistry and went on to receive training as a doctor at the Uniformed Services University of Health Sciences in Bethesda, Maryland.

Hasan's uncle described him as "a gentle, quiet, deeply sensitive man," even going so far as to describe a pet bird that Hasan had once owned, and which he fed by placing the bird in his mouth and offering it masticated food. When the bird died, Hasan apparently mourned it for months. One might think this anecdote explains his attraction to psychiatry. However, Hasan's decision to become a shrink, rather than a surgeon, was prompted by an incident when he fainted while observing childbirth during medical training. He completed his residency in psychiatry at the Walter Reed Army Medical Center, where counseling and extra supervision were required for Hasan because he had some unexplained "difficulties," according to training director Dr. Thomas Grieger.

Hasan's parents died in 1998 and 2001, and in the years following their deaths, he became increasingly devout and interested in the teachings of the Koran. During his senior year of residency at Walter Reed, Hasan gave a presentation titled "The Koranic World View as It Relates to Muslims in the U.S. Military," which was not well received by many attendees. In his presentation, Hasan recommended that the Department of Defense "should allow Muslims [sic] Soldiers the option of being released as 'Conscientious objectors' to increase troop morale and decrease adverse events" (citing "adverse events" such as Hasan Akbar's 2003 murder of two officers at Camp Pennsylvania, Kuwait). He also came to the following conclusions:

- God expects full loyalty. Promises heaven and threatens with Hell.
- Muslims may be seen as moderate (compromising) but God is not.
- "I love the Koran and being a Muslim, but I don't want to live under Islamic rule".

- Fighting to establish an Islamic State to please God, even by force, is condoned by the [*sic*] Islam.
- Muslims [*sic*] [s]oldiers should not serve in any capacity that renders them at risk of hurting/killing believers unjustly → will vary![4]

Due to this presentation and similar comments in which Hasan proselytized his radical ideas, some colleagues doubted Hasan's commitment to the military. One graduate school classmate, Dr. Val Finnell, said that Hasan's presentation "justified suicide bombing" (most likely referring to a slide titled "Comments," which read: "If Muslim groups can convince Muslims that they are fighting for God against injustices of the 'infidels'; i.e.: enemies of Islam, then Muslims can become a potent adversary i.e.: suicide bombing, etc.") and was "anti-American propaganda." Hasan described himself as "a Muslim first and an American second," and this, in conjunction with Hasan's presentation, made Finnell question his loyalty.

Finnell said that Hasan's presentation was off-topic—it was meant to be a presentation on environmental health, but Hasan's project focused on whether the War on Terror was a war against Islam—and that Hasan brought up his religion often and unprompted: "If those topics came up in conversation, it was because he brought those things up," Finnell said. "It was a self-fulfilling prophecy. He made himself a lightning rod by making his extreme views known to everyone."[5] Finnell added he was shocked that someone exhibiting such beliefs was allowed to wear an officer's uniform, but that no one filed a formal complaint against Hasan for fear of appearing discriminatory. He was not surprised that Hasan committed the Fort Hood shooting. He stated: "I had real questions about what his priorities were, what his beliefs were."[6]

Hasan grew increasingly vocal about his opposition to the wars in Iraq and Afghanistan, and he seemed to find it ever more difficult to reconcile military duties and religion. He occasionally complained of harassment, such as an incident in which someone drew a camel on his car and wrote beneath it, "Camel jockey, get out!" Furthermore, a cousin of Hasan's claimed that Hasan was terrified of being deployed after having counseled so many returning soldiers who exhibited post-traumatic stress disorder.

Relatives said that Hasan retained a lawyer in an attempt to get discharged from the Army, but he believed it was impossible. The army had paid for his education, he was in need of mental health professionals, and he was actively attempting to recruit Arab-Americans—he believed his chances of getting an early discharge were slim to nil. Indeed, Bernard Rostker, a military personnel expert at the Rand Corporation, said that Hasan's advancement from captain to major in 2008 was all but certain, explaining that the Army was:

> short of officers, particularly at the major and lieutenant colonel level because of the war, and we're short of psychiatrists .... There would have had to be

> something very detrimental in his record before there would have been a banner that would have said, "No, we don't want to promote him."[7]

Similarly, an investigation conducted by the Department of Defense found that although Hasan had:

> repeatedly failed to meet basic standards set for officers for physical fitness, appearance and work ethic . . . superiors allowed his medical career to advance [because] supervisors were blinded by his resume, believing they had found a rare medical officer: someone with a stellar undergraduate record, prior service in the infantry and intimate knowledge of the Islamic faith . . . . "The Army thought it had hit the trifecta."[8]

In 2001, Hasan began attending the Dar al-Hijrah mosque in the Falls Church area—a mosque also attended at the same time by two 9/11 hijackers, Nawaf al-Hazmi and Hani Hanjour, and by Ahmed Omar Ali, a man convicted of providing material support to al Qaeda and conspiring to assassinate President George W. Bush. At the time, the mosque's imam was Anwar al-Awlaki, an Islamic lecturer and spiritual leader with ties to al Qaeda.

Hasan clearly revered al-Awlaki's teachings, and he sent al-Awlaki as many as 20 emails from December 2008 forward. In his emails, Hasan asked al-Awlaki when jihad is appropriate, and if it was acceptable to kill innocents in a suicide attack. He also wrote that he could not wait to join al-Awlaki in the afterlife. In the months before the shooting, Hasan discussed how to transfer funds abroad without coming to the attention of law authorities. A counter terrorism specialist reviewed the emails at the time and proclaimed them innocuous. The emails were viewed as "general questions about spiritual guidance with regard to conflicts between Islam and military service . . . judged to be consistent with legitimate mental health research about Muslims in the armed services."[9]

However, Hasan had been an active antiwar presence on the Internet for years before his conversations with al-Awlaki. In one Internet posting titled "Martyrdom in Islam Versus Suicide Bombing," Hasan compared a suicide bomber to a soldier who jumps on a grenade to save the lives of fellow officers, in that both were sacrificing their lives "for a more noble cause."[10] This and other postings, however, were not definitively tied to Hasan at the time. After the Fort Hood shooting, al-Awlaki commended Hasan's actions on his website, encouraging Muslims serving in the military to "follow in the footsteps of men like Nidal," whom he called a hero. He claimed that Hasan was simply a "man of conscience," a man who "could not bear living the contradiction of being a Muslim and serving in an army that is fighting against his own people." And finally:

> The fact that fighting against the US [A]rmy is an Islamic duty today cannot be disputed. No scholar with a grain of Islamic knowledge can defy the clear-cut

> proofs that Muslims today have the right—rather the duty—to fight against American tyranny.[11]

Some investigators believe that Hasan's conversations with al-Awlaki were what prompted his actions on November 5, 2009. If so, then Hasan is a classic case of leaderless resistance, à la Timothy McVeigh (Chapter 2) and the ALF/ELF activists (Chapter 4).

9.2 The Shootings and the Legal Proceedings That Followed

On the day of the shootings, at approximately 1:34 p.m. CST, Hasan entered the Soldier Readiness Center and sat down at a desk, bowed his head for a few moments, and opened fire, committing one of the worst mass killings at a U.S. military facility on record. The response to the shooting was deemed "prompt and effective" by the Department of Defense: "Just four minutes and 10 seconds after the first 911 call, the accused shooter was incapacitated and the rampage halted, according to the report,"[12] but the damage was done, and everyone—both the military and the public—was left to question the motivation behind Hasan's actions.

Speculation began immediately, with some citing Hasan's fear of deployment, others his contact with al-Awlaki. An antimilitary activist, Selena Coppa, blamed the military itself, commenting, "This man was a psychiatrist and was working with other psychiatrists every day and they failed to notice how deeply disturbed someone right in their midst was."[13]

U.S. Rep. Michael McCaul (R-Texas), provided one of the most inflammatory remarks on record: "Whether it was domestic or foreign, clearly when a US military base is attacked in this fashion, that is an act of terror in my book."[14] Similarly, Sen. Susan Collins (R-Maine) and the Homeland Security Committee ranking member said, "I am convinced that terrorists are beginning to focus their efforts on smaller-scale attacks, with small arms and explosives such as we saw at Fort Hood, Arkansas, and in India."[15]

These comments beg the questions: Can Hasan's actions be labeled terrorism? Are his actions evidence of a larger trend toward grassroots terrorist attacks? Due to the huge amount of speculation following the shootings and the publicity surrounding the event, a complicated and lengthy trial process was inevitable, and it seemed that questions of terrorism might never be satisfactorily addressed. According to one contemporaneous news source, it would take approximately two years to even reach the military equivalent of a trial—and who knows whether that will occur at Fort Hood or elsewhere—and the outcome would more than likely be muddied by a multitude of appeals. According to Richard Rosen, a former military justice attorney at Fort Hood,

Hasan could still get a fair trial: "There could be a lot of prejudice there .... But experience has been that military jurors are an independent bunch. The military jurists are smart people. The officers will all be college-educated and people with advanced degrees."[16]

Hasan spent several days hospitalized and in a coma in Fort Sam Houston in San Antonio. When he finally awoke, he refused to speak to investigators and requested a lawyer, and was soon being represented by John P. Galligan, a criminal defense attorney and retired U.S. Army colonel.

An Article 32 hearing was conducted and ended on November 15, 2010 (after a three-week delay, as the defense did not want the hearing conducted during the anniversary of the shooting), wherein the defense team called no witnesses, later claiming that they had not received key government reports regarding the case.[17] Several witnesses provided unsettling testimony for the military, however, and the 911 tape from the shooting was also played during the hearing.[18]

Under the Uniform Code of Military Justice, Hasan was charged with 13 counts of premeditated murder and 32 counts of attempted premeditated murder.[19] U.S. Army Col. James L. Pohl presided over the hearing and also recommended a general court-martial for Hasan, and the investigating officer recommended that the military pursue the death penalty.[20] Around December 10, 2010, Hasan began a mental evaluation that would determine if he were competent to stand trial.[21]

After numerous delays involving complex legal maneuvering, similar to what I have described in detail in previous chapters, Hasan finally was tried in the summer of 2013. In August 2013, Hasan was convicted of 13 counts of murder and 32 counts of attempted murder. Following the penalty phase of the trial, he was sentenced to death, a sentence which has yet to be carried out.[22]

Though some believe the Fort Hood shooting to be the "first international terror attack on American soil since 9/11,"[23] Hasan's defense was determined to paint the attack as a spontaneous act, the desperate actions of a mentally ill man.[24] Despite Hasan's contact with al-Awlaki prior to the attack, FBI investigators found that Hasan had apparently acted alone, without outside help or direct orders from al-Awlaki or anyone else to commit the attack on Fort Hood.[25]

When Hasan finally came to trial in 2013, he represented himself and made statements that indicated he considered himself to be a jihadist. Such statements, so late in the game, may have been gratuitous or may have been sincere. They beg the question: Is "terrorist" a subjective or objective term?

"I used to argue it was only terrorism if it were part of some identifiable, organized conspiracy," said Bruce Hoffman, a terrorism expert at Georgetown University. But Hoffman changed his definition, he said, because "this new strategy of al-Qaeda is to empower and motivate individuals to commit acts of violence completely outside any terrorist chain of command." He added, "The nature of terrorism is changing, and Major Hasan may be an example that," Hoffman argued. "Even if he turns out to have had no political motive, this is a sea change."[26]

If "leaderless resistance" is the wave of the future, it may be less lethal but harder to fight; there are fewer clues to collect and less chatter to hear, even as information about means and methods is so much more widely dispersed. It is more like spontaneous combustion than someone from the outside lighting a match. The U.S. Senate's Homeland Security Committee chaired by Sen. Joe Lieberman (I-Connecticut) warned of this threat in a report that asserted, "The emergence of these self-generated violent Islamist extremists who are radicalized online presents a challenge," the report concluded, "because lone wolves are less likely to come to the attention of law enforcement." At least until they start shooting.

It might help if there were at least agreement on what constitutes terrorism; one government study found 109 different definitions. As far as the FBI is concerned, it counts as terrorism if you commit a crime that endangers another person or is violent with a broader intent to intimidate, influence, or change policy or opinion. If Hasan shot people because of indigestion, worker conflict, or plain insanity without a larger goal of intimidation or coercion, it was probably "just" a crime. If, on the other hand, his crime was motivated by more than madness—say, a desire to protest U.S. foreign policy—it was effectively terrorism.

But it's becoming more and more difficult to distinguish between the mentally disturbed lone wolf and the true terrorist, as I explain in Chapter 11 and Chapter 12. Former Homeland Security Secretary Michael Chertoff warned, "We have to be careful not to let our definition of terrorism become too broad" because "once everything is terrorism, then nothing is." However, while the reasoning behind other attacks such as the Virginia Tech shooting in 2007 seem quite personal to the shooter, Hasan had for years been declaring the U.S. war effort in Iraq and Afghanistan immoral.[27] On June 29, 2012, a military judge had decreed that Hasan's trial would begin in August. However, in August it was delayed yet again, this time to await a determination of whether the Army could force him to shave the beard he had grown. It took another year to bring him into the courtroom. In light of these facts, I find it difficult to discredit has claim to being a jihadist, and ergo a terrorist.[28]

9.3 Anwar al-Awlaki and the Yemeni Connection

Anwar al-Awlaki was born April 22, 1971, in Las Cruces, New Mexico. He is a dual citizen of the United States and Yemen. If he had a resume, it might identify him as an Islamic lecturer, spiritual leader, and former imam who inspired Islamic terrorists against the West. According to U.S. officials, he was a "senior talent recruiter and motivator," who also became "operational" as a planner and trainer, "for al-Qaeda and all of its franchises."[29] The U.S. Under Secretary of the Treasury for Terrorism and Financial Intelligence once warned that al-Awlaki "is extraordinarily dangerous, committed to carrying out deadly attacks on Americans and others worldwide."[30] With a blog, a Facebook page, and many YouTube videos, he was described as the "Bin Laden of the Internet."[31]

Al-Awlaki's sermons were attended by three of the 9/11 hijackers. He reportedly met privately with two of them in San Diego. One moved from there to Falls Church, Virginia, as al-Awlaki moved. Investigators suspect that al-Awlaki may have known about the 9/11 attacks in advance.[32] In 2009, he was promoted to the rank of "regional commander" within al Qaeda, according to U.S. officials.[33]

As noted previously, his sermons were also attended by accused Fort Hood shooter Nidal Malik Hasan. U.S. intelligence intercepted at least 18 emails between Hasan and al-Awlaki in the months prior to the Fort Hood shooting, including one in which Hasan wrote: "I can't wait to join you [in the afterlife]." After the shooting, al-Awlaki praised Hasan's actions. In addition, "Christmas Day bomber" Umar Farouk Abdulmutallab said al-Awlaki was one of his al Qaeda trainers, who met with him and was involved in planning or preparing his attack, and provided religious justification for it, according to U.S. officials. In March 2010, al-Awlaki said in a videotape that jihad against America was binding upon every able Muslim.

Shortly after the Fort Hood shootings, news sources revealed that the rogue cleric had escaped to Yemen, apparently due to police incompetence. According to ABC News,

> A felony arrest warrant for radical Islamic cleric Anwar al-Awlaki was rescinded in 2002 a day before he was intercepted as a terror suspect at New York's JFK airport, forcing authorities to release him, according to sources familiar with the case. The warrant was canceled by the U.S. Attorney's Office in Denver, even though Awlaki was on a terror watch list, and even though the office's supervising prosecutor for terror cases—who was later appointed by the Obama administration as the U.S. Attorney in Denver—had been fully briefed on Awlaki's alleged terror ties, according to investigators.[34]

As Awlaki's connections to other would-be terrorists, such as the Times Square bomber (Chapter 10), became increasingly apparent, the Obama administration placed him on its "targeting shooting" list.[35] This in turn led to a lawsuit brought by the American Civil Liberties Union and the Center for Constitutional Rights on August 30, 2010.[36]

UNITED STATES DISTRICT COURT FOR THE DISTRICT OF COLUMBIA

NASSER AL-AULAQI, on his own behalf and as Next Friend of Anwar Al-Aulaqi,
Al-Zubairi Street
Al-Saeed Center Sana'a,
Yemen, Plaintiff,
v.
BARACK H. OBAMA, in his official capacity as President of the United States 1600 Pennsylvania Avenue NW Washington, DC 20500;
LEON C. PANETTA, in his official capacity as Director of the Central Intelligence Agency Central Intelligence Agency Washington, DC 20505; ROBERT M. GATES, in his official capacity as Secretary of Defense
1000 Defense Pentagon Washington, DC 20301–1010, Defendants.
COMPLAINT FOR DECLARATORY AND INJUNCTIVE RELIEF
(Violation of constitutional rights and international law—targeted killing)

INTRODUCTION

1. This case concerns the executive's asserted authority to carry out "targeted killings" of U.S. citizens suspected of terrorism far from any field of armed conflict. According to numerous published reports, the government maintains lists of suspects—"kill lists"—against whom lethal force can be used without charge, trial, or conviction. Individuals, including U.S. citizens, are added to the lists based on executive determinations that secret criteria have been satisfied. Executive officials are thus invested with sweeping authority to impose extrajudicial death sentences in violation of the Constitution and international law.
2. The right to life is the most fundamental of all rights. Outside the context of armed conflict, the intentional use of lethal force without prior judicial process is an abridgement of this right except in the narrowest and most extraordinary circumstances.
3. The United States is not at war with Yemen, or within it. Nonetheless, U.S. government officials have disclosed the government's intention to carry out the targeted killing of U.S. citizen Anwar Al-Aulaqi, who is in hiding there. In early 2010, several newspapers reported that U.S. government officials had confirmed Anwar Al-Aulaqi's placement on government kill lists; these lists amount to standing authorizations to use lethal force. Numerous subsequent reports have corroborated

those accounts. According to one media report, there have already been as many as a dozen unsuccessful attempts on Anwar Al-Aulaqi's life. Anwar Al-Aulaqi has been in hiding since at least January 2010. Plaintiff Nasser Al-Aulaqi is Anwar Al-Aulaqi's father; he brings this action on his own behalf and as next friend to his son.

4. Outside of armed conflict, both the Constitution and international law prohibit targeted killing except as a last resort to protect against concrete, specific, and imminent threats of death or serious physical injury. The summary use of force is lawful in these narrow circumstances only because the imminence of the threat makes judicial process infeasible. A targeted killing policy under which individuals are added to kill lists after a bureaucratic process and remain on these lists for months at a time plainly goes beyond the use of lethal force as a last resort to address imminent threats, and accordingly goes beyond what the Constitution and international law permit.
5. The government's refusal to disclose the standard by which it determines to target U.S. citizens for death independently violates the Constitution: U.S. citizens have a right to know what conduct may subject them to execution at the hands of their own government. Due process requires, at a minimum, that citizens be put on notice of what may cause them to be put to death by the state.
6. Plaintiff seeks a declaration from this Court that the Constitution and international law prohibit the government from carrying out targeted killings outside of armed conflict except as a last resort to protect against concrete, specific, and imminent threats of death or serious physical injury; and an injunction prohibiting the targeted killing of U.S. citizen Anwar Al-Aulaqi outside this narrow context. Plaintiff also seeks an injunction requiring the government to disclose the standards under which it determines whether U.S. citizens can be targeted for death.

JURISDICTION AND VENUE

7. Jurisdiction is proper pursuant to 28 U.S.C. § 1331 (federal question jurisdiction) over causes of action arising under the Fourth and Fifth Amendments to the U.S. Constitution, and 28 U.S.C. § 1350 (Alien Tort Statute) over a cause of action arising under customary international law and treaty law. Jurisdiction is also proper pursuant to 5 U.S.C. § 702 et seq. (Administrative Procedure Act) and 28 U.S.C. § 2201 et seq. (Declaratory Judgment Act).
8. Venue is proper in this district pursuant to 28 U.S.C. § 1391.

PARTIES

9. Plaintiff Nasser Al-Aulaqi is the father of Anwar Al-Aulaqi, a U.S. citizen whose targeted killing Defendants have authorized. Nasser Al-Aulaqi is a citizen and resident of Yemen. He acts on his own behalf and as next friend to his son. He acts in the latter capacity because his son is in hiding under threat of death and cannot access counsel or the courts to assert his constitutional rights without disclosing his whereabouts and exposing himself to possible attack by Defendants. He brings the Alien Tort Statute claim on his own behalf to prevent the injury he would suffer if Defendants were to kill his son.
10. Defendant Barack H. Obama is President of the United States. As President, he is Commander-in-Chief of the U.S. armed forces and serves as Chair of the National Security Council, which authorizes the targeted killing of suspected terrorists who are U.S. citizens. President Obama is sued in his official capacity.
11. Defendant Leon C. Panetta is the Director of the Central Intelligence Agency ("CIA"). As CIA Director, he has ultimate authority over the CIA's operations worldwide. Upon information and belief, Defendant Panetta approves the addition of individuals to the kill list maintained by the CIA, and signs off on individual targeted killing operations conducted by the CIA outside of armed conflict, including those against U.S. citizens. Director Panetta is sued in his official capacity.
12. Defendant Robert M. Gates is the Secretary of Defense. As Defense Secretary, he has ultimate authority over the U.S. armed forces worldwide, including the Joint Special Operations Command ("JSOC"). Upon information and belief, JSOC is involved in carrying out targeted killings, including of U.S. citizens outside of armed conflict. In his capacity as Secretary of Defense, Defendant Gates is also a statutory member of the National Security Council, which authorizes the targeted killing of U.S. citizens. Secretary Gates is sued in his official capacity.

FACTUAL ALLEGATIONS

Targeted Killings by the United States Outside of Armed Conflict

13. Since 2001, the United States has carried out targeted killings in connection with the "war on terror." While many of these killings have been conducted by the U.S. military in the context of the armed conflicts in Afghanistan and Iraq, the United States has also carried out targeted killings outside the context of armed conflict, and it is these

killings that are at issue here. Upon information and belief, both the CIA and JSOC are involved in authorizing, planning, and carrying out targeted killings, including of U.S. citizens, outside the context of armed conflict.

14. The first reported post-2001 targeted killing by the U.S. government outside Afghanistan occurred in Yemen in November 2002, when a CIA-operated Predator drone fired a missile at a suspected terrorist traveling in a car with other passengers. The strike killed all passengers in the vehicle, including a U.S. citizen. The United Nations Special Rapporteur on Extrajudicial Killings later stated that the strike constituted "a clear case of extrajudicial killing" and set an "alarming precedent." Since 2001, there has been an increase in targeted killings by the United States against terrorism suspects outside of Afghanistan and Iraq.
15. The government has publicly claimed the authority to carry out targeted killings of civilians, including U.S. citizens, outside the context of armed conflict. For example, in February 2010, then-Director of National Intelligence Dennis Blair, in response to a question by a member of Congress about the targeted killing of U.S. citizens, stated that the United States takes "direct action" against suspected terrorists and that "if we think that direct action will involve killing an American, we get specific permission to do that." In June 2010, Deputy National Security Advisor John Brennan responded to questions about the targeted killing program by stating, "If an American person or citizen is in Yemen or in Pakistan or in Somalia or another place, and they are trying to carry out attacks against U.S. interests, they will also face the full brunt of a U.S. response."
16. Although the government has publicly claimed the authority to carry out targeted killings of civilians outside the context of armed conflict, it has not explained on what basis individuals are added to kill lists, or the circumstances in which the asserted authority to carry out targeted killings will actually be exercised.

Specific Authorization to Kill Plaintiff's Son Anwar Al-Aulaqi

17. Plaintiff Nasser Al-Aulaqi moved to the United States in 1966 to pursue his studies as a Fulbright scholar at New Mexico State University. Plaintiff's son, Anwar Al-Aulaqi, was born in New Mexico in 1971. Plaintiff remained in the United States with his family for the next seven years, until 1978, when they moved back to Yemen. Plaintiff went on to serve as Minister of Agriculture and Fisheries in the Government of Yemen, and later founded and served as president of Ibb

University and served as president of Sana'a University. Plaintiff currently resides in Yemen with his wife, who is an American citizen, and their family.

18. In 1991, Plaintiff's son Anwar Al-Aulaqi returned to the United States to attend college at Colorado State University. Anwar Al-Aulaqi went on to obtain his master's degree at San Diego State University and later enrolled in a Ph.D. program at George Washington University, which he attended through December 2001. He married and had three children while living in the United States. He moved to the United Kingdom in 2003, and to Yemen in 2004.
19. In January 2010, the Washington Post reported that Anwar Al-Aulaqi had been added to "a shortlist of U.S. citizens" that JSOC was specifically authorized to kill. The same article reported that Anwar Al-Aulaqi had survived a JSOC-assisted strike in Yemen in late December 2009. That strike reportedly killed 41 civilians, mostly children and women. Another January 2010 news report stated that Anwar Al-Aulaqi was "all but certain" to be added to a list of suspects that the CIA was specifically authorized to kill. In April 2010, the Washington Post and other media sources reported that Anwar Al-Aulaqi had been added to the CIA's list.
20. Numerous news reports have corroborated that Defendants have authorized the targeted killing of Anwar Al-Aulaqi and are actively pursuing him. According to one media report, he has already been the target of as many as a dozen unsuccessful strikes. One U.S. official stated that "he's in everybody's sights." In the context of a discussion about targeted killing, Defendant Panetta stated that Anwar Al-Aulaqi is "someone that we're looking for" and that "there isn't any question that he's one of the individuals that we're focusing on."
21. Defendants added Anwar Al-Aulaqi to the CIA and JSOC kill lists after a closed executive process. In the course of that process, Defendants and other executive officials determined that Anwar Al-Aulaqi satisfied secret criteria that determine whether a U.S. citizen can be killed by his own government. Upon information and belief, Anwar Al-Aulaqi is now subject to a standing order that permits the CIA and JSOC to kill him. Upon information and belief, the authorization for Anwar Al-Aulaqi's killing by the CIA and JSOC involved the approval or recommendation of all Defendants.
22. Upon information and belief, individuals placed on the CIA and JSOC targeted killing lists remain on those lists for months at a time. An intelligence official who was questioned about the CIA's kill list stated that individuals would be removed from the kill list if their

names "hadn't popped on the screen for over a year, or there was no intelligence linking [them] to known terrorists or plans."

23. Upon information and belief, Defendants have authorized the CIA and JSOC to kill Anwar Al-Aulaqi without regard to whether, at the time lethal force will be used, he presents a concrete, specific, and imminent threat to life, or whether there are reasonable means short of lethal force that could be used to address any such threat.
24. Executive officials have condemned Anwar Al-Aulaqi's public statements and sermons; they have also alleged that he has "cast his lot" with terrorist groups and taken on an "operational" role in a terrorist organization. The U.S. government has not, however, publicly indicted Anwar Al-Aulaqi for any terrorism-related crime.
25. In response to reports that the United States has placed Anwar Al-Aulaqi on kill lists, Yemeni officials, including the Prime Minister, the Foreign Minister, and the Director of the National Security Agency, have publicly stated that their government's security forces are taking measures to arrest Anwar Al-Aulaqi for possible charge and trial. Yemeni cabinet members have also publicly requested that the United States provide the Yemeni government with any evidence against Anwar Al-Aulaqi to support arresting him and bringing him to trial. The Yemeni government has prosecuted other residents of Yemen for terrorism-related crimes, and the Yemeni government is currently prosecuting at least one U.S. citizen who is alleged to be a member of a terrorist organization. Anwar Al-Aulaqi has in the past been detained by the Yemeni government and was imprisoned for 18 months in 2006 and 2007.
26. Anwar Al-Aulaqi has been in hiding in Yemen since at least January 2010. Plaintiff has had no communication with his son during that time. Anwar Al-Aulaqi cannot communicate with his father or counsel without endangering his own life.

CAUSES OF ACTION

First Claim for Relief Fourth Amendment: Right to be Free from Unreasonable Seizure

27. Defendants' policy of targeted killings violates the Fourth Amendment by authorizing, outside of armed conflict, the seizure, in the form of targeted killing, of U.S. citizens, including Plaintiff's son, in circumstances in which they do not present concrete, specific, and imminent threats to life or physical safety, and where there are means other than lethal force that could reasonably be employed to neutralize any such threat. Plaintiff brings this claim as next friend for his son.

Second Claim for Relief Fifth Amendment: Right Not to be Deprived of Life Without Due Process

28. Defendants' policy of targeted killings violates the Fifth Amendment by authorizing, outside of armed conflict, the killing of U.S. citizens, including Plaintiff's son, without due process of law in circumstances in which they do not present concrete, specific, and imminent threats to life or physical safety, and where there are means other than lethal force that could reasonably be employed to neutralize any such threat. Plaintiff brings this claim as next friend for his son.

Third Claim for Relief Alien Tort Statute: Extrajudicial Killing

29. Defendants' policy of targeted killings violates treaty and customary international law by authorizing, outside of armed conflict, the killing of individuals, including Plaintiff's son, without judicial process in circumstances in which they do not present concrete, specific, and imminent threats to life or physical safety, and where there are means other than lethal force that could reasonably be employed to neutralize any such threat. Plaintiff brings this claim in his own right to prevent the injury he would suffer if Defendants were to kill his son.

Fourth Claim for Relief Fifth Amendment: Due Process Notice Requirements

30. Defendants' policy of targeted killings outside of armed conflict violates the Fifth Amendment by authorizing the killing of U.S. citizens, including Plaintiff's son, on the basis of criteria that are secret. Plaintiff brings this claim as next friend for his son.

PRAYER FOR RELIEF

For the foregoing reasons, Plaintiff Nasser Al-Aulaqi requests that the Court:

1. Declare that, outside of armed conflict, the Constitution prohibits Defendants from carrying out the targeted killing of U.S. citizens, including Plaintiff's son, except in circumstances in which they present concrete, specific, and imminent threats to life or physical safety, and there are no means other than lethal force that could reasonably be employed to neutralize the threats.
2. Declare that, outside of armed conflict, treaty and customary international law prohibit Defendants from carrying out the targeted killing of individuals, including Plaintiff's son, except in circumstances in which they present concrete, specific, and imminent threats to life or physical safety, and there are no

means other than lethal force that could reasonably be employed to neutralize the threats.

3. Enjoin Defendants from intentionally killing U.S. citizen Anwar Al-Aulaqi unless he presents a concrete, specific, and imminent threat to life or physical safety, and there are no means other than lethal force that could reasonably be employed to neutralize the threat.
4. Order Defendants to disclose the criteria that are used in determining whether the government will carry out the targeted killing of a U.S. citizen.
5. Grant any other and further relief as is appropriate and necessary.

Respectfully submitted,
11 August 30, 2010
/s/Arthur B. Spitzer
Arthur B. Spitzer (D.C. Bar No. 235960) American Civil Liberties Union of the Nation's Capital
1400 20th Street, N.W., Suite 119 Washington, DC 20036
Tel. 202-457-0800 Fax 202-452.1868 artspitzer@aol.com
Jameel Jaffer (to be admitted *pro hac vice*) Ben Wizner (to be admitted *pro hac vice*) Jonathan M. Manes American Civil Liberties Union Foundation
125 Broad Street, 18th Floor
New York, NY 10004 (212) 519-7814 jjaffer@aclu.org
Pardiss Kebriaei (to be admitted *pro hac vice*) Maria C. LaHood (to be admitted *pro hac vice*) William Quigley Center for Constitutional Rights
666 Broadway, 7th floor New York, NY 10012 (212) 614-6452 pkebriaei@ccrjustice.org

Thus, as the trial of the Fort Hood killer hanged fire, the man who allegedly inspired Hasan's heinous acts was suing Uncle Sam in an effort to avoid the U.S. government's righteous wrath. One might reasonably observe that only in America can the legal process seemingly be so radically turned on its head.

On the other hand, if indeed no person may "be deprived of life, liberty, or property, without due process of law,"[37] then the U.S. government arguably ought not to be targeting even the worst suspects for summary execution.

As with Jose Padilla's incarceration (Chapter 7), the targeting of Awlaki (or Al-Aulaqi, as the complaint calls him) tested yet again the boundaries of the federal government's police and war powers in light of the U.S. Constitution. And, as I argued in the Preface, ours is not an over-lawyered society. To the contrary, given that Awlaki had not personally pulled a trigger or pressed a detonator button—but, rather, had incited illegal acts, as did the ALF activists tried earlier in the decade in Trenton, New Jersey (see Chapter 4)—he perhaps ought to have been captured, extradited, and tried, just as they were.

The Awlaki suit tested this theory, and in the process test us as a civil society ostensibly committed to civil liberties and fair play.

For its part, the government on September 24, 2010, moved to dismiss, raising a range of fundamental defenses:

> Defendants Barack H. Obama, President of the United States, Leon E. Panetta, Director of the Central Intelligence, and Robert M. Gates, Secretary of Defense, hereby move to dismiss Plaintiff's complaint, pursuant to Federal Rule of Civil Procedure 12(b)(1), on the grounds that Plaintiff lacks standing and that his claims require the Court to decide non-justiciable political questions. Alternatively, the Court should exercise its equitable discretion not to grant the relief sought. In addition, Plaintiff has no cause of action under the Alien Tort Statute.
>
> To the extent that the foregoing are not sufficient grounds to dismiss this lawsuit, plaintiff's action should be dismissed on the ground that information properly protected by the military and state secrets privilege would be necessary to litigate this action.[38]

Stripped of its legal jargon and boiled down to its essence, the motion contended that the federal judge has no business poking a judicial nose into the secret doings of the Department of Defense and the CIA.

The case became moot when al-Awlaki was killed by a drone strike on September 30, 2011.[39]

9.4 Postscript

Meanwhile, the paralyzed Hasan himself may have become the target of either an assassination or perhaps a rescue attempt. In April 2012, the U.S. Court of Appeals for the Fifth Circuit affirmed the conviction of Senan Kahtan Abrahem for making a "material false statement to Defense Department security personnel." The court stated the facts as follows:

> On the morning of January 6, 2010, the Defendant entered the Brooke Army Medical Center (BAMC) demanding to see a patient in the hospital accused in the Fort Hood shooting. He claimed he was the patient's lawyer. Though he did not identify the patient by name, he was referring to Major Nidal Hasan, an army psychologist who was being held as a protected patient at BAMC after shooting several people at Fort Hood several months before. The front desk

volunteers understood that the Defendant was referring to Major Hasan. They informed the Defendant that they did not have the authority to permit him to see Major Hasan, and they notified security. The Defendant became increasingly agitated; he began shouting and banging on the information desk and made various remarks referring to the man he was seeking to see as "my brother," and suggesting that the volunteers "shoot me."

Staff Sergeant Justin White was in the BAMC lobby and heard the commotion. He walked up to the Defendant and moved him away from the information desk. Sergeant White testified that Defendant told him that he was there to see "the psychiatrist," "the one who was shot by the infidels." He testified that the Defendant was yelling various statements, including "Allahu Akbar," and that the man he was trying to see was innocent.

Captain Bielling, the supervisor of uniformed security at BAMC, testified that he responded to the duress alarm from the information desk. Captain Bielling identified himself and asked to see the Defendant's identification, which he provided. Captain Bielling testified that he asked the Defendant what he was doing there, and the Defendant replied that he was there to see the person involved with the shooting at Ford Hood. The Defendant was informed that he was not allowed access to the shooter, and that only lawyers and physicians were able to see him. The Defendant replied that he was the man's lawyer, and he asked if he could see him. Captain Bielling asked the Defendant what his client's name was. The Defendant replied he didn't remember. The Defendant asked several bystanders the name of the person who was involved in the Ford Hood shooting. Somebody said it was Major Hasan, and the Defendant said that's the person he wanted to see. According to Captain Bielling, the Defendant identified himself as a Muslim, said he was the person's Muslim brother, and that he had the right to defend him. In making these statements, the Defendant was cooperative and no longer excited, loud or violent. Captain Bielling informed the Defendant that Major Hasan already had a legal team, and that the Defendant would have to coordinate with them if he wanted to defend Major Hasan.

The Defendant then identified himself as a doctor for Major Hasan and stated he was there to treat him. Captain Bielling asked him what he was there to treat him for and the Defendant responded it was confidential. Captain Bielling told the Defendant that Major Hasan already had a doctor and medical team and if he wanted to treat Major Hasan he would have to coordinate with that team.

The Defendant stated that if he was not allowed to see Major Hasan that day he would come back every day for 15 minutes and cause a disturbance until he was let in. Captain Bielling informed him that he had caused a disturbance already, that he had to leave, and that he was interfering with patient care. The Defendant put his wrists in the air and asked if Captain Bielling was going to put handcuffs on him or arrest him. Captain Bielling said he was not, that he was just going to take down the Defendant's information and that the Defendant had to leave. The Defendant stated he wanted to sit and collect himself for ten minutes. Captain Bielling told him he could wait in his car and that he had to leave. The

> Defendant agreed to leave, stood up, and walked out. Captain Bielling and two other officers accompanied the Defendant out of the lobby. The officers took down the relevant material describing the Defendant's car and gave it to the information desk. The Defendant got into his vehicle and departed.[40]

Hasan survived so that he might die on another day. In September 2023 the U.S. Court of Appeals for the Armed Forces unanimously denied his latest motion to have his death sentence commuted.[41]

Notes

1. "The Troubled Journey of Major Hasan," *TIME*, http://www.time.com/time/photogallery/0,29307,1938816_1988791,00.html; Wikipedia, "Fort Hood Shooting," http://en.wikipedia.org/wiki/Fort_Hood_shooting.
2. James C. McKinley Jr. and James Dao, "Fort Hood Gunman Gave Signals before His Rampage," *New York Times*, November 8, 2009, http://www.nytimes.com/2009/11/09/us/09reconstruct.html?_r=1.
3. Matt Chittum and Jorge Valencia, "Suspected Fort Hood Shooter Maj. Nidal Malik Hasan: Social Awkwardness Kept with Him into Adulthood," http://www.roanoke.com/news/roanoke/wb/225310.
4. These are all statements presented on a PowerPoint slide, as part of a presentation that Hasan made during his senior year of residency at Walter Reed Hospital. See "Hasan on Islam," Washington Post, November 10, 2009, http://www. washingtonpost.com/wp-dyn/content/gallery/2009/11/10/GA2009111000920.html (accessed December 18, 2012). The actual slide show may be accessed at "File: Hasan presentation.png," http://en.wikipedia.org/wiki/File:Hasan_presentation.png.
5. Bob Drogin and Faye Fiore, "Retracing Steps of Suspected Fort Hood Shooter, Nidal Malik Hasan," *Los Angeles Times*, November 7, 2007, http://articles.latimes.com/2009/nov/07/nation/na-fort-hood-hasan7/2.
6. "Clear Warning Signs, Hasan's Colleagues Say," *Associated Press/MSNBC*, November 7, 2009, http://www.msnbc.msn.com/id/33753461/ns/us_news-tragedy_at_fort_hood.
7. Ibid.
8. Julian E. Barnes, "Gates Makes Recommendations in Ft. Hood Shooting Case," *Los Angeles Times*, January 15, 2010, http://articles.latimes.com/2010/jan/15/nation/la-na-fort-hood-pentagon16-2010jan16 (accessed January 17, 2010).
9. Wikipedia, "Nidal Malik Hasan."
10. Drogin and Fiore.
11. "Anwar al-Awlaki: 'Nidal Hassan Did the Right Thing,'" *The NEFA Foundation*, http://www.nefafoundation.org/miscellaneous/FeaturedDocs/nefaawlaki-fort-hoodshooting.pdf.
12. Barnes.
13. Nick Allen, "Fort Hood Gunman Had Told US Military Colleagues That Infidels Should Have Their Throats Cut," *The Telegraph*, November 8, 2009, http://www.telegraph.co.uk/news/worldnews/northamerica/usa/6526030/Fort-Hood-

gunman-had-told-US-military-colleagues-that-infidels-should-have-their-throats-cut.html (accessed November 9, 2009).
14. Wajahat Ali, "Fort Hood Has Enough Victims Already," *The Guardian* (London), http://www.guardian.co.uk/commentisfree/cifamerica/2009/nov/06/fort-hood-shootings-hasan-muslim (accessed November 6, 2009).
15. Patrik Jonsson, "Will Fort Hood Shooting Trial Find Motive—or Link to Terrorism?" *The Christian Science Monitor*, October 19, 2010, http://www.csmonitor.com/USA/2010/1019/Will-Fort-Hood-shooting-trial-find—motive-or-link-to-terrorism.
16. Anthony Spangler, "Trial of Fort Hood Shooting Suspect Could Be Lengthy Affair," November 12, 2009, http://www.mcclatchydc.com/2009/11/12/78766/trial-of-fort-hood-shooting-suspect.html.
17. "Hearing for Fort Hood Shooting Suspect Ends," *Associated Press*, November 15, 2010, http://www.foxnews.com/us/2010/11/15/hearing-fort-hood-shooting—suspect-wrapping.
18. "Testimony Begins in Fort Hood Shooting," NPR, October 15, 2010, http://www.npr.org/templates/story/story.php?storyId=130543304. With permission.
19. "Fort Hood Suspect Charged with Murder," *CNN*, November 12, 2009, http://www.cnn.com/2009/CRIME/11/12/fort.hood.investigation/index.html (accessed November 12, 2009).
20. "Death Recommended for Major Nidal Hasan," *Terror on Trial*, November 17, 2010, http://terrortrials.blogspot.com/2010/11/death-recommended-for-major-nidal.html.
21. Angela K. Brown, "Fort Hood Shooting Suspect Undergoing Mental Exam," December 10, 2010, http://www.wtopnews.com/?nid=600&sid=2032321.
22. "Nidal Hasan," *Wikipedia*, https://en.wikipedia.org/wiki/Nidal_Hasan (accessed December 29, 2023).
23. Jonsson, note 16.
24. Clifford Krauss, "Defendant in Court for Hearing at Ft. Hood," *New York Times*, October 12, 2010, http://www.nytimes.com/2010/10/13/us/13hearing.html?_r=1&ref=nidal_malik_hasan.
25. "Investigators Say Fort Hood Suspect Acted Alone," *Associated Press*, November 9, 2009, http://www.msnbc.msn.com/id/33777070/ns/us_news-tragedy_at_fort_hood/.
26. Mary Thompson, "Fort Hood Highlights a Threat of Homegrown Jihad," *Time*, November 11, 2009, https://content.time.com/time/nation/article/0,8599,1937912,00.html (accessed May 7, 2024).
27. Nancy Gibbs, "The Fort Hood Killer: Terrified . . . or Terrorist?" *TIME*, November 11, 2009, http://www.time.com/time/nation/article/0,8599,1938415-2,00.html.
28. Angela K. Brown, "Fort Hood Shooting Suspect Trial Won't Be Delayed," *San Francisco Chronicle*, June 29, 2012, http://www.sfgate.com/news/article/Fort-Hood-shooting-suspect-trial-won-t-be-delayed-3672205.php (accessed July 1, 2012).
29. Fox News staff, "Congressman Wants Radical Cleric's Citizenship Revoked," *Fox News*, April 7, 2010; Bob Orr, "Al-Awlaki May Be Al Qaeda Recruiter," *CBS News*, December 30, 2009; James Gordon Meek, "Fort Hood Gunman Nidal Hasan 'Is

a Hero': Imam Who Preached to 9/11 Hijackers in Va. Praises Attack," *New York Daily News*, November 9, 2009; Michelle Shepherd, "The Powerful Online Voice of Jihad," *Toronto Star*, October 18, 2009; Tom Sharpe, "Radical Imam Traces Roots to New Mexico; Militant Islam Cleric's Father Graduated from NMSU," *Santa Fe New Mexican*, November 14, 2009.

30. "Treasury Designates Anwar al-Awlaki Key Leader of AQAP," *CNN*, July 13, 2010.
31. Loveday Morris, "The Anatomy of a Suicide Bomber," *The National (Abu Dhabi)*, October 24, 2010; Aamer Madhani, "Cleric al-Awlaki Dubbed 'Bin Laden of the Internet,'" USA Today, August 25, 2010.
32. Joseph Rhee and Mark Schone, "How Anwar Awlaki Got Away," The Blotter from Brian Ross; Fort Hood Investigation (*ABC News*), November 30, 2009; Kelly Thornton, "Chance to Foil 9/11 Plot Lost Here, Report Finds," *San Diego Union Tribune*, July 30, 2003.
33. David Usborne and the Centre for Social Cohesion (British think-tank), "Obama Orders US-Born Cleric to Be Shot on Sight," *The Independent* (London), April 8, 2010.
34. Rhee and Schone.
35. James Gordon Meek, "Experts: Al Qaeda in Yemen May Send American Jihadis, Recruited by Anwar al-Awlaki, to Attack U.S.," *New York Daily News*, February 4, 2010; Usborne and Centre for Social Cohesion.
36. See http://www.ccrjustice.org/targetedkillings#filesn (accessed December 11, 2010).
37. U.S. Constitution, Fifth Amendment, which reads in full:

> No person shall be held to answer for a capital, or otherwise infamous crime, unless on a pre-sentment or indictment of a Grand Jury, except in cases arising in the land or naval forces, or in the Militia, when in actual service in time of War or public danger; nor shall any person be subject for the same offense to be twice put in jeopardy of life or limb; nor shall be compelled in any criminal case to be a witness against himself, nor be deprived of life, liberty, or property, without due process of law; nor shall private property be taken for public use, without just compensation.

38. Defendants' Motion to Dismiss, http://www.ccrjustice.org/files/15-Al-Aulaqi%20 USG%20MTD_09-25-10.pdf (accessed December 11, 2010).
39. Sudarsan Raghavan, "Awlaqi Hit Misses al-Qaeda Bombmaker, Yemen Says," *Washington Post*, October 1, 2012, http://www.washingtonpost.com/world/anwar-al-aulaqi-us-born-cleric-linked-to-al-qaeda-killed-yemen-says/2011/09/30/gIQAsoWO9K_story.html (accessed July 1, 2012).
40. *United States v. Abraham*, 678 F.3rd 370 (5th Cir., 2012).
41. Zamone Perez, "Death Penalty Upheld for Soldier Who Killed 13 in Base Shooting," *Army Times*, September 11, 2023, https://www.armytimes.com/news/your-military/2023/09/11/death-penalty-upheld-for-soldier-who-killed-13-in-base-shooting/ (accessed December 29, 2023).

The Times Square Bomber (2010)

10

In Chapter 9, the main focus of which was the Fort Hood shootings of November 2009, you also met the late Anwar al-Awlaki (aka al-Aulaqi). Widely believed to have been Osama bin Laden's inheritor, Awlaki was successfully targeted by the Obama administration for assassination in 2011. This decision was challenged in a lawsuit brought by the American Civil Liberties Union (ACLU) and others in the District of Columbia's federal trial court. In announcing the suit, ACLU's Jameel Jaffer said:

> The United States is not at war in Yemen, and the government doesn't have a blank check to kill terrorism suspects wherever they are in the world. Among the arguments we'll be making is that, outside actual war zones, the authority to use lethal force is narrowly circumscribed, and preserving the rule of law depends on keeping this authority narrow.[1]

Among the plaintiffs was Nasser al-Awlaki, the target's father, who asserted that his son was American-born and therefore a U.S. citizen.

Commenting on the case, Sam Rascoff, a law professor at New York University, observed,

> Previous lawsuits have focused mainly on the government's power to detain, interrogate, and gather intelligence on individuals as part of the so-called "war on terror." Now, for the first time, the government's authority to kill one of its own citizens is in question.[2]

Al-Awlaki may have been an American citizen and he may have been an imam. But he was also a figure connected by compelling evidence to a whole series of terrorist attempts upon the United States and Europe. These failed strikes included:

- Christmas day bomber: Al-Awlaki and Umar Farouk Abdulmutallab, the al Qaeda attempted bomber of Northwest Airlines Flight 253 on December 25, 2009, had contact according to assorted sources. In January 2010, CNN reported that U.S. "security sources" said that there

DOI: 10.4324/9781003474104-10

is concrete evidence that al-Awlaki was Abdulmutallab's recruiter and one of his trainers, and met with him prior to the attack.[3]

In February 2010, al-Awlaki admitted in an interview published on al-Jazeera that he taught and corresponded with Abdulmutallab, but denied having ordered the attack.[4]

- Fall 2010 cargo plane bomb plot: A British newspaper, *The Telegraph*, reported that U.S. and British counter terrorism officials believe that al-Awlaki was behind the cargo plane bombs that were sent from Yemen to Chicago in October 2010.[5] U.S. Ambassador to Yemen Gerald Feierstein said flatly, "al-Awlaki was behind the two . . . bombs."[6]

And, of course, there was Alwaki's alleged connection to the Times Square bomber, as laid out in the bulk of this chapter. All of which begs the threshold question: How in 2010 did Yemen become "al Qaeda central"? The CIA's *World Factbook* offered the following background information:[7]

Background

North Yemen became independent of the Ottoman Empire in 1918. The British, who had set up a protectorate area around the southern port of Aden in the 19th century, withdrew in 1967 from what became South Yemen. Three years later, the southern government adopted a Marxist orientation. The massive exodus of hundreds of thousands of Yemenis from the south to the north contributed to two decades of hostility between the states. The two countries were formally unified as the Republic of Yemen in 1990. A southern secessionist movement in 1994 was quickly subdued. In 2000, Saudi Arabia and Yemen agreed to a delimitation of their border.

Economy

Yemen is a low-income country that is highly dependent on declining oil resources for revenue. Petroleum accounts for roughly 25% of GDP and 70% of government revenue. Annual real GDP growth has averaged 3–4% since 2000. Yemen has been largely unaffected by and insulated from the effects of the global economic crisis because its financial system is underdeveloped and not well integrated into the international community, but the drop in oil prices since mid-2008 slashed government oil revenues in 2009 by more than 50%, as compared to 2008. Yemen has tried to counter the effects of its declining oil resources by diversifying its economy through an economic reform program initiated in 2006 that is designed to bolster non-oil sectors of the economy and foreign investment. In October 2009, Yemen exported its first liquefied natural gas as part of this diversification effort. The Yemen government in August reaffirmed its commitment to reforms in a plan detailing the country's top ten development priorities. Despite these ambitious plans, Yemen faces difficult long term challenges, including declining water resources and a high population growth rate.

GOVERNMENT

CONSTITUTION:

16 May 1991; amended 29 September 1994 and February 2001

LEGAL SYSTEM:

based on Islamic law, Turkish law, English common law, and local tribal customary law; has not accepted compulsory ICJ jurisdiction

SUFFRAGE:

18 years of age; universal

EXECUTIVE BRANCH:

chief of state: President Ali Abdallah SALIH (since 22 May 1990, the former president of North Yemen, assumed office upon the merger of North and South Yemen); Vice President Maj. Gen. Abd al-Rab Mansur al-HADI (since 3 October 1994)
head of government: Prime Minister Ali Muhammad MUJAWWAR (since 31 March 2007)
cabinet: Council of Ministers appointed by the president on the advice of the prime minister (For more information visit the World Leaders website)
elections: president elected by popular vote for a seven-year term; election last held on 20 September 2006 (next to be held in September 2013); vice president appointed by the president; prime minister and deputy prime ministers appointed by the president
election results: Ali Abdallah SALIH elected president; percent of vote—Ali Abdallah SALIH 77.2%, Faysal BIN SHAMLAN 21.8%

LEGISLATIVE BRANCH:

bicameral legislature consisting of a Shura Council (111 seats; members appointed by the president) and House of Representatives (301 seats; members elected by popular vote to serve eight-year terms)
elections: last held on 27 April 2003 (scheduled April 2009 election postponed for two years)

election results: percent of vote by party—NA; seats by party—GPC 228, Islah 47, YSP 7, Nasserite Unionist Party 3, National Arab Socialist Ba'ath Party 2, independents 14

JUDICIAL BRANCH:

Supreme Court

POLITICAL PARTIES AND LEADERS:

General People's Congress or GPC [Abdul-Kader BAJAMMAL]; Islamic Reform Grouping or Islah [Muhammed Abdallah AL-YADUMI]; Nasserite Unionist Party [Abd al-Malik al-MAKHLAFI]; National Arab Socialist Ba'th Party [Dr. Qasim SALAM]; Yemeni Socialist Party or YSP [Yasin Said NUMAN]; note—there are at least seven more active political parties

POLITICAL PRESSURE GROUPS AND LEADERS:

Muslim Brotherhood; Women National Committee
other: conservative tribal groups; southern secessionist groups; al-Qa'ida in the Arabian Peninsula (AQAP)

None of this information, however informative in a general sense, explains why Awlaki made Yemin his worldwide jihad headquarters. Another leading English newspaper, *The Independent*, offered valuable insights in the wake of the parcel bombs. The newspaper reported on the presence of explosives in two packages headed for the United States, with a suspected 24 more, calling Yemen "the new Afghanistan." The article put al-Awlaki on a par with Usama bin Laden, reporting that he has been linked to three 9/11 bombers, the Fort Hood shootings, the "underpants" bomber, and the Times Square bombing. Sajjan M. Gohel, director for international security for the Asia-Pacific Foundation, called him "the most dangerous ideologue in the world."[8] Armed with this background, we are ready to review the strange tale of the Times Square bomber.

10.1 Background

On May 1, 2010, a mounted New York City police officer was notified of a smoking car, a dark blue Nissan Pathfinder sport utility vehicle (SUV), parked in Times Square. Inside the car were "eight bags of an 'unknown substance' and a pressure cooker-type metal pot containing a 'bird's nest of wires and

M-88 firecrackers,'"[9] as well as "three propane tanks weighing between 15 and 17 pounds . . . [and] two full five-gallon gasoline containers."[10] The car was determined to contain a bomb that had ignited but failed to explode, and the materials were quickly dismantled without causing any casualties. Tests later found the substance to be "non-explosive grade fertilizer incapable of blowing up,"[11] but the intent was clear. Someone had meant to kill a lot of people.

Two days later, 30-year-old Faisal Shahzad was arrested as he boarded a flight to Dubai at John F. Kennedy International Airport.[12] A naturalized U.S. citizen since April 2009, Shahzad was born in Pakistan, and after admitting to planning an attack on Times Square, he told investigators that he had trained in Pakistan at a terrorist camp in preparation. In court, Shahzad proudly stated, "I want to plead guilty 100 times over."[13] But why?

Born of a wealthy family in northwestern Pakistan and the son of a senior military officer, Shahzad had a privileged childhood, "tended to by chauffeurs, servants, and armed guards,"[14] and while he identified proudly with his Pashtun heritage, he lived in many different places. He attended primary school in Saudi Arabia and several schools in Pakistan. By the time Shahzad entered high school, his family had moved to Karachi, a large city in the south of Pakistan. The country was in chaos, rocked by political instability and violence, with many Pakistanis blaming the United States (which was imposing steep sanctions due to Pakistan's nuclear program). Shahzad "came of age during Pakistan's state-sponsored jihad against India's military in the breakaway region of Kashmir—a conflict that granted legendary status to Pakistani jihadists."[15] It is unclear how formative these events of his childhood were.

After high school, Shahzad attended Greenwich University. He was a mediocre student, but he was determined to finish his degree in the United States. He transferred in 2000 to the University of Bridgeport, where more than a third of the university's students were foreigners. There, Shahzad had a wide social circle, unlike most Pakistani students, who tended to socialize together exclusively, and he showed little interest in Islam. According to a fellow Pakistani student, "Back then, it was all about fast cars and becoming something."[16]

However, Shahzad's anger against America was well known to his fellow students. During the 9/11 attacks on the United States, a classmate recalled Shahzad watching footage of the attacks and saying, "They had it coming," and "If these people come to my land, it's not going to be good."[17] He seemed to believe that Western countries had conspired to harm Muslims.

In 2002, after he graduated from the University of Bridgeport with a degree in computer applications and information systems, Shahzad once again seemed focused on his future in the United States. He held down a good job at the Elizabeth Arden cosmetics company in Stamford, Connecticut, while attending night classes at Bridgeport and eventually earning a master's degree.

In 2004, he married Huma Asif Mian in an arranged marriage. He seemed settled, though he complained about the fact that his employer never raised his salary above $50,000. Due to his marriage to a naturalized U.S. citizen, he himself was granted American citizenship on April 17, 2009.[18]

Around that time, Shahzad became noticeably more religious. He began praying five times a day, attending mosque, and pressuring his wife to wear a hijab and to move back to Pakistan with their two children while he looked for a new job in the Middle East. During a visit to Pakistan in July 2009, Shahzad asked his father for permission to fight in Afghanistan, which his father denied with increasing concern. Shahzad told officials that it was during that same visit that he trained with the Pakistani Taliban in North Waziristan to learn how to build a bomb that he planned to detonate in the United States.[19]

10.2 Legal Proceedings and Trial

U.S. Attorney General Eric Holder said: "Based on what we know so far, it is clear that this was a terrorist plot aimed at murdering Americans in one of the busiest places in our country."[20] Seemingly pleased and proud to confirm this preliminary assessment, Shahzad admitted to his part in the attempted bombing and was cooperative with the investigation, providing a wealth of useful information. He willingly pleaded guilty to the ten counts charged against him, all the while smiling and once replying to the judge, "Allahu Akbar" ("God is great"). He exhibited no remorse for his attempted crimes in the following transcript of his court sentencing. (Note that Mr. Weinstein is the defendant's attorney and Mr. McGuire represents the Government.)

The court: Mr. Shahzad?
The defendant: Yes.
The court: I think you should get up. Have you read the pre-sentence report?
The defendant: Yes.
The court: Have you discussed it with your lawyer?
The defendant: Yes.
The court: Is there anything in the pre-sentence report that contains an error that you would like to bring to my attention?
[Defendant conferred with counsel]
The defendant: Yes.
The court: What is that?
Mr. Weinstein: Do you have an objection to it, or not?
The defendant: No.
The court: Very well. Then I will hear anything you want to tell me and anything your lawyer wants to tell me in connection with sentence.

The defendant: OK. My statement should take about five minutes to ten minutes, and I hope that the judge and the Court will listen to me before they sentence me. In the name of Allah, the most gracious, the most merciful, this is but one life. If I am given 1,000 lives, I will sacrifice them all for the sake of Allah fighting this cause, defending our lands, making the word of Allah supreme over any religion or system. We Muslims don't abide by human-made laws, because they are always corrupt. And I had a first-hand experience when on the second day of my arrest I asked for the Miranda. And the FBI denied it to me for two weeks, effecting harm to my kids and family, and I was forced to sign those Mirandas. The sentence by the judge will not mean anything to me, for how can I be judged when the Court does not understand the suffering of my people? They don't understand my side of the story, where the Muslim life of is no value. Therefore, the only true judgment will be on the day of resurrection when Allah will judge between me and you as to who is fighting for the just cause. So decree whatever you desire to decree, for you can only decree regarding the life of this world. The crusading U.S. and NATO [North Atlantic Treaty Organization] forces who have occupied the Muslim lands under the pretext of democracy and freedom for the last nine years and are saying with their mouths that they are fighting terrorism, I say to them, we don't accept your democracy nor your freedom, because we already have Sharia law and freedom.

Furthermore, brace yourselves, because the war with Muslims has just begun. Consider me only a first droplet of the flood that will follow me. And only this time it's not imperial Japan or Germany, Vietnam or Russian communism. This time it's the war against people who believe in the book of Allah and follow the commandments, so this is a war against Allah. So let's see how you can defeat your Creator, which you can never do. Therefore, the defeat of U.S. is imminent and will happen in the near future, inshallah, which will only give rise to much awaited Muslim caliphate, which is the only true world order. Soon the bailout money which is holding your fragile economy will run out and soon you will not be able to afford the war costs.

The court: Do you want to comment in any way in connection with sentence?

The defendant: This is all coming towards the common—towards the sentence, to how I support myself in the whole, what's my motivation for this whole.

The court: All right. You became a naturalized American citizen some years ago, isn't that right?

The defendant: Yes.

The court: Not very long ago.

The defendant: Yes.

The court: When was that?

The defendant: I think it was April last year.

The court: Last year. Didn't you swear allegiance to this country when you became an American citizen?

The defendant: I did swear, but I did not mean it.

The court: I see. You took a false oath?

The defendant: Yes.

The court: Very well. Is there anything else you want to tell me?

The defendant: Sure. I am ashamed that I belong to a slave country like Pakistan, who has accepted the slavery of the West from the day it was born. Bush had made already clear when he started the war on us, on Muslims, he said, You are either with us or against us. And so it's very clear for us Muslims, either we are with the mujahideen or we are with crusading losing Christians. There is no in between. Blessed the immigrants and the leader Sheikh Usama bin Laden, who will be known as no less than Saladin of the 21st century crusade and blessed be those who give him asylum.

The court: How much do you know about Saladin, as you called him?

The defendant: What do I know about him?

The court: Yes.

The defendant: He was the one who fought the First Crusade from the Western European countries.

The court: He didn't want to kill people.

The defendant: He wanted to liberate . . .

The court: He was a very moderate man.

The defendant: He liberated Muslim lands from the Jewish crusade, Christian crusade. And that's what we Muslims are trying do, because you're occupying Iraq and Afghanistan, under the pretext of democracy and freedom. We don't want that. We already have Sharia law, law given by Allah. We don't need human-made laws.

The court: All right. Thank you. Does your lawyer want to add anything?

The defendant: I just want to finish off. I just have like one, two minutes more.

The court: Very well.

The defendant: If you don't mind.

The court: I will listen to what you want to tell me in connection with sentence.

The defendant: Sure. This is towards the end. So, the past nine years the war with Muslims has achieved nothing for the U.S., except for it has waken [*sic*] up the Muslims for Islam. We are only Muslims trying to defend our people, honor, and land. But if you call us terrorists for doing that, then we are proud terrorists, and we will keep on terrorizing until you leave our land and people at peace. But if you don't, then I remind you that we have watches and we have time. We will defeat you with time. And before I end my statement, I want to give you the last message, which is the message of truth, so that when you meet Allah on the day of resurrection, you will not be able to say nobody gave you the message. The message is there is only one God, the lord of the universe; Mohammed, who is the last messenger and prophet; the Holy Koran is the last revelation to mankind, which obligates by its gospel to embrace Islam and become Muslims and save yourselves from the total pain of the last day.

[Defendant spoke in another language]

The court: Very well.

The defendant: Thank you.

The court: Does counsel have anything to add?

Mr. Weinstein: Your Honor, I think as I informed the court in the letter about two weeks ago, Mr. Shahzad has asked that I say nothing.

The court: Very well. You may be seated.

The defendant: Thank you.

The court: I assume the government has nothing to add?

Mr. McGuire: We do, your Honor, briefly.

The court: I don't think it is necessary.

Mr. McGuire: Your Honor, if I may just briefly, just as . . .

The court: A long time ago when I was an assistant United States Attorney, we did not think it was the function of the prosecutor to be heavily involved in sentence.

Mr. McGuire: Very well, your Honor.

The court: The one thing I would like the government to explain is what the forfeiture provisions mean. I don't understand them.

Mr. McGuire: The government's not seeking forfeiture in this case, your Honor.

The court: Very well. I'm glad to hear that, because I do not understand the language of the forfeiture provision in the indictment. So you are withdrawing that, I take it?

Mr. McGuire: That's correct, Judge.

The court: Very well. I have myself examined the pre-sentence report very carefully, and I do adopt the guideline calculation of the probation officer. But I also examine with care the factors to be considered in imposing a sentence that Congress has enacted in Section 3553 of the Criminal Code in setting sentence. A number of the counts carry mandatory sentences, but nevertheless I have, as the law directs me, considered the nature and circumstances of the offense and the history and characteristics of the defendant. The sentence imposed must reflect the seriousness of the offense and the history, and the sentence should promote respect for the law and provide just punishment for the offense. It must also afford adequate deterrence to criminal conduct to those who would be inclined to follow the example of this defendant, and, very important, to protect the public from further crimes of this defendant and others who would seek to follow him. The defendant has repeatedly expressed his total lack of remorse and his desire, if given the opportunity, to repeat the crime. So there is really no basis here for me to believe that somebody who falsely swore allegiance to this country, who swore to defend this country, who took oath a year ago to defend this country and to be loyal to it, has now announced and by his conduct has evidenced that his desire is not to defend the United States or Americans, but to kill them. Those are all serious matters that I must take into consideration in setting sentence. There are ten counts in this indictment, and there are three counts of mandatory life in prison.

Mr. McGuire: Your Honor, I'm sorry to interrupt. I believe there's one count of mandatory life in prison, which is Count Six.

The court: Thank you. In any event, Count Six requires life imprisonment. Counts One and Two and Four and Five and Nine and Ten provide for penalties of up to life in prison.

Mr. McGuire: Your Honor, Counts Nine and Ten have a 20-year statutory maximum. Those can be up to 20 years' imprisonment. The other counts your Honor named do have a life maximum sentence.

The court: There are a few counts which have 20 years in prison as maximums. Those are Counts Nine and Ten. Seven and Eight have penalties of up to ten years. At this time, I set as your sentence life in prison.

The defendant: Allahu Akbar.

The court: I am really not inclined, even though the statute so provides, to have sentences following life in prison. It is the height of technicality for me to have sentences consecutive to life in prison. To the extent that it has any meaning, I adopt the requirements of the statutes, but I do not set any period of supervised release because no release is permitted. I want my sentence to be real, not fictitious, not formulaic. What you have done here, although happily the training you sought in making bombs was unsuccessful and you were unsuccessful in your effort to kill many Americans, you have made it plain that all of the factors that I mentioned before require that you be incarcerated for life. Accordingly, that is the sentence of the Court. Is there anything further?

Mr. McGuire: Your Honor, while understanding that it is a technical matter, and I understand your Honor's point with respect to sentence, the government would just request that the sentence per count as it would be reflected in your Honor's judgment be stated for purposes of the record. There is a proposed . . .

The court: Very well. On Counts One and Two, I sentence you to life in prison each, separately.

The defendant: Allahu Akbar.

The court: I understand that you welcome that. On Counts Three, Four, and Five, I also sentence you to life in prison. What I hesitate to say is they shall run consecutively. On Count Six, life in prison is mandatory. On Counts Seven and Eight, the statute requires ten years on each count, or permits ten years on each count, and those will run concurrently with the sentence on Counts One, Two, Nine and Ten. On Counts Nine and Ten, I set 20 years on each count to run concurrently with Counts One and Two, but the overriding sentence is life in prison. You are a young man, and you will have a lot of time to reflect on what you have done and what you have said today and in the past.

The defendant: My sentence, if you allow me to speak, will be only for the limit that God has given me life in this world. But if you people don't become believers, the life that you would get in the hereafter, which you don't believe in, will be forever. So I'm happy with the deal that God has given me.

The court: Very well. Is there anything further?

Mr. McGuire: Your Honor, with respect to sentence, stating the special and any mandatory conditions of supervised release.

The court: Thank you, yes. There is a mandatory assessment of $1,000, which you are required to pay. It is not a penalty, but it is collectible as if it were. The conditions of supervised release I will not go through because I consider supervised release here a meaningless technical fiction. You appear to be someone who was capable of education, and I do hope that you will spend some of the time in prison thinking carefully about whether the Koran wants you to kill lots of people.

The defendant: The Koran gives us the right to defend, and that's what all I'm doing.

The court: I see. All right. Is there anything further?

McGuire: Your Honor, the defendant should be advised of his right to appeal the sentence.

The court: Thank you. That is correct. You have a right to appeal this sentence. If you wish to do so, you should discuss it with your lawyer. Within ten days, he must file a protective notice of appeal for you, so you can then argue to the Court of Appeals, the next level of court, that your sentence is in error. Very well. There is no forfeiture sought, so I will ignore the forfeiture provision of the indictment. It has been withdrawn. You are now excused.

[Adjourned][21]

10.3 Accomplices and Co-Conspirators?

Shahzad initially claimed to have acted alone, but ultimately, more than a dozen people were arrested in connection to the plot. He later said that he had met members of Lashkar-e-Taiba, a group responsible for the attacks on the Indian city of Mumbai in 2008. He also said that he was "inspired to take up the cause of al Qaeda and radical Islam by the Internet messages of

Anwar Al-Awlaki."[22] Attorney General Holder stated, "The Pakistani Taliban was behind the attack. We know that they helped facilitate it. And I suspect that we are going to come up with evidence which shows that they helped to finance it. They were intimately involved in this plot."[23] President Obama's counter terrorism advisor, John O. Brennan, also stated, "He was trained by them." Brennan added, "He received funding from them. He was basically directed here to the United States to carry out this attack."[24]

Grassroots terrorism has become an increasing worry. In a video, alleged al Qaeda spokesman Adam Gadahn urged "wannabe terrorists" to create their own attacks against Americans, as this October 2010 FBI report asserted:

- Adam Gadahn, Al Qaeda's American Mouthpiece, Tells Wannabe Terrorists to Go it Alone, Urges Attacks in the West (The Daily News, October 23, 2010; AFP, October 23, 2010).
- Californian Adam Gadahn, Al Qaeda's American mouthpiece, urged wannabe terrorists in a new video to act alone instead of trying to join cells attempting 9/11-type spectacular strikes. Gadahn, also known as Azzam the American, was born in 1978. He is a native of southern California and has appeared in several videotapes for al Qaeda since 2004. Wearing a shaggy beard and with an AK-47 rifle within reach, Gadahn hailed Hasan, Abdulmutallab and Times Square bomber Faisal Shahzad, who also acted alone on behalf of the Pakistani Taliban. Gadahn urged individual violent jihad in a 40-minute tape, which endorsed an Al Qaeda ally's call last week for sympathizers to mimic the Ft. Hood killings and attempted bombings over Detroit last Christmas and in Times Square in May. "To my Muslim brothers residing in the states of the Zio-Crusader coalitions . . . know that Jihad (holy war) is your duty as well," Gadahn said in a the Arabic language video. He addressed Muslims in "emigrant communities like those which live on the margins of society in the miserable suburbs of Paris, London and Detroit, or are from those arriving in America or Europe to study in its universities or seek their daily bread in the streets of its cities . . . ." "You have an opportunity to strike the leaders of unbelief and retaliate against them on their own soil, as long as there is no covenant between you and them," he added in the 48 minute, 20 second video, produced by al Qaeda media arm As-Sahab.
- Gadahn urged Arabs to launch "heroic operations similar to the invasion of the American consulate in Peshawar and the bombing of the Danish embassy in Islamabad," in their cities and capitals. However, "it is obligatory to avoid harming Muslims and destroying their properties" when carrying out such attacks, he said in Arabic, with the video providing English subtitles. Six Pakistanis were killed in an April attack on the US consulate in the northwestern Pakistani city

of Peshawar. In June 2008, a car bomb exploded outside the Danish embassy in Islamabad killing at least eight people, including a Dane, and wounding about 27 others. Gadahn also called on Muslims to attack "American military bases spread across the (Arabian) Peninsula, the Gulf, the Levant countries and elsewhere . . . like the one carried out by Major Nidal Hasan," the US Army psychiatrist accused of opening fire on colleagues at Fort Hood, Texas, killing 13.

- The message is significant because Osama Bin Laden's operational goal has long been to kill hundreds, if not thousands, in simultaneous multiple attacks on US targets with cells of extremists—and Gadahn speaks for Al Qaeda. In October, the Yemeni spin-off of Bin Laden's terror network, Al Qaeda in the Arabian Peninsula, released a slick 74-page online "magazine" called "Inspire" with essays by Yemeni-American imam Anwar al-Awlaki urging individual jihad. The Gadahn tape and AQAP publication were obtained by the SITE Intelligence Group.
- The Gadahn tape may be evidence of Al Qaeda, under massive pressure in Pakistan's tribal areas from a CIA drone blitz, being emasculated if it's giving a stamp of approval to AQAP's call for "lone wolf" attacks, one expert said. Awlaki was in contact with and inspired Army Major Nidal Hasan, accused of murdering a dozen at the Texas base, and Umar Farouk Abdulmutallab, the underwear bomber who almost blew up a plane Christmas Day last year. The AQAP how to manual offered suggestions for individual mass murder, such as gunning down feds at Washington lunchtime eateries and welding blades to the grill of a large truck to "mow down" crowds on a street. "Here you are in the battlefield, just like the heroes before you," said Gadahn, who is under federal indictment for treason.[25]

What we have here is a classic case of leaderless resistance à la Timothy McVeigh and the ALF/ELF eco-terrorists. Awlaki hid out in Yemen, while disseminating his poisonous message via the Internet. Receptive Muslims, such as Shahzad—as well as the Fort Dix Six and the Fort Hood shooter—acted either entirely on their own or after reaching out to al Qaeda operatives in Yemen, Afghanistan, Pakistan, or elsewhere for training, seed money, and other support.

This was global terrorism on the cheap. Also, it is a devilishly difficult challenge for law enforcement and national security assets to meet. The best example may be the Boston Marathon bombing in 2013.

> The Boston Marathon bombing was a domestic terrorist attack that took place during the annual Boston Marathon on April 15, 2013. Brothers Dzhokhar and Tamerlan Tsarnaev planted two homemade pressure cooker bombs that detonated near the finish line of the race 14 seconds and 210 yards apart.[26]

Notes

1. Mark Wilson, "CIA on the Verge of Lawsuit," *Seer Press News*, August 5, 2010, http://seerpress.com/cia-on-the-verge-of-lawsuit/3341 (accessed December 12, 2010).
2. Ibid.
3. Jay Kemis, "Wednesday's Intriguing People," *CNN News Blogs*, April 7, 2010, http://news.blogs.cnn.com/2010/04/07/wednesdays-intriguing-people-3 (accessed December 12, 2010).
4. Ahmad Al-Haj and Sarah El Deeb, "U.S. Cleric: Accused Plane Bomber Was My Student," *Associated Press*, February 4, 2010, http://abcnews.go.com/International/wireStory?id=9744188 (accessed December 12, 2010).
5. Sean Rayment, Patrick Hennessy, and David Barrett, "Yemen Cargo Bomb May Have Been Targeted at Britain," *The Telegraph*, October 30, 2010, http://www.telegraph.co.uk/news/uknews/terrorism-in-the-uk/8099345/Yemen-cargo-bomb-plot-may-have-been-targeted-at-Britain.html (accessed December 12, 2010).
6. "Yemeni Radical Cleric behind Parcel Bombs: U.S. Ambassador," *World Times*, November 26, 2010, http://world.globaltimes.cn/mid-east/2010-11/596921.html (accessed December 12, 2010).
7. https://www.cia.gov/library/publications/the-world-factbook/geos/ym.html (accessed December 12, 2010).
8. David Randall and Andrew Johnson, "Yemen, the New Crucible of Global Terrorism," *The Independent*, October 31, 2010, http://www.independent.co.uk/news/world/middle-east/yemen-the-new-crucible-of-global-terror-ism-2121364.html (accessed December 12, 2010).
9. "Suspicious Car Leads to Closure of Times Square," *CNN*, May 2, 2010, http://www.cnn.com/2010/CRIME/05/02/times.square.closure/index.html (accessed May 2, 2010).
10. Ibid.
11. Ibid.
12. Jack Healy, Mark Mazzetti, and Sabrina Tavernise, "Suspect, Charged, Said to Admit to Role in Plot," *New York Times*, May 4, 2010, http://www.nytimes.com/2010/05/05/nyregion/05bomb.html?hp.
13. B. Weiser, "Guilty Plea in Times Square Bomb Plot," *New York Times*, June 21, 2010, http://www.nytimes.com/2010/06/22/nyregion/22terror.html?_r=1&hp.
14. Andrea Elliott, "For Times Sq. Suspect, Long Roots of Discontent," *New York Times*, May 15, 2010, http://www.nytimes.com/2010/05/16/nyregion/16suspect.html?pagewanted=all (accessed May 16, 2010).
15. Ibid.
16. Ibid.
17. Ibid.
18. Ibid.
19. Colin Moynihan and Benjamin Weiser, "Guilty Plea in Times Square Bomb Plot," *New York Times*, June 21, 2010, http://www.nytimes.com/2010/06/22/nyregion/22terror.html?_r=1&hp.

20. "Suspect in Times Square Bomb Plot Faces Terror Charges," *U.S. News*, May 4, 2010, http://politics.usnews.com/news/articles/2010/05/04/suspect-in-times-square-bomb-plot-faces-terror-charges.html.
21. "Read the Faisal Shahzad Transcript," *New York Post*, October 5, 2010, http://www.nypost.com/p/news/local/manhattan/read_the_faisal_shahzad_transcript_zDoUXlGEMoqZMwzsIRrlkM/0.
22. Damien McElroy, "Times Square Bomb Suspect Had Links to Terror Preacher," The Telegraph, May 7, 2010, http://www.telegraph.co.uk/news/worldnews/northamerica/usa/7691929/Times-Square-bomb-suspect-had-links-to-terror-preacher.html.
23. Charlie Savage, "Holder Backs a Miranda Limit for Terror Suspects," *New York Times*, May 9, 2010, http://www.nytimes.com/2010/05/10/us/politics/10holder.html.
24. Ibid.
25. "National Security Threat Awareness Monthly Bulletin," *FBI Newark Division*, October 2010.
26. "Boston Marathon Bombing," Wikipedia, https://en.wikipedia.org/wiki/Boston_Marathon_bombing (accessed December 29, 2023).

The Age of Trump

11

Tuesday, November 8, was Election Day in the United States in 2016. I had voted after driving home from my job at Rider University, had dinner with my wife Joanne, then settled in for the ritual of watching the election returns.

The 2016 campaign season had been an emotional roller coaster, regardless of which major candidate you favored. As some political pundit or other had opined, "Both parties picked the one candidate that the other could defeat." Hilary Clinton was the heir-apparent to Barack Obama. Having elected, and re-elected, the first Black American President, the nation seemed ready to put the first female into the Oval Office. Clinton brought an impressive record to the presidential race: First Lady, New York Senator, Secretary of State. But she also brought an extraordinary amount of baggage:

- The September 11 (of all dates!), 2012 attack on the American diplomatic compound in Benghazi, Libya, by the Islamic militant group Ansar Al-Sharia. That being a presidential election year, Congressional Republicans tried mightily to lay blame for lack of preparedness at the feet of Democratic leadership.[1] Although no wrongdoing was ever laid directly on Clinton, six Congressional committee notwithstanding, "Benghazi" remained a blotch on her record as Obama's Secretary of State right into the 2016 election campaign.
- WikiLeaks:

  > On March 16, 2016 WikiLeaks launched a searchable archive for over 30 thousand emails & email attachments sent to and from Hillary Clinton's private email server while she was Secretary of State. The 50,547 pages of documents span from 30 June 2010 to 12 August 2014. 7,570 of the documents were sent by Hillary Clinton. The emails were made available in the form of thousands of PDFs by the US State Department as a result of a Freedom of Information Act request. More PDFs were made available on February 29, 2016, and a set of additional 995 emails was imported up to February 2, 2018.[2]

- Not only did these vast email dumps provide fodder for journalists, pundits, opponents and the general public to question, criticize, and

DOI: 10.4324/9781003474104-11

> embarrass the candidate, they also precipitated FBI investigations—the second one virtually on the eve of the election. Although the first investigation ended in early July 2016 with a determination that no criminal charges were warranted,[3] this fell far short of a vote of confidence on Clinton's competency.

Running against Clinton was a former reality-TV star and real estate tycoon who repeatedly called her a "crook" and led chants of "Lock her up!" at his rallies. Such rhetoric was heretofore unheard of in a presidential campaign. And Donald Trump's disdain for political correctness was just one of his idiosyncratic characteristics.

Trump launched his campaign for the presidency on June 16, 2015 at Trump Tower in New York City. From the get-go, his campaign was unprecedented.

> Many of Trump's remarks were controversial and helped his campaign garner extensive coverage by the mainstream media, trending topics, and social media. Trump's campaign rallies attracted large crowds as well as public controversy. Some of the events were marked by incidents of violence between Trump supporters and protestors, mistreatment of some journalists, and disruption by a large group of protestors who effectively shut down a major rally in Chicago. Trump himself was accused of inciting violence at his rallies.[4]

Initially, Trump's candidacy was considered by many to be a joke. Indeed, he was frequently the butt of satire and parody every bit as merciless as his own harsh rhetoric. But the tone and incredulity of late night talk show hosts and pundits altered markedly, as they—along with millions more Americans—watched in amazement at Donald Trump's relentless march from the "comic relief" of the campaign to the winner of the most GOP primary contests to the Grand Old Party's nominee to the winner of the 2016 presidential election. Per Wikipedia,

> On November 8, 2016, Trump and Pence were elected president and vice president of the United States. Trump's populist positions in opposition to illegal immigration and various trade agreements, such as the Trans-Pacific Partnership, earned him support especially among voters who were male, white, blue-collar, working class, and those without college degrees. Many voters in the Rust Belt, who gave Trump the electoral votes needed to win the presidency, switched from supporting Bernie Sanders to Trump after Hillary Clinton won the Democratic nomination.[5]

Trump—like most Republican presidential candidates before him—lost the popular vote but won the Electoral College contest: the contest that counts.

Comedian and TV host Bill Maher probably spoke for millions of voters on the other side of the tally when he commented three days after the election,

> He won. He ran a vicious, vulgar campaign and I gave it back exactly in measure—I was also vicious and vulgar—but he won. And he did it his way. Nobody gets to sing that song more than Donald Trump. Everybody told him he couldn't do this, he couldn't do that—and he won. He did the hardest thing in the entire world to do: win the election as the leader of the free world.[6]

11.1 President Donald Trump and the Triumph of the Radical Right

This chapter is not—indeed cannot be—a history of the Trump Presidency. As this *Second Edition* goes to press in early 2024, Donald Trump may be "The Once and Future King,"[7] as all early indicators point to his nomination, which would lead to a rematch between Trump and incumbent Joe Biden.

Rather, this chapter will limit its inquiry to the rejuvenation of the radical right, facilitated, if not encouraged, by the former president.

Aurelian Mondon[8] and Antonia Vaughan[9] of England's University of Bath trace the stages of the American radical right's rises and recessions. Some of the following should seem familiar to you, having read this book's Chapter 2 on McVeigh and Nichols.

- From the end of World War II until the 1960s, racism remained systemic and the right—represented by the Ku Klux Klan, among others—retained an almost mainstream position in American society, at least regionally.
- The successes of the Civil Rights movement—especially the Civil Rights Act of 1964 and the Voting Rights Act of 1965—marginalized the Klan and contributed to a decline of the radical right more generally.
- However, marginalization of the radical right did not mean its destruction. Racism became less blatant but did not disappear—and what remnants of the radical right remained took a more extremism turn (as my Chapter 2 documents).[10]

They continue:

> The 5th era of far-right activity saw groups go "underground and offline" [*cite omitted*], regarding the internet as free from government oversight or control. The far right's online presence was mixed, with innovation dependent on the

> national context: a number of sites took advantage of the affordance of the internet to spread propaganda, expand networks, and connect previously scattered individuals. The online presence of the far right evolved with the internet.[11]

Their assessment of the 2016 presidential election is that the so-called "alt-right," as jubilant cheerleaders for Trump, fueled a venomous discourse. This grew in its viciousness as the campaign moved from the primaries into the general election. Readers will remember Trump's calls to "Jail Hillary." Even opposition conservatives were not immune from the attacks, being labeled "cuckservatives". Recognizing an opportunity and warming to the trend, Trump brought such alt-right heroes as Steve Bannon into his fold. Thus, following Trump's surprising upset victory over Clinton, the alt-right actually had access to the Oval Office, and the discourse of alt-right hate speech entered the mainstream. The fortunes of the radical right came full circle with a restoration of legitimacy not enjoyed since the 1950s.[12]

11.2 Charlottesville, August 2017

Donald Trump's ascension to the U.S. presidency was not the only catalyst of a resurgent right. The resurgence also was intended as a counter to organized efforts aimed at removing the vestiges of the Confederacy, once and for all. This effort was, in turn, a response to the brutal attack on a Charleston, South Carolina church in 2015, when a white supremacist invaded a service and slaughtered the minister (a state senator) and eight parishioners.[13] Among other responses to the travesty, a movement arose to remove the remaining statues and monuments, and change the names of streets and public spaces, dedicated to the Confederacy. One such statue, that of Robert E. Lee, was scheduled from removal from what once had been Lee Park in Charlottesville, Virginia.

A local white supremacist, Jason Kessler, spearheaded the "Unite the Right" rally that would bring all manner of right-wing adherents to his hometown—and that of his alma mater, the University of Virginia (UVA)—in August 2017. Kessler was a man of many parts: blue-collar dishwasher, truck driver and handyman; blogger, poet, and novelist; former Democrat, liberal, and Occupy movement adherent turned neo-Nazi.[14]

Among the assorted groups and ideological true believers brought to Charlottesville for the August 11–12, 2017 rally were:

- The neo-Nazi Traditionalist Worker Party.
- The neo-Confederate League of the South.
- The National Socialist Movement.

- The Loyal White Knights.
- The Confederate White Knights.
- The Fraternal Order of Alt-Knights.
- The California-based fight club Rise Above Movement.
- The Detroit Right Wings (a play on the NHL Detroit Red Wings).[15]

Conducted in the backyard of UVA, the rally predictably aroused a bevy of counter-protestors. Clashes were inevitable, no doubt deemed by some to be desirable. By day two, the situation was so volatile that Virginia Gov. Terry McAuliffe declared a state of emergency and the state police labeled the rally an unlawful assembly. At the event, this was too little, too late. At about 1:35 p.m. on the second afternoon, a self-proclaimed white supremacist, James Alex Fields, Jr. drove his car into a group of counter-protestors, injuring 35 and killing one, Heather Heyer. Fields fled the scene in his auto but was soon apprehended.[16]

Two noteworthy legal actions occurred in the wake of the ill-fated, deadly rally. One was a civil action aimed at Jason Kessler, the second the criminal prosecution of James Fields.

11.3 Jason Kessler, et al.

Kessler, as the lead organizer of the Unite the Right rally, was only the first-named of 14 individuals and ten organizations named as defendants by nine plaintiffs in the civil suit styled *Sines v. Kessler*. It took four years for the case, which was filed almost immediately after the disastrous rally, to come to trial in October of 2021. En route to that trial, the defendants raised a challenge grounded in their alleged First Amendment rights. Ruling on their motion to dismiss, federal judge Norman K. Moon of the U.S. District Court for Virginia's Western District explained the suit and denied the defendants' motion as follows:

> Congress passed a law "directed at the organized terrorism in the Reconstruction South[.]" *Chapman v. Houston Welfare Rights Org.*, 441 U.S. 600, 610 n.25, 99 S. Ct. 1905, 60 L.Ed.2d 508 (1979); *see* 42 U.S.C. § 1985. Over a hundred and forty years later, on August 11th and 12th, 2017, the Defendants in this lawsuit, including the Ku Klux Klan, various neo-Nazi organizations, and associated white supremacists, held rallies in Charlottesville, Virginia. Violence erupted. Charlottesville residents who suffered injuries at the rallies, the Plaintiffs, allege that this violence was no accident. Instead, they allege the Defendants violated the 1871 Act and related state laws by conspiring to engage in violence against racial minorities and their supporters. The Defendants retort that they were

> simply engaged in lawful, if unpopular, political protest and so their conduct is protected by the First Amendment. While ultimate resolution of what happened at the rallies awaits another day, the Court holds the Plaintiffs have plausibly alleged the Defendants formed a conspiracy to commit the racial violence that led to the Plaintiffs' varied injuries. Accordingly, the Plaintiffs' claims largely survive, although one Defendant is dismissed and other claims are pared down.[17]

Following three more years of discovery and motion practice, the suit finally made it to a jury in 2021. For the plaintiffs, it was worth the wait. The jury found for them and awarded them more than $25 million in damages.[18] But, of course, that was not the end of it. It was not until December 30, 2022 that Judge Moon affirmed the verdict, but in the same breath reduced the punitive damages drastically, leaving the plaintiffs with a total award totaling about 10% of the original jury amount.[19] In January 2023, His Honor also granted judgment against some defendants, who were default, but refused to lift the $350,000 punitive-damage cap with regard to the defaulters.[20]

With regard to Kessler in particular, Judge Moon wrote:

> Kessler planned the torch march for months. It would ultimately occur on August 11, 2017, but Kessler kept it secret including from police, who reached out to Kessler about the rally itself planned for August 12 [*cite omitted*]. Kessler also was less-than-forthcoming to the police about the rally—for instance keeping the total number of anticipated number of attendees from the police [*cite omitted*]. (Kessler: "If the police ask you how many people we have coming, don't tell them. If they think we have more than 400 they might be able to help the city pull our permit."). . . .
>
> In other words, Kessler was by his admission a lead organizer of Unite the Right, in which he sought to reprise the violent "Battle of Berkeley" into the "Battle of Charlottesville"; Kessler knowingly invited violent people to Unite the Right, including those like Damigo who gained notoriety for violence in Berkeley; Kessler professed to be "raising an army" for Richard Spencer, for "the cracking of skulls if necessary"; Kessler encouraged attendees to bring signposts, shields and other "self-defense implements" which could transformed from "free speech tool[s] into [] self-defense weapon[s] should things turn ugly"; Kessler believed Antifa (a left-wing, anti-fascist group represented at the event) wouldn't initiate the fight, and so he schemed to provoke violence with Antifa; and after Unite the Right, Kessler tried to delete the record of their digital communications planning Unite the Right on Discord, though he ultimately failed in that endeavor. And after Unite the Right, Kessler reiterated his support for codefendant James Fields, and expressing numerous times that Heather Heyer—who Fields killed in his car attack on August 12, 2017—was to blame for her own death . . . .
>
> Kessler argues that his conduct never amounted to anything more than self-defense or preparing for himself and the other participants in Unite the Right

rally to be prepared to defend themselves [*cite omitted*]. The jury was instructed about Kessler's (and the other defendants') self-defense theory at considerable length [*cite omitted*]. The jury simply didn't believe it. That's unsurprising. The evidence of Kessler's participation in a civil conspiracy to commit numerous unlawful acts—which resulted in widespread violence during weekend of August 11–12, 2017, including Plaintiffs' injuries—was absolutely overwhelming. There's no error in the jury finding Kessler liable for Virginia state law civil conspiracy in Count III.

Finally, Kessler argues that the jury improperly found him liable for racial, religious, or ethnic harassment or violence in violation of Virginia Code § 8.01–42.1, and therefore seeks a directed verdict on Count IV [*cite omitted*]. Kessler argues that the evidence of his activities at the torch march only show him "engaging in First Amendment protected expressive activity" [*cite omitted*]. He asserts that participation in "the torch march itself, without the violence at the rotunda," was "lawful activity," and that he "had nothing to do with the violence at the Rotunda" [*cite omitted*]. Kessler also argues that neither Plaintiff Romero or Willis claims to have heard or seen him at the torch march, further supporting his argument for a directed verdict. The Court disagrees. Kessler is not entitled to a directed verdict on Count IV.

The jury could find Kessler liable under § 8.01–42.1 if it found, by a preponderance of the evidence, that he subjected Plaintiffs Romero and Willis to acts of intimidation, harassment, or violence directed at their persons, and that his actions were motivated by racial, religious, or ethnic animosity [*cite omitted*]. There was such evidence and more in the record. Kessler testified that it was originally his idea to hold the torch march the evening of August 11, 2017 [*cite omitted*]. He planned and organized the torch march in the preceding months, including notifying potential attendees on the Charlottesville 2.0 Discord server and making sure attending groups would have tiki torches [*cite omitted*]. Then, on the evening of August 11, 2017, Kessler, along with Spencer and Kline, *led* the hundreds carrying lit torches and chanting "You will not replace us," "Jews will not replace us," "Blood and Soil," through University of Virginia grounds, down its historic Lawn, and up the steps of the Rotunda . . . . Kessler conceded at trial that the chants used during the torch march, including "Jews will not replace us," and "Sieg Heil," were offensive and intimidating to Jewish persons [*cite omitted*].[21]

When Kessler, leading the torch-wielding marchers, approached the top of the Rotunda steps, he saw a small group of counter-protestors surrounding the Thomas Jefferson statue down below [*cite omitted*]. Those included Plaintiffs Romero and Willis, who had linked arms with others around the statue [*cite omitted*]. Then, Willis described an "ocean of light and flames just starts spilling over both sides of the steps, and it's washing down," and "they basically just rushed the entire area and surrounded all of us in a matter of seconds" [*cite omitted*]. The Unite the Right rallygoers yelled at Romero, Willis, and the other counter-protestors: "go back to where you came from," "stupid bitch," "blood and soil," "Jews will not replace us," "you will not replace us"; and they made "[m]onkey noises" at them [*cites omitted*]. Willis, who is black, testified that he

> "was really scared because it looked like a lynch mob" [*cite omitted*]. Romero testified that the rallygoers threw a torch at her that landed centimeters from her foot and sprayed Mace at her and the other counter-protestors [*cite omitted*]. Willis testified that he was pepper-sprayed, which left him struggling to breathe, and "someone from the direction of the mob threw . . . mysterious fluid" that appeared to be tiki torch lighter fluid at him [*cite omitted*]. He feared the mob was trying "to burn [them] alive." *Id.* After the event, Defendant Spencer blithely acknowledged that the crowd they had assembled refused to let the surrounded counter-protestors leave. . . .
>
> Kessler argues that his involvement was nothing more than conduct and expression protected by the First Amendment [*cite omitted*]. However, conduct that "authorized" or "directed" tortious activity, or speech "likely to incite lawless action," are not protected. *NAACP v. Claiborne Hardware Co.*, 458 U.S. 886, 927 (1982).

11.4 James Alex Fields, Jr.

Defendant Fields received special attention from the jury: "Defendant James Alex Fields is solely responsible for an additional $701,459 in compensatory damages awarded on Count VI, resulting in a total compensatory damages liability for Fields in the amount of $2,004,743."[22]

Based on his actions from the event, the civil judgment was the least of Fields's troubles. Fields was hardly more than a boy when he drove from Ohio to attend the Unite the Right rally in Charlottesville. According to one source, on August 12, 2017, shortly after 1 p.m. EDT, the 20-year-old:

> paused in his Dodge Challenger as he stared at the diverse group at the foot of a road crossing the downtown pedestrian mall . . . . After a moment, police say[,] Fields slowly backed his car up to the top of the hill, then gunned it through a stop sign and across the pedestrian mall.[23]

Fields, who was said to have expressed admiration for Hitler while still in high school, drove 543 miles from Maumee, Ohio, to attend the rally. After he left home on the 11th, he received a text message from a family member, urging him to be careful. His reply: "We're not the ones who need to be careful." He attached a picture of Hitler.[24]

Fields's state court criminal trial began in Charlottesville on November 26, 2018, with jury selection. Wrote a reporter,

> Charlottesville Circuit Court Judge Richard Moore will preside over the trial of Fields. He's assembled a jury pool of 360 people, who will be screened and whittled down to 12 people plus alternates to decide the fate of Fields. The trial is expected to last about three weeks.[25]

Jury selection took three days.

On day four, the prosecutors opened with perhaps their strongest witness, local resident Stephen Simochek, who had recorded Fields's deadly act. Simochek testified that he had not even realized at first that he had the accused killer on video. The jury then got to see the recording.

> Screams, screeching tires and obscenities could be heard as bodies, clothes and water bottles flew through the air. One juror kept his hand over his mouth through much of the brief video. Fields, dressed for court in a dark blue sweater and open collared shirt, showed no visible signs of emotion as the video played.[26]

After presenting extensive testimony from Fields's victims concerning their injuries, prosecutors on day two of the trial introduced DNA evidence that put murder victim Heather Heyer's blood on the Dodge's hood and her flesh clinging to its windshield. The defense had already stipulated that Fields was behind the wheel.[27]

On day three, Dr. Jennifer Bowers, assistant chief medical examiner for Virginia's Western District, described Heyer's injuries in detail. These included broken ribs, punctured lungs, a large bruise to her chest, deep cuts, and the destruction of the main artery leading from her heart. "It was snapped in half," Bowers said of Heyer's aorta.[28]

The trial lasted a few more days. On December 7, the found Fields guilty of first-degree murder and numerous other charges. He would receive a life sentence—but that was not the end. The U.S. Department of Justice also got its turn. The outcome took another year, but was predictable:

> James Alex Fields Jr., 22, the Ohio man who drove his car into a crowd of counter-protestors at the "Unite the Right rally" on August 12, 2017, killing one woman and injuring dozens, was sentenced today in the Western District of Virginia to life in prison for his crimes. Fields previously pleaded guilty to 29 violations of the Matthew Shepard and James Byrd Jr. Hate Crimes Prevention Act, 18 U.S.C. § 249, for the attack.[29]

Confined to a federal prison ever since, Fields apparently is a bit of a handful. In early 2023, it was reported that Fields

> has been fined for allegedly threatening a correctional officer and brandishing what an inmate disciplinary record called a "dangerous weapon" at the prison where he is serving a life sentence. Federal prosecutors disclosed the misconduct incidents in court documents as they asked a judge to order James Alex Fields Jr. to turn over $650 from his inmate trust account to make a court-ordered payment toward restitution to the victims of his crimes.[30]

11.5 Aftermath

On August 11, 2022, the Southern Poverty Law Center's *Hatewatch* commented:

> Five years after white supremacists descended on Charlottesville, Virginia, the statue they came to protect is gone, and the "alt-right" coalition they embodied has imploded. At the same time, the existential threat that far-right extremism poses to the U.S. has arguably never been more severe. Such is the complex fallout of "Unite the Right," where hundreds of extremists immersed a college town in violent conflict, generating shocking images that news organizations continue to broadcast as symbols of the nation's struggle with hate and authoritarianism. They also helped bring the "great replacement" conspiracy theory into mainstream right-wing discourse by chanting, "Jews will not replace us" in viral videos staged on the eve of Unite the Right.

***

When Trump supporters attacked the U.S. Capitol on Jan. 6, 2021, the event embodied a still-evolving cultural shift in far-right extremism, one that left behind many of the men who participated in Unite the Right on August 12, 2017. Still, it's almost impossible to imagine Trump's mob enacting that kind of violence in a world where Unite the Right never took place.[31]

Regarding the "cultural shift" previously referred to, *Hatewatch* has said:

> One year after Donald Trump's supporters stormed the Capitol in Washington, D.C., the hard-right, anti-democracy faction of the Republican base that led the attack threatens to overtake the party for the long term. This hard-right faction, loyal to former President Trump, minimizes, or supports, the violent storming of the Capitol on Jan. 6. They have worked to systemically undermine America's democracy in the months following the attack by installing into positions of power loyal proponents of Trump's Big Lie and by passing a flurry of voter suppression bills. The few Republicans who oppose Trump or acknowledge the wrong that he and others did on Jan. 6 face being ostracized. This group of Republicans also embrace lies and conspiracy theories to spin away what happened that day. Repeatedly, such high-profile Trump backers as Tucker Carlson have opted to further stoke the feelings of paranoia and bitterness that undergirded the attack, rather than work to calm the tensions of a nation in turmoil.[32]

The twelfth and final chapter of this book examines the January 6, 2021 Capitol insurrection in detail.

Notes

1. "2012 Benghazi Attack," *Wikipedia*, https://en.wikipedia.org/wiki/2012_Benghazi_attack (last accessed December 30, 2023).
2. "Hilary Clinton Email Archive," *Wikileaks*, https://wikileaks.org/clinton-emails/ (last accessed December 30, 2023).
3. "Statement by FBI Director James B. Comey Investigation of Secretary Hillary Clinton's Use of a Personal Email System," *FBI News*, July 5, 2016, https://www.fbi.gov/news/press-releases/statement-by-fbi-director-james-b-comey-on-the-investigation-of-secretary-hillary-clinton2019s-use-of-a-personal-e-mail-system (last accessed December 30, 2023).
4. "Donald Trump 2016 Presidential Campaign," *Wikipedia*, https://en.wikipedia.org/wiki/Donald_Trump_2016_presidential_campaign (last accessed December 30, 2023).
5. "Donald Trump Presidential Campaign," *op. cit.*, note 4.
6. Marlow Stern, "Bill Maher Surrenders to President-Elect Trump: He Did It . . . And He Did It His Way," *Daily Beast*, November 11, 2016, https://www.thedailybeast.com/bill-maher-surrenders-to-president-elect-trump-he-won-and-he-did-it-his-way (last accessed December 30, 2023).
7. *See* "The Once and Future King," *Wikipedia*, https://en.wikipedia.org/wiki/The_Once_and_Future_King:

   > *The Once and Future King* is a collection of fantasy novels by T.H. White about the legend of King Arthur. It is loosely based upon the 1485 work *Le Morte d'Arthur* by Sir Thomas Malory. It was first published in 1958 as a collection of shorter novels that were published from 1938 to 1940, with some new or amended material. The title refers to a legend that Arthur will one day return as king.

8. "Aurelian Mondon," *University of Bath*, https://researchportal.bath.ac.uk/en/persons/aurelien-mondon (last accessed December 30, 2023).
9. "Antonia Vaughan (University of Bath)," *Oxpol*, https://blog.politics.ox.ac.uk/author/antonia-vaughan-university-of-bath/?author=antonia-vaughan-university-of-bath (last accessed December 30, 2023).
10. Aurelian Mondon and Antonia Vaughan, "The Trump Presidency and the Mainstreaming of Far-Right Politics," *Gale*, https://www.gale.com/intl/essays/aurelien-mondon-antonia-vaughan-trump-presidency-mainstreaming-far-right-politics (last accessed December 30, 2023).
11. Ibid.
12. Ibid.
13. "Charleston Church Shooting," *Wikipedia*, https://en.wikipedia.org/wiki/Charleston_church_shooting (last accessed December 30, 2023).
14. "Jason Kessler," *Wikipedia*, https://en.wikipedia.org/wiki/Jason_Kessler (last accessed December 30, 2023).
15. "Unite the Right Rally," *Wikipedia*, https://en.wikipedia.org/wiki/Unite_the_Right_rally (last accessed December 30, 2023).
16. Ibid.

17. *Sines v. Kessler,* 324 F.Supp.3d 765 (W.D. Va., 2018).
18. "*Sines v. Kessler,*" *Wikipedia*, https://en.wikipedia.org/wiki/Sines_v._Kessler (last accessed December 30, 2023).
19. *Sines v. Kessler,* 2022 WL 18026336 (U.S.D.Ct., W.D. Va.), appealed, *Sines v. Damigo* (U.S. Ct. App., 4th Cir., 2023).
20. *Sines v. Kessler,* 2023 WL 127213 (U.S.D.Ct., W.D. Va.) (also on appeal to the U.S. Court of Appeals for the 4th Cir).
21. *Sines v. Kessler, op.cit.,* note 22.
22. *Sines v. Kessler, op.cit.,* note 23.
23. Brett Barrouquere, "Neo-Nazi Sympathizer James Alex Fields, Jr., Faces Jury Over Deadly Actions, Decisions at 'Unite the Right,'" *Sothern Poverty Law Center*, November 26, 2018, https://www.splcenter.org/hatewatch/2018/11/26/neo-nazi-sympathizer-james-alex-fields-jr-faces-jury-over-deadly-actions-decision-unite (last accessed December 31, 2023).
24. Ibid.
25. Ibid.
26. Brett Barouquere, "The Five Most Compelling Moments So Far in the 'Unite the Right' Murder Trial," *Southern Poverty Law Center*, November 30, 2018, https://www.splcenter.org/hatewatch/2018/11/30/five-most-compelling-moments-so-far-unite-right-murder-trial (last accessed December 31, 2023).
27. Brett Barouquere, "Five Things to Know from the Second Day of Testimony in the 'Unite the Right' Murder Trial," *Sothern Poverty Law Center*, December 3, 2018, https://www.splcenter.org/hatewatch/2018/12/03/five-things-know-second-day-testimony-unite-right-murder-trial (accessed December 31, 2023).
28. Brett Barrouquere, "Five Things to Know from the Third Day of Testimony in the 'Unite the Right' Murder Trial," *Sothern Poverty Law Center*, December 4, 2018, https://www.splcenter.org/hatewatch/2018/12/04/five-things-know-third-day-testimony-unite-right-murder-trial (last accessed December 31, 2023).
29. "Ohio Man Sentenced to Life in Prison for Federal Hate Crimes Related to August 2017 Car Attack Related to Rally in Charlottesville, Virginia," *U.S. Department of Justice Office of Public Affairs*, June 28, 2019, https://www.justice.gov/opa/pr/ohio-man-sentenced-life-prison-federal-hate-crimes-related-august-2017-car-attack-rally (last accessed December 31, 2023).
30. Associated Press, "White Supremacist Serving Life Sentence Fined for Prison Misconduct," *PBS*, March 1, 2023, https://www.vpm.org/news/2023-03-01/james-alex-fields-jr-fined-unite-the-right-charlottesville (last accessed December 31, 2023).
31. Michael Edison Hayden et al., "'Unite the Right' 5 Years Later: Where Are They New?" *Southern Poverty Law Center*, August 11, 2022, https://www.splcenter.org/hatewatch/2022/08/11/unite-right-5-years-later-where-are-they-now (last accessed December 31, 2023).
32. Michael Edison Hayden, "One Year After January 6, the Hard Right Digs In," *Southern Poverty Law Center*, December 30, 2021, https://www.splcenter.org/hatewatch/2021/12/30/one-year-after-jan-6-hard-right-digs (last accessed December 31, 2023),

The January 6, 2021 Insurrection

12

I have chosen the word "insurrection" to include in this chapter's title. The word means, "an act or instance of revolting against civil authority or an established government."[1] To me, the label seems apt. Others may prefer other labels. All, I think, will agree that the intent of the well-armed mob, thousands strong, on January 6, 2021 was to prevent the vice president of the United States from certifying the votes of the Constitutionally-mandated Electoral College. More than 2,000 individuals would actually break and enter the Capitol building, forcing the Congress and the vice president to flee their chambers and offices, but ultimately failing to halt the counting of the ballots and the affirmation of Democrat Joseph Biden as the 46th U.S. President.

The day of violence began with a rally aimed at bolstering incumbent President Donald Trump's claim of being the real winner of the election. Among the speakers at the rally was the outgoing President himself, who addressed the crowd milling about the National Mall. Speaking for an hour and 11 minutes, Trump asserted that he would "never concede" the race. He admonished his supporters that if they did not "fight like hell, you're not going to have a country anymore."[2]

Trump's audience was substantial, though estimates varied wildly. Rally organizers had told the National Park Service to plan for 30,000. Some in law enforcement and the army pegged the number closer to 80,000. On the opposite end of the spectrum, the Associated Press estimated at least 10,000. The disparities can be explained, at least in part, by the absence of any aerial imagery and the fact that many attendees peeled off and left the Mall when the siege of the Capitol took its violent turn.[3]

Arrayed against this mob were about 1,200 Capitol Police, albeit the number assigned to protect the Capitol building itself was smaller. Just how much smaller is another data point open to controversy.[4]

The Capitol Complex was breached just before 2 p.m. Some Capitol Police, scattered around the Mall, rallied to the aid of those already defending the Complex. It would be another three hours before National Guard troops would arrive to relieve the beleaguered police force.[5]

Depending on who is counting, the death toll was between five and nine.

DOI: 10.4324/9781003474104-12

> Most news sources have officially counted five deaths including Capitol Police Officer Brian Sicknick, who died after suffering two strokes, and San Diego resident Ashli Babbitt, who was fatally shot by Capitol Police while climbing a barricaded door inside the Capitol. But some in Congress – including Rep. Alexandria Ocasio-Cortez (D-N.Y.) – have suggested the number of deaths is closer to nine and should include officers who committed suicide in the days and months following the attack.[6]

The number of injured officers totaled about 140, according to the same source. Damage to the Complex and its furnishings was extensive.

Remarkably, the insurrectionists recorded and photographed their illegal activities and posted them extensively on social media, making identification enormously easier than if they had not apparently considered themselves immune from arrest and prosecution. If that is what they believed—perhaps based upon the President's exhortations—they were wrong. Just how wrong was summarized by the U.S. Department of Justice 2½ years later.

July 6, 2023 Report of the U.S. Attorney for the District of Columbia[7]

Thursday, July 6, 2023, marks 30 months since the attack on the U.S. Capitol that disrupted a joint session of the U.S. Congress in the process of affirming the presidential election results. The government continues to investigate losses that resulted from the breach of the Capitol, including damage to the Capitol building and grounds, both inside and outside the building. As of October 14, 2022, the approximate losses suffered as a result of the siege at the Capitol totaled $2,881,360.20. That amount reflects, among other things, damage to the Capitol building and grounds and certain costs borne by the U.S. Capitol Police.

Under the continued leadership of the U.S. Attorney's Office for the District of Columbia and the FBI's Washington Field Office, the investigation and prosecution of those responsible for the attack continues to move forward at an unprecedented speed and scale. The Department of Justice's resolve to hold accountable those who committed crimes on January 6, 2021, has not, and will not, wane.

Based on the public court documents, below is a snapshot of the investigation as of the close of business Wednesday, July 5, 2023. Complete versions of most of the public court documents used to compile these statistics are available on the Capitol Breach Investigation Resource Page at https://www.justice.gov/usao-dc/capitol-breach-cases.

Arrests made: More than **1,069** defendants have been charged in nearly all **50** states and the District of Columbia. (This includes those charged in both District and Superior Court).

Criminal charges:

- Approximately **350** defendants have been charged with assaulting, resisting, or impeding officers or employees, including approximately **110** individuals who have been charged with using a deadly or dangerous weapon or causing serious bodily injury to an officer.
  - Approximately **140** police officers were assaulted Jan. 6 at the Capitol, including about **80** from the U.S. Capitol Police and about **60** from the Metropolitan Police Department.
- Approximately **11** individuals have been arrested on a series of charges that relate to assaulting a member of the media, or destroying their equipment, on Jan. 6.
- Approximately **935** defendants have been charged with entering or remaining in a restricted federal building or grounds. Of those, **103** defendants have been charged with entering a restricted area with a dangerous or deadly weapon.
- Approximately **61** defendants have been charged with destruction of government property, and approximately **49** defendants have been charged with theft of government property.
- More than **310** defendants have been charged with corruptly obstructing, influencing, or impeding an official proceeding, or attempting to do so.
- Approximately **55** defendants have been charged with conspiracy, either: (a) conspiracy to obstruct a Congressional proceeding, (b) conspiracy to obstruct law enforcement during a civil disorder, (c) conspiracy to injure an officer, or (d) some combination of the three.

Pleas:

- Approximately **594** individuals have pleaded guilty to a variety of federal charges, many of whom faced or will face incarceration at sentencing.
  - Approximately **160** have pleaded guilty to felonies. Another **434** have pleaded guilty to misdemeanors.

- A total of **68** of those who have pleaded guilty to felonies have pleaded to federal charges of assaulting law enforcement officers. Approximately **36** additional defendants have pleaded guilty to feloniously obstructing, impeding, or interfering with a law enforcement officer during a civil disorder. Of these **104** defendants, **76** have now been sentenced to prison terms of up to **150** months.
- **Four** of those who have pleaded guilty to felonies have pleaded guilty to the federal charge of seditious conspiracy.

Trials:

- **98** individuals have been found guilty at contested trials, including three who were found guilty in the Superior Court of the District of Columbia. Another **24** individuals have been convicted following an agreed-upon set of facts. **51** of these **122** defendants were found guilty of assaulting, resisting, or impeding officers and/or obstructing officers during a civil disorder, which are felony offenses, including one who has been sentenced to more than 14 years in prison.

Sentencings:

- Approximately **561** federal defendants have had their cases adjudicated and received sentences for their criminal activity on Jan. 6. Approximately **335** have been sentenced to periods of incarceration. Approximately **119** defendants have been sentenced to a period of home detention, including approximately **19** who also were sentenced to a period of incarceration.

Public Assistance:

- Citizens from around the country have provided invaluable assistance in identifying individuals in connection with the Jan. 6 attack. The FBI continues to seek the public's help in identifying approximately. . .**323** individuals believed to have committed violent acts on Capitol grounds.
- Additionally, the FBI currently has **14** videos of suspects wanted for violent assaults on federal officers and **(ONE)** video of **(TWO)** suspects wanted for assaults on members of the media on January 6 and is seeking the public's help to identify them.

12.1 The Stories Behind the Data

The data in this report is impressive . . . as a skeletal outline of 30 months of intensive investigation, arrests, prosecutions, guilty pleas, and convictions. Now let us add some flesh and blood to this skeleton. The subtitle of this book is *Case Studies in the Courtroom*. And, indeed, the human drama behind these statistics can be found in the numerous court opinions that the investigations, arrests, and prosecutions have generated.

We can best begin with someone not listed in the foregoing dataset, yet the most important actor in this ongoing legal drama: former President Donald Trump.

As previously noted, Trump's 71-minute speech climaxed a morning-long rally featuring his leading lawyer, Rudy Giuliani, and other of his far-right sycophants warming up the crowd. The fundamental question is: "Did Trump incite the violence that followed in the afternoon?" If so, he is guilty of a crime that places his speech outside the First Amendment's ambit. But before this question can be decided by a judge and jury, a threshold issue presents itself: Is the President of the United States immune from any such prosecution?

Ultimately, the Supreme Court will answer this question. However, in late 2023, the high court declined to expedite that answer. This early Christmas present was given to the former president on December 22, 2023. "The ruling is a scheduling win for Trump and his lawyers, who have sought repeatedly to delay the criminal cases against him as he campaigns to reclaim the White House in 2024."[8]

What we have, as this *Second Edition* heads off to the printer, is an opinion by the U.S. Court of Appeals for the District of Columbia Circuit concerning Trump's potential liability for damages in a civil suit stemming from the January 6 insurrection.[9] In the court's December 1 decision, its chief judge began by recalling the seminal case of *Nixon v. Fitzgerald*.[10] The Honorable Sri Srinivasan explained,

> Since the Supreme Court's decision . . . , Presidents have carried out their official responsibilities free from any exposure to civil damages liability. *Nixon* established a President's absolute immunity from civil damages claims predicated on his official acts. The object of a President's official-act immunity is to assure that he can fearlessly and impartially discharge the singularly weighty duties of the office.

This holding, of course, begs the factual question: was then-President Trump acting in his official capacity when he gave that incendiary 71-minute speech to the throng on the National Mall? Continued His Honor,

> The President, though, does not spend every minute of every day exercising official responsibilities. And when he acts outside the functions of his office, he does not continue to enjoy immunity from damages liability just because he happens to be the President. Rather, as the Supreme Court made clear in *Clinton v. Jones*, 520 U.S. 681, 117 S. Ct. 1636, 137 L.Ed.2d 945 (1997), a President's official-act immunity by nature does not extend to his unofficial actions. When he acts in an unofficial, private capacity, he is subject to civil suits like any private citizen.[11]

In what capacity, then, was Trump acting on the morning of January 6? As the President of the United States or as a presidential candidate?

> President Trump himself recognized that he engaged in his campaign to win re-election—including his post-election efforts to alter the declared results in his favor—in his personal capacity as presidential candidate, not in his official capacity as sitting President. That is evident in his effort to intervene in the Supreme Court's consideration of a post-election lawsuit challenging the administration of the election in various battleground states. He expressly filed his motion in the Supreme Court "in his personal capacity as candidate for reelection to the office of President" rather than in his official capacity as sitting President. Trump Mot. to Intervene 3, *Texas v. Pennsylvania*, No. 22O155 (U.S., 2020). And he grounded his claimed right to intervene in the case in his "unique and substantial personal interests as a candidate for re-election to the Office of President" rather than in any official interest in exercising the office's duties. *I*
>
> In arguing that he is entitled to official-act immunity in the cases before us, President Trump does not dispute that he engaged in his alleged actions up to and on January 6 in his capacity as a candidate. But he thinks that does not matter. Rather, in his view, a President's speech on matters of public concern is invariably an official function, and he was engaged in that function when he spoke at the January 6 rally and in the leadup to that day. We cannot accept that rationale. While Presidents are often exercising official responsibilities when they speak on matters of public concern, that is not always the case. When a sitting President running for re-election speaks in a campaign ad or in accepting his political party's nomination at the party convention, he typically speaks on matters of public concern. Yet he does so in an unofficial, private capacity as office-seeker, not an official capacity as office-holder. And actions taken in an *unofficial* capacity cannot qualify for *official*-act immunity.[12]

Blassingame v. Trump is the consolidation of a number of cases brought by members of the House of Representatives and Capitol Police officers in their personal capacities, seeking monetary damages. The December decision denies Trump's motion to dismiss. As such, it is not ripe for Supreme Court review, nor does it determine how the appellate court may decide the same question on a subsequent summary judgment motion by the defendants following the discovery phase of the litigation.

> Instead, we hold only that, taking the allegations in the plaintiffs' complaints as true as we must at this point in the proceedings, President Trump has not demonstrated an entitlement to dismissal of the claims against him based on a President's official-act immunity. In the proceedings ahead in the district court, President Trump will have the opportunity to show that his alleged actions in the runup to and on January 6 were taken in his official capacity as President rather than in his unofficial capacity as presidential candidate.[13]

Another interesting issue, akin to Trump's own immunity, lurks in the shadows. Let us assume that, despite efforts by a raft of Republican opponents to defeat him in the spring 2024 primary elections, and despite some court decisions to actually exclude him from some states' primary ballots,[14] he emerges as the GOP's presidential candidate and he defeats incumbent Joe Biden in November 2024. Could the once and future president pardon some or all of the January 6 insurrections listed in the Justice Department's October 6, 2023 summation? A triumphant Trump might very well welcome this challenge. His supporters would certainly applaud it.

However, this is hardly the only legal issue of note. Adding to federal trial and appellate court dockets across the country are the myriad issues raised by the women and men who invaded the nation's Capitol some three years ago and wound up on the wrong side of a criminal prosecution in the wake of their actions. What follows here are selected decisions that not only illustrate the range of those legal issues, but also in the judges' presentation of the facts of the cases take us inside the insurrection and, indeed, inside the Capitol.

12.2 *United States v. Mario Mares*[15]

Mares, approximately 50 years old, lives in Ballinger, Texas. He was not arrested until August 2, 2023. Following his arrest, a federal magistrate judge ordered him to be detained pending his trial. He challenged his detention, arguing he should be out on bail. Here are the facts, as presented by the district judge who reviewed the magistrate's decision:

> Defendant made three alarming social media posts to a small online group in December 2020. In one, he urged "every #patriot" to "go to your state capitol and local mayors offices heavily armed and drag out and either jail or execute all the known CORRUPT #politicians for treason!" In another, "YOU WANT VIOLENCE! YOU #CELEBRITIES AND CORRUPT #POLITICIANS ARE

> FIXING TO FIND OUT WHAT VIOLENCE IS!! WE ARE FUCKIN TIRED OF ALL YOUR SHIT!! WE ARE GOING TO FIND YOU AND WE THE PEOPLE WITH NO MERCY ARE GOING TO HANG OR EXECUTE YOU!!!" *Id.* at 6. A third read: "Time to start the LYNCHING party!!"
>
> But Defendant's alleged activities on January 6 were more limited than his posts would have suggested. On January 4 and 5, Mr. Mares drove to Fairfax, Virginia, from his home in Ballinger, Texas, with two other individuals. On January 6, the men first attended the "Stop the Steal" rally outside the White House before proceeding to the U.S. Capitol grounds "between approximately 12:15 PM and 2:30 PM." Photographs taken of Defendant that day show a bulge under his jacket on his right hip. The Government alleges that the bulge was a concealed gun; Defendant denies this.
>
> Two-and-a-half years passed before federal authorities arrested Defendant at his home on August 2, 2023. The Government does not allege that Mr. Mares engaged in violent behavior or made any threats during the interim.[16]

Drawing guidance from the Bail Reform Act,[17] District Judge Ana C. Reyes looked at Mares's background and history.

> Defendant's history and personal characteristics persuade the Court that conditions of release could assure the safety of the community.
>
> Defendant has no criminal record, history of drug or alcohol abuse, or mental or physical conditions. These considerations weigh against detention. And unlike Magistrate Judge Parker, the Court has before it numerous letters in support of Mr. Mares from family, friends, and neighbors—many of whom have known Mr. Mares for more than a decade. The letters describe him in favorable terms. His wife describes his efforts to collect and deliver donations for the communities hit hardest by Hurricane Harvey. The assistant pastor at his church, the local justice of the peace, his coworkers, and others describe him as a loyal family man, a financially stable business owner, a law-abiding citizen, and someone who poses no threat to their community. There is no reason to believe that these letters are disingenuous. The Court is therefore persuaded that Defendant has the type of stable and long-established financial, family, and community ties that disfavor detention.[18]

To my mind, Mario Mares is representative of the uncounted thousands who sounded the call to arms and who themselves showed up in Washington in early January 2021. As with the vast majority of these folks, Mares was mostly talk. When push, quite literally, came to shove on the afternoon of January 6, this vast majority never entered the Capitol building. Mares, according to the DOJ's own indictment of him, never brandished his gun, if indeed he carried one; never played a leadership role in the insurrection; never entered the Capitol; never tussled with the D.C. police nor committed any act of vandalism. Consequently, ruled Judge Reyes, he should be out on bail.

Whether Mares and his ilk should ultimately be convicted of crimes and incarcerated seems to be an even tougher question. According to the court's opinion, he believes that the Constitution gives him the right to carry firearms anywhere, anytime. His social media posts during the run-up to the insurrection certainly seem to advocate violence and insurrection. But they do not encourage the reader to rendezvous in Washington, much less to invade the nation's Capitol. And, per the DOJ itself, Mares did not really do anything in D.C., other than to add his physical presence to the mob. Without more, one wonders if he committed a crime at all.

12.3 *United States v. David Krauss*[19]

On January 6, about 20 minutes after rioters first broke into the Capitol and two minutes after Vice President Mike Pence and members of Congress evacuated the chambers, Krauss and two co-defendants entered the building and remained inside for 17 minutes. Those fateful 17 minutes led to four charges against him: For his conduct in the Capitol, Krauss was charged with entering and remaining in a restricted building, in violation of 18 U.S.C. § 1752(a)(1); disorderly and disruptive conduct in a restricted building, in violation of 18 U.S.C. § 1752(a)(2); violent entry and disorderly conduct in a Capitol building, in violation of 40 U.S.C. § 5104(e)(2)(D); and parading, demonstrating, or picketing in a Capitol building, in violation of 40 U.S.C. § 5104(e)(2)(G). Krauss copped a plea, pleading guilty to a misdemeanor. He was sentenced to nine months of probation.

A condition of his probation was that he not carry firearms and that all his guns be removed from his possession for the duration of his probation. This was in September of 2023. Apparently either this condition proved to be intolerable, even for such a short stretch, or—and this seems much more likely—he wants to be a test case. In any event, he reappeared in court shortly after the start of his probation, requesting the no-guns requirement be lifted and asserting his Second Amendment right to bear arms.

In early November 2023, Judge Boasberg issued his ruling, retaining the firearms restriction. In doing so, he used the federal sentencing guidelines to find the appropriate balance between the inconvenience caused the defendant and the welfare of his community. Contrasting Krauss's case to that of another January 6 participant, he pointed out that she and her family were the target of threats, establishing a need to keep a firearm in her home, while Krauss could show no such necessity.[20]

Clearly, Krauss's culpability surpasses that of Mares. The former actually entered the Capitol. Yet, again, the government presented no evidence of any actual vandalism, nor of any altercation with the Capitol Police. Both men are minor players in the tragedy enacted on January 6. Appropriately, neither seems to be suffering severe consequences. Their cases provide us with a glimpse of how the criminal justice systems—which, per the cliché, grinds slow and fine—has sorted through the thousands of identifiable pawns in the "insurrection game."

From Mares and Krauss, let us now turn to two of the major players, one of whom—to continue the chess analogy—was not even a piece on the board on January 6, but nonetheless merited the harshest prison sentence to date.

12.4 Henry "Enrique" Tarrio

The former leader of the Proud Boys was found guilty of seditious conspiracy and sentenced to 22 years in prison, the longest sentence to date. And yet, Tarrio was even at the National Mall on January 6. To the contrary, he had been arrested several days earlier and was in custody when the insurrection took place.[21]

Here are the facts about the Proud Boys, per the Anti-Defamation League:

- **Ideology**: The Proud Boys are a right-wing extremist group with a violent agenda. They are primarily misogynistic, Islamophobic, transphobic and anti-immigration. Some members espouse white supremacist and antisemitic ideologies and/or engage with white supremacist groups.
- **Membership**: There are 119 active Proud Boys chapters across 46 states recognized by the national Proud Boys organization.
- **Notable characteristics**: Members frequently wear black and yellow Fred Perry polo shirts, other black and yellow clothing and tactical vests.
- **Global footprint**: Proud Boys have international chapters in Canada, Britain, Ireland, Germany, Norway, Sweden, Australia and the Philippines.
- **Membership:** Controlled by local chapter leadership and subject to initiation rituals.
- **Tactics**: Public rallies and protests. Members have been known to engage in violent tactics; several members have been convicted of violent crimes.
- **Recent Activity:** Proud Boys members accounted for one of the highest number of extremist arrestees in relation to the Jan 6 insurrection. In 2021, Proud Boys latched on to anti-mask and anti-vaccine activism, showing up at school board meetings as well as related protests and rallies.[22]

For their role in the January 6 insurrection, the Proud Boys have been sued by the District of Columbia.[23] The case is one of many pending before the District of Columbia's federal trial court, which seek to hold the participants in the January 6 insurrection civilly liable; the case against Donald Trump, discussed earlier in this chapter, is another. This case is unique in that it is the District itself, which is suing, rather than individuals. Also named as a defendant is the Oath Keepers. Principally, the city seeks reimbursement of "the costs of deploying D.C. police officers, the costs to treat injured officers, and the costs for paid leave for injured officers."

In a motion to dismiss, the defendants argued that the District has no standing to pursue its claims. Disagreeing, District Judge Amit. P. Mehta held that the District has pleaded a plausible claim of civil conspiracy, as to which acts of assault, battery, and intentional infliction of emotional distress, even if not directly committed by individual Defendants, were foreseeable consequences of the alleged scheme," and its direct expenditures constitute potential damages.

The Southern Poverty Law Center,[24] the bane of right-wing extremists, long ago recognized that the best way to cripple and even destroy such organization is to significant civil-damage suits against them. Witness the following SPLC press release, dated November 14, 2008.

The Southern Poverty Law Center today won a crushing jury verdict against one of the nation's largest Klan groups for its role in the brutal beating of a teenager at a county fair in rural Kentucky.

> The Southern Poverty Law Center today won a crushing jury verdict against one of the nation's largest Klan groups for its role in the brutal beating of a teenager at a county fair in rural Kentucky.
>
> The $2.5 million verdict will likely cripple the Imperial Klans of America, which has 16 chapters in eight states.
>
> "The people of Meade County, Kentucky, have spoken loudly and clearly. And what they've said is that ethnic violence has no place in our society, that those who promote hate and violence will be held accountable and made to pay a steep price," said SPLC founder and chief trial attorney Morris Dees, who tried the case. "We look forward to collecting every dime that we can for our client and to putting the Imperial Klans of America out of business."
>
> The SPLC brought the lawsuit on behalf of Jordan Gruver, who was 16 when he was attacked in July 2006.
>
> The jury deliberated for nearly seven hours before delivering the verdict against IKA Imperial Wizard Ron Edwards and two former IKA members, Jarred Hensley and Andrew Watkins, both of whom served two years in state prison for assaulting Gruver. The SPLC earlier reached settlements with Watkins and one other Klansman.

> The verdict included $1.5 million in compensatory damages—apportioned among Edwards, Hensley and Watkins—and $1 million in punitive damages against Edwards.
> The SPLC argued in court that Edwards and the IKA incited the racial hatred that led to the attack at the Meade County Fair in Brandenburg in July 2006. Several Klansmen were at the fair on a recruiting mission when they spotted Gruver, who is a U.S. citizen of Panamanian descent. They threw whisky in his face and called him a "s—." Gruver, who stood 5-foot-3 and weighed just 150 pounds at the time, was surrounded, beaten to the ground and kicked by the Klansmen, one of whom was 6-foot-5 and 300 pounds. He was left with a broken jaw and arm, two cracked ribs and multiple cuts. He now suffers from post-traumatic stress syndrome and has permanent arm and jaw injuries.[25]

Such tactics will work against the Proud Boys, as well. But, meanwhile, the leaders, such as Tarrio, appear to be prison-bound.

Born in the ominous year 1984, Henry Tarrio is of Afro-Cuban descent and grew up in the "Little Havana" section of Miami. At 20, he had his first brush with law, ending in a theft conviction. In 2004 or 2005, he founded two small businesses, one of which provided companies with GPS tracking. In 2012, he was back in the criminal justice system, this time indicted for a scheme to rebrand and resell diabetic test strips. Tarrio turned state's witness, cut a deal, got 30 months, and served 16 months. The court transcript indicates he worked as an informant for federal and local law enforcement from 2012–2014. Much of this phase did not come to light, until Reuters obtained those court records in—again, perhaps ominously—January 2021.[26]

Tarrio joined the Proud Boys in 2017. In 2018, he was elevated to "fourth degree" in the organization after he physically attacked someone believed to be a member of the far-left Antifa organization. Not long afterward, he assumed the chairmanship of the organization. His predecessor, Gavin McInnes, apparently saw potential in Tarrio—even as a possible political candidate. The two enjoyed access to right-wing "superstars" such as Trump acolytes Steve Bannon and Roger Stone.[27]

Tarrio certainly showed organizing ability, playing a role in the rally "End Domestic Terrorism" in Portland, Oregon, on August 17, 2019. In a prelude to the January 6 insurrection, in mid-December, Tarrio led about 200 Proud Boys to Washington. On December 12, they seized a "Black Lives Matter" banner from a United Methodist church and burned it, and attacked and vandalized several Black churches.[28]

These antics continued into early January, including clashes with leftist groups, which resulted in at least four stabbings. The upshot was Tarrio's arrest on January 4. Consequently, he was indisposed when the "big show" took place two days later.[29] Like Tarrio's reign of mayhem in December 2020 and January 2021, those activities led to what might be considered a sort of prelude.

> In July 2021, part of a plea agreement with prosecutors, Tarrio pleaded guilty to destruction of property and to a misdemeanor count of attempted possession of a high-capacity magazine (the felony counts were dropped as part of the agreement). Tarrio acknowledged that he had burned the banner, but denied that the act was a hate crime. At the sentencing hearing in August 2021, Tarrio said he made a "grave mistake" and wanted to "profusely apologize for my actions." The D.C. Superior Court judge found that Tarrio's claim that he did not fully realize what he was doing was "not credible" and that video evidence contradicted some of Tarrio's claims.[20] Tarrio was sentenced to 155 days in the D.C. Jail, more than the 90 days requested by federal prosecutors. Tarrio began serving his sentence on September 6, 2021. His November 2021 request for early release based on poor living conditions in the D.C. Jail was denied. Tarrio was released from the D.C. jail in January 2022, after serving four months and a week.[30]

Tarrio's "honeymoon" period was brief. Between November 2021 and January 2022, dozens of Proud Boys were rounded up and indicted for their roles in the insurrection. Meanwhile, a rift split the Proud Boys, catalyzed in part by the Reuters revelation that Tarrio had been an informant. Financial services, such as PayPal, severed business relationships with the Proud Boys. In September, Tarrio stepped down from the national organization's chair.[31]

In June 22, a Washington, D.C. grand jury indicted Tarrio and four of his former lieutenants, who in effect were his "boots on the ground" at the National Mall on January 6, for seditious conspiracy. Their trial finally began in January 2023, two years after the insurrection. Among the extensive videos, thousands of encrypted text messages, and chats introduced at trial was Tarrio's clear social media admission of guilt: "Make no mistake. We did this." In a war plan entitled "1776 Returns," the Proud Boy leadership referred to the Capitol as "The Winter Palace."[32]

Found guilty, Tarrio was sentenced in September to 22 years of incarceration. At the sentencing, he reportedly begged the judge, "Please don't take my 40s away from me."[33]

12.5 Stewart Rhodes

The founder of Oath Keepers stands in second place, just four years behind Tarrio, with an 18-year sentence, also for seditious conspiracy. With a patch over his left eye, his piratical appearance seems a good fit with the swashbuckling storming of the Capitol. Elmer Stewart Rhodes was born in Fresno, California in 1966. Like Tarrio, his background belies his right-wing orientation.

Abandoned by their Marine father when Rhodes was only a toddler, he grew up in a Mexican-American household. Rhodes even claimed some Native American blood on his maternal side.[34]

Following high school in Las Vegas, Nevada, Rhodes joined the Army but was honorably discharged after a spinal injury during paratrooper training. After studying political science at the University of Nevada, Las Vegas (UNLV), he landed a spot on the staff of U.S. Congressman Ron Paul (R-Texas). In 2008, he worked on Paul's presidential campaign. Meanwhile, the 9/11 terrorist attacks and the legislation that followed reportedly left Rhodes concerned about what he saw as the erosion of Americans' rights. This may have been one reason why he attended Yale's law school, graduating in 2004.[35]

Rhodes clerked for a justice of the Arizona Supreme Court, then entered private practice. His legal career screeched to a halt in 2015, when he was disbarred by the Montana Supreme Court. But by then, his interests apparently lay elsewhere. In 2009, he founded the Oath Keepers. The launch was theatrical, conducted at Lexington, Massachusetts, scene of "the shot heard round the world."

As for the eye patch, the story goes that Rhodes in 1993 accidentally dropped his .22 caliber pistol, which discharged and shot him in eye.[36]

In the decision that denied defendants' motion to dismiss their indictment—and which teed up the case for trial—District Judge Amit P. Mehta explained the principal charge against Rhodes as follows.

1. HISTORICAL BACKGROUND

> At the start of the Civil War, the national government had limited authority under federal criminal law to detain and punish those who supported the rebellion. The charge of treason, which carried the death penalty, was the primary tool available, but the Constitution defined that offense strictly, and judicial opinions imposed rigorous elements of proof. *See* Catherine M. Tarrant, *To "insure domestic Tranquility": Congress and the Law of Seditious Conspiracy, 1859–1861*, 15 Am. J. Legal Hist. 107, 107 (1971). "As part of the effort to meet the emergency war posed, Congress enacted statutes to define crimes less than treason. Congressmen believed these measures were necessary since no statute law on the subject existed, and the common law was not applicable." *Id.* at 118. Approximately 100 days after the first shots were fired at Fort Sumter on April 12, 1861, Congress passed "An Act to Define and Punish Certain Conspiracies," which eventually would become the seditious conspiracy statute. *Id.* at 118–19. The Act became law on July 31, 1861. *Id.*; *see* Act of July 31, 1861, ch. 33, 12 Stat. 284. One of the bill's sponsors, Senator Lyman Trumbull of Illinois, explained that the "object of this bill is not under any other name to punish traitors, but it is to punish persons who conspire together to commit offenses against the United States not analogous to treason." *Cong. Globe*, 37th Cong., 1st Sess. 277 (1861).

Ten years later, Congress passed the Enforcement Act of 1871, also known as the Ku Klux Klan Act, "to enforce the Provisions of the Fourteenth Amendment of the Constitution of the United States." *See* Act of Apr. 20, 1871, ch. 22, § 2, 17 Stat. 13, 13 (codified at 70 Rev. Stat. § 5336 (1878)). That law contained a nearly identically worded conspiracy provision as the Act of July 31, 1861. *See id.*; *Baldwin v. Franks*, 120 U.S. 678, 693, 7 S. Ct. 656, 32 L.Ed. 766 (1887) (observing that § 5336 "is a reenactment of similar provisions in the Act of July 31, 1861"). This enactment eventually would become the seditious conspiracy statute under the modern federal criminal code. *See* Act of Mar. 4, 1909, ch. 1, § 6, 35 Stat. 1089 (codified at 18 U.S.C. § 6 (1940)).
Now codified at 18 U.S.C. § 2384, the seditious conspiracy statute reads as follows:

> If two or more persons in any State or Territory, or in any place subject to the jurisdiction of the United States, conspire to overthrow, put down, or to destroy by force the Government of the United States, or to levy war against them, or to oppose by force the authority thereof, or by force to prevent, hinder, or delay the execution of any law of the United States, or by force to seize, take, or possess any property of the United States contrary to the authority thereof, they shall each be fined under this title or imprisoned not more than 20 years, or both.

Defendants in this case are not charged with a conspiracy to overthrow the government or to levy war against it. Nor are they charged with attempting to seize property of the United States. Rather, Defendants stand accused of conspiring "by force to prevent, hinder, and delay the execution of any law of the United States." Indictment ¶ 15 [*cite omitted*]. The indictment spells out the "law[s] of the United States" that they allegedly tried to prevent, hinder, and delay: "the Twelfth Amendment and Twentieth Amendments to the Constitution and Title 3, Section 15 of the United States Code," *id.* ¶ 16.

2. "EXECUTION OF ANY LAW OF THE UNITED STATES"

Defendants' assertion that Count One fails to state an offense rests on their reading of the words "execution of any law of the United States." Caldwell MTD at 7–19. According to them, "[s]ince laws do not 'execute' themselves the target of the seditious conspiracy, logically, must be *both* the federal law itself and at least one person attempting to execute that law." *Id.* at 7. Such person must be "authorized" to execute the law, Defendants assert, and under Article II of the Constitution, only the President is vested with the authority to "execute" the laws of the United States. *See id.* at 8; U.S. Const. art. II, § 3 (granting authority to the President to "take Care that the Laws be faithfully executed"). So, Defendants say, because only persons acting pursuant to the authority of the President "execute" laws, members of Congress (including the Vice President acting as President of the Senate), whose offices are constitutionally separate from the Executive Branch, cannot be the object of a seditious conspiracy. Caldwell MTD at 16–17. In other words, because members of Congress on January 6 were not "executing" any constitutional or statutory election-related

> law within the meaning of § 2384, Count One fails to state an offense. *Id.* at 15 ("Count 1 is defective because . . . it fails to identify, as the target of the conspiracy, an *individual* authorized to *execute* the *election laws*.").
>
> The government's response is twofold. First, the government maintains that Defendants' hyper-focus on identifying a particular person as the object of the conspiracy is misguided. Gov't Resp. to Caldwell MTD, ECF No. 123 [hereinafter Gov't Opp'n], at 10. It contends that § 2384 only requires that the conspiracy be directed against the government of the United States as a whole in its execution of its laws. Gov't Opp'n at 14–17. And that is precisely what the indictment charges: Defendants conspired to resist the government's execution of the "law governing the transfer of power," Indictment ¶ 16; Hr'g Tr., ECF No. 159 [hereinafter Oral Arg. Hr'g Tr.], at 39. Second, the government argues that, even if Count One must identify a person authorized to "execute" the law at issue, it does so: the Vice President and members of Congress who gathered for the Joint Session on January 6. Gov't Opp'n at 16–17. The government maintains that the word "execution" in § 2348 carries its ordinary, not Article II, meaning. *Id.* at 14–16. The term's common meaning easily reaches the Vice President and members of Congress carrying out their duties in certifying the Electoral College vote. *Id.*
>
> The court thinks the government has the better reading of the seditious conspiracy statute.[37]

So, what exactly did Rhodes do to merit his conviction and 18-year sentence? According to the U.S. Department of Justice:

> According to the government's evidence, the Oath Keepers are a large but loosely organized collection of individuals, some of whom are associated with militias. Following the Nov. 3, 2020, presidential election, Rhodes, Meggs, and others began plotting to oppose by force the lawful transfer of presidential power. Beginning in late December 2020, via encrypted and private communications applications, Rhodes, Meggs, Harrelson, Watkins, Caldwell, and others coordinated and planned to travel to Washington, D.C., on or around Jan. 6, 2021, the date of the certification of the electoral college vote.
>
> The defendants also, collectively, employed a variety of manners and means, including: organizing into teams that were prepared and willing to use force and to transport firearms and ammunition into Washington, D.C.; recruiting members and affiliates; organizing trainings to teach and learn paramilitary combat tactics; bringing and contributing paramilitary gear, weapons, and supplies—including knives, batons, camouflaged combat uniforms, tactical vests with plates, helmets, eye protection, and radio equipment—to the Capitol grounds; breaching and attempting to take control of the Capitol grounds and building on Jan. 6, 2021, in an effort to prevent, hinder, and delay the certification of the electoral college vote; using force against law enforcement officers while inside the Capitol on January 6, 2021; continuing to plot, after January 6, 2021, to oppose by force the lawful transfer of presidential power, and using websites, social media, text messaging and encrypted messaging applications to communicate with each other and others.

On January 6, 2021, a large crowd began to gather outside the Capitol perimeter as the Joint Session of Congress got under way at 1 p.m. Crowd members eventually forced their way through, up, and over U.S. Capitol Police barricades and advanced to the building's exterior façade. Shortly after 2 p.m., crowd members forced entry into the Capitol by breaking windows, ramming open doors, and assaulting Capitol police and other law enforcement officers. At about this time, according to the government's evidence, Rhodes entered the restricted area of the Capitol grounds and directed his followers to meet him at the Capitol.

At approximately 2:30 p.m., according to the government's evidence, Meggs, Harrelson, and Watkins, along with other Oath Keepers and affiliates—many wearing paramilitary clothing and patches with the Oath Keepers name, logo, and insignia—marched in a "stack" formation up the east steps of the Capitol, joined a mob, and made their way into the Capitol. Rhodes and Caldwell remained outside the Capitol, where they coordinated activities.

While certain Oath Keepers members and affiliates breached the Capitol grounds and building, others remained stationed just outside of the city in quick reaction force (QRF) teams. According to the government's evidence, the QRF teams were prepared to rapidly transport firearms and other weapons into Washington, D.C., in support of operations aimed at using force to stop the lawful transfer of presidential power.[38]

12.6 Conclusion

As this *Second Edition* of *Counter Terrorism Issues* goes to press, the final resolution of the events of January 6, 2021 remains a fluid and elusive goal for the American system of justice. As we have seen in this chapter, the following questions remain unresolved:

- Is former President Donald Trump entitled to immunity from civil liability and/or criminal culpability regarding his role in the events of that day?
- Will former President Donald Trump be the Republican nominee for President, and if so, will he be re-elected—and if so, will he pardon the long list of insurrections who have been convicted or have pled guilty to crimes committed on January 6?
- What will be the outcomes of the inevitable appeals that have sprung, or still will spring, from the insurrectionists' convictions and sentences?
- Who else may yet be identified, arrested, charged, and tried for involvement in the insurrection?
- And, perhaps most acutely urgent of all: What role will the radical right play in the 2024 presidential election?

One thing this author believes he can say with reasonable certainty is this: Whereas the bulk of this book's *First Edition* was dominated by case studies related to international Islamic terrorism, this *Second Edition* shifts the focus toward domestic right-wing terrorist activities. While it would be folly for me to dismiss the continuing threat to America's national security posed from abroad—particularly in light of Hamas's attack on Israel and the harsh Israeli response in the autumn of 2023—the most urgent threat to American democracy in 2024 unquestionably arises from the right.

In 1995, while some (such as the SPLC) sounded the alarm and fought the good fight against the radical right, most Americans saw the Oklahoma City bombing as a tragic but unique incident. Some even believed,[39] and no doubt still believe, that it was an act of international Islamic terrorism. Most thoughtful and knowledgeable scholars have come to appreciate the direct line that can be traced from McVeigh's heinous act nearly three decades ago and the events in Washington, D.C. just three years ago.[40]

This, I will submit, is the greatest challenge currently posed to our law enforcement and national security apparati, and to our system of justice. I believe that in the 1993–2023 span covered by this book, our courts have acquitted themselves admirably in most—if not all—of the case studies presented and examined in these 12 chapters. Faculty and students who use this volume as a text may or may not agree. In the book's *Instructor's Manual*, I've endeavored to pose the questions that may form the basis of lively class discussions and debates, equally lively discussion forums and blogs of online courses, and fodder for further research via term papers and class projects.

Like who killed Kennedy, some questions posed by the case studies in this text continue to defy definitive answers. Some await the unfolding of "future history." Others will forever remain the terrain of conspiracy theorists.

Good luck!

Notes

1. "Insurrection," *Merriam-Webster Dictionary*, https://www.merriam-webster.com/dictionary/insurrection (last accessed December 31, 2023).
2. Jie Jenny Zou and Erin B. Logan, "Key Facts to Know About the January 6 Insurrection," *Los Angeles Times,* January 5, 2022, https://www.latimes.com/politics/story/2022-01-05/by-the-numbers-jan-6-anniversary (last accessed December 31, 2023).
3. Ibid.
4. Ibid.
5. Ibid.
6. Ibid.

7. "30 Months Since the January 6 Attack on the Capitol," *U.S. Attorney for the District of Columbia*, July 6, 2023 (updated October 6, 2023), https://www.justice.gov/usao-dc/30-months-jan-6-attack-capitol (emphasis in original; last accessed December 31, 2023).
8. "Supreme Court Declines to Rule on Whether Trump Can Be Prosecuted for Now," *PBS News Hour*, December 22, 2023, https://www.pbs.org/newshour/politics/supreme-court-declines-to-rule-on-whether-trump-can-be-prosecuted-for-now (last accessed January 2, 2024).
9. *Blassingame v. Trump*, 87 F.4th 1 (2023).
10. *Nixon v. Fitzgerald*, 457 U.S. 731, 102 S. Ct. 2690, 73 L.Ed.2d 349 (1982).
11. *Blassingame v. Trump, op cit.*, note 9.
12. Ibid.
13. Ibid.
14. "Trump is Blocked from the GOP Primary Ballot in 2 States. Can He Still Run for President?" *PBS News Hour*, December 29, 2023, https://www.pbs.org/newshour/politics/trump-is-blocked-from-the-gop-primary-ballot-in-2-states-can-he-still-run-for-president (last accessed January 2, 2024).
15. *United States v. Mares*, 2023 WL 7921972 (U.S.D.Ct., D.D.C.) (emphasis in original).
16. Ibid.
17. 18. U.S.C. §3142(e)–(f).
18. *United States v. Mares, op cit.*, note 14.
19. *United States v. Krauss*, 2023 WL 7407302 (U.S.D.Ct., D.D.C.).
20. Ibid.
21. Sareen Habeshian, "Here Are the Harshest Punishments Yet for January 6 Rioters," *Axios*, September 5, 2023, https://www.axios.com/2023/09/01/jan-6-longest-sentences-list (last accessed January 2, 2024).
22. "Backgrounder: Proud Boys," *Anti-Defamation League (ADL)*, December 11, 2023, https://www.adl.org/resources/backgrounder/proud-boys-0 (last accessed January 2, 2024).
23. *District of Columbia v. Proud Boys International, LLC*, 2023 WL 2733767 (U.S.D.Ct., D.D.C.).
24. "Southern Poverty Law Center," *Wikipedia*, https://en.wikipedia.org/wiki/Southern_Poverty_Law_Center (last accessed January 2, 2024).
25. "SPLC Wins $2.5 Million Verdict Against Imperial Clans of America," *Southern Poverty Law Conference*, November 14, 2008, https://www.splcenter.org/news/2008/11/14/splc-wins-25-million-verdict-against-imperial-klans-america (last accessed January 2, 2024).
26. "Enrique Tarrio," *Wikipedia*, https://en.wikipedia.org/wiki/Enrique_Tarrio (last accessed January 2, 2024).
27. Ibid.
28. Ibid.
29. Ibid.
30. Ibid.
31. Ibid.
32. Ibid.

33. "Former Proud Boys Leader Enrique Tarrio Gets 22 Years in Prison for January 6 Seditious Conspiracy," *PBS News Hour*, September 5, 2023, https://www.pbs.org/newshour/politics/former-proud-boys-leader-enrique-tarrio-gets-record-22-years-in-prison-for-jan-6-seditious-conspiracy (last accessed January 2, 2023).
34. "Stewart Rhodes," *Wikipedia*, https://en.wikipedia.org/wiki/Stewart_Rhodes (last accessed January 2, 2024).
35. Ibid.
36. Aurko Maitra, "What Happened to Stewart Rhodes' Eye? Injury Explored as Oath Keeper is Convicted of Seditious Conspiracy," *SK Pop*, December 3, 2022, https://www.sportskeeda.com/pop-culture/news-what-happened-stewart-rhodes-eye-injury-explored-oath-keepers-founder-convicted-seditious-conspiracy (last accessed January 2, 2024).
37. *United States v. Rhodes*, 610 F.Supp.3d 29 (D.D.C., 2022).
38. "Leader of Oath Keepers and Oath Keepers Member Found Guilty of Seditious Conspiracy and Other Charges Related to U.S. Capitol Breach," *U.S. Dept. of Justice, Office of Public Affairs*, November 29, 2022, https://www.justice.gov/opa/pr/leader-oath-keepers-and-oath-keepers-member-found-guilty-seditious-conspiracy-and-other (last accessed January 2, 2024).
39. See, e.g., Jayna Davis, *The Third Terrorist: The Middle East Connection to the Oklahoma City Bombing* (Nashville, TN: Thomas Nelson, Inc., 2004) (https://www.amazon.com/Third-Terrorist-Connection-Oklahoma-Bombing/dp/0785261036):

> Timothy McVeigh and Terry Nichols were not the lone conspirators in the Oklahoma City bombing-the attack that killed nearly 170 people in a few short seconds. They were part of a greater scheme, one which involved Islamic terrorists and at least one provable link to Iraq. This book, written by the relentless reporter who first broke the story of the Mideast connection, is filled with new revelations about the case and explains in full detail the complete, and so far untold, story behind the failed investigation-why the FBI closed the door, what further evidence exists to prove the Iraqi connection, why it has been ignored, and what makes it more relevant now than ever. Told with a gripping narrative style and rock-solid investigative journalism and vetted by men such as former CIA director James Woolsey, Davis's piercing account is the first book to set the record straight about what really happened April 19, 1995.

40. See, e.g., David Masciotra, "American Terrorism: From Timothy McVeigh to January 6," *Washington Monthly*, May 3, 2023, https://washingtonmonthly.com/2023/05/03/american-terrorism-from-timothy-mcveigh-to-january-6/ (last accessed January 2, 2024).

Index

A

ABC News, 189
Administrative Procedure Act, 191
airport full-body scanners, 178
Air Transportation Safety and System Stabilization Act (ATSSSA), 66
Ajaj, Ahmad Mohammad, 3
Al-Arian, Sami (2005–2010), 108–124
  civil contempt case, 112–116
    contempt citation, 113
    cooperation, 113
    grand jury subpoena, 113
    nearly identical case, 114
    no-cooperation promise, 114
    plea agreement, 113, 115
    standard cooperation provision, 114
    subpoena, 113
  criminal contempt case, 116–118
    house arrest, 118
    hunger strike, 117
    immigration authorities, 117
    immunity order, 116
    International Institute for Islamic Thought, 117
    Muslim Public Affairs Council, 117
    pocket veto, 118
    responsive brief, 118
  final chapter, 118–119
    innocent casualties, 119
    one-page notice, 118
    thought crimes, 119
    website, 119
  First Amendment rights, 110
  grand jury indictment, 110
  Islamic Committee for Palestine, 108
  Palestinian Islamic Jihad, 109–111
  terrorism trial, 110–112
    double jeopardy, 111
    evidence, 111
    plea-agreement hearing, 111
    sentence, 111
  University of South Florida, 108
Alley, Wayne, 25
All Writs Act, 159
Al Qaeda, 47–50
  early attacks, 50–51
  training camps, 49
  Times Square Bomber and, 213–215
  World Trade Centre, *see* World Trade Center bombing (1993)
American Association of University Professors, 110
American Journal of Archaeology, 129
American Civil Liberties Union (ACLU), 203
Ancient Order of Hibernians, 17
Animal Enterprise Protection Act of 1992, 81
Animal Farm, 79
animal law, 95–96
Animal Liberation Front (ALF), 79, 97
Animal rights movement, *see* SHAC 7/Stop Huntington Animal Cruelty (2006)
Anticev, John, 17
Army Court of Military Review, 156
Ashcroft, John, 44, 109
Authorization for Use of Military Force (AUMF), 162
Azzam the American, *see* Gadahn, Adam

B

Beam, Louis, 80
Bentham, Jeremy, 76
Bill of Rights, 157
Bin Laden, Usama, 47
  fatwah endorsed by, 51
  inheritor, 203
  operational goal, 215
Bin Laden of the Internet, *see* Anwar al-Awlaki and Yemeni connection
Black, Hugo, 64
Blassingame v. Trump, 235
Blinkinsopp, David, 85
blogosphere, conspiracy theories, 67, 165
Boston Marathon bombing (2013), 215
Branch Davidians, 24
Brinkema, Leonie, 59
Brooke Army Medical Center (BAMC), 198
Bureau of Alcohol, Tobacco and Firearms, 7, 24

Bureau of Land Management, 99
Bush, George W., 108, 159, 164

C

Capitol insurrection, January 6, 2021
- criminal charges, 232
- Henry "Enrique" Tarrio, 239–242
- pleas, 232–233
- public assistance, 233
- Report of the U.S. Attorney for the District of Columbia 231–233
- sentencings, 233
- Southern Poverty Law Center, 240
- Stewart Rhodes, 242–246
- stories behind the data, 234–236
- trials, 233
- *United States v. David Krauss*, 238
- *United States v. Mario Mares*, 236
- U.S. Capitol attack, 230–231

Cass, Brian, 85
Chertoff, Michael, 188
Christmas Day bomber, 189, 203
The Chronicle of Higher Education, 94
Churchill, Ward, 109
CIA, 195
- kill list, 192
- operational triumph of Cold War, 48

civil liberties, *see* National security vs. civil liberties
Civil Rights Act, 157
Classified Information Procedures Act (CIPA), 72
Clinton, Hilary, 218
CNN, 203
Cohen Act, 23
Collins, Susan, 186
"conflict of laws" principles, 133
Coppa, Selena, 186
Crime Victims Rights Act (CVRA), 66
cyber-terrorists, 84

D

Dallas Morning News, 33
Darrow, Clarence, 27
death penalty, 64
- Americans favoring, 43
- elimination of, from case, 59
- Supreme Court ruling on, 64

Declaratory Judgment Act, 191
Department of the Army, 153
Department of Defense, 183, 185, 186, 198
Department of Homeland Security, 178, 186, 188
Department of Justice (DOJ), 59, 84, 115, 164, 237, 238
Department of State, 141
Department of Treasury, 125
Descartes, Rene, 76
Detroit Institute of Arts, 127
Dirty bomb story, 165
due process of law, 10

E

Eco-terrorists, 215
Egyptian Islamic Jihad, 49
Eichmann, Adolf, 153
Eight Amendment, 64
English common law, 205
entrapment
- incitement and, 214
- techniques of, 207

evidence
- circumstantial evidence, 11
- DNA, 10
- eyewitness evidence, 35
- motion to suppress, 6–8
- World Trade Center bombing (1993), 2

F

Facebook, 189
fatwah, 51
Federal Bureau of Investigation (FBI), 110
- agent testimony, 60
- arrest of Al-Arian, 110
- description given to agent, 31
- forensics expert, 43
- Ruby Ridge incident, 24
- tips to, 30

Federal Rule of Civil Procedure, 198
felony arrest warrant, 189
Fields, James Alex Jr., 225–226
Fifth Amendment, 15, 27, 154, 191, 196
Financial Times, 92
Finnell, Val, 184
First Amendment, 84, 94, 110
Foreign Intelligence Surveillance Act (FISA), 74, 124
Foreign Sovereign Immunities Act (FSIA), 127, 142
Fort Dix conspirators and Underwear Bomber, 170–181
- Fort Dix wannabes, 170–172
  - anarchism, 171

Fu Manchu, 171
mixed bag, 172
Molly Maguires, 171
plotters, 173–177
bagmen, 175
charges, 174
chronology of incrimination events, 176
Fort Dix Six, 175
illegal weapons, 173
informers, 175
law enforcement, surveillance by, 175
Pocono training, 175
questions, 173
sarcastic article, 175
target, 172–173
basic training center, 172
mock Vietnam village, 172
Operations Desert Shield and Desert Storm, 173
War on Terror, 173
Underwear Bomber, 177–179
absurd legal action, 179
airport full-body scanners, 178
carry-offs, 177
frivolous lawsuits, 179
Khalid the Drole, 177
photographic samples, 178
shuffling gait, 177
standby counsel, 178
Times Square Bomber, 179
Fort Dix Six, 175, 215
Fort Hood shootings, Nidal Malik Hasan and (2009), 182–202, 207
Anwar al-Awlaki and Yemeni connection, 188–198
Administrative Procedure Act, 191
causes of action, 195
Christmas Day bomber, 189
CIA kill list, 192
Declaratory Judgment Act, 191
drone strike, 198
factual allegations, 192
Federal Rule of Civil Procedure, 198
felony arrest warrant, 189
Fifth Amendment, 196
international law, 190, 191
jihad, videotape declaration, 189
joint Special Operations Command, 192
jurisdiction and venue, 191
parties, 192
pending suit, 198
prayer for relief, 196
targeted killing policy, 196
"targeting shooting" list, 189
terror watch list, 189
test of civil society, 198
treaty law, 191
United Nations Special Rapporteur on Extrajudicial Killings, 193
background, 183–186
anti-American propaganda, 184
conscientious objectors, 183
Dar al-Hijrah mosque, 185
education, 184
Leaderless Resistance, 186
man of conscience, 185
military personnel expert, 184
off-topic presentation, 184
Rand Corporation, 184
residency at Walter Reed, 183
deployment to Afghanistan, 182
postscript, 198–200
Brooke Army Medical Center, 198
false statement, 198
religious martyr, 182
shootings and legal proceedings to date, 186–188
Leaderless Resistance, 188
military jurors, 187
shifting definition of terrorism, 188
Soldier Readiness Center, 186
speculation, 186
Uniform Code of Military Justice, 187
Solider Readiness Center, 182
Fourteenth Amendment, 157
Fourth Amendment, 195
Fox News, 201
French law, 133
FSIA, *see* Foreign Sovereign Immunities Act

G

Gadahn, Adam, 214–215
Galligan, John P., 187
Gates, Robert, 192, 198
Geneva Convention, 152
Genshaft, Judy, 109, 110
GIS mapping, 98
Grassroots terrorism, 214
Grieger, Thomas, 183
Grotius, Hugo, 152

H

Hadas, Jodie, 7
Hagerty, Angela, 163

Hamas, 121, 125, 247
Hanson, Lee, 65
Hartzler, Joseph, 28–29
Harvard Crimson, 127
Hasan, Nidal Malik, *see* Fort Hood shootings, Nidal Malik Hasan and (2009)
Herzfeld, Ernst, 132
Hoffman, Bruce, 187
Holder, Eric, 208
homegrown terrorists (Tim McVeigh and Terry Nichols) (1995), 22–47
- appeals and execution, 43–44
  - request to die, 44
  - U.S. Court of Appeals for the Tenth Circuit, 43
  - U.S. Supreme Court, 44
- background, 22–25
  - Branch Davidians, 24
  - Cohen Act, 23
  - kindred spirits, 24
  - Persian Gulf War, 23
  - white supremacist, 23
  - witnesses, 25
- McVeigh's trial, 27–43
  - adverse witness, 43
  - Bronze Star, 33
  - CCTV, 27
  - conspiracy theory, 30, 34
  - defense strategy, 31
  - evidence, 30
  - eyewitness evidence, 35
  - FBI forensics expert, 43
  - Federal Prosecutor, 27
  - government burden, 31
  - government witnesses, 34
  - immunity, 38
  - John Doe 2, 30
  - news media, 33
  - notion planted, 35
  - powerful metaphor, 29
  - social call, 37
  - subtle argument, 37
  - tears, 37
  - threshold chore of defense, 32
- Murrah Federal Building, 22, 24
- pretrial proceedings, 25–27
  - controversy, 26
  - defense attorneys, 25
  - Fifth Amendment right, 27
  - grand jury indictment, 26
  - lawyers, 25
  - motion for recusal of the presiding judge, 26
  - writ of mandamus, 26

Huntingdon Life Sciences, 84, *see also* SHAC 7/Stop Huntington Animal Cruelty (2006)
hydrogen bomb, conspiracy theories, 17

I

Immigration and Customs Enforcement (ICE), 140
Immigration and Naturalization Service (INS), 3, 13
Imperial Japanese Army, 153
The Independent, 206
International Institute for Islamic Thought (IIIT), 117
international law, 190, 191
Islamic law, 205

J

Jaffer, Jameel, 203
Jersey Journal, 99
Jewish Defense League, 1
jihad, 48
- Bin Laden declaration, 48
- Egyptian Islamic Jihad, 49
- new direction in America, 207
- videotape declaration, 189

Johns Hopkins Center for Alternatives to Animal Testing (CAAT), 77
Joint Special Operations Command (JSOC), 192
Jones, Stephen, 30

K

Kahane, Meir, 1
Kessler, Jason, 221, 222–225
- "Unite the Right" rally, 221

Khalid the Drole, 177
Koresh, David, 24
Kunstler, William M., 2

L

Laboratory Animal Welfare Act, 77
Leaderless Resistance, 79–80, 186, 188, 215
Lee, Gerald Bruce, 116
legislation
- Administrative Procedure Act, 191
- Air Transportation Safety and System Stabilization Act, 66
- All Writs Act, 159
- Animal Enterprise Protection Act of 1992, 81
- Civil Rights Act, 157

Classified Information Procedures Act, 72
Cohen Act, 23
Crime Victims Rights Act, 66
Declaratory Judgment Act, 191
Foreign Intelligence Surveillance Act of 1978, 74
Foreign Sovereign Immunities Act, 127
Laboratory Animal Welfare Act, 77
Non-Detention Act, 160
Patriot Act, 157–158
Terrorism Risk Insurance Act of 2002, 127
Voting Rights Act, 157
Levin, Richard C., 139
Lieberman, Joe, 188
Linder, Douglas, 47, 153
Local tribal customary law, 205

M

MacMahon, Edward, 59
Manning, Blanche M., 132
Martin, Lawrence, 37
McCaul, Michael, 186
McCoun, Thomas B., III, 117
McParland, James, 17
McVeigh, Tim, *see* homegrown terrorists
Moffitt, William B., 118
Molly Maguires, 17, 171
Mother Jones, 175
Moussaoui, Zacarias (2006), 47–75
aftermath, 66–67
Air Transportation Safety and System Stabilization Act, 66
Crime Victims Rights Act, 66
grand jury records, 66
withholding of exculpatory material, 66
background, 47–50
al Qaeda, 47
communist puppet regime in Kabul, 48
Egyptian Islamic Jihad, 49
jihad, 48
military committee, 49
oath of allegiance, 48
opposition to United States, 48
techno-holy warriors, 48
conspiracy theories, 67–68
Israeli intelligence, 67
master theory, 67
Pearl Harbor, 67
early al Qaeda attacks, 50–51
planning and execution, 51–58
bank accounts, 54
check ride, 57
fatwah, 51
flight training courses, 52
German cell, 51
grand jury indictment, 51
gym training, 54, 55
hijackers travel to United States, 54
immigration charges, 58
preparations for coordinated air attack, 57–58
probable material witness, 58
pretrial legal maneuvers, 59
bifurcated trial, 59
pleading guilty, 59
U.S. District Judge, 59
trial (phase 1), 59–64
defense counsel, 59
jury's finding, 64
key witness, 60
substitute witnesses, 63
testimony, 60
trial (phase 2), 64–65
Eight Amendment, 64
influential concurring opinion, 64
jury deliberation, 65–66
revisionist trend, 65
"Supermax" facility, 65
museums, *see* Persian antiquities cases (2001–2018)
Muslim Public Affairs Council (MPAC), 117

N

National Institutes of Health (NIH), 77
National security vs. civil liberties, 152–170
conspiracy theories, 165–166
blogosphere, 165
Dirty bomb story, 165
John Doe 2, 165
leading theory, 165
logic of theory, 165
Jose Padilla, 158–162
All Writs Act, 159
controversy, 159
double-jeopardy prohibition, 163
interlocutory appeal, 159
material witness warrant, 160
Non-Detention Act, 160
Supreme Court decision, 161
wrong defendant, 162
Jose Padilla's trial and post-trial proceedings, 163–165
alleged subjection to torture, 164

Islamic extremists, 163
post-traumatic stress disorder, 163
pretrial perambulations, 163
rights illegally denied, 164
sole defendant, 164
Stockholm syndrome, 163
laws of war, war crime trials, and combatants' rights, 152–156
Army Court of Military Review, 156
"banality of evil," 153
commission witnesses, 154
court-martial convictions, 156
Fifth Amendment, 153
Geneva Convention, 152
Imperial Japanese Army, 153
International Military Tribunal, 152
Japanese trials, 153, 154
miscarriage of justice, 156
Nazi-controlled territories, 152
pretrial publicity, 156
tribal regions, 152
litigation in the south, 162
authorization use of military force, 162
inherent constitutional powers, 162
second-class citizens and unlawful enemy combatants, 157–158
African-Americans, 157
Bill of Rights, 157
curbing citizenship, 157
"equal protection" clauses, 157
Fourteenth Amendment, 157
German saboteurs, 158
Patriot Act, 157–158
spy, 158
Thirteenth Amendment, 157
New Jersey Department of Homeland Security and Preparedness, 96
Newsweek, 43
New York Supreme Court, 16
New York Times, 5, 10
Nichols, Terry, *see* homegrown terrorists
Nosair, El Sayyid, 1

O

Obama, Barack, 190, 198, 218
Oklahoma City bombing, *see* homegrown terrorists
O'Connor, Joseph E., 175
Ohio Supreme Court, 95
O.J. Simpson murder case, 111
open-records law, 95
O-Reilly, Bill, 109
Orwell, George, 79
Oswald, Lee Harvey, 165

P

Palestinian Islamic Jihad, 109, 111
Panetta, Leon, 190, 198
Path to Paradise, 2
Patriot Act, 157–158
Pearl Harbor, 67
People for the Ethical Treatment of Animals (PETA), 78
Persian antiquities cases (2001–2018), 125–151
antiquity ownership, 139
heated debate, 139
Machu Picchu, 139
odd folks out, 139
Arthur M. Sackler Museum of Harvard University, 128–130
era of tomb raiders, 129
liberated treasures, 130
plaintiffs, 128
Reliefs of Persepolis, 129
developments (2010), 134–138
analysis, 134
court denies motion to intervene, 135–136
legal standard for motion to intervene, 134–135
prerequisites to intervene, 134
"sound bite" anti-terrorism legislation, 138
timeliness, 135
default judgment, 125
defendants' collective stance, 126
denial of defendants' motions, 127
final judgment, 125
Foreign Sovereign Immunities Act, 127
Hamas, 125
Iranian bank accounts, 126
Museum of Fine Arts, 126
primary targets, 126
Supreme Court declines to intervene, 142–143
Terrorism Risk Insurance Act of 2002, 127
triple suicide bombing, 125
Field Museum, 130–131
collections, 131
incorporation, 130
major benefactor, 130
museum campus, 131
Persian antiquities cases (2001–2018), Oriental Institute, 131–134

Choga Mish materials, 131
"conflict of laws" principles, 133
French law, 133
information requests, 131
Nazi Germany, 132
Persepolis Fortification archives, 131
web page statement, 133
postscripts, 140–142
antiques pilfered in Baghdad, 141
artifacts authenticated, 140
Immigration and Customs Enforcement, 140
Supreme Court denial, 142
United Nations, letter sent to, 141
phantom cell structure, *see* Leaderless Resistance
Philadelphia Inquirer, 173
Philadelphia Museum of Art, 127
Pilker, Eric, 7
'pocket veto', 118
Pohl, James L., 187
post-traumatic stress disorder, 163, 184
Precht, Robert E., 1, 5
pretrial publicity, 156

R

Rand Corporation, 184
Rascoff, Sam, 203
Rhodes, Elmer Stewart, 242–246
charges against, 243
Oath Keepers, 242
seditious conspiracy, 242, 244, 245
sentencing, 245
Riches, Jonathan Lee, 179
Riefenstahl, Leni, 153
Rostker, Bernard, 184
Rubin, Jenny, 125, 142
Ruby Ridge, 24
Rumsfeld, Donald, 159
Russell, Thomas B., 179
Ryan, Patrick, 27, 37

S

Salem, Emad, 17
Samit, Harry, 60
Schlesinger, Alvin, 2
Schneider, Joel, 174
Schwarzkopf, Norman, 23
September 11 (2001), *see* Moussaoui, Zacarias
SHAC 7/Stop Huntington Animal Cruelty (2006), 76–107
aftermath, 94–99
animal law, 95–96
Bureau of Land Management, 99
GIS mapping, 98
international fugitives, 99
Ohio Supreme Court, 95
open-records law, 95
tertiary targets, 98
threat overview, 97–98
violent tactics, 98
animal activist philosophy and tactics, 78–84
acts of humiliation, 84
Animal Liberation Front, 79
cyber-terrorists, 84
federal legislation to protect scientists using animals, 81–84
First Amendment protection, 84
gradations of standards, 78
independent cells, 80
Leaderless Resistance, 79–80
People for the Ethical Treatment of Animals, 78
phantom cell mode of organization, 80
pyramid-style organization, 80
sliding scale model, 78
strong animal rights view, 78
utilitarianism, 78
conviction and appeal, 94
First Amendment, 94
sentences, 94
indictments and trial, 89–94
Andrew Baker, 89–90
corporate witnesses, 89
Marion Harlos, 92–93
Molotov cocktail, 94
phone calls, 91
Robert Harper, 93–94
Sally Dillenback, 90–92
roots of animal rights movement, 76–78
anti-vivisection movement, 77
father of Utilitarianism, 76
hippy movement, 77
Johns Hopkins Center for Alternatives to Animal Testing, 77
natural philosophers, 76
organic machines, 76
socio-cultural revolution, 77
Stop Huntington Animal Cruelty (SHAC), 84–89
accomplishments, 86
anonymous bulletins, 86
black fax, 88
evading investigators, 87

Huntingdon Life Sciences, 84
newsletter, 85
PGP, 88
"Top 20 Terror Tactics," 87
UK campaign, 85
video footage of protests, 85
website, 85–89
Shahzad, Faisal, 207
Sharia law, 209, 210
Sixth Amendment, 15, 72
Space Station, 7
Stephenson, Neal, 76
Styer, Wilhelm D., 153
Supreme Court
Eight Amendment and, 64
Fort Dix conspirator case, 176
Japanese trials, 153, 154
refusal to review ruling, 59
Tenth Circuit's decision and, 44

T

Tarrio, Henry "Enrique", 239–242
Proud Boys, 239, 241
Capitol insurrection, January 6, 240
sentencing, 242
Terrorism Risk Insurance Act of 2002 (TRIA), 127
Thierack, Georg, 165
'thought crimes', 119
Tigar, Michael, 25
Time Magazine, 111
Times Square bomber case, *see* Yemeni connection (Times Square Bomber)
Titsworth, Bill, 37
Treaty law, 191
Trump, Donald
2016 election campaign, 219
aftermath, 227
Charlottesville rally, August 2017, 221–222
comic relief, 219
"cuckservatives", 221
cultural shift, 227
Hatewatch, 227
Jason Kessler, 221, 222–225
James Alex Fields, Jr., 225–226
Sines v. Kessler, 222
and triumph of the radical right, 220–221
Unite the Right rally, 221, 222
Turley, Jonathan, 164
Turner, Earl, 23
The Turner Diaries, 23, 29

U

Underwear Bomber, 177–179
absurd legal action, 179
airport full-body scanners, 178
carry-offs, 177
frivolous lawsuits, 179
Khalid the Drole, 177
photographic samples, 178
shuffling gait, 177
standby counsel, 178
Times Square Bomber, 179
Uniform Code of Military Justice, 187
United Flight 93, conspiracy theory, 67
United Nations
letter sent to, 141
organization, 48
Special Rapporteur on Extrajudicial Killings, 193
United States v. David Krauss, 238–239
United States v. Mario Mares, 236–238
University of Michigan, 127
University of South Florida (USF), 108
unlawful enemy combatant, U.S. citizen declared, *see* National security vs. civil liberties
U.S. Constitution Bill of Rights, 157
Eighth Amendment, 64
Fifth Amendment, 15, 27, 154, 191, 196
First Amendment, 84, 94, 110
Fourteenth Amendment, 157
Fourth Amendment, 191
Sixth Amendment, 15, 72
Thirteenth Amendment, 157

V

de Vattel, Emerich, 152
Virginia Tech shooting, 188
Voting Rights Act, 157

W

Waco, 30
War on Terror, 173
Yemeni connection, 192
Washington Post, 173
Weaver, Randy, 24
Western Federation of Miners (WFM), 27
Westphal, Carl, 165
White, Justin, 199
Whitehurst, Frederic William, 43
Winthrop, Grenville L., 127–129
witnesses
corporate, 89

criminal trial of World Trade Center bombing, 8, 10
homegrown terrorists, 25, 34, 43
substitute, 63
World Trade Center bombing, 8, 10
Wooley, James, 18
World Trade Center bombing (1993), 1–21
acquittal, 2
background, 3–5
Camp Khaldan, 3
code, 4
first target, 4
Immigration and Naturalization Service inspectors, 3
joint bank account, 4
smokeless powder, 4
terrorist kit, 3
urea nitrate and hydrogen gas truck bomb, 3
bizarre verdict, 2, 16
blind Sheik, 3
civil trial, 16
conspiracy theories, 16–18
Atomic Annie cannon, 17
counter-theory, 17
Egyptian informant, 17
hydrogen bomb, 17
Molly Maguires, 17
PBS interview, 18
ragged fringe of, 17
eyewitness, 2
first criminal trial, 8–12
blunt impact trauma, 10
circumstantial evidence, 11
DNA evidence, 10
dramatic moments, 10
due process of law, 10
eyewitness testimony, 10
government inferences, 11
jury selection, 8
test of endurance for legal counsel, 10
witnesses, 8, 10
Home Box Office docu-drama, 3
insanity defense, 2
last word, 18
pretrial proceedings, 5–8
incriminating remarks, 7
Mohammad Salameh's bail application, 5–6
motions to suppress evidence, 6–8
public defender, 5
Space Station, 7
storage shed, 7
videotape, 6
public defender, 1
radical lawyer, 2
subsequent criminal trials, 12–16
airliner, 13
bomb preparations, 13
convictions, 14
Fifth Amendment right to due process, 15
grand jury indictment, 14
sentencing, 14
Sixth Amendment right to counsel, 15
terrorist training camp, 13
weak case, 2
Wrinn, Joe, 127

Y

Yamashita, Tomoyuki, 152
Yemeni connection (Times Square Bomber), 203–217
accomplices and co-conspirators, 213–215
Arabic language video, 214
Azzam the American, 214
eco-terrorists, 215
evidence of Al Qaeda, 215
global terrorism on the cheap, 215
grassroots terrorism, 214
heroic operations, 214
Leaderless Resistance, 215
"lone wolf" attacks, 215
online magazine, 215
wannabe terrorists, 165, 214
ACLU, 203
"al Qaeda central," 204
background, 206–208
airport arrest, 207
education, 207
religion, 207
upbringing, 207
cargo plane bomb plot, 204
Christmas day bomber, 203
CNN, 203
economic reform program, 204
government, 205
legal proceedings and trial, 208–213
court sentencing transcript, 208–213
Sharia law, 209, 210
war on terror, 203
Yoo, John, 164
Yousef, Ramzi Ahmed, 3
YouTube, 17, 189

www.ingramcontent.com/pod-product-compliance
Lightning Source LLC
LaVergne TN
LVHW011117300926
849160LV00008B/415